WRITING
THE WAR

WRITING
THE WAR

CHRONICLES OF A
WORLD WAR II CORRESPONDENT

EDITED BY
ANNE KILEY AND THOMAS PELLECHIA
WITH DAVID KILEY

Prometheus Books

59 John Glenn Drive
Amherst, New York 14228

Published 2015 by Prometheus Books

Cover design by Grace M. Conti-Zilsberger
Cover images courtesy of the authors

Inquiries should be addressed to
Prometheus Books
59 John Glenn Drive
Amherst, New York 14228
VOICE: 716–691–0133
FAX: 716–691–0137
WWW.PROMETHEUSBOOKS.COM

19 18 17 16 15   5 4 3 2 1

Library of Congress Cataloging-in-Publication Data Pending

ISBN 978-1-63388-104-4 (HC)
ISBN 978-1-63388-105-1 (ebook)

Printed in the United States of America

For Charles, Ned, Paul, and John
(the rest of the ball team)

"*Death is but crossing the world, as friends do the seas; they live in one another still.*"

William Penn, from *More Fruits of Solitude*

CONTENTS

ACKNOWLEDGMENTS

We extend our thanks to a number of people for their help and encouragement during the long process of putting this book together.

David Gardiner of the *Stars and Stripes* was extraordinarily helpful and generous with his time. Steven Mitchell of Prometheus Books played an essential part in the book's production. Chuck Keeton, script doctor extraordinaire, was the first to read the book's manuscript, and we are grateful for his invaluable suggestions.

Special thanks go to Jean-Yves Simon, good friend and author of *The Stars and Stripes in Normandy*, a scholarly study of the US Army newspaper in France during the first months after D-Day.

This book's many Facebook fans helped us immeasurably with their appreciation and comments.

We also want to thank Paul Kiley for spending much time with the wartime editions of the *Stars and Stripes*, picking out stories and recording them for transcription, and to John Kiley for helping with the proofreading. Special thanks and appreciation go to Joanne Buchanan, Warren Gray's daughter, for sharing her research on her father's war experiences.

We also acknowledge the World War II veterans who read and appreciated the *Stars and Stripes*, and who wrote millions of their own letters home.

INTRODUCTION

A Jersey City, New Jersey, newspaperman and sports writer who had reported on Babe Ruth, Joe Louis, and Red Grange, Charles Kiley was drafted just before the start of World War II and went into the war as a soldier expecting to fight. Before his US Army unit, Company H, 135th Infantry, 34th Division, was deployed to North Africa from Northern Ireland in 1942, he wired a few stories to the *Stars and Stripes*, the US Army newspaper in London. When that paper switched from a weekly to a daily in November 1942, the editors remembered the soldier from Company H and requested him for their staff. Charles moved to London while the rest of his unit went to North Africa.

The *Stars and Stripes* was written and edited by enlisted soldiers, men with civilian newspaper experience, with only a rare officer here and there. Its stories were subject to potential military censorship but not military editorial control. The paper was always a tabloid both in format and in feel, featuring stories about enlisted soldiers told from the soldier's point of view. Each edition invariably included an extensive sports section and comics. A newspaper of that name was briefly published during the Civil War, but the real beginning of the *Stars and Stripes* was during World War I when it was published weekly in Paris from 1917 to 1919 for the American Expeditionary Forces (AEF). Publication of the Army newspaper was resumed in April 1942 in London, at first to serve the ever-increasing number of US military personnel pouring into England and Northern Ireland.

Beginning in late 1942, Charles reported on the war from London and from all over Great Britain until the D-Day landings in 1944. He wrote about everything from the WAC deployment in England to the Army Rangers' rigorous training program in the Scottish highlands. He trained as an aerial gunner so he could accompany and report on bomber crews as they flew to targets in Germany and Norway. Reporting on the air war together, Charles and *Stars and Stripes* reporter Andy Rooney (later of CBS's *60 Minutes*) began a life-long friendship. The two shared rooms in London, in Air Force bases as they covered the air war, and they waited together in Bristol, England, for embarkation orders for the Normandy invasion.

After the invasion, Charles was part of a small team designated to set up the first continental edition of the *Stars and Stripes*; while he waited for the fighting to advance from the landing areas, he wrote and produced a single-sheet mimeographed beachhead edition of the paper and distributed it himself to soldiers up and down the beaches. He worked at the paper's Paris edition, then the Liege, Belgium, edition when the Allied ground forces got to Germany.

While Dwight Eisenhower was the commander of the Allied invasion force, he insisted that only one reporter would have direct access to him, and that the reporter had to be from the *Stars and Stripes*. In April 1945, Charles Kiley was assigned to be that reporter. He was the sole news source for the surrender negotiations between the Germans and Allies that culminated on May 7, 1945. Charles's story of the surrender appeared in the *Stars and Stripes*. His account was also picked up by major international news services and was included in the best-selling book about the surrender, *The Day the War Ended*, by the leading British historian and official Churchill biographer Sir Martin John Gilbert, who interviewed Charles for the book. Historians consider Charles's story the primary contemporary source of what happened during the surrender negotiations.

/////

Billee Gray was just twenty-one when she met Charles while he was in basic training at Camp Croft, South Carolina. She lived in Asheville, North Carolina, the city famously described by Thomas Wolfe in *Look Homeward, Angel*. Billee and Charles were in each other's company only three times before he proposed marriage, right before he shipped out to Europe in April of 1942. They were separated and wrote to each other for two and a half years before they were able to marry, and then were separated again and wrote for another eight months, until Charles finally returned to Billee at the end of the war in Europe.

After Charles was first deployed overseas, Billee moved to Ohio to work in the defense industry, and then to New Jersey where she witnessed blackout conditions, encountered wounded veterans, and volunteered as a plane spotter.

In February of 1943, Billee had to write Charles to console him for the sudden death of his mother.

Charles was an experienced and colorful writer. Both his stories for the *Stars and Stripes* and his letters to Billee, in which he tells her the story behind the stories, particularly his coverage of the air war, D-Day, and the German surrender negotiations, make for fascinating reading. Billee was an avid reader; her letters provide an intimate and unusually literate description of her home-front experiences and reflect the charm and inner strength that Charles had fallen in love with.

Charles and Billee's romance was confined almost entirely to the written word. Their letters show the combination of war and distance, not to mention the censorship that made sure information was delayed or missing altogether. The introduction of V-mail made it faster to send and receive mail, but not by much. When Charles's mother died, he didn't get the news for three weeks.

Early in 1944, Billee went back to an Asheville transformed by an enormous military presence. After she and Charles were married in August of that year, Billee lived in New York City while waiting for Charles to return from his final deployment. She worked first for the magazine *Time* and then as a secretary at Standard Oil. In Manhattan, Billee roomed with the wife of another *Stars and Stripes* staff writer, and spent time with the wives of more of Charles's Army newspaper associates, living with the rationing of food and clothing in big city wartime conditions . . . and writing about it all in her letters to Charles.

During World War II, over one billion pieces of mail were exchanged between those in uniforms and their loved ones at home. Charles Kiley and Billee Gray's letters to each other, nearly eight hundred of them, were written on every kind of paper: acid-laden wartime paper, now brown and crumbling; thick, pre-war rag stationery, still good as new. Flimsy blue airmail paper, tiny V-mail letters, commercial paper samples cut with a scissor, folded and folded again to fit in mismatched envelopes. These seventy-year-old letters tell the story of two people who met in the upheaval of war, fell in love fast because they didn't have much time, and then were separated for years. The letters also reveal their families, their friends, their longing for each other, and how the two changed over their long separation in the face of a world war.

Charles and Billee's wartime experiences, captured in their letters, were shared by much of the country, and, indeed, much of the world. Theirs is a universal story of love in the time of war, of a people's upheaval from the known to the unknown, and their strange and difficult work in the face of adversity.

/////

A note on the editing of this book:

The letters that were used for this book have been edited and excerpted. Many of the letters exchanged by Charles and Billee are interesting to family members but not to the general reader. Including all of the letters would have given us a book at least five times as long as this one.

The letters were first digitally scanned, transcribed, and then edited. In some cases, sentences were merged for clarity; spelling, grammar, and punctuation were also occasionally altered for the same reason.

Charles and Billee routinely and repeatedly addressed each other as "dear" and "darling" in their letters. While endearments like this were meaningful and important to both of them at the time, to read them repetitiously is tedious; they were mostly edited out.

The letter excerpts appear in chronological order. We have included a number of excerpts from Charles's *Stars and Stripes* stories, as well as from stories by other *Stars and Stripes* staff writers; these stories for the most part also appear in chronological order by publication date. In 1942, Charles kept an intermittent diary; some of those diary entries appear in this book.

Editors' notes in the text of the letters appear in [brackets].

About Billee's name . . . "Billee" is a French name, pronounced "Bill-LAY" with the emphasis on the second syllable. In the United States, the name is unusual. Billee's family always pronounced it "BILL-ee," as if it were spelled "B-i-l-l-y."

PROLOGUE

*I've wondered many times since that night what might have happened
if I hadn't decided to invite myself to that party. I remember sitting
beside that empty chair and wondering who was going to occupy it.
Then, I saw you making your way toward our table and thought,
"Mmmm, he looks nice. Maybe he's the one," and you were.*

[Billee to Charles, March 1942.]

*The first time I saw you, the first words we spoke. I remember I
didn't catch your name when you introduced yourself. It didn't seem
to matter because I was much more interested in the girl. Then, I
remembered I'd have to know your name...*

[Charles to Billee, March 1942.]

In 1941, Charles Kiley, twenty-seven, was a sports reporter for the *Jersey Journal*, in Jersey City, New Jersey, where he had worked for seven years. A handsome man with a charming and gregarious personality and a wide circle of friends known as the "gang," Charles came from a close blue-collar Irish family; his paternal grandparents had emigrated from the Waterford area in the 1880s. He still lived at home, as did his younger brother and two younger sisters. They all worked full time and helped to support their parents and to pay off the mortgage on their house. His older brother, John, had been ordained a Catholic priest in 1939.

His father, also named Charles but always known as "Pop," was a steamfitter for US Steel. An honors student, Charles had to leave high school after his junior year when his father's work was cut during the Depression. At first, he worked pickup jobs on the Bayonne docks. He went to night school to learn journalism and started at the *Jersey Journal* as a copy boy.

In October 1941, Charles was drafted into the Army. Only six weeks shy of twenty-eight, then the cutoff age for the draft, his request for an economic hardship exemption was denied. The *Jersey Journal* held a banquet in his honor and promised to keep his job open for him, his "gang" gave him a loud party that went on all night, and Charles caught the bus to Fort Dix along with other Jersey City draftees.

Charles Kiley—Camp Croft, South Carolina, October 1941. (Kiley Family)

He arrived at Camp Croft, South Carolina, in early November for basic training and was assigned to Company H, 135th Regiment. During his training, he received a sharpshooter medal, learned to be a radio operator, and, typically, made many friends. On Sunday, December 7, Charles was enjoying a weekend pass in Tryon, North Carolina, with two of his army buddies when the news of Pearl Harbor came over the radio.

Charles wrote home frequently during his time at Camp Croft, especially to his brother John. His letters were full of concerns about his mother, Ella, whose health was not good; the news of Pearl Harbor made her frantic with worry for Charles and her youngest son, Eddie, just twenty-one years old and sure to be drafted.

Charles had another pass scheduled for the third weekend of January 1942. He and a group of his army friends decided to go to Asheville, North Carolina, about seventy miles on the bus from Camp Croft. They got rooms at the George Vanderbilt hotel, where they heard about a canteen party and dance to be held at the Asheville YMCA on Saturday night, January 17.

Billee Gray's mother, Elizabeth, had grown up in a Pennsylvania coal-mining town; all four of her grandparents had emigrated from Wales in the 1860s and '70s. Billee's father, William Gray, was born and raised in Delaware, where his family had lived since the 1700s. He was an engineer who had made a specialty of installing the large electrically powered doors on dirigible hangars. In the 1920s and early '30s, the greatest period for both commercial and military dirigible flight, Billee, with her mother, two sisters, and a brother, often accompanied her father wherever his many jobs took him. The family always traveled by car in that time before straight, smooth highways on roads barely paved or not paved at all. They lived in rented rooms and houses; the children changed schools frequently. Whenever the family was not following William from state to state, they lived with Elizabeth's oldest sister Katharine and her husband, Fred Gilbert, in Massillon, Ohio.

William and Elizabeth divorced in 1934, and Billee's mother moved with her children to the mountain resort town of Asheville. She bought a large house and turned it into a tourist home and boarding house called Oak Lodge that could accommodate about twenty-five people per night. Asheville's mountain climate drew many summer visitors from Florida and the other southern states in that era before air-conditioning; the town had been a health resort attractive to tuberculosis patients since before World War I.

Billee Gray—Asheville, 1941. (Kiley Family)

Charles and Billee the morning after they first met—Asheville, January 1942. (Kiley Family)

By 1941, Billee Gray, twenty, had been living in Asheville, North Carolina, for seven years. Her two sisters had married and left home when each was just eighteen. Her brother, then seventeen and still troubled by his parents' divorce and the absence of his father, was living in Ohio with Aunt Katharine and Uncle Fred.

Very attractive, yet shy and introverted, Billee worked full time in the billing office at Ivey's, a well-known Asheville department store, at a job she got right out of high school. She also helped her mother run Oak Lodge, taking reservations, cleaning, making beds, doing laundry, and serving breakfast and dinner. Some guests were long-term residents: Billee had become very close to one, New Jersey native Marguerite Heuser, who worked at one of the local banks. On December 7, Billee, Marguerite, and Elizabeth were listening to a live symphony orchestra concert on the radio when the announcer broke in with the news about Pearl Harbor.

Asheville was affected by the war almost immediately. A group of Axis diplomats and civilians were interned with their families at the Grove Park Inn, a hotel of international reputation at the heart of Asheville's identity as a mountain resort, and which could be seen in the distance from the front porch at Oak Lodge.

Billee celebrated her twenty-first birthday on December 26th; by mid-January she had started a first-aid course, "just in case," and was worn out from long hours at Ivey's, finishing up the store's billing after the Christmas holiday shopping and the January white sales. In the days before credit cards and computers, this was a considerable job. She had attended a few canteen parties at the Asheville YMCA for the growing number of soldiers stationed in the vicinity. At first, she thought she didn't have the energy to go to the one scheduled for January 17 . . . and then she changed her mind.

CHAPTER 1

JANUARY–APRIL 1942

I can hear a soldier playing, "You Made Me Love You," on the piano in the Recreation Hall next door. It seems appropriate because it reminds me of Asheville. Not that you did make me love you—that was as natural as the rising and setting of the sun.
                                                    [Charles to Billee, March 1942.]

///////

The War: Following the 1941 bombing of Pearl Harbor, the Congress strengthened presidential war powers. The *New York Times* complained that war messages out of Washington, DC were confused, but to the men in uniform—as well as their friends, parents, siblings, girlfriends, wives, and young children—it was clear that thousands were being trained at military bases to fight war in Europe and in the Pacific.

Under the War Production Board, the manufacture of civilian consumer goods took a back seat. Women who had never worked before outside of their homes were encouraged to take defense production jobs; with gasoline and tires rationed, many rode bicycles to and from work. To save electric power, in January President Roosevelt signed the Daylight Time Act, extending daylight for one hour; it was scheduled to last only until the war's end.

On January 2, the Japanese army pushed Filipino and American forces onto Bataan and then Corregidor; soon thereafter, Libya fell to Germany's Field Marshal Rommel's Afrika Korps. With Germans in uniform blanketing the European continent, the one ray of hope to the Allies was the ill-equipped German Army bogged in the snow on the Russian front.

While the sighting of two Axis submarines in the Gulf of Mexico prompted a complete blackout along the Texas coast in late January, the first units of the newly established American Expeditionary Force arrived in Northern Ireland as the result of the US decision to build up American forces in Great Britain.

/////

LEONARD E. JONES, MANAGER

1-18-42

THE
GEORGE VANDERBILT
HOTEL
ASHEVILLE, NORTH CAROLINA

Evenin' Honey-Chile:

I thought I'd like to drop in and say, "Hello", tonight and to remind you to be a very good girl until Saturday when I give the command, "Present — Arms"!

Give my sincere thanks, again, to mother and my best regards to Miss Heffernan, Marguerite, Evelyn and the rest.

Bye for awhile

Charles's first letter to Billee. (Kiley Family)

[Charles to Billee, written in Charles's hotel room while Billee waited for him in the lobby.] January 18, 1942—Asheville

Thought I'd like to drop in and say "Hello," tonight and to remind you to be a very good girl until Saturday when I give the command, "Present arms!"

Give my sincere thanks, again, to mother and my best regards to Miss Heffernan [a long-term guest at Oak Lodge], Marguerite [Billee's friend], Evelyn [Fragge, an Asheville friend] and the rest.

[Charles to Billee] January 22, 1942—Camp Croft, South Carolina

I had the inclination to drop in and see you tonight but I suppose the least that can be done under the circumstances is a little chat by mail.

You may have seen the news in the paper, or heard it on the radio, that Uncle Sam is instituting a full six-day week for the Army. I haven't heard yet whether it will affect us. However, if it does, I'll still be heading for Asheville [this] Saturday night.

I called home Monday night and gave my mother a description of the Gray hospitality. She asked me to thank your mother again, for her.

Do you know, I spent another restless night [last] Sunday. Seems like I wanted to turn back the clock to Saturday night. I wish such things were possible.

[Charles to Billee, written after their second weekend together in Asheville.] January 26, 1942—Camp Croft

I was wrong, but I wish I was right; which is to say, you didn't keep me awake last night. Yes, I did sleep like a baby, just as you said, but you were the last one I thought of before the sandman dropped by. Strange, or is it . . . you were still in my mind when I awakened at 5:30.

As I write this, I'm listening to the radio over which a broadcast from Ireland is coming, describing the arrival of the first detachment of the AEF to Europe [Allied Expeditionary Force]. I can't help feeling a thrill to hear that at last we are doing something concrete about giving peace and serenity to our people.

But we can find nicer things to talk about, can't we?

For instance, I'm looking forward, so much, to next weekend. With a visit to the Grove Park Inn cocktail lounge, not to mention approximately 21 hours with you. I'm certain it will be a weekend I'll never forget. I believe I won't want to go to sleep, in fear of awakening to discover I've been dreaming for these weeks.

///////

[Charles to Billee, written after their third and final Asheville weekend, before the transfer to Fort Dix.] February 2, 1942—Camp Croft, S.C.

We haven't much to do today except give the barracks a final scrubbing and there isn't anything I would rather do more than "talk" to you. That is, unless I could be with you in the flesh.

Do you know, we were the victims of a conspiracy? As soon as the bus got over the mountains last night the heavens were as clear as spring water and the moon was full, and oh, so big! Then I could only look and miss you some more. Somehow, I couldn't think of much other than "our moment" Saturday night outside the Inn. Things like that just happen once in a lifetime—to me, at least—but I'll always remember and look ahead to the time when we can go to the same spot, contented instead of being restless with anxiety.

///////

[Charles to Billee] February 3, 1942—En Route to Fort Dix, N.J.

I hope to cover my trip in chronological order so I'm starting from the beginning. The time now is 2:30 and we are on the train waiting for it to pull out of camp. Johnny Joyce [a Jersey City friend and also a private in the 135th Infantry, 34th Div.] and I are seated together.

3:00 p.m.—The train pulls out with over 1,100 men aboard and the band plays "Auld Lang Syne." I have a funny feeling of wanting to stay behind, to rush to Asheville and be with you. I can't remember ever missing anyone the way I miss you now. John has a wistful look on his face, too, as he looks over the camp for the last time.

5:00 p.m.—We have passed Gastonia and Gaffney and have been served a hasty dinner. Not very good but there are only a few grumbling.

7:00 p.m.—I have been playing cards and reading to pass the time but now the porter is making the berths and I'll have to leave you for awhile again.

9:30 p.m.—We are stopping for 15 minutes at Danville, Va. so it is a good time for me to get a sandwich and coffee in the station if we can.

10:00 p.m.—We have "turned in" and before I put the light out, stare out the window as the night and trees rush by, and think of you, I'm going to kiss you goodnight.

7:00 a.m.—(Wednesday) I woke at 6:00 to discover we were stopping briefly in Washington. Can't see much because the capital is blacked out. We passed the huge printing offices, which apparently work 24 hours.

Baltimore–Wilmington–Philadelphia–and Fort Dix!

7:00 p.m.—(Wednesday) We all arrived safely and sound, but forgive me if I sound a bit bewildered. It's difficult to piece things together: I mean, what has transpired within the last few hours. As I said, 1,100 of us—radio operators, intelligence units, message center company, electricians, etc., all specialists—came home from Croft. But we have all been put into different outfits. That's all I can say now.

If you don't hear from me as often as you know I would write, it will not be because I have forgotten you for a moment but only because I am not in a position to write. As it is now, I don't believe we will be seeing each other for that Easter date [in New York City]. But wherever I am, you will be with me in spirit. Please remember that I'll be back for you some day.

[Charles to Billee] February 4, 1942—Fort Dix, N.J.

I was moved over to Headquarters Company from Company H, which puts me in radio again. I don't know how long I'm going to be here so I suggest you send mail to my brother [John] and he will forward it to me. He will know where I am and will be easier to contact when and if I move. I told him all about you and from my description he is very anxious to see you.

I'll keep you posted as to my whereabouts and my work. Incidentally, our 135th Infantry, 34th Div. is supposed to be one of the "fight'enest" outfits in US military history. There are 13 "major battle" streamers in our standard.

Johnny Joyce (left) and Charles training in radio operations—Camp Croft, November 1941. (Kiley Family)

/////

[Billee to Charles (Billee's first letter)] February 7, 1942—Asheville

I have just finished reading your most welcome letter.

Yes, I'm at home. Those symptoms turned into the real thing and caught up with me yesterday. So here I am, all greased up and covered in flannel for the duration of this pesky cold. It has its advantage, though. I have that much more time to think about us and these past few weeks.

I still have to stop and wonder if it isn't all a pleasant dream, but then I have your perfume and your emblem on my coat too. There is a certain indescribable element within me that wasn't present before. I feel almost complete. There's more than just a corner of my heart reserved.

Marguerite was so sweet Sunday night after I came home. I went to her room and we talked a long time. Of course, I'll have to admit you appeared more than once in the conversation.

We're having real Dixieland weather: yes, snow and lots of it. You spoke of the moon being so bright Sunday night. Marguerite and I sat on the settee Monday night and watched it come over the mountain.

There are so many things I could say about your letter and what it means, but what would be the use. All we can do is grin and bear it, and hope for the best and that it won't be long before all this will be over and we can go back to our normal living. Perhaps it is just as well we don't have that Easter date. It would only make things harder, but then I guess we can take it. I think I'll come anyway even if you aren't there and maybe I'll go and see your mother.

I'm sending you a picture, the one you forgot. I was afraid it wouldn't fit in your wallet, hence the folder. There's room on the other side for your other girlfriend but you'd better not let me see it.

This letter seems to be going on and on. I hope I'm not boring you and that you aren't disappointed in me as a letter writer. I have five from you and this is my first. I'm not going to read it over. I might tear it up if I do.

[Billee to Charles] February 8, 1942—Asheville

I kept thinking "this time last Saturday night" and "this time last Sunday."

My sniffles are still with me. One advantage my cold has, I've caught up on my knitting and reading. I did the back of an army sweater and a sleeve-and-a-half on a child's Red Cross sweater. You must have given me incentive.

I can't seem to forget anything. All I do is remember. I have such a lost feeling not knowing where you are, because, of course, I realize the address you gave me is just an address.

I hope you received the picture and my letter safely and that this one reaches you as well. I sincerely hope you were able to spend some time with your family. I know how much it meant to you.

I'll have to close now, no more paper and yet I am very reluctant to leave you.

/////

[Charles to Billee] February 9, 1942—Fort Dix, N.J.

I may be only 70 miles from home but I'd give anything to be back in Camp Croft. They said Croft was a model camp. Now I can understand it more than ever. So far, we have had snow, rain and freezing weather. Moreover, we still haven't been located with our proper outfits. I had been with one company, moved to another, and then moved back to the first one.

Nothing has been said about our radio work and we are only hoping it is cleared up soon so we can get down to serious work. Of course, there are plenty of rumors, good and bad, that are too numerous to list.

I was fortunate in getting a pass to go home over the weekend. Mother, Dad and the "kids" were overjoyed at the family reunion. My younger brother [Eddie] had received his notice to report for induction so he will have his uniform in a couple of weeks.

I believe I told you not to count too heavily on seeing me if you came north for Easter. If I am here, there isn't anything I would want more than to just hold you in my arms for days. But everything is too indefinite. I can honestly say I don't know if I'll be here for a day, week, month, or a year. This is a combat unit and is liable to take off at any time. It is not fully organized yet, but then again, I can't say when it will be ready. At any rate, I'm going along doing my best in whatever I'm told and hoping the day is not too far off for us to make up for lost time.

Do you know, at 11:00 o'clock Saturday night I excused myself from the family to go out on the porch and stand there alone wishing I was back at the Grove Park Inn with you held close to me. There will be one of our anniversaries the 31st of each month—together with the 17th, the day I first looked into your eyes!

[Billee to Charles] February 9, 1942—Asheville

Here I am again, but so relieved to know you are still somewhere close. You don't know the visions I had: boats, airplanes, tanks, etc.

It's nice to be with a company that has such a reputation. I know you must feel proud, especially since you are back in radio. I'm so glad you are able to spend some time with your family. I was worried, for fear that you wouldn't, and how awful that would have been.

[Charles to Billee] February 13, 1942—Fort Dix, N.J.

Your "little bit of heaven" reached me Wednesday night—letter, picture, case and all—and I wish I could get one every day. Don't take that too seriously, but it *is* the way I feel. It told me so many things I wanted to hear.

I wouldn't dare put anyone else's picture [in the case], not only because you wouldn't want it, but because it just wouldn't belong.

It appears as if I would be here for a while yet. How long, I can't say. About your Easter visit . . . Mother will be happy to see you whether I am still here or not.

I'm writing this, hoping you get it by the 17th—our first month's anniversary. It seems as though we've known each other a lifetime instead of a few short weeks.

The picture case Billee sent to Charles. Charles carried it in his pocket all through the war. (Kiley Family)

/////

[Charles to Billee] February 16, 1942—Fort Dix, N.J.

It's raining tonight, but I can smile, since I have your last letter to read over and over again. Mother, Dad and my brother were here to visit me yesterday and your letter came with them, too.

Billee, I guess we both have that same "lost feeling." This past Saturday night, for me, was so terribly lonesome. I would have given ten years of my life to have you with me if only for an hour. But then, I do have "you" in the picture case next to my heart.

And, as I've said before, no matter where I am and what I'm doing, I'll be thinking only of the time when I can hold you oh, ever so tightly. Because, you see, I do love you so much, Billee Ruth! Like you, I can scarcely believe it happened, and, so suddenly. There were people who interested me in the past, but none who made my pulse quicken whenever I looked at her, none of whom I could say, "This is it!"

///////

[Billee to Charles] February 17, 1942—Asheville

You'd laugh if you could see where I'm at this minute, perched up on the last flight of stairs going to the roof. It's the only quiet place I could find. Our [work] lounge is something like a bedlam let loose during the lunch hour and you have about as much chance of relaxing as a monkey in a cage.

If my letter was "a bit of heaven," yours was the sunshine we didn't have yesterday. What a day. Rain . . . literally buckets of it all day long and far into the night. I don't as a rule mind rain, but coupled with the bad [war] news we've been getting, it was a little more than I could take.

You're sparking me with your letters, Charles. I've had one almost every other day since you left. I'm not complaining. I love it and your letters. They are so much like you and few people can do that. I can close my eyes and almost hear you say what's written.

I'm sending a little something along with this to help keep those Yankee breezes away. I'm hoping that it fits. The size was a guess and I had to be the model since we don't have any men-folk around to try things on. If it doesn't fit, give it to someone it does.

One of our large schools near Asheville is being turned into a naval academy. There is also talk of the building of an Army airfield to be used for training purposes, that is, to familiarize pilots to mountain flying.

I showed our picture [taken the morning after they first met] to Mom and, of course, she turned it over to the back [where Charles had written a note], and this is what she said: "My, he certainly made up his mind in a hurry."

I've had to move from my perch, and I'm really writing under difficulties. We have so many sick in our office that we are all having to do double duty. I'm in the tube room where all the sales tickets come, trying to make change and write in between.

Please, stay 'till [*sic*] Easter.

/////

I've been trying to write this since Thursday, but without much luck. Thursday night we had company and Friday night I went to first-aid class and the movies afterward. Last night we had company again.

Hank Gornicki's [major league baseball pitcher with the St. Louis Cardinals] wife and baby are here to stay while he is in spring training camp. I know Wynne Gornicki quite well. We have been quite a merry household. It's a very pleasant change to have a little one around again.

Charles, I enjoyed your letter so much and your picture arrived safely. I was so happy to see "you" again. I put it on my dresser so that when I open my eyes in the morning, you're the first thing I see.

I am getting excited at the prospect of seeing New York again, but more at the slim chance that you may still be in the vicinity. I'm trying hard not to count too much on you being there so that I won't be too disappointed.

I do so want to see you again before they send you away. I miss you a lot, Charles, but I'm not lonely because I feel you are always nearby. Many times, I feel that if I closed my eyes and reached out my hand, you would be there to take it.

/////

I thought I'd be able to write over the weekend, but I was able to get a pass and spent Saturday p.m. and Sunday at home. Even then, I started to write twice but I was interrupted both times. It seems as though everyone wants to see a soldier when he is home.

I received the sweater and, Billee, you couldn't have sent anything I would appreciate more, except your picture.

Your letters lift me up so much. So, don't ever worry about me getting too many or that they are too long. If my little remembrances make you smile, or bring home the thoughts I send, it makes me happy. I want to make you the happiest girl in the world.

All this may sound rather small, coming from someone who, just now, isn't in a position to make anyone happy. Still, I'd like to believe I can one day. I don't mean to get heroic, or wave the flag, but I *do* know that what I have to do now must come first. You can understand that, can't you?

I showed your pictures to the family as well as several friends. In fact, I showed them to everyone I met since I received them. And I have yet to hear any of them say I didn't "strike gold" in Asheville. Mother's opinion was that you were "so sweet." My sisters, Eleanor and Bette, just said, "Ah!" I did take a bit of ribbing from my brothers, Ed and John, but I loved it. Ed, by the way, expects to be in the service by March 16.

Don't worry about discouraging news about the war. Everything will be all right soon. And when we start rolling, it will be over in no time at all.

[Charles to Billee] February 26, 1942—Fort Dix, N.J.

I received your latest "bit of heaven" yesterday morning, and, although I wanted to write immediately, I was prevented because of guard duty. However, I have the chance now and I'm going to make the best of it.

You ask if I'm not "being hasty in declaring myself." And I can very easily understand the question. It *is* hard to believe such a thing could happen when we have known each other for so short a time. When you consider the barriers we face, it becomes a more difficult problem, doesn't it? But if this is any more assurance, I know I have never been as certain of anything before as I am in loving you.

I didn't mention this before because I wasn't sure it would work out, but we are publishing a company paper and I've been doing some work on it. I'll send you a "first edition." It won't be so good because it will be mimeographed and practically all of the fellows never had experience in publishing. I'll let you know how I make out.

[Billee to Charles] February 28, 1942—Asheville

The only reaction I had today from your letter was to hop a plane and come the fastest way possible to reassure you that there isn't any doubt in my mind as to your feelings or mine. Like you, I have never been impulsive, although I've always wanted to be, but that practical side always rose above it . . . then the exception had to come someday. Besides, I'm tired of being practical.

It's strange how different people can be. There never has been anyone I could talk to or write to the way I am doing with you. That must be complete understanding.

Charles, I've meant to tell you before how much I admire your spirit and reaction to your present position because it is definitely a sacrifice. It would be different if you were just out of school, but you were making a career for yourself and you haven't said anything or written anything that would lead me to believe you felt sorry for yourself.

I finished my first-aid course; now all I have to do is work for my grade and certificate from Washington and I'll be all prepared. I'm going to take the air raid warden's course next and the advanced first-aid course. I sincerely hope I never have to use it, but then, anything can happen.

I bought my Easter bonnet for our Easter date. I tried to look at it from a man's viewpoint but I doubt if I'm succeeding. Anyhow, it is cute and definitely an Easter bonnet.

///////

[Billee to Charles] March 1, 1942—Asheville

Everyone is curious about your [regimental] button on my coat, but it's still too wonderful to talk about. Besides, so many of them are just curious and not interested: you might know, working in a large department store. Of course, I have a few special friends that know a little and to whom I showed your picture. They all agreed you were definitely smooth, nice and they liked your looks.

Do you remember going by that rock house on the mountain and me saying it was rumored a Nazi spy lived there? They caught him the other day . . . in fact, a whole gang. The fences and gates were all electrified and they had to kill four large dogs before they got in. They found a high-powered sending and receiving set plus other damaging evidence. It hasn't been published, but the information came from an authoritative source. They were all taken to Washington. The man who built the house has been in Asheville several years, but the house was built last fall. He lived at the Inn all last winter. I imagine he's been under surveillance for some time.

[This is possibly reference to a raid on the house of William Dudley Pelley, founder of an American Christian fascist organization called "The Silver Shirts," modeled after Hitler's Brown Shirts, with a membership at its height in the 1930s of around fifteen thousand people in twenty-two states. Pelley lived in Asheville for several years and did build a house near the Grove Park Inn. In April 1942 he was tried for sedition and insurrection and served fifteen years in a federal penitentiary.]

[Charles to Billee] March 2, 1942—Fort Dix, N.J.

I'm not waiting for your letter to write tonight. It is a rather unusual setting, too, because I'm on guard duty again and I'm writing this during my four hours off, in the guardhouse. I can hear a soldier playing, "You Made Me Love You," on the piano in the Recreation Hall next door. It seems appropriate because it reminds me of Asheville. Not that you *did* make me love you—that was as natural as the rising and setting of the sun—but we danced to that song so often, didn't we?

There were 300 men moved out from our regiment yesterday—destination unknown—but none from my company. I hope they continue on that scale until after I see you, and hold you again. Fellows with whom we trained in Camp Croft were among those leaving. They were notified Saturday night to pack their bags and left yesterday morning. That's how it happens.

It's almost time to get out to my post again so I'll have to leave you for a while.

Remember me to all and take care of yourself. By the way, do you know the words to "Only Forever"? Well, I'm thinking of them now: "Do I long to be with you as the years come and go . . ."

/////

[Charles to Billee] March 4, 1942—Fort Dix, N.J.

I've been lying on my bed for the past hour or so, reading your letter so many times, just being happy and so much in love with you. Billee, I wouldn't share my happiness with anyone tonight, unless it was with you. So, I preferred to remain "in" with my radio and you.

I want to tell you what I felt when you said, "you are necessary and important to me," and, "I am entrusting all my love and sincerity to you without question." I'll do everything humanly possible to be ever worthy of that trust, believe me. It is something like that I want to tell you while you are close to me, instead of writing about it.

Billee, it certainly was a surprise to hear that the "man in the mountain" was actually a spy. I recall that I had mentioned it was a good spot for a short-wave radio.

Now, about the company paper: it was 50 percent worse than I expected, and I did feel pessimistic. I couldn't expect to accomplish much with the meager equipment, time and help but things turned out pretty badly from my standpoint. However, everybody else thought it was a good effort considering our handicaps. In other words, instead of making a good thing of it, the idea of the paper is to give the men a little more interest in extra-curricular activity. In the end, I had to write, edit and rewrite practically everything. Because I wasn't on hand to watch the printer, he made several mistakes. Well, as long as we're happy, we'll get by.

/////

[Billee to Charles] March 5, 1942—Asheville

I expect you have read about our mountains being isolated by snow . . . 18 inches in fact and that is a snow here. They really make much of it down here. The war news almost took the second page. They closed the store at noon Tuesday—no business—so we all went home and played in the snow.

The fire department closed the theaters until the snow leaves the roofs. They are afraid that it is too heavy for the roofs to hold ... imagine. We've all been saving our money. I haven't been going quite so often. I used to go twice a week, but sometimes I don't go at all. It is just a habit I guess.

For the first time since you left, I heard "our song" [Tonight We Love, based on Tchaikovsky's Piano Concerto #1 and recorded by Tony Martin in 1941] yesterday morning just before I got up to go to work. Mother turned the radio on and that is what they were playing. I closed my eyes and felt you take my hand in yours, and remembered how many times we had heard it together.

Oak Lodge in the big snow—Asheville, March 1942. (Kiley Family)

/////

[Charles to Billee] March 6, 1942—Fort Dix, N.J.

Just now, I'm listening to Kate Smith's program and she's singing, "She'll Always Remember, So Don't You Forget." My happiest moments during the day are those spent thinking of our few weekends together. I don't know how many times I've covered the time, from our first moment together until the last.

Our first dance . . . do you remember the song? (Kate is singing, "Miss You.")

The first time I saw you, the first words we spoke. I remember I didn't catch your name when you introduced yourself. It didn't seem to matter because I was much more interested in the girl. Then, I remembered I'd *have* to know your name and found it on your tag.

I remember, too, how I sat in your living room, pretending to read the paper on Sunday morning, all the while watching you wherever you went. Wondering why you were out of my sight so long when it was really only for a moment or two.

I remember our night at the Inn and how proud I was of you at the President's Ball [at the Grove Park Inn]. The Sunday mornings in church, and how I longed to hold your hand but didn't think it would be very dignified. How much I missed you during the week, trying to speed up the time when I could see you.

/////

[Billee to Charles] March 6, 1942—Asheville

I'm sitting in our chair wishing I could turn the clock back to a certain Sunday afternoon so I wouldn't have to write. Instead, I'd be laying my head on your shoulder and whispering all the things I want you to hear. That would be so much better than trying to write. You'd laugh if you could hear all the plans I've made . . .

We are going to have our first air raid practice Monday. It seems hard to realize that anything could happen in this isolated place. But then, anything can happen and we'd best be prepared for what may come.

We had a birthday party for Mrs. Davidson [another long-time Oak Lodge guest]. She was 80 years old. We had cake and ice cream for her and Marguerite and I bought her cut flowers. She fairly beamed, she was so surprised. She is such a sweet old lady.

I should close and go to bed. I'm so sleepy and it is way past my bedtime. I had all good intentions of figuring my income tax and getting that off and here I am still writing. I'm so happy that I reassured you properly. I love writing to you. I guess I could go on and on. I know I'd better close now. They are beginning to tell ghost stories on the radio and I have much more pleasant thoughts than that, so off it goes and me with it.

//////

[Charles to Billee] March 9, 1942—Fort Dix, N.J.

You said you were looking forward to meeting the Kileys. Well, they are anxious to meet Miss Billee Ruth Gray. I might introduce them, briefly, now.

Dad . . . he's Charles, Sr. . . . is the best in the world to me. The head of a family of six children (a daughter passed away 13 years ago), he has worked hard to give his family the best possible, and I think he has done a fine job.

Mother . . . my best girl, since I have a sweetheart now, is to me what your mother is to you.

Then, there is John, Father John, the eldest of the children, and the pride of the family. He was ordained [as a Catholic priest] four years ago. Eddie, just 22, is next. They say he looks like me. He will be inducted one week from today, and uppermost in my mind is the effect it will have on Mother. I hope it won't be too bad. Eleanor, the "beauty" of the family, I claim, is 20 and worth her weight in gold. Bette (she was Betty until a year or so ago . . . you know how girls are) is the "baby." She is a little more shy than El and 18, but she has a disposition that can't be beat. Well, there they are. I may have been a bit prejudiced.

//////

[Billee to Charles] March 10, 1942—Asheville

I started your letter Friday night listening to Kate Smith's program, too. You have a better memory than I, since you say "Miss You" was the first tune we danced to. I always connected that with us, but I didn't know why.

I've wondered many times since that night what might have happened if I hadn't decided to invite myself to that party. I remember sitting beside that empty chair and wondering who was going to occupy it. Then, I saw you making your way toward our table and thought, "Mmmm, he looks nice. Maybe he's the one," and you were.

I can't remember having such wonderful times as those three weekends. I remember our first kiss. Somehow I knew you were going to and I didn't make any effort to prevent it and the thought went through my mind, "He'll think I'm a fine one that I just go around letting everyone kiss me." It was such a rare moment. I was afraid to move for fear I'd spoil it all, and then I wanted you to do it again.

I especially remember that afternoon we dropped in the drug store and played all the records, songs I'd heard so many times but they never meant as much to me as at that moment, and you holding my hand.

I made up reasons to come back to the living room. I just couldn't believe it all happened. I kept saying to myself, "This can't be me . . . watch your step or you'll be falling," but that was a laugh. I had already done that. That last night I can't even write about. There just aren't words to describe how I felt. I'm still afraid it's all a dream and maybe that's what you have fallen in love with. I want so much to see you again, not to reassure myself, but you.

///////

[Billee to Charles] March 12, 1942—Asheville

You made me so happy with your call last night and letter today, I feel even more reassured after hearing you tell me yourself. Charles, I wanted so much to tell you, too, what you told me but I couldn't make you hear without everyone in the house knowing, too. It is still much too wonderful to share with anyone yet. Then, too, it will be so much more wonderful to be with you and tell you how much you mean to me. The only thing is, I'm afraid when the moment comes I'll be so tongue-tied I won't be able to say it.

My cousin enlisted in the Marines and is at Parris Island, S.C. He is to have six days at the end of his first six weeks so his family is going to meet him here—

[his mother is] one of Mother's older sisters—so we'll have a family reunion soon.

I had to laugh at Mom last night after you called. She said, "Hmmm. He must have it bad." And then a little later, "At last I think you have met someone that appreciates you." She asked me if I was to see you in New York and I said I wasn't sure and she said, "I don't see any point in going, then."

[Charles to Billee] March 13, 1942—Fort Dix, N.J.

It meant so much to me to talk with you the other night. I suppose I shouldn't have been so outspoken by telling you how much I love you, not realizing that someone would be within earshot of your voice, preventing you from saying things that perhaps you wanted to say.

One of the fellows was outside the phone booth when I called and later remarked, "Wow, you dropped so many quarters in I lost count!" I told him it was only $1.10 but was worth many more times that.

Billee, I'm enclosing our regimental insignia, another of my forget-me-nots, which you may hold for safekeeping. Better still, you may wear it if you wish. It is the standard insignia of the 135th Regiment. The colors are blue and silver. The cloverleaf in the center signifies the "Minnesota Volunteers" who formed the first 135th prior to the Civil War and who fought seven major battles in that war. The crossed swords signify action during the "Philippine Insurrection," while the figure on the right was carved during the Spanish-American War. The "fleur de lys" on top was earned in World War I. The motto, "To the last man," was adopted and incorporated in 1929 and was taken as the result of action when our regiment was sent into battle to hold a key position. After weeks of intense warfare, the battle was won and the 135th reported every man present or "accounted for." I am told there were more casualties in the 135th in that action than there were in any other regiment in any battle during the last three wars.

It may sound grim, but those are the things we are supposed to uphold.

[Billee to Charles] March 15, 1942—Asheville

This is just a note that I hope you will receive in time for our second anniversary. I am enclosing a little something I picked up last week [a shamrock charm]. You were all I could think of the moment I saw it and since it's St. Patrick's Day, it is very timely. I hope you will like it. You don't have anything lasting except the sweater and that will wear out. I hope it will bring you good luck always.

The war is coming home to us here. We have lost four boys in the community: one I went to school and worked with for several years. That is the hard part of it all.

My girlfriend in the office went on her vacation to Columbia, S.C. to visit her cousin and 60,000 soldiers. We had a lot of fun teasing her, but she has a good sense of humor.

We had word from my young brother [Warren Gray, who was living in Ohio] and he will be home for the Easter holidays. Mom is getting quite excited. He is the only boy and the pride and joy of the family. He is so grown up now with his job and newly assumed responsibility. It seems hard to realize . . . he was such a little fella for so long.

I'm tired tonight for some reason or other and I'd give a lot to have your shoulder under my head for a little while. I know I could relax. I have done quite a bit today, and I've been up since 8:00 a.m. getting breakfast, helping with dinner and supper, the usual Sunday routine.

[Charles to Billee] March 18, 1942—Fort Dix, N.J.

I visited my brother here at the Reception Center. He was inducted Monday. Poor kid, he looked a little bewildered by everything. I guess I looked the same way once. Mother and my elder brother came down today and I took them over to the Reception Center to see Eddie. He will be leaving here in a day or so for his training camp.

Only two and a half weeks now. Your plans sound swell. I'll do what I can to elaborate on them. First of all you can count on me getting a pass from 1:00

p.m. Saturday the 4th until 6:00 a.m. on Monday, the 6th. If things break right, I may be able to get a pass the following weekend, too.

/////

[Billee to Charles] March 20, 1942—Asheville

I just finished listening to the war correspondent from Melbourne telling of MacArthur's arrival. It was quite stirring and so realistic, I felt as if I were there. He certainly has made history in the very short time. His escape was something you only expect to find in fiction and not real life.

[MacArthur had an active public relations department in the Philippines working overtime in the weeks before America's surrender there, to influence public opinion in favor of his rescue; the public relations officers were part of the rescued party. MacArthur abandoned an entire standing army, including over 100 Army nurses, which was starving along with the Philippine civilian population; the Axis powers took delight in calling him a coward.]

I know how your Mother must feel with both her boys in the Army now. It's a help, though, that you are together for just a little while. Perhaps he will be sent South. I'm wondering how long it's going to be before my young brother will go. He will be eighteen in July. My mother will certainly take it hard, he being the only boy and the baby in the family. I dread it.

Two weeks from tonight this time, I'll be speeding through the night on my way to you and our weekend. It hardly seems possible.

/////

[Charles to Billee] March 29, 1942—Fort Dix, N.J.

Your letter of Thursday came at noon today in time to keep me company over the weekend, since I'm staying in camp this week in order to ensure my pass next week.

I haven't forgotten that ever-so-big "little item," that you love me. Nothing can make me forget it. If I never see you again, which terrifies me to even think of it, and I live to be 1,000,000, I'd love you then, as now. Whenever I haven't something military on my mind, I can only think of plans for us to catch up on the happiness we are missing now.

I was able to get to a nearby town for a moment last night, in order to call home. Mother told me my younger brother left camp last Sunday and she hasn't heard from him since. I have an idea he may have gone to the West Coast for his training, which would explain the delay in notification. They may have heard from him today.

/////

[Charles to Billee] March 31, 1942—Fort Dix, N.J.

When you receive this I will have spoken with you on the phone and received the latest details on your train reservations, etc. So, we won't have to discuss much of that, will we?

Charles and Billee on top of the Empire State Building—New York City, April 1942. (Kiley Family)

The only thing I am vitally interested in is getting to see you as fast as my feet and other transportation will carry me.

All my love and kisses, forever and always, C.

[This was the first time Charles signed off with "forever and always." It became his singular signature closing to nearly every letter he wrote to Billee.]

CHAPTER 2

APRIL–OCTOBER 1942

We lost our boss this week to the Army Air Corps. Everything happened so suddenly . . . We all kissed him goodbye and sent him on his way with a new Elgin watch as a farewell present. He said he'd only be gone a few months.

[Billee to Charles, August 1942.]

/////

The War: In the Philippines, Corregidor was under siege in April and lost in May. Thousands of prisoners were forced on a death march to POW camps, where the Japanese saw their surrender as weakness and subjected them to maltreatment of all kinds. Soon, the Solomon Islands also fell to the Japanese. One bright spot was the US Navy air success at Midway in June. In September, as battles heated up at Guadalcanal in the Pacific, a Japanese seaplane launched from a submarine made it to southern Oregon, and dropped incendiary bombs in a forested area, but did little damage.

In North Africa, German and Italian forces swept through Libya to Tobruk, where they captured more than thirty thousand Allied troops.

A combination of substantial losses in the Atlantic and Hitler's order to bomb historic British towns put pressure on Winston Churchill's leadership. He retaliated by sending Royal Air Force bombers to Hamburg and Essen. Meanwhile, the first German U-boat sinking by a US destroyer took place in mid-April. Despite U-boat activity, convoys made frequent trips.

In late June, General Dwight D. Eisenhower was appointed commander of US armed forces in Europe. By July, four million US soldiers were serving the war effort. In response to this US buildup of forces in Britain, German Field

Marshal von Rundstedt devised the Atlantic Wall, a fortress along the coast of France.

[On April 30, a convoy carrying nineteen thousand troops left New York harbor for the British Isles. Charles Kiley was on board one of the ships, the *Aquitania*. During his trip, Charles kept a sporadic diary; excerpts from this diary are included in this chapter.]

/////

[Billee to Charles] April 14, 1942—Asheville

We arrived in Spartanburg on time at 5:50 a.m. Then I had to wait two hours and a half for a train to Asheville.

My take-off was a little lonely, with no one to see me off. I blew a kiss your way when we passed Trenton about 6:30.

There was a lot of gold braid on the train, both Army and Navy. They were all plastered before the evening was over. I never saw so much scotch.

Mom is in the midst of housecleaning. I've told her about us and she doesn't seem to mind, just that I should be very sure. [On April 4, while the two were in New York City, Charles had asked Billee to marry him.] There isn't any doubt about that.

Not being able to sleep, it is only natural that my vacation with our two perfect weekends should be constantly in my thoughts. There aren't words to describe what they meant to me. It took such a lot to go out of that station Sunday night. I ran practically all the way back to the hotel. I was afraid to go slow; I knew I'd never get there.

The mountains were simply gorgeous coming in. The dogwood and mountain pinks are all in bloom, and the new leaves all coming out ... definitely a spring picture. There isn't any place like it. When all this is over, I'm really going to show them to you in all their glory. I love them so. Outside of Mom, that's all I'd miss here.

Now I'm going to pray for a furlough soon, and our happiness.

[Charles to Billee] April 15, 1942—Fort Dix, N.J.

If I could have one wish granted it would be that we could be married tonight. I want it so much it scares me! And don't you dare say, "Fraidy Cat."

But that isn't what I had planned for us, Billee, a "hurry-up" wedding, so to speak. You deserve everything that goes with it and I mean to give it to you. Yes, I know our time is short, and I'll be honest with you. I'm out on a limb, trying to weigh the merits and demerits of taking advantage of our time . . . now, or waiting. Like you, sweetheart, I'm not afraid of what will happen but I do think we must be sensible in anything we do. It will be the biggest thing in our lives and we have to have both feet on the ground when we decide.

I've seen fellows in the service married and I thought them insane, if only because of the terrific handicap thrown on the girl's shoulders. Finding myself in the same position, I wonder whether or not they were right. It must have been after one o'clock before I could sleep last night, trying to arrive at a decision. Finally, I realized we must wait until we can see each other again.

[Billee to Charles] April 17, 1943—Asheville

Just three months ago. It doesn't seem possible . . . so much has happened.

Marguerite is leaving permanently. As you know, her mother has been quite ill, hence her decision to go home to take care of her. I am going to miss her so very much. She has been more than a friend and so much closer to me than either of my sisters.

Now, to get down to business. I had no idea such a simple thing as getting married could cause so much trouble. I don't mean that the way it sounds.

My darling "Fraidy-cat," I appreciate no end your concern for what I deserve. I have such a warm feeling knowing you think of me in that respect. It wouldn't be a "hurry-up" wedding. It's been planned for years. I've just been waiting for the moment and you. Now that I've found you, there's just the moment.

I've thought it over from all angles. Maybe you will be different when you come back. Perhaps you won't think the same . . . that I'm the one you want.

This has been going through my mind since I came home. You will probably have had so many experiences that will change you.

I wish, sitting here in our corner, that I could turn the clock back two weeks. I would be speeding through the night on my way to you. Better still, if I could turn it ahead five years. We would be in our own living room with all this worry and anxiety behind us. You with your newspaper and me not so far away with my knitting and somewhere in the distance, Junior crooning himself to sleep. There'll be no rocking in this family, not with a ball team in the making.

P.S. Dreamed all last night I was making you chocolate cake.

[Charles to Billee] April 17, 1942—Fort Dix, N.J.

Billee, if you had followed me into Penn Station on Sunday night, you would have seen me find a secluded corner and stare into space, afraid to look behind me in fear of finding you there. If you had followed me, I don't believe I would have gone back to camp that night. I was even afraid to move because if I did it may have been back to your hotel.

This afternoon I was thinking of us three months ago. Honestly, I can't suppress the feeling that we've known each other ten times three months. There are two dates I'll want to remember always, January 17 and April 4.

PS: Baseball note: Jersey City had a paid admission of over 55,000 yesterday for opening day, the largest crowd in baseball for 1942. Last year it was over 60,000. The stadium can hold 30,000 crowded. But they can still sell 55,000 tickets!

[Billee to Charles] April 19, 1942—Asheville

I thought last night would never end. I ironed the good things I took to New York and put them away in tissue paper and sachets until the next vacation, wrote you a letter and tore it up . . . fine way to spend a Saturday night.

I've been trying to imagine what your weekend has been like. The family probably came to see you today. I hope so. They are such a nice family. I hope they like me as much as I do them. I've been engaged two weeks now. Isn't that wonderful? I celebrated by doing your ring [a class ring of Charles's acting as a temporary engagement ring] up in fresh adhesive so it's all bright and shining.

/////

[Billee to Charles] April 20, 1942—Asheville

One of the girls in the office had a letter from a boy in the Army she knows. It was sent from Alaska, and the letter took two weeks by airmail and half of it was cut out with a scissors here and there. Didn't make much sense. In fact, it looked like a lace doily. She didn't know much after she read it . . . some four pages.

You know I've always wondered about these people that write letters to the same people every day and what they could write about. Now I know.

I know you must have wished that you were there for that opening game. Oh, well, there will come a day when you'll be able to write all about them again and probably with me tagging along behind. Oh, I forgot about our "ball team."

Don't worry about me. I don't want to be a hindrance to the defense program. That would be sabotage.

/////

[Billee to Charles] April 22, 1942—Asheville

I'm sitting on my bed with your picture in front of me and when I'm not writing, I'm just looking and marveling that anything so wonderful could happen to me.

I sent Mom off to the movie, one I had already seen—*Remember the Day*. A lot like us except about the last war and he didn't come back.

I feel so helpless down here, not doing anything very worthwhile, but I guess there are a lot like me just waiting and trying hard to do it with a smile. I want to see the day when we'll be able to smile with our eyes, too . . . laugh and love . . . when all this is over.

When I made my very brazen proposal that last Sunday night in the station [Billee had suggested that she stay in New York so they could be married at once], it was for a purely selfish reason. I felt that I could stand the waiting better knowing I really belonged to you. It isn't easy to explain, but I think you know what I mean. Regardless, I'll be somewhere around, waiting, when you come back.

PS: Don't know whether you saw the papers or not, about the sabotage down here. 12,000 acres in Pisgah Forest burned by set fires. They have caught three that they suspect. In the meantime, three defense factories have had to close for two days and two dams are endangered. The fire is still going on in some parts, but they have it pretty well under control now. The original fire was an accident, they think, but during the night additional fires were set.

[Charles to Billee] April 23, 1942—Fort Dix, N.J.

Jack Donnell [an Army friend from Camp Croft] came over to see me tonight and tell me he was married last Saturday in Brooklyn to Theda Franklin. When he told me all about it, I was amazed to find their case is almost an exact replica of ours. Only, they did something about it.

She is starting back to Asheville on Sunday, I believe, and she'll stay there until he comes back for her. She is staying at the Asheville Y.W. He thought she would be lonely and would enjoy your company. You can decide what to do about it.

Jack was so happy, telling me about it, and it wasn't jealousy I felt, but envy. You see, they made plans a long time ago.

That's one of the things I'll consider when I think of us, Billee. We deserve a four-star wedding and everything that goes with it. We deserve a honeymoon to rank with any and as a good start. We won't have those things now and I wonder if you won't miss them?

[Charles to Billee] April 25, 1942—Fort Dix, N.J.

Forgive me for using a typewriter, but I have news tonight, good and bad, and I can get it off to you a bit faster.

By reading my return address on the envelope you must know by now that a promotion came through today. I'll have to wait a little while longer for my corporal's stripes, but I took a step in that direction today by earning my one stripe as Private First Class. They tell me I have to go through the stages of a Pfc. before getting two stripes. What's more, it means six dollars more a month, more for me to save and send you.

Now the bad news is . . . I can't say. I want to tell you more but it would come under the heading of censorship. My plan is to call you either next Thursday, Friday or Saturday nights. If I don't call, you'll know our time ran out.

[Billee to Charles] April 29, 1942—Asheville

I have your airmail that came via special messenger. Theda called me tonight and said she had brought both the radio and letter with her. Of course, I didn't waste any time getting to the Y. We talked for a bit and she told me all about her wedding and how it all went off like clockwork. She looks so happy. She said she didn't mind leaving Jack as much this time as before, even though it was under such uncertainties. She also told me a little of what prompted your letter, and how well you looked and what a nice tan you have. I was envious of her, having been able to see you just this past Sunday.

I'm so proud, I feel like they pinned a stripe on me, too. It won't be long until you have another to go with it. Now I want a picture, if possible, to see if you've changed.

My darling, I'm just sitting here in "our corner" with my pen poised. All I can think of now is how very much I love you. I always seem to end up with that. It's the only thing I'm really sure of . . .

Left Fort Dix by train at 3:30 p.m. Passed through Jersey City at dusk. Had a last look at Journal Square and Downtown where people cheered from windows and streets as we passed. Boarded ferry at Exchange Place to uptown New York where we embarked on *Aquitania*. Saw *Normandie* in next pier still lying on its side. [Seized by the United States after the German invasion of France, the *Normandie* caught fire in February 1942 while being refitted as a troop carrier, capsized and sank at Pier 88 on the Hudson River in Manhattan.] Our quarters leave much to be desired. Walters and Rabbitt bunked above me with Sgts. Styrlund, Reberg and Blackie Oliphant on the other side [members of Charles's unit]. Some of Coast Artillery were pushed in with us. Someone said we were to be in "C" deck staterooms but someone made a mistake.

/////

[Billee to Charles] April 30, 1942—Asheville

Your letter came this afternoon. It couldn't have been held up very long. I waited tonight until after 9:30 hoping just by accident you might have been able to get a call through.

I keep trying to wonder where you might be and I always end up with you beside me, reaching out for my hand. That's the way it will always be.

We aren't being punished. This is just what you might call an interruption before our life begins. I love you so much. Nothing will ever change that and I'll be here patiently waiting until all this is over . . . one day we'll look on this as just a bad dream.

/////

[From Charles's diary] April 30, 1942

Awoke at 6:50 a.m. to learn we were passing the Statue of Liberty. Had boat drill at 9:45 and then spent most of the day watching our convoy. The CO passed on info to non-coms that we will be part of the largest convoy in history. Present plans seem to be to go first to Halifax before starting over. The meals are terrible: mutton, bad corned beef, badly cooked vegetables, etc. Everybody's griping about something.

Two cruisers, at least 10 destroyers, and an aircraft carrier form our protection. One of the other transports is the *Cathay*.

[From Charles's diary] May 1, 1942

Noticed the colder weather during the night when I awoke a few times. Spent quite a bit of time on deck again. During the afternoon, a destroyer dropped three depth charges and a transport fired two shells from what appeared to be a six-inch gun. Bombers can be seen circling convoy occasionally. The carrier sent two planes up to hunt the sub. Report mail will be picked up tomorrow at Halifax. I've written several letters tonight. I'm wondering if Billee will come to New York.

[Charles to Billee] May 2, 1942—"Somewhere at Sea"

This will be censored and probably held until we reach our destination, but at least it is good to "talk" with you again.

You will forgive me for leaving so abruptly, won't you? And, too, you'll have to pardon Uncle Sam for interrupting our plans. If I had been there when you came back, we would surely have gone through with our "miracle." I know I couldn't have said, "Wait," anymore. John came to see me two days before I left and I told him I was determined.

Now, about our trip:

[LARGE PORTION CENSORED]

Looking at the full moon last night I could only wish this was a different situation and we were on our way to a [CENSORED] honeymoon. But how different it really is!

/////

Arrived at Halifax this morning at 7:30 a.m. Rocky cliffs on both sides of the straits. Gulf of St. Lawrence lies ahead. Nova Scotia looks cold and bleak but peaceful. Guns are emplaced atop cliffs at entrance to harbor. Also, a submarine net. Two tankers sunk in harbor. My mail was censored quite a bit. The company moved to better quarters aft at night.

/////

Convoy left Halifax at 8:30 a.m. after refueling and taking on water. During the afternoon, a destroyer dropped six depth charges, marking the second "attack" so far. The vibration from the bombs is remarkable. Three more charges were dropped at 9:00 p.m. while Rabbitt, Solow, Gee and I were playing cards. Weather cold. Time was pushed up one hour today.

/////

Our censor was kind enough to tell me there were some parts of my first letter that had to be eliminated so I'll endeavor to keep this one "clean."

It's not necessary, but I'll tell you again that I miss you so very much, and that I love you more than ever.

Our company was moved to more comfortable quarters since my last letter and the trip is getting more enjoyable than ever. I've been reading quite a bit since I left, our training manuals and Reader's Digest, mostly. Today our company assembled for a highly interesting talk by one of the chaplains aboard about the customs of the people we will meet, the change in currency, etc.

Our boat drills continue along with the enforced rule of wearing life belts at all times. While there isn't any immediate danger, there is always the possibility of an emergency. The company received commendation from the colonel for the cleanliness and orderliness of our quarters yesterday and today the general passed on favorable comments on the cleanliness of the deck we are to keep in order.

/////

[From Charles's diary] May 4, 1942

Sea is getting rough although it isn't felt until the convoy changes course. Fog has settled and is "pea soup." Unable to see any other part of the convoy. Bulletin says, "Cleveland leading A.L. after winning 12 straight. Dodgers running away with N.L."

Weather mild.

/////

[Billee to Charles] May 5, 1942—Asheville

I couldn't help but remember that yesterday was one of our anniversaries. Just one month ago that we started out on that memorable weekend . . . remember?

I went to a movie last night. It was cute and very timely. Ray Milland and Paulette Goddard in *The Lady Has Plans. Jungle Book* is coming this week. Every time I pass the billboard I think of how we sat in the last row like a couple of school kids holding hands [in New York]. I loved every minute of it . . . couldn't tell you now what the picture was about except maybe for the snake.

/////

[From Charles's diary] May 5, 1942

During lunch, seven depth charges were dropped. Men take it as a matter of routine now. Passed a fishing schooner, which led me to believe we are near the coast of Newfoundland.

Met some quartermasters who have been in the army only six weeks!
Fog continues to be thick.

Company had manual of arms on deck today. Seemed silly to me.

[From Charles's diary] May 6, 1942

Big news today was the rumor the *Aquitania* had been sunk!

Fog continued with intermittent rain.

Played bridge at night with Solow, Rabbitt and Quentin. Orchestra from 135th Regiment band played and sounded OK—but good!

Forgot to mention before ... "Cap," police dog of "G" Co. is aboard and quartered over us. Could write a good story about him.

Time went ahead one hour for the second time.

[Billee to Charles] May 7, 1942—Asheville

I'm enjoying your radio, carrying it out to the kitchen, in the yard to sit, etc. I'll try not to wear it out before you come back. Mom just loves it. She doesn't see how anything so little can have such volume.

[From Charles's diary] May 7, 1942

Fog lifted but rain fell from cloudy sky. Dreary all day. Haven't seen the sun in four days. Saw schools of porpoises this afternoon. Put my watch up another hour today! Speed of ships said to be 12 knots. Sea swells are rocking boat all day.

Counted 11 ships in convoy: 10 destroyers, an aircraft carrier, cruisers and battleship. The latter prepared to launch plane at 4:00 p.m. but I didn't stay on deck to see it. Another bridge game tonight. Guard duty for me tomorrow.

/////

[From Charles's diary] May 8, 1942

Routine day until I went on guard at 10:00 p.m. It was an eerie feeling to be alone on "A" Deck forward for four hours. Saw a sky full of stars for the first time. It was cold! The convoy looked like black bugs on the water. Complete blackness.

Man put in brig for KOing British sailor who said United States was coming over to get glory again. Lt. Nelson put man in brig for striking cigarette lighter. Ship is equipped with forty 50mm guns, I'm told.

Corregidor has fallen!

Britain takes over Madagascar!!

The ship's cat had four kittens!!!

/////

[From Charles's diary] May 9, 1942

Battleship, two destroyers, and part of convoy went to Iceland during the night. Report says we'll be in Belfast on Monday morning. Expect air raids tomorrow.

Three depth bombs dropped at 12:50 p.m. and nine more at 6:15! This makes sixth attack of trip by subs.

Listened to lecture on Ireland at night and it looks like we're in for a rough time during our stay.

"H" Company will man the 50s tomorrow.

Had frankfurters and beans for dinner. Hurray!

English £ (pound) is worth $4.04.

/////

[From Charles's diary] May 10, 1942

Mother's Day . . .

Beans bad. Even catsup couldn't kill the taste.

Claim two more sub attacks during night making nine in all.

RAF bomber picked up convoy in afternoon.

Gen. Daley said to have flown over in Clipper and will meet us in Belfast tomorrow. Brig. Gen. Collins in charge here.

We will be billeted in Bally Mena, 20 miles from Belfast.

[From Charles's diary] May 11, 1942

Land sighted at 6:00 a.m. Passed shores of Scotland and Northern Ireland. Anchored in harbor several miles from Belfast. Reported five-hour air raid on Belfast last night, which indicates MI leaked out. Ireland looks beautiful from harbor. Patch-quilt scenery all around us.

Another sub attack at 2:00 a.m. today. Woke everybody up. Rumor has us going to Scotland instead of Belfast. Can see ship sunk in harbor we now occupy. Co. H on guard. I'm with officers' quarters.

[From Charles's diary] May 12, 1942

On guard from 2:00 a.m. to 6:00 when ship pulled anchor at 4:30 and steamed out of harbor at 4:45 accompanied by two destroyers. Rest of convoy stayed at Belfast. Report says Belfast was so badly damaged *Aquitania* cannot be docked. Our destination said to be Glasgow. Three RAF planes joined us at 7:30.

Anchored in Firth of Clyde 3 miles from Glasgow at 9:15. Loch Lomond said to be nearby. What we can see of Scotland from here is beautiful. I wish I had a camera! Seaside resort on our left is Dunoon, on our right is Greenock. Battalion boarded tender at 8:00 p.m. Sunset will be at 10:00 p.m. Daylight ends at 11:30 p.m.!

[From Charles's diary] May 13, 1942

Slept on table in salon, awakened at 3:00 a.m. by several depth charges. Tender was full speed zig-zagging. Had Class "C" rations for breakfast. My first taste of rations. Scenic beauty left me breathless when daylight came. Passed Ballynage, Brook Hall, Boomhall, Crook, Clooney, St. Columba and finally docked in Londonderry. Was transported by bus to Bally Castle, about 50 miles away. Passed Coleraine where other troops are stationed.

/////

[Billee to Charles] May 15, 1942—Asheville

My cousin and aunt arrived on Monday and are staying through next week so we've really had almost a family reunion. I haven't seen either in several years. You'd like my cousin. I had a day off today and we went to Chimney Rock. That was my first trip up. There weren't but just a few up there and we couldn't even get a ride down. We really had a ten-mile jaunt . . . getting in training for the Army. Ha.

We now have Germans and Japs in our Grove Park Inn for the duration [Axis nation civilians caught in United States when war was declared]. Isn't that something? Makes me mad every time I look up there.

My boss is leaving for the service. I don't know what is going to happen to our organization. Everyone is leaving.

/////

[Billee to Charles] May 16, 1942—Asheville

The weather has turned a little cool. I hope it doesn't frost and spoil Mom's garden. She had some 200 tomato plants set out besides potatoes, corn and string beans. We still have another plot to plant. We will have quite a garden. Mom is going to get some chickens, too. That will save a lot. She serves a lot of fried chicken in the summertime. I'm only hoping that we will have some people to feed. It doesn't look any too bright now.

I must go and get dressed. It will soon be time to go to the show. We are going to see *The Invaders* [British film also called *The 49th Parallel*, starring Lawrence Olivier and Leslie Howard, about a Nazi submarine attack on Canada]. I know it will be a pleasant diversion. Ha.

/////

[Charles to Billee] May 17, 1942—Northern Ireland

Yes, this is our anniversary and while you are not actually with me, you have been by my side more than ever today. I've been reading your letters, those I still have, in place of mail I hope will be forthcoming soon. We have been here only a short time and this is the first time I've been able to devote to writing. It is Sunday and we have the day to ourselves.

The voyage was something to remember. I will not give you all the details until I see you. But, I can say it was thrilling at times. We are quartered here in homes formerly occupied by residents. There are [CENSORED] in our particular base. We have to be housekeepers as well as soldiers. You would have enjoyed seeing me wrestle my wash this afternoon. There is a scarcity of laundry soap, so, instead of "Luxing" my undies, I "Woodbury'd" them!

There are several mess halls available within a short walking distance and a building with enough showers to take care of the men. Then, of course, we have bathtubs but hot water is pretty hard to get. We use what we can for washing and shaving.

The weather? So far we have been fortunate in getting more sun than rain. It is said that it rains quite often. The scenic beauty is something to behold. I'd want to describe it but it is not permissible. However, I will say, whatever you have heard about Irish beauty did not do it justice. Extreme homeliness can best describe the people.

Radios are very rare. I've heard only one. Our electric irons and razors, etc., aren't any good because of the different current. Dry cleaning is not available; sugar is rationed along with meat, chocolate and most everything else.

The girls, I've noticed, are very muscular besides being homely. A pretty girl in this section is very rare. A dance was held the other night and I was surprised to see how quickly some of the girls caught on to the American style. It wasn't for me because I was an MP on that night, stopping in at the dance only occasionally to see that everything was in order. An RAF orchestra supplied the music.

/////

[Billee to Charles] May 17, 1942—Asheville

Four months today. Remember, life began for us only to end for a little while.

My cousin Ann and I went to "Lucille's" last night for a little while with a bunch. I couldn't help but remember the times we were there together. I'm afraid I wasn't very good company.

Ann and I just came back from going up to the Inn. Of course, we couldn't go in the grounds, but we went up behind the Inn, up Sunset Mountain a way. We saw a couple of the prisoners. They have restricted the area a lot more for those than the others and it is all barbed-wired in.

/////

[Charles to Billee] May 20, 1942—Northern Ireland

I understand we may send cables now and I'll send mine to Father John tomorrow. It will merely consist of a "safe arrival" note in the event my previous letters were delayed.

I don't believe I could describe our beautiful surroundings, as I said Sunday. The beauty is here but the presence of our military life takes just a bit of an edge from it. Did I mention that we have a fireplace in every room in our quarters? Well, they are rather small. Still, they help to keep you in my mind. I'd give anything to be with you in our corner in front of the fireplace we know so well [at Oak Lodge].

Billee, the people here are most friendly and hospitable. We realize how little they have and appreciate their fine spirit more. Stylish clothing and anything but necessities in food are extremely rare because of rationing, etc. The

Irish appear to be splendid people, though going through life with an almost silent attitude. Perhaps it only seems that way to strangers.

As in the USA, our "working day" is long and quite active. We have "reveille" at 6:30 a.m. before starting our schedule at 8:00. "Recall" in the evening isn't until 5:30 p.m., one hour later than it was in Fort Dix. Daylight appears at approximately 6:00 and stays with us until almost 11:00 p.m. at this time of the year. It is 9:00 p.m. now and the sun is still shining!

We haven't had a salary since the first of April but we are expecting one any day. We are to be paid in local currency, I'm told. That means we will be weighed down with coins because when you have the equivalent of a dollar in change, it feels like five dollars or more in your pocket.

A baseball game between companies is being arranged for tomorrow and the people have been invited to watch a demonstration of the great American game.

[From Charles's diary] May 20, 1942

There is so much, and yet so little to write about our life here. We have been on two afternoon marches that were honeys! Our guns are here and that means gun drill. Looks like our marches will be four days a week. One of our marches took us to the top of Fairhead Mountain, the northernmost point in Ireland.

The people here are as gracious as people could be in their own silent way. The women are extremely muscular, probably because vehicular traffic consists mainly of bicycles. The cars here are a little bigger than our Austins. Still everyone appears to be very hospitable.

We haven't been paid since the first of April. Consequently, everybody is low on funds. I borrowed 8 shillings, fourpence from Johnny Quentin today for a cable to John but the Post Office was closed. I'll try again tomorrow.

The CO said tonight we would soon have an overnight march that would take us to the Giants' Causeway—one of the Seven Wonders of the World.

[Billee to Charles] May 25, 1942—Asheville

Mom hasn't been well and I've been home since Friday, getting in practice for our ball team. I have seven to cook for and I haven't been getting any complaints, either, so maybe I'll come up to the standard of a new bride without having you go through indigestion, etc., the first few months. To top it all off, our maid left the first of last week so that left me to be chief cook and bottle washer. Tonight for dinner, I made an Irish stew and all that goes with it, and a strawberry shortcake. I made the cake myself and it was edible. I can't wait to experiment on you.

[Charles to Billee] May 25, 1942—Northern Ireland

I couldn't possibly love you any more than I did when the mail orderly handed me your mail. It arrived with the first mail our company had received. I read the letters in order as if I was getting them one at a time.

I've been trying for three days to send you a cable, but every time I get a chance to go to the post office it is too late. You see, we have our working day up to 5:30 most of the time and the PO is closed then.

By the way, I'm to be our battalion reporter for the *Stars and Stripes,* the official paper of the US Army's Northern Ireland Forces (USANIF) and it will be taking up some of my extra time.

We were paid Saturday and I have already started to save.

P.S. Censors require that letters are to be written on one side of the paper. Can you send me a box of stationery? It's extremely scarce here.

[Billee to Charles] May 27, 1942—Asheville

The official news of your arrival came today via Father John.

What an experience you are having. I know you are taking advantage of it despite the circumstances that exist. Things will soon be rolling "over there."

Now I have a story. I didn't want to say anything about it before, until I had all the facts. Mom has been in the hospital since Sunday. She had seven hemorrhages from the throat in three days. They made tests and they all came out negative. A specialist in nose and throat was called in and he found a blood vessel had burst in the larynx. She is out of danger now and the vessel is healing. He doesn't seem to know what caused the trouble. I've been home since Saturday, being chief cook and bottle washer, but I haven't minded, just so Mom gets better. It's good training and I'll be needing it later on.

The men [working as guards at the Grove Park Inn, and quartered at Oak Lodge] brought some flowers from the Inn, from their rose gardens up there, for Mom. They stole them and carried them home in their lunch buckets. They told me to say the Grove Park Inn sent them. I thought it was sweet of them to think of her. They are all so nice and have been so patient since I've been running things here. They haven't seemed to mind my cooking.

The first women today applied for officers' training [in the Women's Auxiliary Army Corps, the WAAC]. I wanted to go, but I couldn't leave, and besides, I have to be sure of Mom before I do anything. Mom says to tell you your little radio has been a lifesaver. I took it to the hospital for her.

[Billee to Charles] June 1, 1942—Asheville

We brought Mom home today from the hospital and it was swell having her in the house again. There was such an empty place here without her. She is getting along fine, but she'll always have to be conscious of her throat and she won't be able to do any strenuous work.

I'm sending the *Sporting News* [a weekly magazine covering baseball] along with this. Thought you might like to see it.

[From Charles's diary] June 1, 1942

I sent the cable home to John on the 21st. We did not see the Giants Causeway and pulled out of Bally Castle on May 29. Moved on to Castle Parnoon from the 29th through the 31st. Our homes were tin huts amid a woodland camouflage. Whereas we had traveled in buses, we took to a truck convoy to go on to Omagh on Sunday, May 31. In Omagh our company is quartered in a huge former work house that was built in 1841!

[Billee to Charles] June 6, 1942—Asheville

What better way to spend Saturday night than writing to you? As usual, I'm missing you so much and I keep looking back to two months ago tonight. We had another anniversary Wednesday but I can't help making them fall on Saturday nights. Saturday nights seem so important to us. You know we never have spent a weekday together.

Mom is getting along fine now, but we don't know when there will be a recurrence. She thinks so much of you, Charles. She realizes that this isn't any flirtation. Every day she asks, "Any word?" When I'd go to see her in the hospital, she'd write on her tablet the same thing. They wouldn't let her talk for ten days. That was really an effort . . .

I keep wondering . . . what are you doing this minute? I have been so restless, I almost wish I could fly to wherever you are, even if it's only for an hour or a moment, just to see if you're all right, to hear you say, "Hello, sweetheart."

The news has been so encouraging today in the Far East and in Europe. Maybe it won't be so long after all.

[Charles to Billee] June 6, 1942—Northern Ireland

One of the boys is playing "Miss You" on his guitar and it puts you right beside me where I can be with you while I write.

At times my letters may sound vague. That's because, as I write, I try and eliminate all military information. Perhaps I'll be thinking of one thing and writing another.

In our present location, we are more settled. There are four theaters for entertainment, more shops to visit, etc. During the week, I saw *Hit Parade* and *Married Bachelor*. Tonight I intend to see *Dive Bomber*. We are eligible for passes every second or third night. During the past week, I have spoken to several British soldiers who are in training and a few of the ATS girls (Auxiliary Territorial Service). The girls are trained for work as ambulance and truck drivers, cooks, orderlies, etc. They wear uniforms that I must say gives them the appearance of being too masculine. There have been a couple of dances but I passed them up. I doubt if I could enjoy myself. I would probably be thinking of us all evening. Yes, I believe I'll save all my dances for you.

Last night we received our second batch of rations: five packages of cigarettes, three bars of candy, three cans of beer, three bottles of Coca-Cola and a can of fruit juice. Other things available are toilet articles, cigars, tablet stationery, Kleenex, shoe polish, sardines, sewing kits, etc. These supplies come now and then and are deducted from our salaries, that is, according to how much one takes.

[From Charles's diary] June 6, 1942

So far, so good in Omagh. This is Tyrone County whereas we were in Antrim before. This is Saturday and we haven't had rain since Tuesday—a record! During the week, I attended a field day for the British soldiers—the Royal Ulster Rifles and the Inniskilling Fusiliers—as well as the Auxiliary Territorial Service (ATS). It was very dull!!

The coast artillery band has a concert every night outside the "Y" and it looks like the people enjoy the march music in contrast to the British bands. Saw two movies during the week. Prices range from front to rear: ninepence; one shilling, fivepence; two shillings.

[Billee to Charles] June 7, 1942—Asheville

I had a strange dream and I felt so close to you that I had to write.

To begin with, I was so restless last night, as if something was going to happen that concerned me. When I went to sleep . . . I don't know where I was but it was dark and it was raining hard. I walked for blocks alone in some place, town or city. The streets were deserted and there was such a deathly quiet. On the side streets as far as I walked, and it seemed like miles, there were troops standing at attention, all equipped to move somewhere, countless number of tanks, trucks and jeeps. Finally I awakened and I was so cold . . .

Do you believe in mental telepathy? I can't seem to shake the feeling that it all concerns you. Sounds crazy, doesn't it? I seemed that much more close to you. There are times when your presence is so near I have to catch my breath.

/////

[Billee to Charles] June 14, 1942—Asheville

We have been having a convention here [in Asheville] of the House of Brethren Church . . . 2000 delegates. The house is filled to the top. In fact, I'm sleeping on the sofa.

Father John sent me a very welcome note today, bringing me the good news of your second telegram and the message it carried for me. It came just at the right time. I see where troops landed again, so you will probably get some mail.

I'm knitting again . . . this time for Bundles for America. They have combined with Bundles for Britain so it's all the same now.

The aliens checked out of the Inn this week and it is open for business once more. I was cleaning out my drawer tonight and down in the bottom I found the little cocktail napkin I kept from up there that last night we were together here.

I called Theda this morning. She said she had received two letters from Jack that had been written on the boat but that she couldn't make much of them. I'll be getting one from you soon, I know.

Father John told me of the good news that Eleanor [Charles's sister] and Tom [O'Connor] are to be married September 12.

Don't laugh, but I went to see *Gone with the Wind* again . . . the fourth time. Believe it or not, I enjoyed it just as much as the first, second and third times. Sounds silly, but I believe it's the picture of all time.

/////

[From Charles's diary] June 15, 1942

Opportunity to catch up on writing and rest comes today while I nurse a bruised elbow. Baseball team lost to 133rd at Caledon on Sunday and I was a casualty. Had ambulance ride to Castle Urban yesterday for X-ray. Medics have amazing facilities in tin huts there.

Getting weekly rations of cigarettes, beer, Coke, etc., now.

Attended United Nations service yesterday.

Sent cables to John and Billee within the past week. Story from Washington says men can send cables for $.60 but we are still paying at least 8-4. Airgraph service, also supposed to be in effect, has not reached us.

/////

[Billee to Charles] June 17, 1942—Asheville

Your cablegram arrived first thing this morning. I fairly squealed for joy. If it weren't for the law of gravity, I'd be beside you . . . really. That is how high up in the clouds I've been riding today.

I had such a lovely letter from your mom yesterday. She scolded me a little for not telling her that I knew you had left. She told me about Eleanor and Tom's wedding in September and asked me to come. I'm really going to try and go. I'd love to see them all again.

Our company and delegates from the House of Brethren convention left today so once more we are alone, Mom and I. We've had thirty people in the house for a week and what a relief for them to be gone. I can sleep in a bed for a change. I can really sympathize with you.

I haven't had any mail but I guess I will in a few days.

/////

[Charles to Billee] June 19, 1942—Northern Ireland

This is my first letter by V-mail, which has been inaugurated recently for the
United States Army Forces in Northern Ireland. In fact, I should say it has been
devised for all men attached to the AEF II.

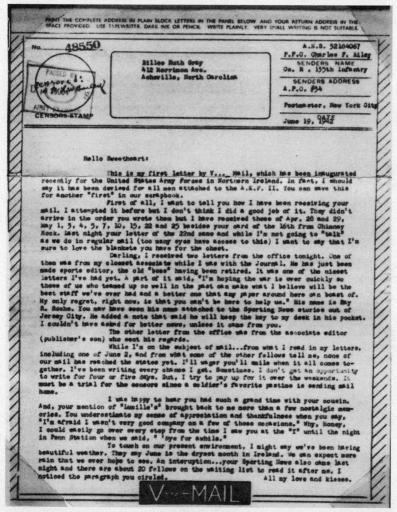

Charles's first V-letter to Billee—Northern Ireland, June 1942. (Kiley Family)

While I'm on the subject of mail . . . from what I read in my letters, including one of June 2, and from what some of the other fellows tell me, none of our mail has reached the states yet. I've been writing every chance I get. Sometimes, I don't get an opportunity to write for four of five days. But, I try to pay up for it over the weekends. It must be a trial for the censors since a soldier's favorite pastime is sending mail home.

To touch on our present environment, I might say we've been having beautiful weather. They say June is the driest month in Ireland. We can expect more rain than we ever hope to see. An interruption . . . your *Sporting News* also came last night and there are about 20 fellows on the waiting list to read it after me.

/////

[Billee to Charles] June 20, 1942—Asheville

I've moved into my summer quarters. It's a storage room that gets all cleaned out once a year for me to move into. I have a window, a single bed, dresser and closet space, and room to turn around once. I don't mind. It's mine and I know where everything is. Your radio is right by my ear. Dick Jergens is playing. They are singing "Johnnie Doughboy Found a Rose in Ireland." I don't like that song.

I washed my hair just a bit ago and that always makes me that much sleepier. It isn't rolled up on curlers either. I never will forget how funny that struck me. The second date we had and out of a clear blue sky, you asked me if I slept in curlers.

/////

[From Charles's diary] June 21, 1942

Tobruk falls to Rommel.

Southern Irish ports said to be opened on F.D.R.'s demand. [The Republic of Ireland was neutral during WWII, although the Irish government did cooperate with Allied powers; ironically, the small Irish merchant fleet was routinely attacked by both sides.] Fleet of United States planes said to have been ferried to Northern Ireland.

Parliament screaming for reason of Libyan failure just as they have for other losses.

/////

[Billee to Charles] June 24, 1942—Asheville

At long last, two letters. Just the sight of your handwriting changed the whole day for me. They were both written onboard ship and the first one looks like confetti almost. You'll have to tell me what they cut out.

Bad news . . . something went wrong with your little radio. Plays swell on the battery but not a bit on the electricity. The electrician at the store says it must be the converter in the tube or else the resisters, so it's being fixed. I miss seeing it on the dresser beside you [a photograph of Charles]. Since Mom and I have separate rooms, I let her take mine and I have yours.

It's quiet out tonight except for the birds singing, and in the distance, I can hear children playing. Occasionally a stray car goes by. They get more scarce every day, with the tire and gas situation. We aren't at all affected, since we haven't had a car in years.

I've been sewing . . . part of my economy program. It is so much cheaper. I've made two dresses last week and this and they didn't cost me but two dollars in all. I'm also making baby clothes for my sister's new arrival in August and having the most fun . . . getting in practice for our "pitcher" to be.

When the time comes, I want to be married in Jersey City in your church. You have so many more friends than I do. All mine are scattered so, and it will be just as easy for the family to go there as come down here. I think that will be quite proper. If my father were here, it would be different. [Billee's father, William Gray, lived in California; she saw him very rarely.] I'll have to give myself to you, darling. Will you mind?

/////

[Billee to Charles] June 26, 1942—Asheville

I'm so filled up inside I can hardly write. Four of your letters arrived today. I wanted to laugh with joy and ended up crying.

The stationery went forward to you today. I tried to proposition the shipping clerk to crate me up and send me along with the stationery but I didn't have much luck.

We all found your letters so interesting. I read the parts about the people and how you were getting on. I envy your experiences. Since it is happening to you, I feel that it is happening to me, too. I know it is stretching the point, but I don't see how marriage could bring us any closer than we already are.

I can't wait to hear more in detail about the people and their customs and the conditions under which you are living. Your letters tell so much. I was especially interested about the girls. We hear so many tales over here about how pretty they are and so many of the boys are marrying them. It must be propaganda.

Your radio is fixed now and playing some very soft semi-classical music. I had to have a new set of resisters put on it. So here I am, curled up in the middle of the bed with all your letters spread out before me and your pictures just a few feet away. It's almost as if you were here.

Your letters came on the afternoon mail and I dashed across to the drug store to read them . . . found a quiet spot. I got through the first two all right, but when I got to the third, the one you wrote after you received my letters, I had to quit or else make a fool of myself in front of everyone.

I'm so proud of your new job. Any chance of me getting your paper?

[From Charles's diary] June 27, 1942

Fired mortar for first time three days ago, after which "H" Co. and "E" Co. staged an attack problem for the benefit of all officers in the division yesterday and today.

I was to go to Belfast for this weekend but came in from problem too late. Mail still coming—mostly from Billee.

/////

[Billee to Charles] June 28, 1942—Asheville

I went shopping for you tonight at the supermarket. We are going to bake cookies tomorrow and fix up your box. The contents will be: 1 flat 50 Chesterfields, 1 pkg cheese, 1 pkg crackers, 1 jar jelly, 1 can salted peanuts, 1 can prepared cocoa, sweetened and with powdered milk, 1 box tea balls, 4 bars Ivory soap, 1 bag candy, cookies.

I'm also going to send the *Sporting News* with it and a couple of magazines. I'm going to mail it Monday. I hope it doesn't take too long getting to you.

We heard last night after I mailed you a letter about the King and Queen reviewing the troops. She spoke to a fellow from Asheville in the Navy and another fellow she spoke to was from Elyria, Ohio. I used to live there and two of my aunts live there now.

We picked our first peas and beans from our victory garden. Mom was so pleased.

They just announced that eight Nazis had been arrested for attempted sabotage. They had been landed from submarines by rubber boats. They had lists of all the places they were to bomb. I guess our FBI is on the job. Four were landed at Long Island and four off the coast of Jacksonville, Fla. That's really bringing the war home. They had enough money and ammunition to last two years.

[Two members of the German sabotage group had no intention of going through with the plan. On June 15, one of them phoned the New York office of the FBI from a pay telephone in Manhattan. The agent he spoke with figured he was a crackpot; the German man hung up. Four days later, the German checked in to the Mayflower Hotel in Washington, DC and then walked into FBI headquarters and asked to speak with J. Edgar Hoover. After being passed to many agents, the man was again dismissed as a crackpot. He finally convinced the agents after he dumped $84,000 on the desk of Assistant FBI Director D. M. Ladd and told him that was the group's budget to plant bombs.]

[Billee to Charles] June 30, 1942—Asheville

Of all things . . . me worried for fear you'll get shot or something and you get hit with a baseball. I'm glad it wasn't serious. Your writing didn't seem so shaky, but I know it must have been painful. It's probably better now, I hope. Telling me to be careful . . . practice what you preach, please.

They had the final registration today for boys 18–21. Warren, my brother, just missed. He will be eighteen July 5.

/////

[Billee to Charles] July 4, 1942—Asheville

Before I forget, your cable came yesterday. I answered it with one of mine. I hope you have it long before this reaches you. The Postal Telegraph has a new service to the Expeditionary Forces anywhere in the world . . . pretty nice.

Today has been quiet. Mom was very disappointed that we didn't get any guests. A year ago we had thirty-seven and filled all the neighbors' spare bedrooms. It's to be expected with the gas and tire situation the way it is. We're going to have to change our way of life.

I know what your cable must mean. Of course, I know they didn't send you over there to pick shamrocks, but I've been putting the action off in my mind. The only trouble is, I don't know whether this was held up and you are already where you are to go. We had word yesterday via Berlin that our troops were in Egypt.

All the magazines came out this month with a waving flag for a cover. It is very impressive except you have to look twice to see what magazine you are getting.

/////

[Billee to Charles] July 9, 1942—Asheville

I may have mentioned in my last letter that I thought the aliens were coming back. They did yesterday. The three guards that were here before brought seven more with them and one man's wife and child. Now our little family has expanded to sixteen. You can imagine how excited Mom and I were. That's the way this business goes . . . like gambling. Much as I hate having those darn aliens in our Inn, as the old saying goes: an ill wind always blows someone good.

Victor Borge is playing "You Are to Me Everything;" expresses my thoughts so well.

Lately so many people have asked me if I'm Irish. That never happened before. You must have brought all my Irish out where people could notice. They say my eyes give me away.

I went to see *Shores of Tripoli* last night. It was taken at the [CENSORED]. [The movie was partially filmed at the Marine base in San Diego, and was an effective recruitment tool for the Marines in 1942.] Very good . . . you must have gone through practically the same . . . that is, the basic training.

[Charles to Billee] July 11, 1942—Northern Ireland

Now, before going any further, may I say I love you so much! Remind me to give you a special reward for each letter received. They are priceless, but I'll try to find something. I cabled 10 pounds to you today ($40.20) and each month I'll be sending more. I'll be getting $67.20 a month now and I'm sure I can put $50 of it in our "hope chest."

Mom told me she had asked you to visit for El's wedding and I do hope you can be there. El thinks a great deal of you and she would be awfully pleased to have you there. Since Tom may be drafted, they have decided to live with Mom and Dad for the time being.

Your *Sporting News* was certainly appreciated but then you always know what I want.

[Billee to Charles] July 17, 1942, Our Anniversary—Asheville

Today was declared Heroes Day and we had a parade and a special breakfast. In accepting the invitation, you had to buy a $500 bond. They set the goal for Buncombe County for $125,000 for today and at last report, about 5 p.m., they had accounted for $300,000 . . . not bad. I relieved at lunchtime in our booth on the first floor and sold $1,050 in an hour. I nearly passed out when this man passed over $375 in cash. I could hardly write out the application; five minutes later along comes another man with a check for the same amount. I felt as if I'd done away with an army of Japs.

I saw a swell movie tonight. I had to do something to celebrate. *This Above All*—it is Eric Roberts' story that appeared in Literary Digest in condensed form. Perhaps you read it. There was a line in it that I want to remember. "God blesses a man and woman that truly love each other. They are the luckiest people in the world." I think that must be us.

A Florida guest, brought home a croquet set the other day and we've been playing. I'd forgotten how much fun it was . . . such a strenuous game . . . ha! By the way, all our guards left again. They took away so many of the aliens and the government has to pay for those rooms anyway that they decided to move all the guards up there until they get some more aliens. As I've said before, this business is like gambling.

We are beginning to eat out of our victory garden. I've eaten string beans until I think they'll come out my ears most any minute, besides the Swiss chard and beets. The tomatoes aren't quite ripe yet, but we have bushels. I guess we'll can from now on.

/////

[Charles to Billee] July 18, 1942—Northern Ireland

I was unable to suppress a shout when I read your inventory of the package that is on the way. You thought of just about everything, didn't you?

And since you spoke of your dream, I want to wish you happy ones. The one you described frightened me a bit because I know how it disturbed you.

Funny thing, though . . . as much as I have you on my mind, I don't dream at all any more.

I will not be able to write for a week or so because of the same thing that prevented me from writing a couple of weeks ago [maneuvers]. Still, I'll be back with you as soon as I can.

/////

[Billee to Charles] July 18, 1942—Asheville (V-mail)

Just received your first V-letter, so here goes my first. It certainly isn't very private but anything is fine, so long as we get our letters through to each other. I don't care if President Roosevelt, himself, has to read them. The post office issues three blanks per person. We just received ours here. I had my name down to be called when they arrived.

We've been busy planning for a picnic Tuesday night that is for the office force. We're going to post a notice in the USO Headquarters and see what happens. There aren't many in town during the week so we probably won't have any luck. I love picnics.

This has been such a lovely weekend so far, with your cables and check and today your letter. Almost like being with you.

This is almost the end. I guess when I want to write more than one page, I'll have to write "continued . . ." like a magazine story.

/////

[From Charles's diary] July 19, 1942

A great deal has taken place since my last entry.

First, there were the division maneuvers from July 2 through the 9th. On the first day out, July 3, I experienced what I believed was the most miserable day in my life.

We had entrained from Omagh to Cookstown in the night of July 2 and bivouacked there. The following day we walked approximately 30 miles in a continuous rain. We bivouacked and slept in the rain. Built fires, ate in the rain. I'll always remember July 3 for that.

We returned to Omagh on the 8th, tired, dirty and thankful.

Shortly afterward, Sgt. Thompson was moved to a machine-gun platoon, possibly for failing to produce on the maneuvers. Sgt. Pepper is our new platoon sergeant, although he may not know as much of the mortars, as Thompson is a better man.

On the 15th, we had our company party in town. What a party! The regimental orchestra sounds better than ever. Walters, Solow, Rabbitt, Savarese and I put on a skit, lampooning the officers!

Yesterday the battalion went on a problem to test the Home Guard and our men never left the carriers.

Tomorrow the battalion goes away for a week for combat firing and maneuvers.

I might say this, while I have it in my mind, that our firing is about 25 percent of what it should be if this battalion is an example.

Perhaps it is my outlook that is wrong, but I honestly can't see the 34th being any help at all in this war if the enemy is even half as effective as it is said to be.

/////

[Billee to Charles] July 20, 1942—Asheville

It's late but I'm not sleepy and there is some good dance music on your radio. I'm propped up in bed writing on my knees. That's usually where I end up writing.

They must be having maneuvers around here somewhere. We have had pursuit planes chasing each other around all day.

They are taking the applications now for the buck privates in the WAAC. I can't make up my mind what to do on that score. I know there isn't anything I can do until I finish off my debts, and then there is Mom. The officers began their training today. I think they will be a big help to do all the deskwork so as to release men for active service. I think that if I went in, I could get a specialist rating with the kind of work I do.

[Billee to Charles] July 24, 1942—Asheville

The new *Life* this week carries pictures of the AEF in Ireland. I'm saving it for you. Also, there are pictures of an Atlantic convoy going across to England. [This was the convoy in which Charles sailed.]

We had a sale today [at Ivey's department store], the first in quite some time. The women were waiting outside both doors to get in. I haven't seen such a wild scramble in years. You should have seen them tackle that merchandise in nothing flat. They just stripped tables and racks.

I'm anxiously awaiting the arrival of that box so I can send another. You know I had to put it all in two boxes to conform to regulations. I have since learned that you can't send but one a week, so perhaps one was held up somewhere.

/////

[Billee to Charles] July 25, 1942—Asheville (V-mail)

There was an article last night about our boys in Ireland and what they were doing about their spirit and how anxious they were to get started. The only thing they missed was letters from home.

This is USO day. The "Junior Commandos" paraded. They are a group of young girls and boys that have collected scrap and donations for the USO and they have been given that title. They were so proud, marching along with a police escort. The reports haven't come in yet as to whether or not they raised their quota.

I've practically worn your last letter out reading it over and carrying it around in my bag. I always carry the last one that I get until another comes, so I'd better hurry and get another . . .

/////

[From Charles's diary] July 26, 1942

Back from what I thought was maneuvers for the benefit of rifle companies mostly. Mortars were practically forgotten. The battalion's set-up of squad tents was good but that rain ruined everything. Scarcely a meal was eaten in dry weather.

Col. Drake apparently was far from satisfied. Maj. Swenson to Capt. Kanstrup caught hell!

Maj. Swenson, who says we may soon have to open the second front "to get the dog off the Russian's back," uses the most picturesque, foul language I ever heard.

/////

[Billee to Charles] July 27, 1942—Asheville

I tried to write yesterday and made several attempts but gave it up as a bad job. Seems that I missed you so much this weekend, I was afraid to tell you how much.

Saw a swell movie yesterday, *Mrs. Miniver*. You know, Jan Struthers' bestseller. Greer Garson and Walter Pidgeon certainly scored another hit together.

I'm starting in the Red Cross Room Wednesday night. This is the first time they have been open at night . . . 7:30 to 9:30, to roll bandages. Seems that the Red Cross furnishes 90 percent for the Army and Navy. I had no idea that it was that much.

/////

[Charles to Billee] July 28, 1942—Northern Ireland

I started to write last night but felt the need of a walk. It developed into a movie: *Adam Had Four Sons*. How many will we have? Nine? Earlier this evening another fellow and myself met a very sweet fourteen-year-old girl, Gwen Magee. She was one of the most fascinating youngsters I've ever met. She was evacuated from Dover, England, two years ago and sent to Wales from where she came to her present home with relatives. Her father has been in the British army for three years. She claims the "Yankee" soldiers have been so pleasant and courteous, she understands why she has heard so many people wanting to come to America. Coincidentally, we received our "luxury" rations tonight and I gave her three bars of candy for being such a charming companion. She refused, rather vehemently, at first, but accepted them. Later, she said the candy would be a real treat since she doesn't have much of it. She recalled how her Daddy once brought her candy and wondered if he ever will again. I doubt if many American children her age could speak so intelligently with elders.

Gwen Magee—Northern Ireland, 1942. (Kiley Family)

/////

[From Charles's diary] July 29, 1942

The company has been shuffled and I move into the 2nd platoon for machine gun work. Lt. Bailey said I would receive good news shortly which may mean a corporal's rating. Received a nice letter from Sgt. Jones of the *Stars and Stripes* re: possible connections on the staff.

/////

[Billee to Charles] July 31, 1942—Asheville

Went to the Red Cross workroom Wednesday to make bandages and met a girl from the store . . . a bride. Her husband ferries bombers. All the time we were working, we kept praying neither of you would need our bandages. There were ten of us and we made 200 bandages.

There is a couple here on their vacation from Newark and they keep teasing me about Jersey City, as if I were a native already.

I'm sending the *Sporting News* tomorrow. There is a paragraph that suggests bringing the World Series teams to the AEF overseas in transport planes to play exhibition games. Swell idea if it works.

/////

[Billee to Charles] August 2, 1942—Asheville

Mom and I were talking just now and if we can't get enough business this winter, we will close the house and go home [to Ohio] for a while. Between the two of us, we will be able to make the payments, because we have to hang onto it. I think the change will be good for both of us. The only thing . . . I'll miss you, because you were here and we were together many places that I go and I can't forget. I don't know whether I could find you up there. Here, all I have to do is close my eyes and I see you in the chair as you were those Sundays with the paper, waiting for dinner or sitting on the sofa in "our corner."

The report came tonight from Moscow that America and England had decided on a second front for 1942. I don't know whether to be glad or unhappy.

/////

[From Charles's diary] August 2, 1942

Mail coming slow for me.

None from Billee in a week or more.

A box of cookies and Billee's stationery arrived during the week.

Also, we were paid two days ago ($85.00) for me, including June's raise. This was our first pay under the raise to $50 base pay, plus 20 percent for overseas.

/////

[Charles to Billee] August 4, 1942—Northern Ireland

Great day today. Your letters, one from Mother, and . . . I was notified I have been made a corporal. Furthermore, before your letters arrived I had filed an application to buy a bond a month, $37.50 to be deducted from my salary. Of course, you are co-owner, to do whatever you see fit with them. They will be mailed to you from Washington.

I hope you don't get the idea that I've developed into a millionaire, but I have set my mind on saving as much money as possible now. It will help to give us a good start. Why, we may have a bit left over to start a "college fund" for the team. But then, I'll bet they are so good they will all get scholarships. With your looks and your brains, how can they miss?

At the end of this month I will draw a salary of $79.60, I believe. From that will be deducted $6.90 (premium on $10,000 insurance) and about $3.00 for canteen supplies (cigarettes, candy, toilet articles, etc.) Then, I will send at least $50.00 to you, possibly more. The bond money will be deducted starting with September's salary. Even with that deduction, I'm sure I will be able to send a little more back to you each month. Have you got a sharp point on your pencil or do you think we should hire a bookkeeper?

While I'm in town, I might see *Shepherd of the Hills*. The last picture I saw was *This Man Reuter*, with Edward G. Robinson. It was a story concerning the first news service (one that is still in existence) and was especially interesting to me. I couldn't help but give a start when, during Reuter's younger days, his wife remarked, "It isn't fair." I'll never forget those words, whispered atop the knoll surrounding the Inn. It is little things like that that keep you with me constantly.

Judging by your sale of $1,050 worth of bonds, I'd say you were a super-saleswoman.

Honey, about the WAAC ... I wouldn't try to influence you in any way if you had your mind set but I do think you should stay with [your] Mother, just as I advised when we were in New York. You have a job to do watching over her. You just keep selling bonds and the home fires burning. We can do the rest.

[Billee to Charles] August 4, 1942—Asheville

I'm going to have to learn not to let my imagination run away with me. Here I had you in Russia or somewhere and all the time you were right there.

Before I forget, this is the first mail I've had in a month with the exception of that V-letter that arrived on the 18th, so you see how the mail is coming through. I believe it is being held in New York ...

Mother says she doesn't see how I can write so often without saying the same things.

[Charles to Billee] August 8, 1942—Northern Ireland

The V-mail was the first of its kind I have had and it was a novelty to me. It gave me an opportunity to see how mine look when you get them.

In my cable today, I told you I had been made a corporal. I've been so busy of late, I can't remember whether I wrote during the week and told you of it.

I wanted to tell you of our visit to Baronscourt, the vast estate (27 miles by 9) of the Duke of Abercorn, during the past week. I can give you an outline now, but I hope to get out a story on it for the *Stars and Stripes* and I'll send the details on the story, if and when it is used.

The estate is a mass of woodland, glens, trails and has four lakes. It houses so many rabbits I can't start to guess the number, plenty of deer, fish in the lakes, etc. You almost expect to see Robin Hood, Friar Tuck and the rest of the Sherwood Forest boys swing down from the trees.

There are approximately 90 rooms in the main house, 28 of which were ruined by fire two years ago and are now in the stages of reconstruction. Two of the Duke's daughters are ladies in waiting to the Queen and Women of the Queen's Bedchamber. Sounds funny, but it is an enviable position.

Unfinished Business (Bob Montgomery and Irene Dunn) is playing in a nearby theater (cinema, I should say) and I'd like to see it. Afterward, I'll try to get the story off to the *Stars and Stripes*.

/////

[Billee to Charles] August 8, 1942—Asheville

We lost our boss this week to the Army Air Corps. He went into the Administrative Division as a First Lieutenant . . . pretty nice. He is very capable and I'm glad he was able to get what he wanted. We are like a ship without a pilot since there has been no replacement. Everything happened so suddenly that I am still a little bewildered. You see, I've never worked for anyone else, so this will be a new experience. He has been such a wonderful boss, I don't see how anyone could take his place. We all kissed him goodbye and sent him on his way with a new Elgin watch as a farewell present. He said he'd only be gone a few months.

We are fairly busy now [at Oak Lodge] and have prospects of being that way for the rest of the month. I'm so glad for Mother's sake. She gets discouraged so easily these days. I have to keep her well before all things. I think we are going to close the house for the winter and go home [to Ohio]. We both can get work and I think the change will do her good. She can get to know her grandchildren before mine, or rather ours, come along and confuse her.

/////

We experienced our first blackout last night and it was a huge success . . . all of western N. Carolina. I was home alone when we got the alarm. I locked everything up and went out in the yard. What a night! There must have been a million stars out twinkling . . . really a sight.

The manager of the store said that all those girls who wanted to visit husbands or sweethearts in the camp would be given the time off. I'm going to see what he can do about managing a trip "over there." Wouldn't you be surprised!

/////

I think when you come back that I will want to go dancing every night for a month, or else to just sit and look at you. What will you want to do?

The little girl [Gwen Magee] sounds nice. Seems strange that a bar of candy should represent so much . . . something that we take for granted. We have too many things, I'd say.

We had a long letter from our boss today. They have already taken two inches (he is quite a big man) off his waistline in a week. He says it is hard, but he likes it very much. They are stationed at the Embassy Hotel, one of the finest in Miami.

Kaltenborn [H. V. Kaltenborn, a well-known announcer on NBC radio] was on a little while ago. He just returned from over there. From his description, he must have spent some time with you all. He said he talked with a New York boy that was headed for home on the next boat for a leave. I hadn't thought of that possibility. I wonder if that is too much to hope for.

[Charles to Billee] August 17, 1942—Northern Ireland

I would like to say now that my airmail letters will be fewer, at least for the time being. My Lieutenant gave us permission to send letters home and to our sweethearts by air, but the others (unless they are important) should go by V-mail or regular mail. There has been such a flood of airmail letters from the troops that the plane service, or I should say the airmail service, has been slowed down. That is the probable answer as to why you hadn't heard from me in a month. The family hadn't heard for the same period. So, while I will be able to send one airmail letter or so a week to you and to the folks, the rest will have to wait a while longer for theirs.

/////

[Billee to Charles] August 22, 1942—Asheville

I see you have received my stationery. That's good. Probably by this time, you will have received the boxes. There is to be no more food sent through the mail . . . new regulations. They must have seen what I sent you .

Your trip to Baronscourt sounds wonderful. Another reason I'm enjoying your experience . . . at least this part of it.

/////

[Charles to Billee] August 22, 1942—Northern Ireland

This is another of our Saturday nights. I wonder if you have picked up your pen yet to keep our date. It is only 7:30 . . . a little early for you, perhaps. Your letter of Aug. 8 came last night. With it came the Journal [*Jersey Journal*] and your *Sporting News* of July 17. The packages are still among the missing, but I'll be looking for them.

So, your boss is in the Air Corps. I envy him. But then, if my age hadn't prevented me from enlisting, "we" wouldn't be, would we? I hate to even think of that. When he said he would be gone for only a few months, I believe he was a little too optimistic.

You speak of the beautiful sunshine, warm evenings, etc. I'm sure I can get 1,000 men who would give 10 years of their lives for one hour of that. Rain, chill and mud have been the order of the day for so long now.

/////

[From Charles's diary] August 24, 1942

Left Omagh on Aug. 22 and arrived at Eli Lodge, five miles outside of Enniskillen on the afternoon of the same day. We are now in County Fernmanagh, situated beside Lake Erne, a beautiful spot, scenically speaking. Our tin huts, erected by Americans, are vast improvements over the British huts. The mess hall is the best we have had, even to the extent of having an ice cream freezer.

Lt. Bailey, Sgts. Thompson and Wiseman are transferred to the 108th for training in Scotland. My OTS blank will wait for time being. Heard Joe Higgins is on his way back to the States for OTS in Signal Corps.

We were on maneuvers again from Aug 12 to 17—rain, mud and hardship all over again. During it, I was attached to 1st, 2nd and 4th platoons.

Mail showing up again with only Billee's letters keeping up.

Said "Goodbye" to Gwen and Bertie, the Magee kids in Omagh, and I'll miss them.

/////

[Billee to Charles] August 25, 1942—Asheville

You're still head man in this family. You're making $5.20 more a month than I am. How about that? I think I'll join the army.

There was a soldier from England on Sunday a week ago on the Army Day program who said that he thought their raise should be kept on this side for them, that they didn't need all that money over there. Too, that it created a feeling of animosity between the British soldiers and the Americans because the British didn't have as much money to spend.

I'm saving all I can, but it won't be as much as you are, naturally, since I have to pay my own way.

I had to leave you for a while, since eight extras came in and five of them had to have lunch. They are all tucked in for the night now and the tables all set to serve 17 for breakfast. Just like old times before Pearl Harbor.

I saw *The Pied Piper* last night, with Monty Woolley. The story ran in *Collier's* last winter … a story of occupied France and an Englishman trying to return to his country. An excellent story and so well cast. Sunday I saw *Orchestra Wives* with Glenn Miller's orchestra. Really smooth and very entertaining. There is a new song in it that just hits right … "At Last." That's what you are … my "at last."

My brother, Warren, will be here Saturday. Mom is getting excited. We probably won't see much of him since he has a girlfriend here that he has kept in close contact with since he left home. She is a nice girl, but they are so young. He was only 18 in July.

/////

[Charles to Billee] August 29, 1942—Northern Ireland

Let's you and I dream a while. Let's pretend I'll be back in a month … What would we do? That month would give you time to pack and get ready to move, yes? Then, I would want about a week to get straightened out with the Journal, replenish my wardrobe and look at you. If you were already in J.C. [Jersey City] … fine. If not, I'd cut my week to two days then take a plane to wherever you are, then start back to J.C. If we had enough to go ahead, the wedding date would be set as soon as possible, if not sooner. In between, we could do our shopping and whatever else was necessary.

How about the honeymoon? Of course, that would depend on what we had, but I believe I could spread your wings and fly you around a bit. It would depend on the time of year … Miami, Berkshires, Adirondacks, perhaps a trip to the coast, Atlantic City if you prefer, or Asheville! How about Bermuda if you like boats … Miami on a train … a trip by car to anywhere? What appeals to you?

Have you awakened from the dream yet? Nice, wasn't it? I can see us lying in the Miami sand … hot days and cool nights … standing on the rail on the Monarch or Queen of Bermuda, on our way; maybe dining on the porch of the

Le Bourget at Lake Placid or driving along Lake Champlain to Fort Ticonderoga. While we were in the vicinity, we might stop at Cooperstown. We may stand on the same spot outside the Grove Park Inn, looking ahead instead of saying "Goodbye."

I have been too busy to devote much time to the *Stars and Stripes* but I have sent a couple of "quickie" stories that haven't been published yet. There was a note from them today asking for more copy. The stuff I sent wasn't very good, mainly because material is scarce.

/////

[Charles to Billee] August 31, 1942—Northern Ireland

A fellow from West Virginia and another from Indiana accompanied me on a visit to Belfast [on a weekend pass]. The ride, in rather ancient trains, was an experience in itself. When we arrived late in the afternoon, our first stop was at the American Red Cross headquarters. There we were given a ticket for lodging at the US Consulate building. The cost . . . one shilling (20 cents). The beds were stretched out on one floor, dormitory style. It felt so good . . . soft mattress, fresh linens, etc. A cold chicken dinner preceded a second (for me) attendance at *Gone with the Wind*. G.W.T.W. is, or was, playing its second week. Seats were 2, 3 and 4 shillings.

On Sunday, we boarded a double-decker tram (trolley) for Bellevue Park, one of the "things to see."

Oops, forgot something . . . the blackout. When we came out of the theater, we had to walk hand in hand in order to stay together. When they say blackout over here, they mean it.

/////

[From Charles's diary] August 31, 1942

A weekend in Belfast with Bob Paulus and Earl Reagan. Stayed at US Consulate Building. Saw G.W.T.W. and visited Bellevue Park. Damage done by air raid 16 months ago very evident. Bought camera and film for 14s. Train fare: 6s return.

Al Jolson & Co. to be here Thursday.

Billee's packages arrived with everything in them.

Charles (center) with members of his squad enjoying the snacks Billee had sent—Northern Ireland, August 1942. (Kiley Family)

///////

[Billee to Charles] September 3, 1942—Asheville

Don't laugh, but remember you falling up the stairs coming out of the subway? Well, I did the same thing except instead of stairs it was the curb, and I didn't have anyone to hold on to. Consequently, I fell flat on my face, practically crippling myself. I've been hobbling around all week. My knee is a little better tonight but still pretty sore.

We've had word of the trouble in Belfast [IRA riots]. I know you won't be able to tell me, but I've prayed you avoided any trouble while you were there.

There have been rumors that there is to be a registration of women this month, for occupation, I presume. [This remained a rumor.]

Our move north is pretty definite and gets more so every day.

/////

[Charles to Billee] September 5, 1942—Northern Ireland

One of the fellows with us had his "dream come true" a few days ago. He had applied for officers' training quite a while ago and was finally accepted. His orders were to report to Camp Croft! Could I ask for anything more?

Last week, some of us handed in requests for furloughs. I'll confess, I was astonished when the request went through and I signed the papers. All that remains is official approval and I'll have nine days with which to visit London. One of the fellows who went with me to Belfast is going, too. The furlough will start either Sept. 29 or Oct. 6. After a somewhat active summer, the furlough will be a blessing; the activities, of course, are not for publication.

How would you like to have a 15-minute chat with, let's say Merle Oberon and Patricia Morrison? Besides informal interviews with, oh … Al Jolson, Frank McHugh and Allen Jenkins? I'm not trying to be subtle but that was my happy lot the other evening. They appeared at our camp in a show, which is touring the service units in the British Isles. As the *Stars and Stripes* representative here, it was my lot to handle a story on the show and the cast. Being a little rusty, I was a bit uneasy at first but before long we were talking as informally as a couple of soldiers.

I sat backstage with the women for 15 minutes before the show and for a while during the show. They were swell, Billee. More gracious and more willing to talk than the men. Jolson was a smooth hit. I didn't have an opportunity to see him long, since he sat in the audience until he went on.

What did we talk about? Mostly of their tour. A little about our life here. The orchestra was making so much of a racket on the stage it was difficult to speak with any degree of intelligence.

I trust it doesn't give the impression that my mental attitude towards the finer things in life is turning blasé. But when the show was over, I should have been elated for having had the opportunity to interview such personalities. Yet, I wasn't. I just don't know why, either. I've been more excited over less important things.

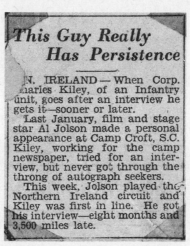

This Guy Really Has Persistence

N. IRELAND — When Corp. Charles Kiley, of an Infantry unit, goes after an interview he gets it—sooner or later.

Last January, film and stage star Al Jolson made a personal appearance at Camp Croft, S.C. Kiley, working for the camp newspaper, tried for an interview, but never got through the throng of autograph seekers.

This week, Jolson played the Northern Ireland circuit and Kiley was first in line. He got his interview—eight months and 3,500 miles late.

Clipping from the *Stars and Stripes* London edition—September 1942. (US Army/*Stars and Stripes*)

/////

[Billee to Charles] September 5, 1942—Asheville

I heard the prettiest song yesterday. Occasionally, my girlfriend and I haunt the music counters at lunchtime. She has a Victrola so we really buy records now and then. She bought this one yesterday, "Just as Though You Were Here"— Russ Morgan's arrangement. She is going to get the words to it. It might have been written for us. One consolation . . . we aren't alone in the world.

I see you so many times . . . stretched out with your hands clasped behind your back. I remember you telling me that was how you listened to the radio back at Dix and thought of me. I always go to sleep thinking of you, where you might be, what you are doing and wishing a little, dreaming what we could be doing.

Did I feel good when one of the girls held up that familiar airmail envelope and said "Billee . . . from some corporal."

/////

[Billee to Charles] September 8, 1942—Asheville

You should have the Congressional Medal of Honor pinned on you for spreading so much sunshine. Yes, your letter came today, the one concerning our honeymoon and I'm still smiling. You're crazy, but I love you just the same.

I spent a very quiet holiday [Labor Day] at home. I slept until 12 o'clock, something that I haven't done in months, then helped around the house, topping the evening off by seeing *Wake Island*. What a picture, based on the actual records sent out by the CO during the siege. They had the Marine recruiting officer in the lobby all week, taking enlistments, but they wouldn't take girls. That picture was enough to make you want to get a gun and start out.

/////

[Billee to Charles] September 12, 1942—Asheville

As usual, I'm tucked in for the night and very sleepy and tired. Sleepy because of the bottle of beer Mom and I just had and tired because I've really been put through the mill today. We haven't had a full office force in so long, I'm still filling in. I'm going to get me a nice quiet job on an assembly line, where I have to worry only about doing *my* job.

I have another *Sporting News* I'm sending along with this. There is talk of holding a lottery for the World Series. Some man has cooked up a scheme by which the government would profit by six billion dollars.

Mom and I are planning your Christmas/birthday box. This time it will be a surprise, but you can rest assured there'll be no extra non-essential trimmings. The Post Office has issued an order that the boxes should be mailed by October 1 to assure delivery on time.

The girls and the rest of the force in the shipping department were all glad to hear that you received the boxes in such good time and that everything was still edible. They have been asking all along if you received it.

I'm beginning to make preparations to wind up my affairs here so I can plan to leave by the fifteenth of next month. We will stay with my aunt. She has a large house and is there by herself practically all the time, since my uncle travels a lot. Talk about baseball fans . . . those two are. My uncle is an old ball player from a long way back. He played on one of the first professional teams. You'll like them . . . my favorite aunt and uncle.

#####

[Charles to Billee] September 17, 1942—Northern Ireland

Father John wrote the other day, telling me he was having difficulty trying to decide whether or not he should enlist as a chaplain. Mother told him to use his own judgment but he is worrying about the effect it would have on her, with three sons in the service.

The trouble in Belfast did not concern us. It happened a week or so after I had been there. The city was put "off limits" for US forces until the storm had passed over.

About the *Stars and Stripes* . . . the latest issue will be on its way tomorrow. My story didn't get a byline and it was cut a bit because it ran long. But you may enjoy it.

Didn't you say something about sending stationery? It will be useful now. I'm almost out of the last box, but will use other paper until it arrives. Since I didn't get mail today, I'm going to read some of your letters again.

#####

[Billee to Charles] September 17, 1942—Asheville

We have our first football game tomorrow night, so fall is officially ushered in. I'll really see some good football at home. You have, no doubt, heard of Massillon's famous high school team. Nothing but champions turned out. The town built a stadium to take care of the population of the town—30,000.

The Cardinals are ahead tonight. Wonder what the outcome will be. I'd love to see a World Series game. I sure would like to see Billy Southworth make it this time. He was awfully nice to me once.

We're having our bond rally tonight. Jane Wyman and John Payne are officiating. Up to the time of the rally tonight, they had sold $457,000. I think that's marvelous. It's more than the last time and all the figures aren't in.

[Billee to Charles] September 24, 1942—Asheville

I received your cable Monday and your letter of September 5, and was I pleased. The cable carried a different address, in fact, it said "Sans Origine." Heretofore, they have had "Great Britain." Makes me wonder, but that's all I can do.

I enjoyed your letter so much . . . bringing such good news. A furlough and interviewing such notables! Al Jolson just arrived in New York today.

Your furlough sounds exciting. Suppose I meet you there at, let's say, Westminster Abbey, and we'll see the sights. I'd love to see the Tower of London, Buckingham Palace and take a boat trip on the Thames. I'd love to go to all the little out-of-the-way places that people don't ordinarily visit. I realize, too, that it will be a changed London and not the London we've been reading about for years. Still it will be a trip for our memory book, in spite of the changes. I'm so happy for you, that you are going to be able to have a rest and change.

The Home Guard is marching up Merrimon. I just watched them go by and couldn't help but see that harvest moon peeking over the top of the mountain. I'm going to miss that when I go home. Yes, I gave my resignation today to the general manager. We are still without a boss. He said, of course, that he was sorry I had to leave, but if I didn't like it when I got to Ohio to write him a letter and I could have a job any time I wanted it.

I think I know why you didn't feel elated over your interviews, or excited might I say. If that had happened under normal circumstances, it would have been different, but circumstances change situations. What you are doing is so much more important than what they are doing. Don't worry about your mental attitude towards the finer things going blasé. That has nothing to do with it.

About Al Jolson, you really owe him a lot. It's a long story but I'll cut it short. When my mom and dad were courting, he was quite a popular figure on the stage. They were both living in Philadelphia at the time and, of course, used to take in vaudeville quite often. Mom had to be home early this one night, and, when they tried to leave, Jolson had the spotlight turned on them and asked them, "What's the hurry?" They couldn't think of an excuse, being very young, so he had the orchestra play the wedding march and, since they had front row seats, they had to march the length of the theater to that tune. Were they embarrassed! Dad, fortified by that experience, popped the question and so they were married!

[Charles to Billee] September 27, 1942—Northern Ireland

My letters to you and those going home will be written as often as possible but the others will have to wait until I can devote more time to them. You will probably be able to tell from my writing that I'm not in a very comfortable position. But, if I have to stand on my head and try to write in the dark I'll continue my visits to you.

The weather is getting cold. We had a few snowflakes the other day. I doubt if it is as cold in the States. I inquired about my impending furlough last night and was informed that everything was in order. Instead of going on the 29th, which is next Tuesday, or on Oct. 6, it appears we will have to wait for a date suitable to division HQ.

By this letter, you know I missed our date last night. I'm making a promise right now that we will never have a dull Saturday night. There will always be something doing on Saturday. Just now, I'd like to be on my way to Princeton, West Point, the Yale Bowl or one of the other fields to see a football game. The weather is just right for it. We're going to see lots of them, with dinner and a show afterward.

[Billee to Charles] September 29, 1942—Asheville

I'm trying to get this in before our blackout begins. We are to have one some-time between 7 and 11. It's now 8:30. The last was downright gruesome, so here we go again.

I saw the cutest movie Sunday, with Ray Milland and Ginger Rogers . . . *The Major and the Minor*. She gets stranded in New York with not quite enough to go home to somewhere in Iowa so she dresses up very convincingly as a twelve-year-old and buys a half-fare ticket. Her adventures from there on are really something. I enjoyed it so much, but then I've always thought Ray Milland smooth.

I'm really believing that we are leaving. Now all I have to do is get Mom convinced. She says she's going, but I know she doesn't really believe it.

I'm enclosing a clipping about the Cardinals. I'm so happy for them and what I wouldn't give to see that opening game. Box seats are going for fifty per. That's one of our musts except that you might have to put a muzzle on me before the game's over because I get awfully excited.

[BLACKOUT]

I can hardly see after sitting in the dark for an hour.

We had a long letter from our boss today. He is in Salt Lake City tempo-rarily, minus 18 pounds and 5 inches off his waistline. He is a big man in his early 40s. The calisthenics accomplished what he's been trying to do for a long time.

I'll bet your friend Bill Daly [from Jersey City] feels bad about the Dodgers losing. He is a Dodger fan, isn't he? I remember you telling me about how sore your ribs were after seeing a game with him.

/////

[Charles to Billee] October 3, 1942—Northern Ireland

There were a million stars in the heavens last night . . . It was a night that cer-tainly was not made for war; rather, it was a crescent-moonlit darkness that surely should have us together.

Don't mind if I feel a bit dreamy this afternoon. I am surrounded by one hell of an atmosphere for dreaming, but my thoughts of you make almost everything all right.

Billee, it appears as though I'll be leaving Tuesday, three days from now, on my furlough. That means I will be unable to send any mail for nine or ten days. I'll write in London, telling you just about everything I can, but I will have to wait until I rejoin my company before the letters are censored.

I'm wondering today how the World Series is coming. This time a year ago, I was running back and forth between Yankee Stadium and Ebbets Field. I remember I took Bill Daly to the series' opener in the Stadium. It was the first series game he had ever seen.

I'd like to root for Billy Southworth but I'm afraid you are stuck with a dyed-in-the-wool Yankee fan. Tell you what . . . you take the Cards and I'll have the Yanks in the series. The winner, between us, can have anything he or she wants on the day of the first series game we are together . . . bet? I haven't heard the results of any series games yet.

/////

[Billee to Charles] October 7, 1942—Asheville

I'm enclosing copy on the World Series. I'm so thrilled the Cardinals won, I don't know what to do. The Yankees still don't know what happened. Time someone else had a chance to win; they've had the honor for many years.

I received a long letter from your mom Monday with snapshots of your sister's wedding and the letter was about the wedding. Now they are all talking about ours.

We have only Mrs. Davidson with us until next Thursday and then Mom and I will be by ourselves to get the house in shape for closing. I get dizzy when I think of all that has to be done.

By the time this letter reaches you, we will be there. How I wish the move was made and this suspense was over. A new job and all . . .

[Charles to Billee] October 17, 1942—Northern Ireland

Yes, I'm back on the job after a super-swell "vacation," safe and sound. We are having a bit of trouble with our lights and this is coming to you by candlelight.

Diary of a Furlough . . . or . . . Johnny Doughboy Visits London

Accompanied by Bob P. and three others, including our First Sgt., I had an uneventful 24-hour trip to London. I'm not at liberty to discuss the means of transportation or the routes we used. But we arrived in London at 9:15 a.m. on October 7.

WEDNESDAY: Having confirmed our reservations at the Hans Crescent Club (a former hotel now being operated by the American Red Cross) we set out to make a short tour. While walking along Piccadilly about noon, we espied a sign, "American Bar," where I had my first sidecar in ever so long. Bob and I took advantage of the Club's offering of tickets to a BBC Quiz Programme broadcast that night and set forth to the Overseas League House where the broadcast was to take place. We were the only "Yanks" in the audience and were asked to take part in the broadcast. There were 10 guests, all servicemen. Two RAF, a flier from Rhodesia, another from Nigeria, two British officers, an Australian sailor, and Canadian soldier joined Bob and myself. We were divided into two teams, and our side won . . . 4-1/2 points to 4. The prizes were cigarettes, gifts of two women in Wichita, Kansas. I had two questions to answer. The first was one concerning the purchase of Manhattan Island by the Dutch settlers from the Indians for $25.00 and the other was something about a window, 6 x 8 . . . how can it be made 8 x 10 or something. I knew the first and with the help of a kibitzer got 1/2 point for the second, although I didn't and still don't have the faintest idea of what it was about . . . It was a Trans-Atlantic broadcast, 6:30–7:00 p.m., or, 12:30–1:00 p.m. EWT. I still wonder if anyone I know heard it. The introductions were simple (Corp. Charles Kiley of New Jersey, USA) and we didn't have time to say "Hello" or anything like that . . . Together with the two RAF's, Bob and I accepted an invitation to attend a lecture by a Member of Parliament at the English Speaking Union after the broadcast. We had dinner at about 9:30 (stumbled into a would-be nightclub) in the blackout.

THURSDAY: Ahhhhh . . . so good to arise at nine . . . hot tub . . . breakfast (served by the Red Cross women) and a visit to the House of Parliament. We all went, conducted by a Mr. Phillips Price, MP. Very interesting visit ... House of Commons, House of Lords, a good view of the Thames, a glimpse of the Prime Minister ... Lunch at Toni's on Regent St ... Visited the *Stars and Stripes* HQ in the afternoon to say "Hello" to those I've been sending my stories (as few as they have been). In the evening, *The Man Who Came to Dinner*, starring Robert Morley at the Savoy Theatre.

FRIDAY: Played table tennis with Bob most of the morning at the Club ... dropped in to the Eagle Club and the Washington Club, other places operated by the Red Cross. Visited the Tower of London in the afternoon [before] seeing Anton Walbrook and Diana Wynyard in *Watch on the Rhine*, a very good show that had quite a run on Broadway. Trying to find a restaurant in the blackout, Bob and I found ourselves in a Chinese place ... So, what else could we say but "Chop Suey."

SATURDAY: A most memorable visit to Windsor Castle, in Windsor (23 miles from London) ... the main buildings, residence of the King and Queen ... Frogmore, where the Duke of Kent was buried recently and where many English kings and queens are interred. King George V, King Edward VII, Queen Alexandra, King Henry VIII and Jane Seymour are among the many buried in St. George's Chapel. Sculptured marble likenesses of them all, lying in state, are placed above the spots under which they were buried ... A hurried trip to Eton College, within walking distance of the Castle, passing the house in which Gray penned his "Elegy." Looking at the names of many great men carved in the panel-work of a room at Eton ... 19 former Prime Ministers, Shelley, Sir Anthony Eden, Fox, Gray, etc. ... Unable to keep from smiling at the sight of the very young students parading about in their top hats, striped pants and "tails" ... Tea in a quaint place near the station and back to town in time to see a marvelous film, Noel Coward's *In Which We Serve*, a tale of the present activities of the Royal Navy.

SUNDAY: A 45-minute ride to Sudbury Town where Bob and I were guests of a Capt. Elliot on a really tough golf course. Darling, my 114 put me in a class with the worst duffers of all time. A dance at the club in the evening was interesting for about 30 minutes to us ... without having a dance (didn't feel like it, to be truthful, since I was thinking of *our* dances). So, another hot tub (No. 1,001) and to bed.

Bob Paulus and Charles on furlough—London, October 1942. (Kiley Family)

MONDAY: Morning and afternoon we browsed about ... me on the lookout for a gift I could get for you. Everywhere it was "No coupons, sorry." Or everything worthwhile was so expensive it would have been silly to get it. I did get my Christmas cards though, and before the day was over had them all addressed (44 of 'em). Got a special one for you ... it hit me just right since it was titled "Solitude" ... on Sunday night I had been sitting at the window of my room, staring into the darkness that was pin-pricked in a very few places with lamp lights (I never thought such a complete blackout could be achieved in such a large city). Still, one needs to simply glance about to see why the city is as cautious as it is ... It was then that I wanted to share my vacation moments with you so much, but sweetheart, you seemed so far away. I don't think I realized how far it was until then ... the States did seem a million miles away that night. When I did go to bed, I re-lived "our" lives again for the millionth time ...

TUESDAY: I should say now that the weather was beautiful during the entire trip. We had rain ... all of five minutes of it one night. So, on this day Bob and I spent the morning in Hyde Park feeding the pigeons (peanuts we had brought with us). Everybody seems to get to Hyde Park and we must have seen every Allied nation in uniform parading before us that morning ... male and female ... Saw *Gay Sisters*, a film with Barbara Stanwyck and George Brent in the afternoon ... after dinner at the Lancastershire House (veddy swank, oh yes) we couldn't resist *Doctor's Dilemma* with Vivien Leigh, another hit on Broadway.

WEDNESDAY: Vacation almost over ... slept until 10:30 ... lazybones, yes? ... but still time to catch *Mrs. Miniver*, very good wasn't it?, at an early matinee before catching a late afternoon train back ...

And that just about winds up this "Gulliver's Travels."

/////

[Billee to Charles] October 21, 1942—Massillon

As you can probably see by the postmark, I am in Massillon. We arrived yesterday, several days sooner than expected. We had to close the house in a hurry. Friday my uncle called to say that my sister's oldest boy has been stricken with infantile paralysis [polio]. He's not three yet. Naturally, we were heartsick, because he's such a dear little fellow. He is in the best of care and his age and healthy condition are in his favor.

The trip was uneventful except for the fact that connections were so close we nearly starved on the way up. It's good we had to leave in a hurry. It didn't give either of us an opportunity to lament over our leaving.

This is really like home. I've been coming to this very house since I was just big enough to put in a dresser drawer. I've grown up with all these surroundings, and I know more people here than I do in Asheville. It's going to be fun to start looking up the kids I went to grammar and junior high school with . . .

I'm taking this week to rest. Next week I'll look for a job. There seem to be plenty here. I think I'll try and get a factory job. I'm a little fed up with office work and I'd feel I'd be doing something worthwhile, too, since I can't join the WAAC. I'll probably join the army of girls in slacks. How would you like that?

Father John mentioned something to me when I was up in the spring about going into the Navy. He was afraid your mom wouldn't be able to take it. I can well imagine how he must feel, especially since there is such a need for chaplains now.

We received definite news that my cousin in the Marines is in the Solomons.

Billee with her mother, Elizabeth—Massillon, October 1942. (Kiley Family)

/////

[Charles to Billee] October 22, 1942—Northern Ireland

While I'm sitting here "talking" with you, perhaps you would like to know what we do with our nights. Well, as for the "family" in our billet: Bob is stretched out reading a *Coronet* [magazine]. Stan has the top of his pen in his mouth trying to think of something to say to his wife; Jerry, Earl and Russ are playing three-handed bridge; Elvy is saddle-soaping his shoes; Erv is out trying to find a place to have my furlough pictures developed; and here I am. There is a movie in the mess hall but I felt like visiting with you. I could pretend the fireplace is glowing and that we are snug in our corner. Think you'll be able to find a corner for us in Massillon?

There are so many things I want to see . . . now. I want to see you standing at the head of the stairs at Penn Station. I want to see you walking from the hotel elevator in that cloud of white. Gosh, you were beautiful, Billee. I want to see you sitting at the table in the Asheville "Y," wondering who those two soldiers were walking in your direction. I want to see you in the cocktail lounge of the Inn. I want to see you walking away from me at Penn Station because if I did, I would go back after you and never let you go again.

/////

[Billee to Charles] October 25, 1942—Massillon

I've had a full weekend, with two heavy dates . . . with my brother. He took me dancing Friday night with a crowd. He hasn't told them yet that I'm his sister. I put a ribbon in my hair and no one knew the difference. Warren gave me a name . . . Billee Kiley from Jersey City. How's that? He said I may as well get used to it.

Last night we went with another couple to see Ted Lewis and his show in Akron. We went riding afterwards and took the fellow's girl home and ended up at a drive-in eating 12 inch hotdogs.

I had forgotten how football crazy this town is. You start a conversation and sooner or later it ends up football. They don't seem to have anything but champions . . . seven years they have held the title.

Eleanor and Tom's wedding picture came today and it is beautiful. Warren tickled me . . . I asked him if he'd give me away and he said that only for me would he wear one of those monkey suits like Tom has on.

/////

[Billee to Charles] October 30, 1942—Massillon

My social security card finally arrived on Tuesday so I started out with that and my birth certificate and both knees shaking. My first stop was Republic Steel Corp., which is the biggest around here. My brother works there. I filled out an application and was ushered into the big boss's office . . . thick carpets and a huge desk that was polished so you could see yourself in it. He seemed to like my qualifications and took up nearly an hour of my time.

From Tuesday until last night I talked to scores of people, took a trip to Canton and filled out applications over there. Last night at suppertime, one of the bosses at Republic called and asked if I could come to work Monday. You can imagine how relieved I was. You know I've never been out of work before . . . it was beginning to get me.

I start Monday afternoon at 3:30 and work until twelve. But, I'll change shifts and it's only five days unless I have to put in overtime. I don't know exactly what the nature of the work is, but it's in the order department of the mill, so I'll be in the midst of all the activity. I feel like I'm joining the Army . . . all the fingerprinting and examinations I'm to take and all the papers I've already signed. The salary isn't quite as much as I wanted to start with, but I don't think it will be long before I'll get a raise and the overtime will make up for the difference.

Mom has been working since Tuesday in the big Mercy hospital in Canton doing nurse's aide work. She took the Red Cross home nursing course two years ago so it is paying dividends now. She has a nice starting salary and her meals.

Little Billy was somewhat better tonight. He has the use of almost both arms now and his shoulders. His legs are completely gone . . . that is, the muscles. It is going to take time, but they are performing miracles with this new Sister Kenny treatment so we can't help but feel encouraged.

Last night Warren took me to a coed dance his club held at the "Y." The kids were fairly young . . . his age and not many older than I. I've done more dancing in the past ten days than any time since New York and Asheville when you were there, and am I rusty! The jitter-bug craze is still going strong here. You should have seen them last night, "zoot suits" and all. We went dancing elsewhere after that, and didn't get home until three; then, I was up at 5:30 to get Warren off to work. I'm laid out now.

My dancing brought you that much closer. I couldn't help but think how wonderful and how much more fun it would be if it were you I was dancing with.

CHAPTER 3

NOVEMBER 1942–FEBRUARY 1943

*The RAF made a mass raid on Berlin last night and it looks as if
"Jerry" is going to repay the compliment.... There they go! A look
out the window made me feel as though I was at the World's Fair
watching the fireworks display.*

[Charles to Billee, January 1943.]

///////

The War: In November, the Allied Expeditionary Forces forced Rommel
to retreat from Egypt and then from Libya. Rommel wanted to evacuate
North Africa; Hitler said no. At the same time, Russian troops were poised to
retake Stalingrad from the German Sixth Army—next stop, Leningrad.

The *New York Times* reported in December that a Victory Committee had
organized 1,141 American theatrical artists from stage, film, and radio, who
made 6,828 appearances over the previous year to entertain the troops, both in
the United States and in the European Theatre of Operations (ETO).

By January 1943, the Allies believed the tide of war was turning in their
favor. In December, the German armies that were not surrounded began to
retreat from Russian territory in the Caucasus, and in January the Japanese
planned to withdraw from Guadalcanal.

In Europe, 1943 began with the first RAF raids on Berlin since 1941, and
the RAF also attacked U-boat bases at Cherbourg and Lorient, France. Luftwaffe planes retaliated over London; the RAF bombed Hamburg. In February,
the RAF and the USAAF established around-the-clock bombing raids over
Germany—the RAF at night, USAAF's Flying Fortresses and Liberators by day.

In mid-January, Roosevelt and Churchill met in Casablanca (Stalin could
not attend because he was needed during the Russian advances). At Casablanca,

it was decided that an Allied assault on northwest Europe would be delayed. Gains in North Africa led to an Allied sweep across the Mediterranean region, with the aim of removing Italy from the Axis. The RAF bombed Milan.

The German army at Stalingrad surrendered in February.

In the United States, Roosevelt sought a longer workweek to increase military supplies for what seemed like a winning war effort.

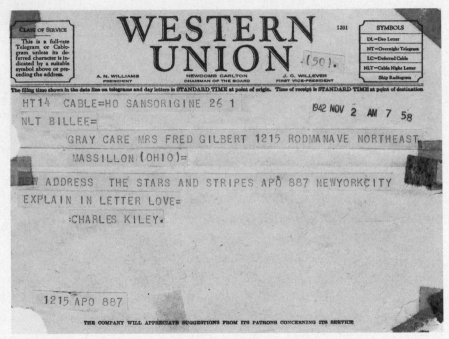

Charles's cable to Billee about his transfer to the *Stars and Stripes*—November 1942. (Kiley Family)

[Charles to Billee] November 3, 1942—London

The cable I sent yesterday must have been as much of a surprise to you as my sudden move here was to me. To sum everything up in a short space of time, I'm with the *Stars and Stripes* headquarters now and enjoying my work immensely.

Whereas the paper was published as a weekly since April, it became a daily today. You can realize how much work it will mean for the staff. Still, there is a very capable group of men to do the work and I'm sure it will be a great success. Bob Moora and Bud [Oram] Hutton, two members of the editorial board, were former *N.Y. Herald-Trib[une]* and *World-Telegram* men.

One of the first assignments I had was an interview with Col. (Mrs.) Oveta Culp Hobby, director of the WAAC. I'm sending today's paper to you so you can read the results for yourself. Wish me luck.

Now that I've had a bit of good fortune in getting back in the "game," as it were, I miss you more than ever because I want to share my good fortune with you.

/////

[FROM THE *STARS AND STRIPES*, November 2, 1942]

BRITISH WOMEN CAN TEACH OURS PLENTY, SAYS WAAC HEAD HERE

by Cpl. Charles Kiley (Staff Writer)

America has a lot to learn from Britain's women at war.

That is the conclusion of Col. Oveta Culp Hobby, director of the Women's Auxiliary Army Corps in America, who has been making an inspection tour of ATS [Auxiliary Territorial Service, the British Army women's service], WAAF [British Women's Auxiliary Air Force] and WRNS [Women's Royal Navy Service, commonly known as "Wrens"] establishments in England...

Although she accompanied Mrs. Roosevelt on a flying trip across the Atlantic and has been with the First Lady on a few visits, Col. Hobby has devoted most of her first week here to studying the operations of the British women's forces.

"Enthusiasm does not describe their efforts," said Col. Hobby. "The better word is 'devotion.' Our girls will derive much from the example set by the women of Britain."

... She referred to the type of training afforded by the centers at Des Moines, Iowa, and Daytona Beach, Fla., where a girl's future in the WAACs is largely determined by what she did in civilian life.

England's women's services, on the other hand, include a "superb" non-specialist training course, Col. Hobby said, whereby a stenographer, for instance, may be training in cooking, or an interior decorator may learn about motor transport.

... Col. Hobby revealed that the present strength of the WAACs is about 6,400, including those in training and the few already in the field.

A reserve list of 5,600 has been maintained, Col. Hobby said, including those who have enlisted and are awaiting orders to report to training centers. The capacity at Fort Des Moines is 7,200, while the newly-opened center at Daytona Beach will house 8,000.

The present setup covers four basic courses for the WAAC— "administration," "communication," "motor transport," and "cooks and bakers." But, with the addition of Daytona Beach as a training center there will be nine courses.

... The WAAF and ATS each have about 652 specialized courses for their women.

After her first week of inspection, Col. Hobby said she had found only a few differences in the operational system of the ATS and WAAF and the WAAC— for instance, WAAC women must be governed by their own officers, whereas the British women may have males as their superior officers.

One of her most emphatic statements during the interview was Col. Hobby's observation that "absolutely nothing is wasted in Britain, from what I can see. Everything is used for something. Even the smallest and, ordinarily, the most useless item is put to some good somewhere."

[Billee to Charles] November 4, 1942—Massillon

How do I rate a cable and two letters since Monday? The only thing I can make out of the cable is that you have been made one of the staff members of the *Stars and Stripes*, but where? Ireland or London? I can't wait to get the letter telling me all about it.

I started to work yesterday on that 3:30 to 12:00 shift. When I think of the responsibility I had at Ivey's, and the little bit I've got here, I have to laugh. I think they figure on working us in on the jobs that quite a few young fellows have, since they will be called for service before long. The job is in the order department where all the orders from the different companies are typed, filed and figured, etc. The office is right in with the steel mill. They are to take new ones through the mill on special days so we can appreciate what we are doing.

It's almost like an army or something around here. You know they work three shifts and there is always someone either going from or coming to work. You see everyone with a lunch basket. This is the production army I've heard and read about.

Since it is only five days, I was called to the Mercy hospital where Mom works . . . they wanted me for full time, but I had already accepted the job at Republic Steel, so I am going to work over there on Saturdays. It will mean about $15 extra a month and that isn't to be sneezed at, eh?

Little Billy played patty-cake last night. His dad is so thrilled. His legs haven't shown much improvement.

I hope to be able to go to our Canton–Massillon game. That's always a battle royal here, and I haven't seen a good game since I left. They even close the stores here on the days of home games so everyone can go. Everything closes except the mills.

It is about a quarter of two, but I didn't get home until twelve-thirty from work and Warren and I had a lunch. He is working 3 to 11 this week.

Talking about "solitude," my dear, you're always with me . . . when I walk along the streets by myself, going to church, even dancing with someone else . . . you're there.

///////

[Charles to Billee] November 5, 1942—London

There were times when you were with me on Irish moonlit nights (the few we had), on days and nights during maneuvers when we all didn't know how we'd ever come through it, through rain and mud . . . now, you're still with me in a different atmosphere, which makes me feel good all over again.

The delay in mail is due, no doubt, to my transfer since I haven't had any from Co. H yet.

Yesterday, I handled a visit by American soldiers with the Mayor of Hammersmith, a London borough. I arrived about an hour before the men and had a very enjoyable chat with the Mayor and his wife (she's called a "Mayoress" over here). His son met a Newark girl in Bonn, Germany, a few years ago, married her and settled in Newark. They gave me their home address and extended a standing invitation to visit them when I have an opportunity, and gosh knows when that will be. He said he enjoys speaking with Americans a great deal. I guess I was a good listener.

/////

[FROM THE *STARS AND STRIPES*, November 13, 1942]

MAYOR ASKS YANKS TO TEA AND WINDS UP AS A GUEST

by Charles F. Kiley, *Stars and Stripes* Staff Writer

"Who's t'rowin' dis party for who?"

Mayor Richard H. Kent, of Hammersmith, a London borough, might have asked this question Wednesday afternoon if he had lived in Newark, N.J., USA.

But he doesn't live in Newark—he's Mayor of one of London's cities-within-a-city—so the question had to be asked with a broad "A."

It seems Mayor Kent asked the Red Cross to bring him a group of American soldiers from his favorite US city, Newark. Only one Jerseyite came, and when the party got going, the Mayor said, the soldiers did most of the entertaining.

Mayor Kent's son, Harold, lives in Newark, N.J., and it was for this reason the mayor specified Newarkians. His son, he said, married a Newark girl, Doris Adams, after they met at Bonn, Germany, in 1939. They went to the United States, and still live in Newark, where the son is helping with air raid protection.

The one Newarkian in Wednesday's party of nine Americans was Sgt. Harry Goode, Air Force. Sgt. Goode, it developed, attended the same high school in Newark where the mayor's daughter-in-law was a teacher when she met her husband on a European holiday.

After Mrs. Kent had served tea with peach and apple pie, in the official parlor, the Mayor led the Yanks through the almost palatial City Hall.

Sgt. Goode, who at home lives under the paternalistic eye of Boss Hague, took one look at the teak-paneled council room and sighed:

"Jeest! Frank Hague'd give his eye-teeth for this joint!"

[Billee to Charles] November 8, 1942—Massillon

I've had a pretty full week: five days at my new job and one day at the other new job in Canton.

Next week they start taking us through the mill so we'll know our way around if we have to go on errands and so forth when the fellows are gone. I'm looking forward since this is the closest I've ever been to a steel mill. Night before last I spent part of the time watching them make steel in one of the mills close by that I can see from our office window, the twenty-four-inch mill I believe they call it.

You'd laugh if you could hear the girls and me over lunch boxes, fighting the war and what we are going to do afterwards. One girl is married and her husband is stationed near Seattle; the other girls both have boyfriends in the service, so we have a high old time hashing and rehashing—a real hen party.

The atmosphere at the job in Canton in the hospital is entirely different. Everything is so quiet that you can almost hear yourself think.

My sister's little boy turned over in bed himself the other night when they took the packs off his legs. We are all so thrilled and pleased, and very grateful. A few nights before that, he reached up and scratched his head. You can't imagine little things like that meaning so much.

[Charles to Billee] November 12, 1942—London

In a few days, I'll have a few more articles to send to you. I had one on a fellow here whose dad is a private in the Army, another on the CWACs (Canadian Women's Army Corps) who recently arrived in Britain and a review on the Alaska–Canada Highway. The CWACs, or "Quacks" as they are called, are just about the closest thing to American girls you'll find. That's only natural, I guess.

I'm sending you as many copies of the *S. and S.* as I remember to. I say that because sometimes I forget a lot of things during the rush of a working day. Everything except you.

The other night I had to check on the arrival of Kay Francis, Martha Raye, Carole Landis and Mitzi Mayfair. They are here to entertain the troops. One of the fellows covered them at a press conference last night and agreed with me that Mitzi was the nicest.

[FROM THE *STARS AND STRIPES*, November 16, 1942]

"THAT'S MY POP" IS PRIVATE TO CPL. OGLE

[No byline]

Remember the times your old man led you into the woodshed and blistered your seat? Or when he interrupted some of your very confidential sessions with Mary on the front porch and chased you to bed?

With this in mind you probably never thought you'd see time march on to the day when you out-ranked the old man in the Army and were able to shout, "That's my pop!" as he answered your question with "Yes, Corporal."

Well, T-5 Wayne Ogle, Idaville, Ind., is in that enviable position. At present, he's stationed in Britain while his dad, Pfc. Clifford Ogle, is at Fort Benjamin Harrison, Ind.

"You never can tell, though," says Wayne, hopefully and smilingly. "I might meet up with him soon. Gosh, I'd love to see his expression when I said, 'Ogle, your uniform isn't neat,' or 'Straighten your cap, rookie.'"

Still, Ogle's father isn't an ordinary rookie. Make no mistake about that. True, he's been in the Army only two months, during which time he made Pfc.

Ogle, Sr., is a 44-year old veteran of World War I. He has stood at attention longer than his son has been in the Army and is qualified to give the "kid" pointers on soldiering.

Pfc. Ogle took part in several major battles during his 21 months in France. Wounded three times, he was decorated with the Purple Heart and Victory Medal . . .

[FROM THE *STARS AND STRIPES*, November 20, 1942]

HERE'S A PREVIEW OF OUR OWN WAACS— AND THEY'RE NICE

by Charles F. Kiley, *Stars and Stripes* Staff Writer

She's about 5-3, weighs 110 pounds, is 23, uses lipstick, speaks our own "slan-guage" . . . and brothers, she's nice!

That's a picture of the average CWAC (Canadian Women's Army Corps). If you haven't met her yet, you will. More than 100 of them just arrived in Britain with the first detachment to proceed overseas, and there's more on the way.

Like a lot of us, you're wondering what our WAACs will be like when, and if, they get over here. The CWACs give you the nearest thing to a preview of our gals inasmuch as the only line that separates them is the 49th Parallel, and that's only imaginary.

Don't get a wrong slant on this, buddy. The ATS are swell. So are the WAAFs and WRNS. But these Canadian girls are as close as you'll get to the one who's waiting back home . . . you hope.

. . . As far as discipline is concerned, Army regulations are enforced in so far as they can be made applicable to women. The CWAC is disciplined by its own officers but in the event of adequate punishment beyond the powers of a CWAC officer, the offender may be tried by an Army officer.

. . . And, mates, they are living in style.

They arise to a 7 a.m. reveille, have a 7:45 breakfast in mess-hall style, repair to their rooms for last-minute rouging and hair-combing before falling out for work.

Visiting a boudoir was something new but the girls didn't seem to mind since the "intrusion" was properly chaperoned.

It sounded like New York when one of the girls piped, "What's cookin' America?"

/////

[Billee to Charles] November 14, 1942—Massillon

Yesterday brought a letter from your mom. They have evidently heard from you since I have because your mother wrote, "What do you think of Charles being a war correspondent? Isn't it wonderful?" I'm so thrilled and excited for you because I know what it means to you. You're a lucky guy.

Warren just came in so things are buzzing around here now. I think he is going to enlist very soon. Mom hasn't said very much. We were talking about it last night and she seems to think he is right. I'm so glad that she feels that way, because it will make everything easier when he goes. He is in the heat-treat department of the metallurgy laboratory where they make up the formulas and test them. I believe he is thinking about going into the metalsmith division of the Navy Air Corps.

Warren wants me to join the WAVES [during WWII, the women's division of the US Naval Reserve; the acronym stood for Women Accepted for Voluntary Emergency Service]. They passed a bill to say that those women wouldn't be sent out of the country. There was a WAAC in the office yesterday. She looked good in her uniform and seemed to like Army life. She was a former employee in the bookkeeping department . . . in the hospital, I mean. I would consider joining, but I'm afraid I might land in Timbuktu by the time the war is over, and you'd come back before I would. I don't like to even think about it.

/////

[Charles to Billee] November 21, 1942—London

Saturday night . . . not anything unusual but it is one of our date nights. And, I can't forget it is two days before my birthday. I'm afraid it's going to be a rather dull birthday, too.

The best birthday present I could receive from you came two days ago . . . your letter of Nov. 4. Apparently, you had written some before it that I haven't received yet because until I read that letter I didn't know you were working for Republic, I didn't know Mother was with Mercy hospital, I didn't know about little Billy and I can't remember hearing what you wanted for winning the Series' wager. However, I expect that letters that have been delayed will give me the answers.

Often I think I can tell you all the things that are in my heart but when I read my letters, they still sound so inadequate. At night I still try to create a little consolation by thinking about us . . . when we'll be together, how long it might be, wishing I were near you in whatever you were doing, worrying about you, and cursing Hitler for the day he was born.

I said I was worried about you. Without sounding like an old woman, I am concerned about those gosh-awful hours you work. I know there is work to be done and Republic has to function, but Billee, please don't let it run you down.

/////

[Billee to Charles] November 23, 1942—Massillon

Happy birthday! I sent you a wire today that should arrive in a few days. Really meant to do it several days ago so that it would arrive in time but the days went by too quickly. I hope my card arrived in time to be with you today.

The biggest upset of the year—Massillon lost to Canton for the first time in eight years, and its only loss in heaven knows when. 35–0. You can imagine what a blow that would be. They've had regular riots here since Saturday. Canton hasn't stopped celebrating yet. We have two high school kids in jail and the school is on a walkout until they are released. People have been stoned in the street by Canton passersby in their cars. Anyhow, the Yankees and Massillon got beat this year. What upsets!

/////

[Billee to Charles] November 26, 1942—Massillon

Happy Thanksgiving. It's very early but still Thanksgiving morning and I know this will be the only opportunity I'll have to write.

This place will really be buzzing a little later on when the rest of the family gets here. We expect 20. Warren and I are going to a dance later on in the evening. He is waiting on his birth certificate so he can get his enlistment papers. It won't be so long now. I'm going to miss him. We get along well together, and I'm really just beginning to know him. His year away from home has changed him and made him older than his eighteen years.

They are starting to break in the girls on the day shift, on the jobs of some of the fellows who have already received [draft] questionnaires, so it won't be long now. Some of them are very complicated jobs. I've got my fingers crossed.

How am I going to stand up against such competition as all these celebrities, I want to know. Carole Landis, Kay Francis, Martha Raye and Mitzie Mayfair. I wonder if I could rate a seat on a clipper to spend Christmas. I'd be entertaining a soldier and anyone else you might happen to have around. Christmas in London with you. What would we do?

/////

[Billee to Charles] November 28, 1942—Massillon

Do I catch just a note of discouragement in your letter? Everything will be all right one of these days and you'll be back in your own little groove again, a bit crowded since I'll be there, but all this will be just an interlude.

Yesterday brought the article on Alaska, by far the best. I enjoyed it so much. The family enjoyed it, too. My uncle's comment: "Hmmm, for a sportswriter, he doesn't do bad at all."

Why couldn't I hop a plane and be with you over there? I wouldn't get in the way, not even to tag along if it couldn't be done at that time. I could file orders over there just as well as in Republic Steel here. I think they have a subsidiary over there. I'll look into that. I know I'd get pretty far: "I want a transfer to England, please."

Don't worry about me. You have enough to do. I'm all right and a little hard work never hurt anyone.

I hope my Xmas package arrives in time to be with you and that Davy Jones doesn't have the pleasure of unwrapping it.

[FROM THE *STARS AND STRIPES*, November 16, 1942]

AMERICA'S BURMA ROAD

by Charles F. Kiley, *Stars and Stripes* Staff Writer

While American munitions trucks rumbled across French North Africa today, more US transport was moving against the Japs—this time in icebound Alaska, an ocean and a continent away.

The Alaskan Highway—America's Burma Road from Seattle to Fairbanks—is open for fighting men.

Up there, US Engineers—and with them Canadians and civilians—have fought an ugly, unglorified battle against big timber, mud, cold, deer-flies, mosquitoes—every imaginable hardship and danger outside of actual bombs from enemy planes—to push the big road through and get 'em rolling . . .

The 1,671-mile highway leading from the American frontier across Western Canada to Alaska is speeding traffic from arsenals of the United States to bases established as springboards for attack against Japan. Another crushing demonstration that the people of the New World can do it, anywhere, any time, the vital trunk line was open months ahead of schedule.

Under 48-year-old Brig. Gen. William Morris Hoge, the engineers completed this amazing triumph over wilderness, mountain and swamp in six months, after it was estimated it would take 18 to 24 months. Completion of the route means that troops and equipment will reach Fairbanks, Alaska, from Edmonton, Alberta, in 80 hours, whereas it previously took nine days by sea and rail from a West Coast port . . .

An army of 7,000 soldiers and 2,000 civilians, working 16 hours daily, pushed the road forward at the rate of eight miles a day.

They worked in cold, 25 below zero; slept in pup tents or anything considered "quarters." They withstood the pestering mosquitoes, "no-see-'ems" and other insects which fortunately did not carry malaria. They died on the Alcan while bulldozers ploughed on and power shovels groaned and strained. Gales ripped down the valleys and tore army camps to shreds . . .

There were no furloughs or leaves for the soldiers. They knew from the start what they were up against.

As a result, America now has the chance to drive the Japs off Kiska and the tip of the Aleutians, used by them to ravage Pacific ship lanes between America and the Soviet Union, as well as being able to dispatch long-range bombers from numerous airfields to Tokyo, 2,547 miles from Dutch Harbor . . .

Furthermore, it has been stressed that with a safe ferry across the Bering Strait from Nome, a prospect is opened for a transportation route linked with the Trans-Siberian Railway in Russia . . .

[Charles to Billee] November 29, 1942—London

I could say that I love you more than ever, but I wouldn't be telling the truth. It's because I couldn't feel any closer to you than I do now, no matter what happens.

You may wonder, why this opening flood of "amour"? Is it because the Christmas packages arrived? In a sense, you'd be right. The packages did come the other day while I was away on another three-day trip and they were almost too much to ask for. Now that I have dispersed the contents, I can't remember whether it came in one or two packages, I was that excited.

I'm wearing the gloves—perfect fit. I needed the hankies so bad I couldn't believe my eyes when I saw them. Oh, just everything was swell.

Now, the cake—my, oh my. I'm letting you in on a secret that you'll have to promise to keep. Naturally, I shared it with the boys; then, I typed a little testimonial to Mother's baking and had the fellows sign it.

This afternoon, a new Red Cross center was opened here. By this afternoon, I mean early evening, Vivien Leigh, Diana Wynyard and Miriam Jordan as well as an Army glee club and orchestra were on a transatlantic broadcast through NBC, 6:30–7:00 p.m., our time over here. That would make it 2:30 to 3:00 Eastern War Time, I believe. Ralph Martin, who accompanied me on my recent trip, covered the story.

Incidentally, while Ralph and I were on the trip, we stumbled on a good story. Kay Francis and Mitzi Mayfair, here on tour with Martha Raye and Carole Landis, were in an Army hospital down with colds, etc. Mitzi sustained a sprained shoulder while tossing a sergeant over her shoulder during a jitterbug act. We were allowed to see Mitzi, whom we had met before, but not Kay. As usual, Mitzi was very pleasant. We chatted for 45 minutes and then phoned the story into the office. To our surprise, nobody else had the story. It was good from our angle because they were forced into the hospital as the result of entertaining the troops.

(l–r) Charles, Vivian Leigh, Diana Wynyard, and Ralph Martin—London, November 1942. (Kiley Family)

/////

[Billee to Charles] December 2, 1942—Massillon

They wouldn't accept Warren in the Navy because he stutters when he gets excited or overtired. He's lots better than when he was younger and I think in time it will leave him entirely. The recruiting officer suggested the Navy Reserve. I hope they accept him because he will be so disappointed if they do not. As much as I don't want to see him leave, you have to look at it from his side, and he does want to go so badly.

Little Billy, my nephew with infantile paralysis, wiggled his little toes the other night for the first time and moved his one leg by himself. That means so much progress. My sister is feeling a little better.

Warren enjoys your *Stars and Stripes* so much. He takes it off me when he comes in, before I've had an opportunity to finish reading it. How do you like that?

Warren took me to a Thanksgiving dance Thursday night and some of the kids were quite a bit younger than I and, don't laugh, I got stuck with a high school graduate. He took it for granted I was as old as he was and did I have a time. That brother of mine, instead of answering my S.O.S., sat in the corner and made fun of me. I'll get even with him yet. I'll think twice before I go to one of those again.

We had some bad news over the weekend. My cousin I told you about, in the Marines, was killed in action at Guadalcanal. We're hoping and praying they've made a mistake. He was quite outstanding in sports in high school and played football three years at LSU. I still can't believe it. It's certainly bringing the realization of it all home to us.

/////

[Charles to Billee] December 6, 1942—London

Letters, which will follow, may reach you before Christmas. Perhaps they will not. At any rate, I do hope this gets to you before Dec. 25.

I want to try and say some things that I would be tempted to say on such an occasion. We won't pretend we are together, in Asheville visiting the places we knew together or sitting in "our corner," clinging to the things more realistic than hope, or in New York and Jersey making our Christmas a never-to-be-forgotten one. And we won't pretend we are in Massillon with the folks I am so anxious to meet and know.

Instead, let us face the situation just as it is. I'm here and you are there, thousands of miles apart yet as close to each other as we have been and will ever be, everything considered. By that, I mean you and I are part of each other now and no matter how many miles separate us we will know that everything is "normal."

About Warren enlisting: there isn't much anyone can do about that these days. Letters from home tell me how all the kids are getting the itch and nothing keeps them out. Yes, a great many of them are young, but I've seen real youngsters over here doing the job of men. Some of these RAF lads, veterans of many flights, are barely in their 20s. If Mother wants to, she might be able to stall Warren for a time but if he has a mind to get in, he'll go. As for enlisting, we carried a story yesterday saying that all manpower in the Army and Navy will be handled by Selective Service. In that case, he won't be able to enlist, even if he wants to.

As for me, I'm still as busy as ever. First, I'll tell you of my "flat." I don't believe I told you in my last letter. In fact, I don't believe I had it then. We were put on subsistence, inasmuch as we have to work pretty much like the civilian war correspondents, traveling out of town, working unstable hours, etc. I have a swell room, in a nice residential section, overlooking a park. There's plenty of closet space, a bureau, desk, table and bathroom, all part of a room-and-a-half "flat" as they call it here. I have breakfast served in my room every morning (oh my, yes). Since rooms are hard to get here, I enlisted the aid of a very sweet woman, a volunteer in the Red Cross. Her husband is an officer in the British medical corps (skin specialist in civilian life) who is now in North Africa. She knows everybody from generals on down, is quite well-to-do, mixes in a set with Lady So-and-So, etc. But she is a peach. She tracked down this place and sent me to it. In return, I'm trying to buy a doll for her only child, a daughter of six. Dolls are as scarce as can be, believe it or not. She mentioned once that she had been trying, without success, to get one before Christmas, I don't know how successful I'll be with it.

/////

[Billee to Charles] December 6, 1942—Massillon

We had a big Saturday night last night giving my brother a sendoff. Yes, he was accepted in the Air Corps, Maintenance Division. He goes to Columbus Tuesday for his final examinations. He looks like such a kid to be going. Poor Mom, she's not showing it but she's heartbroken, especially since the news of my cousin. She and Warren are downstairs visiting.

They have taken my nephew out of isolation so that's good news. He isn't so lonely now, what with ten other small children around him to talk with and play with as much as they can.

/////

[Billee to Charles] December 9, 1942—Massillon

Warren is in Columbus at the induction center. He passed his physical in Akron but we don't know how he made out in Columbus. Mom is taking it pretty well, better than I expected. She started a new job [at Republic Steel] yesterday.

I'm breaking Mom in on the same kind of work I'm doing—well, a part of it. Seems so funny, but she's catching on quick. The evening work won't make her miss Warren so much because that's about the only time she saw him.

Mom and I are lucky. We've found a ride in the neighborhood back and forth to work. That makes it swell in bad weather because we had about 1/2 mile or better to walk on the mill property before we got to the mill office.

We've just learned another cousin of mine is in the Solomons. He's in the Marines, too. He's on my father's side. I knew him very well as a young boy, but I haven't seen him in about nine years.

[Charles to Billee] December 10, 1942—London

As usual, I've been buzzing around here and there. I'm enclosing two stories. One concerned the graduation of the first class of the first Officers' Candidate School ever established outside the United States. While simple, it was a very impressive ceremony. One of the graduates was a fellow from Newark. I chatted with him for a while, talking of mutual acquaintances. During the conversation, I learned that he had proposed to his wife at 1 p.m., on Dec. 7, 1941. Minutes later the headwaiter told him that Pearl Harbor had been bombed. Recently he received a wire telling him he was a daddy.

In handling the assignment, I had to travel on a General's train. Comfortable Pullman accommodations overnight, etc. On the return trip, I beat Dave Scherman, *LIFE* photographer, five straight games of Casino. He said the only other man to beat him was a Marine who was shipwrecked with him on an island in the South Pacific a year or so ago.

///////

[FROM THE *STARS AND STRIPES*, December 10, 1942]

43 CADETS GET BARS AT OCS

[No byline]

OFFICERS' CANDIDATE SCHOOL, England, Dec. 9—In a small gymnasium before a handful of onlooking officers and enlisted men, 43 members in the first class of an Officers' Candidate School ever established outside the United States yesterday were commissioned second lieutenants in the US Army . . .

The candidates, from 24 States in the Union and representing 13 branches of the service, listened to an address by Maj. Gen. John C. H. Lee, commanding officer, Services of Supply, from whom they received their diplomas.

The graduate with the longest service record was Lt. Ed Rhoades, 34, who has been in the Army for 17 years. He was the only one in the class without a listed hometown.

"The Army's my home," he said . . .

The graduates represented the Infantry, Air Force, Engineers, Signal Corps, Quartermasters, Field Artillery, Coast Artillery, Ordnance, Transportation Corps, Chemical Warfare, Armored Corps, Military Police and Paratroopers.

[FROM THE *STARS AND STRIPES*, December 10, 1942]

THEY KEEP SUPPLIES ROLLING

by Charles F. Kiley, *Stars and Stripes* Staff Writer

A QM DEPOT IN ENGLAND, Dec. 9—This is another story about the "little guys" in the Army—the soldiers who clothe, feed, house and equip their buddies from Alaska to Guadalcanal, from Iceland to North Africa.

It is a story of an army "nerve center," the Quartermaster Corps.

Typical of QM depots throughout the war theaters of the world is one located in the heart of England . . .

On the surface, this depot doesn't look like much. It is simply a group of plain, square buildings. But, inside, it's a high-gear place, for this unit has its work cut out in supplying 27 camps and hostels that care for American fighting men . . .

To grease the machinery of six warehouses, a huge cold storage plant, garages, carpenter shops, offices, etc., there is a staff of 84 skilled men doing a big job, on the double . . .

One of their big jobs is to handle 110,000 pounds of meat per month in a storage plant that covers 5,000 square feet. Another is to roast and grind a ton of coffee a day.

These QMs also stock check and dispatch from warehouses thousands of items of clothing, food, furniture, stationery, typewriters, files, canteen supplies and a thousand and one other things . . .

Every commanding officer, from the company CO to the chief of staff, realizes its value and shouts it 24 hours a day:

"Supply!"

[Billee to Charles] December 14, 1942—Massillon

Today brought a letter from El. I suppose you know by now you are to be an uncle. How do you feel? She has taken Tom's going away [he was drafted into the Army] so hard that maybe this will ease the misery and give her something else to think of.

We went to Elyria to see my aunt yesterday, the one whose son was killed. We decided to have a quiet Christmas together here. At least we can be together, as many of us as there are.

Warren called Saturday morning from Columbus and told Mom goodbye. He didn't know where he was being sent and we've had no word yet.

[Charles to Billee] December 19, 1942—London

During most of the week I have been busy rounding up the Red Cross Christmas plans. It was quite a job. Too, I went out of town for a day, traveling almost 100 miles only to discover, when I got there, that the story I wanted wasn't available.

Enclosed is a recent story on fellows with oversized feet looking for shoes.

I haven't any plans for Christmas. Many fellows have accepted invitations to spend the day with British families; others will be having parties for orphans, underprivileged children, youngsters of British soldiers overseas, etc. If Ralph Martin were here, we would be able to cook up something between us but he's with our staff in Africa now.

Ralph Martin and Charles in the *Stars and Stripes* office—London,
December 1942. (Kiley Family)

/////

[One of the most popular features of the *Stars and Stripes* during WWII was
the "Help Wanted" column, which featured a shoes and clothing "swap" section
especially for hard-to-fit soldiers. There were quite a few feature stories in the
paper about this service.]

[FROM THE *STARS AND STRIPES*, December 14, 1942]

THERE'S ONE LESS SHOELESS SOLDIER

by Charles F. Kiley, *Stars and Stripes* Staff Writer

It was a quiet Sunday afternoon. Typewriters banged away in the office. Suddenly a rumble was heard. Beginning of another blitz? No sound of planes. The rumble developed into a roll of thunder that grew uncomfortably close.

A figure loomed in the doorway. It was clad in the khaki of an American soldier. The noise ceased when the figure's feet grew still.

"The name is Palumbo," the soldier said. "I am given to understand that the *Stars and Stripes* would like to see every soldier with a pair of shoes. I am one of those guys who needs 'em, but bad."

Timidly someone asked for the gentleman's size.

"I might squeeze into the pair of 13 EEs you're holding for that guy Dewey, who ain't showed up," Palumbo answered, casting anxious eyes around a room for a box big enough to hold such brogans.

A conference was hastily called and a unanimous verdict rendered in four seconds. Palumbo would get the coveted gondolas. Of course, the fact that T-4 Anthony J. Palumbo, New York City, reaches six feet into the air, weighs 260 pounds, is built like a T-2 tank, and had to come through the door sideways had nothing to do with the hurried decision. Neither did the fact that he described himself as a wrestler in civilian life. Not a . . . well, maybe just a little bit.

Before Palumbo departed with the 13EEs firmly grasped in his hands, he revealed that the QMs at Fort Dix spent three weeks getting clothes to fit him. He wears a 19 1/2 shirt . . . They did find two pairs of gun-boats for him but his duty as "heavy equipment man" with the Engineers is tough on the tootsies. He wore one pair down to his socks four months ago. The pair he was wearing had been repaired four times . . .

All of which means that Pfc. Dewey P. Livingston, who originally subscribed for the shoes, and Pvt. Otis L. Martin who had a bid in for them will have to wrestle Palumbo for the shoes. If they keep in touch with this office it will try to get them their 13EE leather lorries.

Other requests to reach the desk of the unhappy "Shoes" editor have been for a pair of 15Ds for S/Sgt. Everette Black, Air Force, and a pair of overshoes to fit 13B shoes for a "certain Lt." at a QM depot.

Sgt. William Spencer, Texas, presently hospitalized, asks for a pair of 13 1/2 AA COWBOY BOOTS! He says he is in the hospital, has flat feet and wears 14 1/2 AA shoes but can use a size smaller in boots. He needs either the boots or shoes, "very, very badly." Spencer describes himself as being 34, 6 ft. 4 in., weighing 200.

This is no job for a guy with—excuse me—8 1/2s. I think I'll go down to the Lamb and Lark for a Guinness. Everybody's got shoes down there.

[Billee to Charles] December 19, 1942—Massillon

Warren called last night. He had ten dollars stolen from him and we were to wire him some more. He says if he's still in Columbus Tuesday, they'll send him home for Christmas.

We're having awful weather. It starts to thaw and then it snows again. We've had the ground covered for about three weeks now. The highways are just sheets of ice. It's awful to try to drive. I don't have to worry about that. A car is a worry now, what with gas rationing, no tires and what have you.

I got good and mad today, but I held my tongue. Going to Canton on the bus this morning there were quite a few older people on the bus. I don't mean to be nosey, but I get a kick out of listening to the snatches of conversation that come my way, but today the general trend of the conversation was that this younger generation couldn't take the hardships that were coming our way, that we were too soft. Now, how do you like that?

[Billee to Charles] Christmas, 1942—Massillon

Christmas really began yesterday with your lovely flowers, by far the nicest present I ever received. Mom is so thrilled and pleased with her poinsettia plant. You can't imagine how beautiful it is, nearly a yard high with six blooms that are easily eight inches across. She's going to write you a note.

We're enjoying the *Stars and Stripes* so much. Several more arrived yesterday with your story about Ludmilla Pavlichenko.

[FROM THE *STARS AND STRIPES*, November 7, 1942]

MEET LT. PAVLICHENKO, RED ARMY SOLDIER

[No byline]

Introducing Junior Lt. Ludmilla Pavlichenko.

But you don't need to "give the little gal a hand," gentlemen, because this good-looking officer in the Russian Army is entirely capable of taking care of herself.

Here by bomber from a tour of the United States, this heroine of Odessa and Sevastopol received the Press yesterday at the British Ministry of Information . . .

The Press, for once, was careful. However, she was smiling and pleasant enough. Modest, too.

"I'm really nobody," she said, "compared to Sgt. Maria Bardia." Maria was killed after machine-gunning 400 Germans and disposing of 11 others in hand-to-hand combat.

"The women of Russia," Lt. Pavlichenko said, "are volunteers for combat service. There are no separate units of feminine fighting forces. In this respect we fight side by side with our men.

. . . She was introduced as one who typifies the courage of Russian women, having been wounded four times in combat as an officer in the regular army.

. . . Ludmilla wears a medal of the Order of Lenin, and the medal of the decoration, Hero of the Soviet Union.

One of her companions, 23-year-old Lt. Vladimir Ptchelinstev, has the

Order of Lenin and a Hero medal, too. He is another sniper expert, credited with using 154 bullets in killing 152 Huns.

. . . Since arriving in Britain the USSR delegation has visited again with Mrs. Roosevelt, who was Ludmilla's sponsor on a tour of 43 American cities . . .

After that, Junior Lt. Ludmilla Pavlichenko, modest heroine of the Soviet, will go back to Russia—"for just a few more."

/////

[Charles to Billee] December 26, 1942—London

In England, this is Boxing Day, derived from the custom of placing alms in boxes for tradesmen and needy people. It is also the day after Christmas, 364 days before the old man with the white whiskers comes around again. More important than anything else, today is your birthday. I missed your last one by 21 days. I'm missing this by about 4,000 miles!

I had been out of town for three days and arrived home Christmas Eve. Stopping at the office, I met one of the men who works here on the [London] *Times*. I have known him since I've been here so it wasn't a casual invitation he extended to spend Christmas with him and his family. I was happy to accept.

He lives in a cottage in Kent, 12 miles from London, has a daughter in the WAAF (a radio operator), a son who works in an aircraft plant and a younger daughter, 12 years old.

I went out there Christmas morning, met the family (the WAAF was home on furlough), had a Xmas dinner (turkey and all the trimmings) and had a most enjoyable day and night just sitting in front of the fireplace talking about a million and one things. They seemed to enjoy my impressions of Britain in comparison with America. The younger daughter was a veritable question box. Wanted to know all about Hollywood, New York, etc.

I stayed overnight and came back to the office for a few hours today. Before leaving, I had to promise to go back tonight and spend another night there.

I felt rather ashamed, not having time to bring a gift or two with me but I'm going to remedy that today. I've packed some of my candy (received in packages) and a couple of cartons of cigarettes with me tonight. If I can get it, I'll bring a bottle of sherry with me, too. Wine and liquor are pretty hard to get here, you know.

On Christmas night, Mr. Frost's daughter gave me an example of a WAAF's skill in wireless by taking 22 to 24 words a minute in Morse code. It was coming over a short wave station in French. This was the first time she had been home in six months and I was tempted to ask her to go to a stage play here in London before she goes back, in part payment for the hospitality I received there. But I remembered that this was your birthday and decided perhaps another night next week would do. I'll let you know what develops. If it takes place it will be my first date in the British Isles, and honestly, I'm afraid I won't know how to act.

And with that I'll have to kiss Mrs. Gray's very beautiful daughter good-night, and while saying "Happy Birthday," I'll mean so much more than that.

/////

[Billee to Charles] January 1, 1943—Massillon

We spent a very quiet New Year's Eve. The biggest part was spent here in the office until 12:00; then, home we went. My uncle made us a highball and put a little extra in Mom's. I thought we'd never get her to go to bed. She talked her head off.

I was twenty-two last Saturday and spent it by myself. I took in a double feature when I finished work at the hospital about 7:30. Saw two good pictures, *Once Upon a Honeymoon* with Ginger Rogers and Cary Grant, plus *Falcon's Brother* with George Sanders and Tom Conway, who really are brothers. They weren't very diverting. Both concerned the war and espionage. When I finally got home about eleven-thirty, I found Mom had baked me a birthday cake and my sister and brother-in-law were waiting for me to come and cut it, so we had a party after all.

If I had seen you yesterday, I could have cheerfully pinned your ears back. To begin with, I've had no mail for five weeks, unless something comes tomorrow. Yesterday an envelope came that I thought contained a letter only to find there were some pictures in it. I'm afraid there were a few tears of disappointment shed, but I just couldn't help it. Please, after this put a little note in those "free mail" letters, even if they only say, "Hello."

/////

Taking advantage of my day off today, I went to the "cinema." Saw *Major and the Minor*. I liked it even though it lagged at times. I started the day off on the wrong foot, trying to check the marriage of Carole Landis and a Major in the Air Force. We carried the story a week ago, saying they might be married Jan. 1, her birthday. Later, we heard it was a publicity gag. I called her last night and she said it might come off early next week and asked me to come up and see her (not in the Mae West style). I called her this morning but she was "rushing off." Have to check again with her tomorrow night. Somebody ought to kick her where it would do her the most good. Mind if I try it?

My New Year's Eve was very dull. Worked until 9 or so, stopped for *a* drink and was home early. I remember last year. Just seventeen days later . . .

/////

My whole outlook has changed since this morning. See what you do to me? I'm afraid that we are going to have to resort to V-letters, since that seems to get preference over personal airmail. There is a girl in the office whose husband is in England, too, and for every V-letter he sends, the next one he sends airmail, and all she has received in the past month or six weeks are the V-letters.

You're having quite a time running around interviewing all these stars and celebrities. Quite different from covering football games and following baseball teams and players around. Which do you like better, or should I ask? You ought to be able to get on the good side of one of them and see about getting a ride for me on one of those bombers or let me conveniently stow away and come over for the duration. We could set up housekeeping in London as well as North Arlington, in a pup tent or bomb shelter, or just any old thing.

Saturday night I met one of the girls after work, the one whose husband is a Marine, and we went to see *Yankee Doodle Dandy*. Hope you get a chance to see it because I know you would enjoy James Cagney in that role. You should see him dance! Afterward, we went to a restaurant. We ate and talked until it closed at one o'clock. We talked about her husband and about you. She has been married about 18 months but her husband enlisted before their first anniversary in June. He left in May. They went together seven years before they were married—not a whirlwind courtship like ours.

[Charles to Billee] January 7, 1943—London

Your letter of the 6th told what I had been wondering about Warren. I hope your mother continues to bear up. You don't have to tell me how she felt when he left because I'll always remember Mom the day I went away. She tried so hard to make it easy for *me*. Yet, it wasn't difficult to see how she really felt. You said Warren tried to appear so grownup. He will be fully grown after a year, perhaps, in service.

Carole Landis married a captain in the Air Force the other day and C.F.K. turned society reporter for a day. To use a worn-out expression, "she was a beautiful bride."

You may wonder, when you read the story, where, why and how I got the fashion details. Yes, I had to ask someone. Mitzi Mayfair, the bridesmaid, arrived at the church about ten minutes before Carole, giving me a chance to get what I wanted. When I asked her, she laughed and said, "I'll bet the boys are dying to know what we are wearing!"

[FROM THE *STARS AND STRIPES*, January 6, 1943]

CAROLE LANDIS WEDS US PILOT: EIGHTH AIR FORCE FLIERS AT EAGLE VETERAN'S MARRIAGE

by Charles F. Kiley, *Stars and Stripes* Staff Writer

Carole Landis, film actress, and Capt. Thomas C. Wallace, Eighth Air Force Fighter Command, were married yesterday afternoon in the Church of Our Lady of the Assumption and St. Gregory, Warwick St., W.I., London.

The simple ceremony, lasting only 12 minutes, was performed by Rev. J. P. Waterkeyn and attended only by friends of the bride and groom and a handful of people who were in the church when the ceremony began.

Mitzi Mayfair, who co-starred with the bride, Kay Francis and Martha Raye, in the USA Camp Shows, Inc., that toured Army establishments in Britain for two months, was bridesmaid. Best man was Maj. Richard Ellis, San Francisco, Cal., a fellow pilot of the groom in Fighter Command. Capt. Wallace, whose home is in Pasadena, Cal., and Maj. Ellis were schoolboy chums.

The bride was attended by Miss Francis, and wore an ivory satin wedding gown in Grecian lines, tulle veil with orange blossoms and carried a bouquet of white carnations and orchids. Miss Mayfair wore an applicade [sic.] organdie dress and carried a spray of carnations and orchids.

The few guests present included Bebe Daniels and Martha Raye, five nurses who attended Miss Landis while she was at the station hospital [having an emergency appendectomy], several officers from the Eighth Air Force and Theatrical and Cinema Division, Special Service Section.

The plans of Miss Landis and Capt. Wallace include only a brief honeymoon before he resumes his work with Fighter Command and she her Hollywood career.

[Billee to Charles] January 7, 1943—Massillon

I keep trying to wonder how you spend your days and nights—what you do. Your job takes up a lot of your time, I know, but that's the kind of work you like, so that's all right. I never mind spending extra time on work I like. I can imagine you're probably the same. Like going to Africa—I know you want to go and that would be a wonderful opportunity, despite the circumstances.

[Charles to Billee] January 13, 1943—London

You said the lack of mail gave you that old "miss you" feeling again. Yes, and I could tell by reading the letters. Still, we'll have to get used to it, Billee. By that, I mean the longing for each other.

We like to think our troubles will be over soon but one day follows another and it still looks far away.

I was interested in your remarks about overhearing the conversation surrounding the inability of "this younger generation" to take it! I wish those people could accompany me to one of our Bomber Command airdromes and watch the Flying Fortresses coming back after a raid. I'd like them to see for themselves how much those fellows of "this younger generation" can take it, and dish it out.

PS: The censor "hates" you for not liking typewritten letters. Told me to tell you so.

PPS: I was only kidding! *The Censor.*

[Charles to Billee] January 17, 1943—London

This afternoon I walked a bit on my holiday. I stopped for an hour or so along the Thames embankment near Waterloo Bridge. I went back over the past year, month by month, until the night of Jan. 17, 1942.

The RAF made a mass raid on Berlin last night and it looks as if "Jerry" is going to repay the compliment. I can hear the ack-ack guns starting to boom a few miles away and it appears as if the batteries in the city will open fire soon. There they go! A look out the window made me feel as though I was at the World's Fair watching the fireworks display. The planes seem to be on the other side of the city, judging from the anti-aircraft activity.

A couple of batteries started firing a few blocks from here and, if you will excuse me, I'll be getting out of here for the time being. On the top floor of a corner building, I am in a very unhealthy position. I'll be back soon . . .

It's all over for the present. I went down the street a few blocks to one of the Red Cross clubs and watched the fun from there. It lasted two hours. That is, the alert did, but the planes were over for only 10 minutes. Some bombs were dropped on the other side of the city, but I won't know until morning how much damage was done. Couldn't have been much . . .

It's 10 a.m., [Jan. 18] and I have seen the morning papers. But first, listen to another tale of woe. At 4:45 a.m., "Jerry" came back again. This time the barrage was noisier but the Luftwaffe didn't stay around very long. The papers say there was damage to a few houses, a few stores, and several people were killed. A few were killed by falling shrapnel from our own A.A. guns. I did get dressed when the guns started earlier this morning but was too sleepy to leave my room. Charlie White, one of the *Stars and Stripes* boys who has a room next to me, and I sat up for 45 minutes, smoked a couple of cigarettes and went back to bed.

And so ends our anniversary—a rather lively one.

/////

[Billee to Charles] January 17, 1943—Massillon

I couldn't help but remember the first Sunday and you were waiting for me— and then going home. I was so afraid you'd feel out of place in our old ladies' home, but everything went well: our turkey dinner and I even remember you coming back for seconds on Mom's pudding.

We went back to your hotel and I waited in the lobby while you gathered up your belongings. Couldn't help but wonder why you were so long, but the letter the next day explained, of course. Then we waited, listening to the radio for time to go by until your bus left, looking forward to the next weekend as if we had always known each other. Tonight it seems just like yesterday or last weekend.

We had a letter from Warren. He's still in Miami Beach but not for long. He will go to Radio and Mechanics School in Illinois for six months. In his letter, he had just finished KP duty, seven hours of peeling onions besides all the other work, but he still likes army life. Mom is very pleased about him going to school.

We received word that little Billy will be home in six weeks or two months, able to walk. Isn't that wonderful? He will have to take treatments for a year, but even at that, it is miraculous. We didn't expect him to live.

[Billee to Charles] January 19, 1943—Massillon (V-mail)

We were awarded the Navy and Army "E" for Efficiency today, so I have a medal, too, to show to our baseball team; then, I went in to the boss to ask for my release so I could take a job at Goodyear. They are trying desperately to hang onto me, much to my surprise, and I think they will come to my terms. I'm beginning to find out that he who squeaks the loudest gets the most.

I have to laugh at Mom now, washing out her hose and undies along with me every night. She used to laugh at me but now, since we've made a business gal out of her and she dresses up every day, she has to spend more time on herself. She's even taken to wearing lipstick.

[Charles to Billee] January 23, 1943—London

The excitement over London has ceased for the present, so I don't believe we will be interrupted as we were last Sunday night. The bombers, the few that got as far as London, were back on Monday and Tuesday. The biggest damage was done to a school not very far from the office, in which 45 children lost their lives. It happened shortly after noon while the kids were having lunch.

[Billee to Charles] January 23, 1943—Massillon (V-mail)

We didn't have our date this weekend, a pretty busy one for me. I worked until 8:00 Saturday night and then went to a party our department had for three boys that left for the Army on Monday. Both Mom and I went and had a swell time. I looked for her once and there she was with two of the big bosses by the piano singing "Daisies Don't Tell."

I had a letter from your mom today. They are busy buying baby clothes already. Tom wants a girl so he can name her Eleanor, and she wants a boy so she can name him Thomas, Jr.

[Billee to Charles] January 25, 1943—Massillon (V-mail)

The party Saturday night was the main topic of discussion today. Practically all the fellows are married and they had their wives with them so we all had a good time together. We paid $1.00 apiece and the fellows brought the liquor. Out of that, we paid for the hall and gave the two fellows that left $15.00 apiece. I'll have to admit I got to feeling a little better than I should have, but that is because it's been so long since I had anything to drink that I couldn't take it. The girl I work with, whose husband is in the Marines, and I stayed pretty close together. She'd take a drink and say, "This one is for George," and then she'd say to me, "You take one for Charles." She says we have to get together after this is over, in New York. She's so cute, about five foot and blonde; her husband is six foot two inches.

I started on new work tonight. It's a little complicated, but I think I'll catch on. Little by little, the making of steel is soaking in my brain, but there are so many things to remember. I don't know what good it will do me after this is over, but I'm stuck now unless I go home. That's the only way I'll get a written release from the company. I might as well be in the Army.

[Billee to Charles] January 28, 1943—Massillon (V-mail)

Warren is still in Miami Beach, but expects to leave in a few days. He likes it a little better. They have moved 2700 WAACs down there and he's having quite a time, what with USO dances and all, besides his basic training. Said in his last letter that he had danced with a WAVE. This training will do him a world of good. He had a good job, but a little too much money to spend. This will tend to settle him down a bit. Not having a father around during the years he really needed one has made a difference, too, so I think he will benefit from all this. Continued in the next [v-] letter.

[Billee to Charles] January 28, 1943—Massillon (V-mail)

Here I am again, but I couldn't say all I wanted to in the other one. Damn Hitler for making me have to write like this. Damn Hitler, period.

I guess things will start to move after this N. African parley [the Casablanca Conference attended by Roosevelt, Churchill, and DeGaulle, which produced a unified Allied statement demanding the unconditional surrender of the Axis countries]. Everyone was so excited about what the news would be. They kept announcing several days before the news broke that there would be this very special news at 10 o'clock Tuesday night. We sneaked a radio in, so we could listen. I couldn't have been any more surprised than if they had said our president was in Timbuktu. I had an idea he was out of the country, but never expected it to be there. I hope they got results or will get it, anyhow. We are all feeling pretty optimistic.

[Charles to Billee] January 30, 1943—London

A few hours ago, I returned from a two-day trip. The purpose of it was to look into a huge athletic program undertaken by one of the units in Britain. I say "unit" because censorship forbids the mention of company, battalion, regiment, or division. However, the program is big enough to have almost 1,000 men taking part in a boxing tournament, many more in a basketball tournament and a large group in rugby and rifle competition. I had the occasion to discuss it with the commanding general, a great sports enthusiast. Athletics are compulsory for these men; one hour a day, seven days a week. You can see fellows taking part in a dozen or more sports.

Before I left on the trip, there was America's first bombing of Germany, when the 8th Air Force's Flying Fortresses and Liberators paid a visit to the naval base at Wilhelmshaven and the industrial sites in Northern Germany. I accompanied 18 other correspondents to Air Force HQ and from there went to a bomber station, arriving just in time to see the first Fort coming in. It was a great sight. After the crews were interrogated, I had time to talk with four of the crews before leaving for London. I had to hustle like hell to get the story up. It was one of the best days I've had overseas.

/////

[FROM THE *STARS AND STRIPES*, January 28, 1943]

US BOMBERS BLAST GERMAN NAVAL BASE: ATTACK IN DAYLIGHT FIRST AMERICAN BLOW ON GERMANY PROPER; FLYING FORTRESSES SMASH WILHELMSHAVEN, SURPRISE NAZI WARSHIPS; LIBERATORS HIT TARGETS IN NORTHWEST

by Charles F. Kiley, *Stars and Stripes* **Staff Writer**

American bombers in daylight yesterday struck their first blow of the war at Germany proper, dropping tons of high explosives on the Nazi naval base at Wilhelmshaven and other targets in Northwest Germany.

Flying Fortresses bombed Wilhelmshaven, 380 miles to the east of London on the northwestern coast of Germany in what headquarters, Eighth Air Force, termed a "large scale attack."

Liberators "bombed other targets," according to a communique.

The big USAAF bombers were unescorted and encountered enemy fighters, "a number of which were destroyed," according to the official announcement.

Returning from Wilhelmshaven, one American formation discovered a large German fleet at sea off the naval base. Bomb racks emptied over Wilhelmshaven, the Fortresses were unable to attack the fleet, but reported back that they had sighted as many as 18 to 25 heavy ships. One observer said most of them were of "10,000 tons or better, and one appeared to be a pocket battleship."

Some bombardiers reported "good hits" on the target at Wilhelmshaven, but in general "results were difficult to observe," the Eighth Air Force communique reported.

Wilhelmshaven is perhaps Germany's most important naval base. It lies a short distance up the Jade, a channel three miles wide, from the North Sea. Dry docks, submarine pens and construction yards surrounded the basin into which have been launched most of Germany's larger ships, such as the *Tirpitz* and the pocket battleships. It has been bombed heavily by the RAF.

American crews returning to their bases in Britain reported encountering both light and heavy flak, over the target areas and along the coast. The northwestern German coast is sheltered by the Frisian Islands on which are based concentrations of ack-ack defenses.

Most of the fighter opposition over the targets was from FW190s and Me109s, the crews said, but reported that many of the Nazi fighter pilots were apparently novices.

It seemed likely that the raid, coming in broad daylight a scant 12 hours after the joint declaration by President Roosevelt and Prime Minister Churchill that the enemy would be hit and hit hard this year, took the German defenses by surprise.

The American daylight attack with bombs still blasting at U-boat production and repair, although hundreds of miles to the west of the French coast bases which had been their targets until yesterday, followed a night raid by the RAF Tuesday on the submarine pens at Lorient, in Nazi-held France.

/////

[Billee to Charles] February 2, 1943—Massillon

By the time this reaches you, you will have heard the sad news from Father John about our mother. I feel I can say that because she would have been my mother, too. [Ella Kiley had fallen on an icy sidewalk in front of her house, suffered a stroke and died; she was fifty-two years old.]

I've never been so shocked. Only yesterday, a letter came from Eleanor telling me she was fine, especially since she had received your letters and cable.

What can I say or do to comfort you? You are so close and yet so far away. I'm going just as soon as I receive the funeral arrangements.

All I can think of is how wonderful she was to me when we were in New York and how much her letters have meant to me since we have been corresponding. Then, I think how alone you are over there.

This is a difficult letter to write, my dear. I can't seem to think of the right words to say.

/////

[Billee to Charles] February 8, 1943—Massillon (V-mail)

Another hard letter to write, but I told Father John that I would write the details following your mother's death. Writing it makes me think I'm in a daze, it is still so unbelievable.

I'll start with my arrival Thursday morning in Jersey City about nine o'clock. Father John came and picked me up. He was so wonderful about my coming. I didn't know at first whether I did right or not but I feel now that I did, that you would have wanted me there.

It just seemed like you had to be there, my dear. Everywhere I looked, I could see you and feel you near. Eddie came downstairs about eleven. He arrived by plane from California about three in the morning. The arrangements were made through the Red Cross. He didn't know until he arrived that it was all over. Tom had come in on Tuesday to be with Eleanor for which I was very glad.

They have all stood up wonderfully. I don't see how they did it. Of course, there were several times that they started to break but Father John was right there at that moment to give them courage and comfort. I knew at the time I was there last year that he seemed to be all and more of what you told me of him, but in my estimation, there isn't anyone like him. If you could have seen him through all the ordeal, how wonderful he was to them all when I know how he must have felt himself.

The people were beginning to come in when I arrived and kept coming all day and night. She must have been well loved because they were all friends. The flowers were gorgeous and I've never seen so many. The mass cards were still coming when I left, hundreds of them.

This is getting down to the bottom of the page, so I'll finish this with another. I started to take a chance on airmail but knew you would want to know as soon as possible. I'll never get one of these [V] letters that I won't think of the message one carried to you, but Father John thought that would be easier than a cablegram, leaving you without any details. I know the shock must have been very great as it was, but it would have been so much harder to have received just a cable.

Friday after the funeral and when the house was straightened, the people all left and we were alone. That evening we were all together. While the family was going over the mass cards and making lists, Father John and I had a long talk, the first opportunity we had—a little of everything. He told me quite a bit about his work and, too, of his desire to enter the service. I don't think he will do anything until after the baby is born, at least I hope not. I can understand the way he feels, but it will be hard for them to see him go.

It was so hard to tell them goodbye. Eddie has until the seventeenth and then he has permission to ask for an additional ten days if necessary. I like him; he is like you in some ways but he is quieter. He likes the Army very much from the way he talked to us about it.

If I could just be [with you] for an hour. It seems like such a little thing to ask.

[Billee to Charles] February 12, 1943—Massillon (V-mail)

Perhaps I didn't tell you, but Warren has been moved to Tyndall Field, Florida, to aerial gunner school. When he finishes his six-week course, he will have a staff sergeant's rating and if he doesn't wash out will go on from there to officers' training school. The training is very rigorous and he has very little leisure time. In fact, his outline for one day left him with one hour of leisure between nine and ten. He would love hearing from you. I've told him so much of you that he almost knows you.

Will you have your commanding officer write out a letter or permit to send you a package so I can show it to the post office? New requirement now. Tell me something that you would like to have—something you need. It's so hard to know just what to put in and what to leave out.

[Billee to Charles] February 14, 1943—Massillon

For some time I have been dissatisfied with my job and there doesn't seem to be much that I can do about it. In a way, I have been frozen, that is, to go to another war plant in the vicinity, and the non-defense plants don't pay enough salary, so consequently I am stuck. I feel, with my qualifications, that I could be doing so much more good elsewhere, doing the kind of work that I know how to do. I have had it in the back of my mind to go to New York for some time. Then, the trip to Jersey City and the circumstances and all has made up my mind. I don't think I'd have any trouble finding what I want there and the salaries are much better.

Mom has decided to stay here for the duration. We have written back to the company holding our mortgage to see if they won't be able to rent it to some private family who would want to sublet the apartment and cottage. I'm waiting to hear about that. Mom and I have been very close for a long time, ever since our family broke up about eight years ago. I have been the only one who stuck by her. [This] seems to be the first opportunity that I have had to leave her, now that she is here with the rest of the family and her sister.

The other angle is that something tells me that it won't be so terribly long before you'll be home. I don't have any wild visions of this year or anything like that. I'm trying not to be too optimistic about it, but now, since your mom won't be waiting for you in Jersey City when the time comes for you to come home, I want to be there.

/////

[Billee to Charles] February 15, 1943—Massillon

Received two letters from Warren today. He's so enthused over his gunnery training. He always did have a yen for guns. His training will take quite a long time. Mom is a little upset over the fact that he will have to learn to fly but she'll have to get used to the idea. I'm very envious of him, because I'd love that, too. From the way he writes, his training will extend a way over six months. I wonder what six months from now will bring.

Little Billy is sitting up in bed feeding himself, for which we're very grateful. He will be home in another two months. That will be a happy day.

/////

[Charles to Billee] February 17, 1943—London

It has been four days since Father John's letter and yours of Feb. 2 arrived simultaneously, telling me the news of Mother's passing. I wanted to write immediately but, truthfully, I wasn't up to it. In fact, I haven't been "up" to much since Sunday.

However, I'm pretty well straightened out now and I'm rather ashamed to admit I felt too sorry for myself during the past few days. It was a terrible shock.

Your letter was so well done, Billee. If I needed comfort, that gave me more than I could hope for.

/////

[Billee to Charles] February 16, 1943—Massillon

One of the fellows said to me last night, "Who do you go with in Massillon?" I said, "No one." "You aren't married, are you?" he says. I answered, "No, I'm engaged." "Even though you're engaged, you could go out, couldn't you?" I said, "No. I'm not interested." He says, "That's funny. Aren't many like you."

Incidentally, he's married, as most of them down there are. Like one of the younger fellows says (he's still in high school and works seven hours on our shift), "A bunch of wolves that got married," but we manage to keep them in their place. They aren't a bad lot, just aren't used to having so many girls around to work with.

I dreamed about you last night. Couldn't be that you were the last one I thought of before closing my eyes. Seems we were in New York. You were in uniform and we were riding in one of those hacks in Central Park and we went to some apartment. I couldn't tell whether it was mine or not. I'm always sorry when I wake up.

Do you remember me telling you about Marguerite's sister's husband who was a captain in the engineers on Corregidor? They just received word recently after months of not a bit of news that he is a Japanese prisoner. They don't know where, but he was on Cebu when it fell. The word came via the Red Cross in the form of a letter from him. When I hear things like this, I'm grateful you aren't somewhere like that.

[Charles to Billee] February 20, 1943—London

Just now I'm looking ahead to next week when I visit the Rangers for a while. As you know, they are the American commandos. Yesterday I went out to an airfield and had an opportunity to talk with some of the boys who went over to St. Nazaire the other day. On Monday I'll be going out to see the GI boxers I covered all last week. The tournament ends Wednesday but I'll only be able to stay for the semi-finals before getting back for the trip to the Rangers.

When my old outfit went to the place where you suspected I was [North Africa], the letters stopped. I haven't heard from any of them since. Another fellow, stationed here now has been writing to them but can't get answers. We assume mail is being delayed.

[Billee to Charles] February 25, 1943—Massillon (V-mail)

I think that before long I will be in New York or Matawan. I had a long distance call and special delivery from Marguerite. There is a vacancy in her bank as of the fifteenth of March and I am being considered for the position. A wonderful opportunity and right up my alley: savings department teller beginning at $110 a month and I'm having a week's vacation thrown in. I really feel if I am accepted that I shouldn't let the opportunity slip by.

Marguerite is making arrangements for me to stay with her, of course on the same basis she stayed with us [as a paying guest].

I had a letter from my brother today and he is writing to you, too. He has about seventeen more days at Tyndall Field and then to radio or armor school. He is getting along fine and I don't think, with the grades he has been getting, that he will wash out. He was letting his mind run away from him in one of his letters and I had to give him a little lecture. He was concerned about learning and studying so much just to learn to kill, but I think I straightened him out. He's a good fellow even if he is my brother.

The darn space is running out. Oh, by the way, the wife of Lt. Jack Gompf, one of those flyers interned in Lisbon, works in the adjoining office and she wondered if it would be possible to find out anything more about him or the whereabouts of the fellows. She hasn't read or seen any more about them. I told her I'd ask. [In early 1943, a group of fighter planes en route to North Africa were forced to land in Lisbon because of engine problems. Because Portugal was neutral, the crews were interned for several weeks before the American Attaché in Lisbon could arrange for their release, an arrangement that included a deal to allow Portugal to keep the planes.]

[Charles to Billee] February 27, 1943—London (V-mail)

I've been able to keep our Saturday date after all. When I left the other day for Scotland, I didn't expect to be back so soon but the job was completed quicker than I figured.

The trip, from which I just returned, brought me over to Scotland to watch our Rangers in training. They are the US equivalent of the British Commandos. In fact, both the Rangers and Commandos are trained in the same camp and by hard-bitten British instructors. I'll go on record as saying the Rangers come out of that camp as the toughest fighting men in the Army and possibly in any branch of American service. In my story, I'm going to try and describe what a rigorous training course they go through. I only hope I can paint the true picture.

[Billee to Charles] February 28, 1943—Massillon (V-mail)

I have [the] job in the Perth Amboy National Bank as savings teller. I received the telegram yesterday telling me the job was mine on my terms. There was an unexpected vacancy in the bank where Marguerite works and she recommended me. I will stay with Marguerite for the present time. Have you ever felt as if you were being led? That's the way I have felt ever since Marguerite called me. I feel sure that what I am doing is right.

I had a long letter from Father John and he thought my decision was all right. He didn't know at the time that I had the job, but then I didn't either. He said Pop had received a cablegram from you. He suggested my staying with them, but I don't believe I had better. I know I would be welcome, but I would rather be on my own. He mentioned that Eddie was being transferred to Tennessee.

CHAPTER 4

MARCH–JULY 1943

Funny, the memories are so vivid, each moment of the time we spent
together stands out alone until I know almost to a sigh what we said
and did and yet it seems like such a long time ago.
[Billee to Charles, July 1943.]

/////

The War: In the Pacific, US bombers hit the Aleutian Islands heavily at Attu; American troops eventually captured the island from the Japanese.

In North Africa, General Patton was given command of the US II Corps; twelve days later, the Tunisian city of Gafsa fell to them; then, the Allies took Tunis and the rest of North Africa, as well as 250,000 Axis prisoners. Defeat of Italy seemed in plain sight: in May, Allied bombing of Sicily and Sardinia was accelerated; in June, their leaders told southern Italians to evacuate.

In Europe, Hitler survived two assassination attempts in March 1943. That same month, Mussolini withdrew troops from the eastern front; within a few days, more than 200,000 Italians staged a protest strike against the Italian leader. US and British advances and the bombing of Rome led to a July 24 vote in the Eternal City to remove Mussolini from power. On July 25, he was arrested and Italy descended into chaos.

In April, France evacuated children and non-essential civilians from Le Havre, Dieppe, Cherbourg, St. Malo, and Brest. Also that month, a joint British-US command was established to plan a major assault landing in Europe. In May, British intelligence duped the Germans with Operation Mincemeat, a corpse floating ashore off Spain bearing papers that showed the Allies planning a major invasion through Greece.

At Torquay, England, a German bombing raid hit a church, killing twenty children and five adults. Damage in Germany from Allied bombs was even more severe at Hamburg and Essen.

At home, a wage disagreement sent about 500,000 coal miners on strike, kicking off a wave of criticism both at home and on the battlefields.

As of July 1, 1943, the Women's Auxiliary Army Corps (WAAC) officially became part of the US Army and was renamed the Women's Army Corps (WAC).

Also in July, the *New York Times* reported that President Roosevelt publicly acknowledged that the Jews in occupied Europe needed saving, yet no particular course of action by America was agreed upon.

/////

[Charles to Billee] March 4, 1943—London

Here goes: you admit having made up your mind to go to New York. If I advised you not to go, you would be disappointed. You would wonder why I protested.

So, I'm going to say, go ahead. I didn't think it was wise for you to go a year ago because you would be leaving Mother. She still needs you and always will. She will miss you terribly. But you have ambitions, and I'll never be the one to try and stifle them. I don't know how conditions have changed since I left New York, but I would say there is a better opportunity there for you. Still, it will be lonely. New York can be the loneliest place in the world.

As for being there, waiting for when I get back: wherever you are will be my first stop. It doesn't matter whether it is in New York, Jersey City or Fort Worth.

/////

[Billee to Charles] March 7, 1943—Matawan (V-letter)

Surprised to see the above address? I start tomorrow morning on my new job. Marguerite's sister, Agnes, is going to break me in. My sister and her husband saw me off. Mom wouldn't go to the station.

I feel so much closer to you already. I do feel so right about what I have done. Mother will understand better as time goes on. I hope I haven't hurt her. I tried so hard not to.

/////

[Billee to Charles] March 11 and 12, 1943—Matawan

I like the banking business. So far, I've been getting along fine.

I had a thought today, listening to all these Jersey accents going on around me. What if you by chance get an English accent along with your Jersey one, and me with my half southern and half mid-western accent. What is that ball team going to sound like?

Haven't heard from home yet this week. Seems funny being away, as if I might be someone else.

Going to work on the train [from Matawan to Perth Amboy], we ride across part of the bay—Raritan Bay—and as I look across to the horizon, out across the ocean I can see in the distance, I can't help but feel that much closer to you. Tomorrow I go to see your family.

I see your friend, Dan Scherman the *Life* photographer, has in this week pictures of pinup girls he found in the barracks in England. Hmmm.

/////

[Billee to Charles] March 15, 1943—Matawan (V-mail)

I know, my dear, how you must have felt [about the death of his mother]. Your letters to the girls, El and Bette, were wonderful. I found them all well, and Pop, too. We had a long talk Saturday night accompanied by a couple of glasses of beer. He talked to me quite a bit about Mom. He is missing her very much, but he does wonderfully looking after the girls, and he cooked Sunday dinner.

Pop told me quite a few of your escapades, such as rolling the inkwells along the floor in school and being scolded by the sisters. Mind if I adopt your dad? I like him an awful lot. This is the first chance I've had to really know him.

I'm anxious to hear of your trip to visit the Rangers. Hope that isn't the new scene of your operations. The *New York Times* carried a list of correspondents taking training to go over with those bombers. Among the names were a couple of staff members of the *Stars and Stripes*.

I can imagine how you must feel over there. I met a soldier on the train [from Ohio]. He made a statement that he'd never be able to find the person he was before the war, that he had completely lost himself in the Army.

[Charles to Billee] March 17, 1943—London

The past week hasn't been very active. I'm working on a story concerning the MPs here: tips on what they don't like soldiers to do on leave and how they enforce military law. Last night I had a nice chat with a lieutenant colonel, provost marshal of London, and then spent an hour riding around in one of the patrol cars. The latter have radio hookup with Scotland Yard.

I played golf last Saturday on my day off. Went 18 holes with Mr. Frost, with whom I spent Christmas. Honestly, I'm getting old. After the first nine, I wanted to quit. At the 15th, I staggered and when we finished, I practically collapsed.

Did I tell you I received a letter from Jack Kenny's brother recently [a Jersey City friend]? He's in Honolulu. If and when I get a letter from China, I will have "circled the globe." I've had some from Africa, Alaska, Hawaii, Bermuda, and Australia. The one from Africa came from Ralph Martin, who left here to work with the North Africa bureau. He's having a helluva time down there, but he's content.

[Billee to Charles] March 22, 1943—Matawan (V-mail)

I started to write a V-letter this afternoon at work, but the typewriter refused to work, so I'm resorting to pen and ink again.

Warren is in Sioux Falls, S. Dakota, and a sergeant. Isn't that something? He'll be there for five months. Had a long letter from Mom today. My two sisters have been giving her a lot of attention for which I'm very grateful. Warren and I keep her busy writing now. She's doing very well at it, too.

I saw in Friday's paper that your friend Ralph Martin was one of the first to enter Gafsa [in Tunisia]. I saved the clipping and will send it to you. I'm glad you're still in London.

//////

FROM THE *NEW YORK SUN*, March 19, 1943

GAFSA FELL TO BROOKLYN: NEW YORKERS PLAY LARGE PART IN CAPTURE—BRONX SOLDIER AND THE *SUN*'S REPORTER AMONG THE FIRST IN.

by Gault MacGowan, Special Cable to the *New York Sun*

On the Tunisian Front, March 18 (Delayed).—A rugged band of New York and Jersey soldiers, veterans of the Kasserine Pass fighting, lead the way into Gafsa and today are pushing on through torrential rains that are flooding the wadis, turning the sands into quagmires, bogging down our army and providing another providential respite for the Axis in southern Tunisia.

Gafsa itself was taken three times: first by a reconnaissance patrol under Capt. Richard Ciecolella, Brooklyn; next by the battalion of Lieut.-Col. John Mathews of Bridgeport, and finally by a party of war correspondents under an English relations officer. Each of the correspondents claimed to be the first to enter the deserted city, and even posed for his picture under the battered walls of the ancient "Beau Geste" fort.

With Ralph G. Martin of the Bronx, a soldier-reporter for the *Stars and Stripes*, I crossed a mine field and an abandoned road barrier, the modern type of city gate, behind Col. Mathews who was leading our local boys. A formation largely composed of Brooklyn men took positions northwest of Gafsa as protection against a counter-attack.

Staff Sgt. Ralph G. Martin covered the Casablanca conference for the *Stars and Stripes*, his father, Hyman Goldberg of the Bronx told the *New York Sun* today. Sgt. Martin legally adopted his present name after using it as a pen name in writing for the City College newspaper and, after his graduation from there and from the School of Journalism at the University of Missouri, in writing as a staff member of a daily paper in Utah.

/////

[Billee to Charles] March 23, 1943—Matawan

Today brought a letter from my sister. She says that Billy is crawling on his hands and knees in bed now so the paralysis is practically gone from one leg. She says Mom is well, but she won't talk much about me being away.

I got an S.O.S. from my brother yesterday. Couldn't figure out why I should get two letters in a row. That's right: a ten spot was needed so I sent it posthaste. He should get a good pay the end of this month, with his sergeant's stripes. He's supposed to draw a hundred and twenty, less the deductions for Mom's allotment and incidentals, so I gave him a little lecture along with the ten dollars, about what he should do with his next pay. Can you picture me in the role of a big sister?

I'm getting a little more used to being on my own and away from home. I still have to pinch myself to believe that I actually made the break, and that I'm not dreaming. I guess you must feel like that sometimes.

/////

[Billee to Charles] March 28, 1943—Matawan (V-mail)

I just finished reading *I Saw the Philippines Fall*, by Lt. Col. Carlos Romulo, an aide to MacArthur. A wonderful book and tells so clearly what happened from Pearl Harbor to the fall of Corregidor. It was especially interesting, too, due to the fact that Marguerite's sister's husband is a prisoner of war there now. She knows definitely that he was on Bataan and then was in the retreat to Corregidor and now it has been confirmed by the Red Cross that he is a prisoner there.

[Charles to Billee] March 29, 1943—London

I received a card from Bob Paulus the other day, datelined from Tunisia. He said he had to use the card because most of his possessions were lost as "the result of several mishaps." I answered him immediately, and also got off a letter to his mother. I don't believe Bob has much time to write these days.

Coming up tomorrow is a three-day basketball tournament here at Albert Hall, to decide the European Theater of Operations title. There are 16 teams from all over the British Isles entered. I'll probably meet some fellows who played on teams I covered at home. It's going to be strange watching basketball at Albert Hall, with its red plush seats, grand tiers and whose walls have listened to some of the world's best music. It might be compared to a basketball tournament being held in Carnegie Hall.

The other day I went out to a B24 (Liberator) station to handle the return of a bomber group that left Britain last December, took part in the African campaign and is ready to resume operations from this theater.

[FROM THE *STARS AND STRIPES*, March 30, 1943]

TEN-DAY JOB BECAME A CAMPAIGN: LIB AIR CIRCUS FOUND AFRICA SOFT TOUCH AFTER ETO

by Charles F. Kiley, *Stars and Stripes* Staff Writer

A US BOMBER STATION, England, Mar. 29—Enemy fighters are tougher in the European Theater of Operations than they are in North Africa. The biggest menace to American bombers down there comes from flak and weather conditions; up here they fight flak, weather and the best fighters in the Luftwaffe.

Those are the opinions of "Ted's Traveling Circus," a USAAF bomber group of four-engined Liberators, back in Britain after one of the outstanding exploits by an air force unit in the war's mission to Africa. Scheduled to last ten days, it turned into a campaign of three months lending air support to the British Eighth Army's march across the desert, bombing Tripoli, Gabes, Sfax, Sousse, Bizerta, Bone, with precision raids on Naples, Crotone, Palermo and Messina in Italy and Sicily.

Operating part of the time from a desert base with only a handful of maintenance men to keep the ships in the air. Using spare parts taken with them for the "ten-day mission." Living in their planes, in small tents made for two but which had to accommodate three or four. No clothes, other than what they had on their backs.

The first heavy bombardment unit to span the Atlantic, the "Circus," commanded by Col. Edward J. "Ted" Timberlake, of San Antonio, Tex., made its first raid from its base in Britain Oct. 9 on Lille. Early in December Col. Timberlake was given eight hours to get his men off to Africa. They expected to be back by Christmas, but the mission extended to weeks and then months.

When the Circus arrived back in Britain Mar. 2, the men found tons of mail and Christmas packages waiting for them. They hadn't received a letter while they were away from "home."

///////

[Charles to Billee] April 4, 1943—London (V-mail)

I'll have to pass along congratulations to Warren. He got those three bars in a hurry, didn't he? Looks like all the brains in the Gray family aren't confined to the females.

A letter from El told me you had called a few times. Also had one from Eddie. To repeat part of what he said: "Wonder if you can tell me where I can find a girl like Billee?" I told him it was hard enough to find one without looking for two.

We're having an early spring. It's nice enough in the city but the English country is grand. Seems like everybody's hobby is flowers, judging by their lawns and gardens.

This morning for our [engagement] anniversary, I had breakfast at one of the Red Cross clubs and walked about two miles to the office. I passed Knightsbridge, Hyde Park, along Piccadilly, down St. James Street to St. James Palace, along the Thames Embankment to Waterloo Bridge, Blackfriars Bridge and finally to Queen Victoria Street and the *Times*. The longest walk I've had since the 15, 20, 25 and 40 mile marches we had in Ireland.

/////

[Charles to Billee] April 8, 1943—London (V-mail)

I'd like to tell you of a letter I received today. It was one of commendation from Brig. Gen. Rogers, commanding office of London Base Command, as the result of a story I did recently. The story dealt with tips on how soldiers can stay out of trouble while on leave. I had to spend three days getting suitable pictures to illustrate the story and two more gathering material from the Provost Marshal. It was a question of persistence more than anything else. I'm forwarding the letter to you. I'd like Dad to see it. You'll bring it to him when you visit 195, won't you? [Charles's home, 195 Lexington Ave, Jersey City]

Say, have you had a chance to see the Yankees in spring training at Asbury Park or the Giants at Lakewood? They're practically in your back yard, you know. I'll bet the boys who were accustomed to covering the clubs in the sunny south are burning up. Yet, I hope that's all they have to suffer from in the war.

Went out to a bomber station again yesterday. Story concerned a T/Sgt. awarded the Distinguished Service Cross and two others the Legion of Merit. The DSC winner is missing from operations and one of the others is a prisoner of war. So it goes.

/////

[FROM THE *STARS AND STRIPES*, April 2, 1943]

HOW TO STAY OUT OF TROUBLE: BAD BOOZE, FROWZY DAMES SPELL WOE FOR GIS

by Charles F. Kiley, *Stars and Stripes* Staff Writer

The Provost Marshal says the small percentage of soldiers on leave who get into trouble in London usually do in one or more of six ways:

Drunkenness.

Associating with females of questionable character.

Failing to observe rules of proper uniform.

Becoming involved in arguments with civilians or soldiers of other nations.

Flashing too much money, particularly in pubs.

Failure of officers to check-in with proper authorities when they arrive on leave.

Of course, these aren't the only ways a soldier gets into a jam, but they constitute the sources of most trouble.

The Provost Marshal, Lt. Col. Marvin Charlton—no copper at heart but a cowpuncher and oil man from Del Rio, Tex.—doesn't figure that MPs are running a Sunday School; and this newspaper isn't holding up a platform of moral reform for guys just in from weeks of slogging in the mud, crawling in and out of tanks or risking their lives on raids over the Reich.

As a matter of fact, the PM wants to see soldiers on leave raise all the hell they have in them, yet steer clear of the MPs. So he passes along these tips on how to stay out of trouble.

In regard to the drinking situation, Col. Charlton says some of the stuff sold nowadays is positive dynamite and can bring a load of grief to the drinker.

"I've seen men who didn't remember what happened to them after a few drinks," he declares. "They were easy prey for pickpockets and victims of street-walkers, and usually woke up in the detention barracks."

The high rate of venereal disease, up 70 per cent in Britain since the outbreak of war, is another potential stumbling block for the over-enthusiastic soldier on leave.

A reminder that rules pertaining to proper uniform must be observed is one of the PM's tips. Enforcement of these rules makes the MPs more unpopular than the man who redlines you on payday, says the Colonel.

The PM frequently walks about town, stopping in at the Red Cross clubs to note the things soldiers do, the problems they have and what can be done to correct them.

"I've been through the mill in two wars," he says, "and I know what a leave is to a soldier. I'll go out of my way to see he has a good time, but he has to play ball with us."

The PM is authorized to order a summary court martial in London 24 hours after a soldier is charged. It can mean 40 to 60 days in the jug, a stiff fine and a climb to the top of "the list" in his organization.

Another tip is to avoid arguments, especially in pubs.

Col. Charlton says there have been cases of soldiers reporting incidents where they were slugged and relieved of everything they had. It may have started in a pub where a soldier begins to celebrate his furlough.

These tips apply to officers as well as enlisted men, the PM says.

Officers are reminded to avoid a "date" with the PM by checking in with proper authorities when they come to London. He advises them to report whether they are on business or leave.

Ever since the Army's first military police unit was organized, MPs have been something out of this world and only their best friends won't tell them, but Col. Charlton says they aren't as bad as all that. They are just good soldiers, that's all, with a cop's job to do.

[Billee to Charles] April 11, 1943—Matawan

This has been a busy Sunday. We started right in moving furniture. I still feel like I've caused a lot of trouble, but Marguerite wanted me to stay with her. I had in mind going to stay with a private family, but she said, only if I didn't *want* to stay here. Now her room looks like a dormitory. We have three beds in here. Luckily, it's quite a large room. Now the furniture is all moved and we each have a bed of our own.

You know, it's a year ago tonight, or rather tomorrow night, that I last saw you. I'm in one of those rebellious moods tonight, against circumstances that keep us apart.

Coming east has helped me a lot. I don't know what it was—the job or what. I don't think I've ever been so lonely in my life, and there was no reason for it. The lonely feeling is gone now and I feel lots better, both mentally and physically.

//////

[Charles to Billee] April 17, 1943—London

I've been away for the last few days but got back in time to drop in for a Saturday night date with you. It's a perfect spring day again today and since I'm no different than anyone else, my fancy more than lightly turns to thoughts of you, and us. You were with me during the last few days when I was traveling through the English countryside, still beautiful and picturesque despite war.

My out-of-town assignment during the last few days concerned sports. Tournaments in four sports were winding up at a division base. Next week all-star teams in boxing, softball and soccer, from this division and the Canadian Army meet in a carnival of sports program. I met another one of our generals earlier last week, Maj. Gen. Key, Provost Marshal General in the ETO, regarding a story on an MP school. A couple of days later I traveled 80 miles to attend another graduation of officer candidates. Then came the long trip. Don't know what next week will bring.

[Billee to Charles] April 19, 1943—Matawan

Little Billy is at home now. While he is much improved, there is a long way to go before he walks: three times a week to the hospital besides the home treatments, for some months to come yet.

I'm looking forward to spending Easter weekend with the Kiley family. I haven't been there in nearly three weeks.

Agnes, Marguerite's sister, received word from the Red Cross that the cable she sent her husband in the Philippines passed the censors and will be delivered to him. He is a captain in the Engineers and has been a Japanese prisoner since the fall of Bataan. It cost her $16.12 for four words, but then it was worth it—at least it would be to me.

[Charles to Billee] April 26, 1943—London (V-mail)

I have so many things to tell you I scarcely know where to begin. I've been away again on a flying trip to Scotland, returning yesterday in time to catch Easter sunset and so tired I couldn't even sit down and write an Easter letter to you.

I should tell you now that there will be a period of two weeks in which I won't be able to write. I'm going away at the end of this week and I'll have to wait until I get back to tell you about it. Nothing to worry about, so don't start wondering what it is.

You said you were thinking of having a picture taken for me. I'd love to have one. I still have the one you gave me in the picture case, in a place where I can see you when I'm home. When I go away I bring it with me. In a way, you've seen a great many things. For instance, on the trip from which I just returned you were in a plane for about 10 hours in all. You had a glimpse of Loch Lomond and saw a pub in which Bobby Burns [Robert Burns, eighteenth-century Scottish poet] quaffed his ale. Every time I come to the office and your picture is in my pocket you see the spot where Shakespeare made his debut on the stage. You see, just outside the door of the *Times* is the site where the Blackfriars Theater once stood, way back when, in the 16th century.

/////

[Billee to Charles] April 26 1943—Matawan

The letter of commendation was swell. I took it to 195 this weekend and they were as pleased as I. You should rate a promotion or maybe a "furlough," an extended one that would bring you to the States. I called Ray Roche [Charles's co-writer at the *Jersey Journal*]. He decided to come by before going to the baseball game. He took the letter along with him, together with the article, to put in the paper.

He stayed about an hour talking to Father John and the rest of us. They are having quite a problem getting help. He mentioned, too, about baseball, that he didn't expect it to last through Decoration Day. He was down to Lakewood for seven days and found no news at all. As he put it, they had a lot of "humpty dumpties" running around the field. No news at all and that the crowds had been very small. That seems a shame, but then all the good players are in the service now, so what can you expect?

My weekend at 195 was fine. I couldn't help but remember last Easter and how scared I was walking down that street with you, to meet them all for the first time. Do you know what Father John's latest idea is? That I should join the volunteer Red Cross organization and ask to be sent to London. I think he wants to see you as badly as I do. He said yesterday that he'd give almost anything to see you and talk with you.

My brother sent me a picture of him in his uniform. He looks so terribly young. I told you, didn't I, about his engagement to the girl from home? He wanted to announce it and asked me what I thought. I told him, but definitely, and I had an answer back this week. Seems I gave him something to think about, and there will only be an "understanding" until after the war. Tickles me. He says he can always depend on me for the right kind of advice about such matters.

[Billee to Charles] May 5, 1943—Matawan (V-mail)

Your trip has aroused my curiosity naturally and I'm wondering where and when and, as always, praying that you will be safe wherever it is. I didn't know you were flying on your trips. I had an idea, but this is the first time you mentioned it. The recent plane crash in Iceland has me wondering, since there has been no names published other than that of General Andrews and the Bishop, but I'm praying that wasn't the "trip" you took. [On May 3, 1943, US Army Lieutenant General Frank M. Andrews, commander of US forces in Europe, was killed in the crash of a B-24 bomber in Iceland. Andrews Air Force Base was named in his honor. "The Bishop" was Methodist Bishop Adna W. Leonard, en route to England to visit Methodist chaplains.]

I'm glad to hear that you have been writing Mom. She will love hearing from you. She's worried quite a bit about Warren. He is going to try for Air Cadet School when he finishes his radio course.

A report just came in that the sole survivor of that plane crash was a staff sergeant.

Don't ever feel your efforts are futile because they aren't. I know it has been a year since we were together. Sometimes it feels like a long time, and then again, it seems like yesterday. Time has gone by so fast. Don't worry about the slow materialization of your dreams. Please don't get discouraged.

[Billee to Charles] May 9, 1943—Jersey City

We just came in from a walk to the cemetery. We bought some azalea plants and set them out, pink and white ones. El wasn't able to go. It's too long a walk and the buses too bouncy.

Yesterday I made the one-twenty into Newark and did some shopping. I bought that dress I was talking about. It's blue and white—nothing spectacular, just something I can wear on weekends and to the bank, too. Oh, I bought some navy and white checked material to make a suit. It's taffeta, so I'll rustle. You'll hear me coming.

We had something of a jam session here today. Bette was showing me how to jitterbug. I didn't think I could move that fast. The twins from next door came in and did their stuff, so we had quite a time. Bette said I didn't do too badly for the first time.

I saw an article in the paper about a school that has been opened in England for war correspondents, to teach them invasion tactics, map reading and first aid. Twenty-five war correspondents are now enrolled. It makes me wonder if that is your new "assignment."

[Charles to Billee] May 11, 1943—London (V-mail)

Back "home" again from the trip I mentioned in my last letter, and it sure feels good.

I was taking part in the training of US Rangers, American counterparts of the Commandos, at the Commando Depot, "somewhere in England." My stay with the Rangers was the toughest experience I've yet encountered and hope to encounter. I'll never know how I lasted as long as I did. But it was surprising to learn how much human endurance one can stand. Let me just say I didn't have my clothes off for 11 days (you sleep with 'em on), didn't have a shower until I stopped overnight in [CENSORED] on my way back, have bruises on both legs, hips and left arm. Still, I feel great and, now that it's over, I'm glad I went through with it. In a way, I sympathize with the boys who are still there. I only took part in part of the training. They still have a bit to travel.

It all started when the office wanted a volunteer to train for a period with the Rangers and do a piece on it. My hand went up and off I went. I didn't want to tell you about it until it was all over because it is risky business and there wasn't any point in worrying you about it.

There were cold nights, wet ones and pretty bad days in the field. But you were near me always. To say I love you more than ever is inadequate.

Have you noticed the promotion? [The "sender" line of the V-mail reads "Sgt. Charles F. Kiley.] Learned of it when I returned from the trip.

[FROM THE *STARS AND STRIPES*, May 22, 1943]

THE DIARY OF AN AMERICAN RANGER: A GI ASSEMBLY LINE TURNS OUT EXPERTS IN DESTRUCTION

In the desolate valley of a snow-covered mountain range in Scotland is a war industry. It develops ordinary soldiers into specialists in destruction of enemy lives and property; men who tumble off the assembly line fighting fit, tough as steel and superbly disciplined.

It is the training base of US Rangers and their British counterpart, the Commandos. Those who are accepted for this training—and survive—go through what American and British military authorities agree is one of the toughest courses anywhere.

Charles Kiley, *Stars and Stripes* Staff Writer, went through part of the Ranger course. What follows is the first installment of his diary. It could be written by any Ranger on "Death Valley," as he calls it, or "Bloody Hell," if you listened to the Commando.

by Charles F. Kiley, *Stars and Stripes* Staff Writer

FIRST DAY—Three weeks ago we volunteered for the Rangers, were accepted and embarked on a preliminary training course that was to prepare us for the stiff test at the Commando depot. During that period there was plenty of time for each man to think out all the angles of the job he had asked for.

In our midst now are soldiers from the Infantry, Artillery, Engineers and Media Corps, some who had soft jobs and others who had tough ones. They are privates, corporals, sergeants, lieutenants and captains whose service records say that, in civilian life, they were farmers, clerks, students, lawyers, musicians, brokers, married men and single. They were aides to the commanding general and blokes who did a couple of hitches in the "glasshouse [prison]." They came from the regular army, National Guard and Draft Board 13 in Falling Rock, W. Va. Some of them served as volunteers in the Canadian Army.

The attraction in the Rangers, for some, may be the flashy paraboots or the red and black shoulder badges that tells everybody you are a Ranger. The majority, however, are drawn by the adventure that surely comes to a Commando or Ranger.

You remember when you were interviewed as a prospective Ranger and qualified as being "under 30, able to swim and in good physical condition."

These things go through your mind today when you arrive at the Commando depot, ready to start a training schedule that is said to be one of the most severe tests to a soldier's endurance.

Nobody has to tell about the frigid weather that reigns practically all year round here. The bleak, rugged, snow-capped mountains that stand guard over this valley refrigerate your blood just to look at them. If there is a more isolated camp in the British Isles it hasn't been reported.

The prospect of living in tents is a blow to those who expect the comforts of Nissen huts, at least. And, the tents look old enough to have been used in the Boer War, but each of them is "home" for four men as long as they are here.

That isn't all. Sgt. Maj. George Pickering, broad-shouldered Commando instructor attached to the Rangers, comes around with the glad tidings that there won't be any cots or beds.

"You'll have to sleep on the floor, lads, with six blankets," he says. "These will be arranged for display every morning and boots will be shined bright enough to see your face in them. Any questions?"

More good news from the Sgt. Major. He says before we leave here, men will wish they never heard of the Rangers when they are covered with mud and wet to the skin almost every day, when lungs are bursting on speed marches or when they are half way up the side of a wind-swept cliff in a cold sweat looking for a foothold, when they have to shower with ice water from a stream that's fed by snow or when they're cut and bruised on assault courses and instructors drive and drive and drive.

After a couple of beers in the NAAFI [British military "Navy, Army, and Air Force Institutes," similar to the US military "PX"], you remember you tried to sleep on the baggage rack in the train and turn in.

Nobody bothers to take their clothes off at night. It's spring, but they haven't heard about it here. Before long you discover that the baggage rack was a feather bed compared to these quarters.

During the night it rains and water seeps through the tent, soaking the top blanket. Somebody wakes up in the tent, probably remembers the warm barracks he left and shouts, "I must be nuts."

/////

[Billee to Charles] May 11, 1943—Matawan

Everyone is jubilant over the African victory. Surely, this is the turning point and it won't be too long. I have visions of another year in the European Theater and heaven knows how long in the Pacific. Everyone is expecting the invasion now at any day and Churchill's presence in Washington makes it all the more likely.

I called Mom Sunday night late. She will be going back to Asheville in a few weeks to make arrangements about the house. She hinted that she might stay.

Little Billy is recovering rapidly. He crawled off the couch and they found him on the other side of the room. Being home and having his mother's care has helped a lot.

Agnes and I decided to take in a movie in Keyport, particularly to see those captured Japanese newsreel pictures of the fall of Corregidor, hoping we might see Jack, but no luck.

My conscience is beginning to hurt. Enlistments [in the WAAC] have fallen off considerably and the plan itself has proved so successful. You should hear Father John on the subject. When I first arrived in Jersey he was all for them and then, a month ago, he said I could just give up any idea of enlisting. It seems a chaplain friend of his related some happenings that went on in Washington and they were anything but nice.

[Note: this persistent rumor about WAAC morals was repeatedly proved unfounded. It was a deliberate slander campaign on the part of US-based soldiers, some of whom were apprehensive that their safe, stateside Army jobs would be taken by women, freeing those soldiers for combat duty overseas. The slander did slow WAAC enlistment drastically.]

We just had some excitement: an air raid alert which meant sending the customers away and putting all our money in our bags and down to the vault in the basement we all went for about forty-five minutes. Everything was very orderly. I happened to be talking to a customer on the phone and had to practically insult her to get her off the line. Thank heaven it was only an alert and not the real McCoy. We're so close to the shore, though, that anything can happen.

[Billee to Charles] May 15, 1943—Matawan

I called El tonight. She says she feels fine. Your dad is working again at night. His vacation will begin soon so he'll have two weeks to rest but I'm afraid there will be little rest for him since he plans on doing his room over for El. I only hope Tom will be here. He says he will go AWOL if he has to, and I wouldn't be surprised.

Eddie said that after he finished maneuvers that he would probably be sent nearer home, I imagine to an embarkation point.

Things are really happening. All the activity gives us new hope that maybe this will be over soon. Didn't take them long to finish off North Africa. Tonight the news of the offensive in the Aleutians makes me think we will hear more from that place and that soon those yellow b____ will be off Uncle Sam's soil or else in it.

///////

[Charles to Billee] May 15, 1943—London

"It's still the same old story, a fight for love and glory, a case of do or die. The world will always welcome lovers, as time goes by."

Funny way to begin our date tonight, darling, but it is being played on the radio and is a song that brings you close to me.

The first of the WAACs (enlisted "men," or enrolled members as they call them) arrived here during the week. There were only five of them. One of the boys, Phil Bucknell [another *Stars and Stripes* staffer] and I accompanied them on a tour of blitzed areas and spots of interest yesterday. Felt good to talk "American jive" again.

(l–r) Phil Bucknell, unknown, two sightseeing WAACs, and Charles—London, May 1943. (Kiley Family)

My eyebrows went up like twin elevators when one of them said I was actually acquiring a British accent. What she meant was that I was using a few British expressions. Can't you picture me coming back and saying, "Actually, dear, I've missed you terribly, don't you know?"

It has been beautiful here during the week. Roses grow here like corn in Iowa. I wish I could send you a carload.

Just now, the midnight news is coming over. Bombers of the 8th Air Force carried out their third record raid today, blasting the harbor at Emden; yesterday they blitzed the naval base at Kiel; and the great news in Africa continues to develop.

[FROM THE *STARS AND STRIPES*, May 19, 1943]

THE WAACS TAKE A PEEK AT LONDON: THEN GET IN GAB FESTS WITH BRITISH GALS AT GI DANCE

by Philip Bucknell, *Stars and Stripes* Staff Writer

The WAAC said, "Try my lipstick." The member of the ATS said, "Ta!" and the two WAAFs moved over to make room in front of the mirror. The maidens in uniforms were holding an allied military conference in the ladies' powder room at Rainbow Corner [a Red Cross club].

Sgt. Claudia M. Couch had a lot to talk about. She had just finished her first sight-seeing tour of London. Her feet, she said, had been danced off the last two nights at club dances. She had been run around all over the place and she was tired. But with the gallantry one expects from a soldier of the United States, she was coming up for the third dance.

Yet it was not of social activities the girls were talking. "How I envy you," Claudia was saying. "Here we've been going around with our blouses on (blouses in the military meaning) and we've been noticing how you ATS are allowed to carry your blouses. We have to keep ours on the whole time."

The British girl soldier explained that they were allowed to go around blouseless (ATS call them "tunics") in the summer time as long as they had their sleeves rolled up.

To the WAAFs the sergeant from Georgia explained that there was no separate women's outfit for the air force. WAACs, she explained, were attached to the Army Air Force in various capacities, but there was no separate command.

Earlier in the day the WAACs had met some of the WRENS, and they considered that the Wren officers looked "just like the WAVES."

When the girls set out on their tour there were certain definite things they wanted to see: Westminster Abbey, of course, and St. Paul's, the bomb ruins and Polish officers.

Londoners who were at first curious about their uniforms soon got the idea and they gave them plenty of welcoming waves—so did the GIs.

Even MPs softened up. When, it is said, a bull remarks to a soldier "We'll take you," that soldier is an unhappy soldier (no unhappy soldier is a good soldier!). But Pvt. Harry Parker, of Chicago, and Pvt. Adam Korvalski, of Detroit, said "We'll take you" when Sgt. Couch asked directions, and no particular unhappiness was noticed in any party.

In return for the courtesies shown them, the WAACs showed a keen regard for military courtesy. "We are perhaps, even keener on discipline and regard for procedure than men soldiers," said Sgt. Violet Bachman, of Long Island, N.Y., primly.

As a natural result of the dances they had attended at the Liberty and Crescent clubs, the girls had dates for the evening dance at the Rainbow Corner. They say they were never late on formation, but they were late for their dates.

MP Pvts. Elder C. Diels, of Milwaukee and Larry H. Ziemer, of Phillips, Wyo., were able to give Joy Dunlop her directions. They even escorted her to the Rainbow Corner. It was as well they did. Soldiers crowding the doors almost held up traffic.

Now sight-seeing and social flings are over for a time. The WAACs came here to do important work. They are doing it as from now.

Billee to Charles] May 20, 1943—Matawan (V-mail)

Sergeant Kiley—sounds swell, doesn't it? I feel like they pinned the stripes on me.

So you have to go and get knocked around with the Rangers to get the realism of their training. I know you must have a satisfied feeling, despite the bruises, that you can "take it." What happened to the fellow who wanted to collapse after eighteen holes of golf? Did you leave him at the desk at the *Stars and Stripes*, or in a foxhole somewhere in the British Isles? I'm praying now that you only have to use the training for the article and nothing else. I imagine they will play an important part in the coming invasion that we are hearing so much about now, and expecting it every time the paper comes out or we turn the radio on.

Two pleasant surprises in one day is something. Your letter, and my favorite uncle paid me a visit [Fred Gilbert]. He just walked in the bank and up to my window. I nearly fell off the stool from shock. He came home with Marguerite and we had a spaghetti dinner. He can go back and tell the family how I'm getting along. He will be in New York several more days, so I'll go in either tomorrow or Saturday and we'll take in a show and dinner.

We had a terrible storm last night, the first electrical storm I've been through in years. Of course, I couldn't sleep. I just lay there and watched the flashes of lightning and listened to the thunder, thinking of us and comparing all the turmoil that is keeping us apart to the storm.

[Charles to Billee] May 22, 1943—London

The Wizard of Something-or-other, meaning yours truly, is off again tomorrow for another week, which means no mail and no opportunity to write. I won't even be able to tell you where I've been and what I have done during this trip.

Ben Price [another *Stars and Stripes* staffer] and I are taking a place off Fleet St., about five minutes from the office. We were very fortunate to get it. Places in London are as scarce as oranges. Ben made a connection and we move in June 5. That will be just about a week after I get back from this upcoming trip.

Time to rush. I've got to gather equipment and get stuff in shape for tomorrow. Forgive me, again. That must make about the millionth time I've asked for it.

[Billee to Charles] May 23, 1943—Matawan

I have a million things I should be doing but you can see what an attempt I'm making. The sun is shining for the first time in days so I'm in a lawn chair under a tree, taking advantage of the sunshine. Everything is so green and clean-looking after all the rain we have had.

I called El yesterday and she is still feeling fine. Every time I call now I don't know whether she will be there or not. Bette answered. She was up in the clouds. Her Eddie was in for the weekend. Lucky her. Tom is being sent back to Virginia. I don't like that too well. He just has to be here for the big event. Eleanor is going to need him.

There goes a beautiful airplane. The sun is catching the silver color of the wings. There are a lot that go over here in a day.

Both Agnes and I were in that "rebellious" mood last night. We turned the radio on and that was worse, because it was some good dance music. So we turned the d___ thing off. At least I have the advantage over her. I do have contact with you. I don't see how she has stood it all this time, not having any direct word from Jack, but I guess you can get used to most anything—not used to it, but able to readjust your life to the facts.

I had a $1,000 bill in my hands yesterday. It's pretty, except it didn't look like that much money. The head teller had quite a few of them. Working in a place like that, money doesn't seem the same. They all call it "crap."

//////

[Billee to Charles] May 24, 1943—Matawan

So the WAAC thought you had acquired an English accent? Just bring all your "aitches" back with you and, well, how shall I say it—the way you came bounding up the stairs in Penn Station—enthusiasm?

Doesn't seem like there could be much left of the continent the way the RAF and USAF has bombed the h___ out of it. It's time Germany was getting a dose of her own medicine. I see the latest news tonight is "Biggest Raid Yet on the Reich."

/////

[Charles to Billee] May 30, 1943—London

About a half hour ago, I arrived back from my week in the "sticks." It actually felt good getting back in the field again, sleeping under the stars, eating field chow (which, incidentally, is good) and mixing with the boys. That was all part of the seven-day job for about a score of correspondents and photographers as well as cameramen. What took place? It's MI, but I'll save it for you. I'm still clad in field uniform, leggings and all, munching on cheese and biscuits salvaged from a "K" ration kit. I intended to wait until tomorrow to write, then realized I had about an hour to wait for my 12:15 a.m. train and couldn't think of a better way to spend it than to be with you.

Benny, who is sitting here with me waiting for the train, tells me clearly enough that I was promoted to Staff Sergeant during my absence. You have my sanction to go out and celebrate right now.

/////

[Billee to Charles] June 1, 1943—Matawan

I went to 195 and found everything fine there, and all waiting on pins and needles for the big event. Your dad is home as it's his vacation. We had a pleasant time together Saturday evening. El went to bed early and we sat up 'til all hours talking, a little about everything. I like him such an awful lot. On Sunday we sat around and crocheted some. The conversation always drifted back to the O'Connor infant while your dad cooked dinner. (I'm wondering if I can train you along those lines.)

Your dad starts redecorating his room today. El wants him to take the little bed down but he said absolutely no. "The boys will be coming home soon and we'll make other arrangements. This is only temporary." He said to me Saturday night, "Do you think they might be home this winter," and then, "Guess not."

Pictures again, yours will soon be on its way. I'm afraid my nose still tilts. I can't seem to do anything about that, but since you like it so much, I'm glad it does and I never felt like that before. I was always a little envious of those girls with nice straight noses.

/////

Ben and I moved back to town this week—bedroom with twin beds, living room, bath, and tiny kitchenette. We are supposed to be very fortunate to even get a place let alone one for a "reasonable" rent—$96 a month. Taxes are so high, living conditions the same, that people are forced to pay prices like that. Can you imagine what we could get for that rent?

As soon as I can get straightened out on moving expenses, traveling expenses, etc., I'll make a budget and see if I can't supplement our savings with some cash. Every time it looks as if I'll see a little, I go off on a trip like the one last week and donate to the good and welfare of hotels, restaurants, etc. While we were with the troops on maneuvers, most of the time we did have to maintain a room in a centralized hotel for headquarters purposes. And hotel rates over here are really something.

/////

[FROM THE *STARS AND STRIPES*, June 1, 1943]

US ARMY SEEMS READY FOR INVASION: MOCK BATTLE AGAINST LARGER BRITISH FORCES PROVES METTLE

by Charles F. Kiley, *Stars and Stripes* Staff Writer

A force of hard-hitting and aggressive American soldiers, among those slated to form part of the invasion spearhead when the Allied blow on the Continent is struck, today bears the stamp of ably-trained troops, as fit for battle as any the United States ever sent into action, following recent large-scale maneuvers in which it operated against a larger force of British armor, infantry and provisional units.

In the role of an Allied army, charged with destroying a German army in flight, the British armored force was three times as large as the defenders, played by American infantry and artillery supported by a regiment of British Lancers' reconnaissance gun carriers.

Without a tank corps of their own to make a stand and fight, the Americans were forced to use speed and deception, carefully camouflaged anti-tank and artillery positions in a delaying action. They operated so well they delayed the scheduled finish of the "battle" for almost 12 hours.

An example of the Americans' hard-hitting spirit was displayed by a detachment of Rangers, commanded by Maj. Randolph Milholland, of Cumberland, Md. The unit carried out a night raid and was credited with "annihilating" an electrical maintenance unit used as a workshop of the armored force, "destroying" all equipment and causing casualties among its personnel.

The Rangers, with blackened faces and using rubber-soled shoes, struck swiftly across a distance of 40 miles by truck and through cross-country to make the attack.

The American artillery, under Maj. Al Gardner, of Baltimore, used reconnaissance planes for observation and frequently caught the advancing forces off guard.

Col. Philip Wood, of Bar Harbor, Me., commanding all American forces, played a major role in the action by skillfully placing anti-tank guns at crossroads and junctions and holding up tank columns for hours at a time.

Infantrymen, armed with bazooka guns and hidden in positions off the road, were credited with knocking out a number of Bren carriers and disabling tanks.

Other infantrymen scattered anti-tank and personnel mines, as well as booby-traps wherever the British forces were expected. Smoke bombs were used as Molotov cocktails and grenades in crippling tanks.

Small blocks of TNT "destroyed" bridges at several main crossings, forcing British engineers to bridge the streams with pontoons and newly-devised equipment.

In the air RAF and USAAF fighters and fighter-bombers were used by both sides for ground-strafing troops and tanks, as well as blowing up bridges.

[Billee to Charles] June 4, 1943—Matawan

We are in the middle of my first heat wave. I took a shower about 30 minutes ago and I should go back now for another. I perspired more in two days than I have in seven years. We all got together tonight and took turns pushing the lawn mower. Rain made the grass grow so fast. I took a hot then a cold shower and felt like a new woman.

There was an article in the *Tribune* about your Lt. Moora concerning the strike situation [coal miners' strike in the United States]. Really, I'm ashamed for them, and what the fellows on the other side must think. I saw in the same paper where fifteen in one mine refused to walk out since they had boys in North Africa. I can't understand why they would do such a thing now when everything is leading up to a swift victory. More than I can understand.

[Charles to Billee] June 5, 1943—London

This is our first night in our new place and since you can't be present for the housewarming, we can do the next best thing, can't we? I said it was a house-warming—rather private—Ben writing to his wife and me spending a "date night" with you. Let me describe our place as I see it from here:

This room—the living room—is nicely furnished with two easy chairs, small dining table, coffee table, side table, floor lamp, red rug, daybed, and imitation fireplace. To my left is the "kitchen." It is so small—there were three flies in there this afternoon and one of them had the nerve to complain he was too cramped. The bath is roomy—everything just right. The bedroom has twin beds, plenty of closet space, chest of drawers, night table, and phone.

Things were rather quiet for me during the past week—since I returned from the maneuvers. Big news during that time was the coal strike. It had a bad effect on the boys here, I'm afraid. Everywhere they talked of men who would walk out over a job like that in wartime.

Now today, I see 20,000 workers in the Packard engine plant in Detroit struck because three Negroes were hired. What the h—l's going on in the minds of those people?

/////

[Billee to Charles] June 7, 1943—Matawan

Don't tell me those stripes have gone to your head? All joking aside, I never felt more like celebrating—Staff Sgt. already. I'm very proud. We'll celebrate all those stripes when we are together once more.

I can just see you, in your field uniform. Do you have a hat too, like they wear, the new style? The boys in the field aren't rationed so much and you are having your taste of rationed food living in London. But then, we are too.

You haven't been able to tell me much about what you are doing, but you have given me enough hints, together with what we read in the paper, that the big push is due to come anytime now. I feel, too, that this week was more or less for conditioning you to go in with the troops. I can't help but be frightened at the thought of it. I rather imagined or was consoling myself with the thought that you wouldn't see "action" in this work, but now I'm not sure.

The strike situation is settled for a little while. I think, when you fellows come back, you're going to have another battle on your hands, and it will be at the gate of Washington. I'm thinking they are going to need some settling up there, and then you're going to have to take over. Seems they are getting a little out of hand.

/////

[Charles to Billee] June 8, 1943—London

Honey, I have a complaint to make. I don't get enough pictures of you. While waiting for the enlargement, I could stand some snapshots.

Upcoming this week for me are the boxing championships between the American and British armies at Royal Albert Hall. Our boys have a couple of scores to settle but will have a tough job to do. Back in 1935 at Yankee Stadium and in 1936 here at Wembley Stadium, British amateur teams gave American boys more than the once-over-lightly. They should be good scraps.

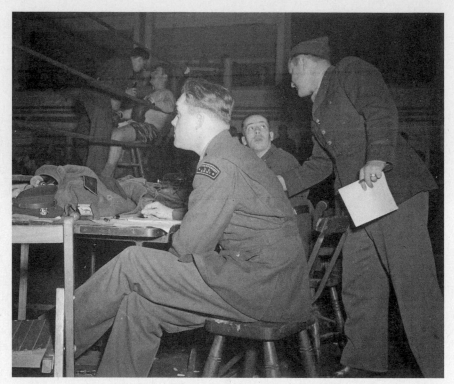

Charles (center) covering the boxing competition at Albert Hall (note the US Army Correspondent shoulder patch)—London, June 1943. (Kiley Family)

[FROM THE *STARS AND STRIPES*, June 11, 1943]

KOZAK AND KINGSLAND HEROES OF THURSDAY'S RING TRIUMPH

by Charles F. Kiley, *Stars and Stripes* Staff Writer

The boxing champions of the United States Armed Forces in the ETO defeated the British Army titleholders, six bouts to five, at Royal Albert Hall, London, last night before a howling crowd of 6,000.

The team honors were not decided until the final bout, when husky Pvt. Vince Kozak, unbeaten ETO heavyweight king, pounded out a close decision over Bdr. [bombardier] George Preston, British titleholder from the Commandos.

The judges were in hot water with the crowd all night. Decisions in at least four of the 11 bouts, including the deciding final, were disputed by the spectators.

The Tommies took a five to four lead before the light-heavyweights and heavies climbed into the ring but after Pfc. Bill Kingsland, of Redondo Beach, Cal., squared the count in the 175 lb. class, Kozak came through with a climacteric victory that had the crowd roaring from bell to bell . . .

There's a bit of Hollywood news (always interesting to the ladies) around that you may like, angel. Burgess Meredith is in London as a public relations officer for Air Transport Command and Adolphe Menjou is due in tonight with the USO Camp Show group. I'm assigned to the latter and will let you know more about it.

Our Andy Rooney did a swell job on a mass interview with Capt. Clark Gable the other day. Contrary to public opinion, Gable is not on operational duty but working on a training film for gunnery instruction. He has been on one mission as an observer to get first-hand information on gunnery and isn't likely to go on any more.

[FROM THE *STARS AND STRIPES*, June 7, 1943]

CLARK GABLE IS JUST A TWO-BAR JOE DOING A JOB: HE'S MAKING A FILM TO TRAIN MORE AIR GUNNERS; NO PUBLICITY SEEKER, SO HEREWITH OUR LAST REPORT

by Andrew A. Rooney, *Stars and Stripes* Staff Writer

Last summer he quieted a rumor that he was going to accept a direct commission as a major by enlisting as a private in Los Angeles. On Oct. 28, after completing the air corps OCS at Miami, Fla., he was commissioned second lieutenant. He served at Tyndall Field, Fla., for a while, and later was shipped to a mid-West field. He came to England about seven weeks ago, has been on one raid (Antwerp, May 4), and his job here is to make a training film for aerial gunners. He is 42 years old, six feet one inch tall, his hair is grey. He seems like an OK guy.

With the possible exception of the German Army, no one is having a tougher time trying to fight this war than Capt. Clark Gable.

A few hundred thousand relatives of privates in the infantry who have been fighting in North Africa want to know why Clark Gable isn't a private in the infantry fighting in North Africa. Mothers of Marines on Guadalcanal want to know why he wasn't a Marine on Guadalcanal. The fathers and mothers, sisters and friends of the staff sergeants on combat crews of B17s and B24s want to know why he is a captain instead of a staff sergeant. And some of the boys wonder.

He is not a captain doing a staff sergeant's job. He is a captain doing a job that has been done by majors and better, and he went from a second lieutenant to a captain in less than six months, not because he had a direct pipe-line to the commanding general, but because he is an intelligent man doing a good job for the Air Force.

He is in England on the orders of Brig. Gen. Luther S. Smith, director of the Air Force training program. With him are 1/Lts. Andrew J. McIntyre, former MGM cameraman, and John Mahin, who wrote several of the script for Gable's pictures.

Together the three of them, with the help of several veteran gunners, are putting together a film they hope will be some help in the training program for aerial gunners. In the film, Gable interviews men, gets opinions and observations on equipment and combat problems. He appears in some of the scenes—does not appear in others.

He went on the Antwerp raid so that he could talk through something besides his hat about raids.

Herewith ends the report on Capt. Clark Gable. For our money he is an OK Joe fighting a war, and, until he bites a dog or figures in a legitimate news story, just like any other Joe, the *Stars and Stripes* will leave the guy alone, as he would like to be left, for the duration.

[Charles to Billee] June 9, 1943—London

There has been something on my mind for a long, long time now, and, after deliberating a great deal I came to the conclusion that I should tell you before another minute goes by. It came to me only a matter of minutes after I met you—17 months gone by. It has been with me every day since I've known your lovely face. Many times, it kept me awake at night. It distracted me from work, made me wonder if I could ever tell you and make you understand. What I'm trying to say, and hope you didn't expect the worst—is that I love you—and so much!

Listen, because my dad is qualified to cook dinner is no reason to believe his son inherited that ability. I can make a bad cup of coffee but that's about all. Speaking about housekeeping, the maid service I mention consists of a woman straightening up our flat after we've left for the office.

I mentioned in my V-mail of yesterday that Adolphe Menjou was due in town. I met him last night when they had a press interview for him. The enclosed story will tell all.

/////

[FROM THE *STARS AND STRIPES*, June 9, 1943]

ADOLPHE MENJOU HERE TO STAGE SHOWS "AS LONG AS ARMY WANTS"
VETERAN FILM STAR READY TO BEGIN TOUR OF ETO CAMPS

by Charles F. Kiley, *Stars and Stripes* Staff Writer

Adolphe Menjou, motion picture star, is in Britain to entertain troops as long as the US Army's Special Service Section and USO Camp Shows, Inc., have work for him.

Menjou is here after touring camp areas in America for five and a half months. Master of several languages, he was used by the Office of War Information on broadcasts to foreign countries, and during the North African invasion spoke on radio programs to Germany, Italy, Spain, Portugal, Turkey and occupied Poland. His work in Britain will be chiefly concerned with entertaining troops, he said last night, and any other activity will be up to the Army.

In the last war, Menjou enlisted in the US Army as a private and rose to the rank of captain. He served overseas in the Fifth Division and saw action at St. Mihiel and in the Argonne-Meuse sector. During two and a half years of duty he also served with the French and Italian armies as an interpreter.

Menjou pointed out that most audiences in America are favoring comedy escapist pictures, mainly because of the flood of war pictures recently produced in Hollywood. He said they call its war films "Stetsons," because when they come on the screen, people reach for their hats.

/////

[Billee to Charles] June 12, 1943—Matawan

How are you taking the quiet life now after all your traipsing around, sleeping under the stars "roughing it"? Will you be ready to settle down after all this is over to a dull life living in a 2 x 4 and going to the office every day with nothing more exciting than maybe the Jersey City basketball team winning with a shut out?

The strike news has settled down again for a time. I sympathize with the miners. They deserve all that's coming to them but still, this isn't the time to assert their rights when we need all the cooperation from labor we can get. I'm afraid the American people have to see or feel real "blitz" before we can be all out for a total war. We are a selfish nation, thinking too much of our own personal needs and wants.

/////

[Charles to Billee] June 13, 1943—London

I've had two reports from old Company [H] (CENSORED), darling. The other day, while looking over a list of wounded, I noticed a Cpl. and Sgt. Then, today I had a letter from Harold Gee, a boy from Winston-Salem, who told all he could about the climactic finish [of the fighting in North Africa]. He indicated all of my particular friends were safe. I'd like to know how Jack Donnell came through so I'm planning to get something off to him in a day or so. Also had a letter from Ralph Martin, an old one that was delayed.

Big news today, honey, is the fall of Pantellaria and Lampedusa, not much but a couple of more steps in the right direction. Also, over 300 Flying Forts had a crack at Bremen today. And, the other night the RAF sent out about 1000 four-engined bombers to hit Duisburg and Munster in the Ruhr area.

/////

[Billee to Charles] June 17, 1943—Matawan

You probably know the good news by now that El is the mother of an 8 pound baby girl. I'm disappointed that it was a girl, but then that's what Tom wanted. I hope my first is a boy. Bette said your dad was so excited. She wasn't exactly calm when she talked to me. I've certainly been keeping the wires busy between here and 195.

How does it feel to be settling down again to interviewing celebrities? No more Rangers or Commandos. Which do you like best?

Tuesday night Agnes and I went to see *Casablanca*. After so long I finally caught up with it. I think I remember you mentioning that you had seen it. Really swell, wasn't it? If you never liked "As Time Goes By" before, you have to like it after seeing the picture.

/////

[Charles to Billee] June 18, 1943—London

At long last, a cable from Bette today broke the good news—a baby girl and both doing well. If I had to wait another day to get word I would've had a baby myself, maybe twins. Why do people have to have babies? Can't they have eggs and hatch them? It would save a lot of trouble for the uncles.

I can't blame you for wanting to celebrate the promotions. How do you think I felt? Still, like you, I can wait. And when we do celebrate it won't be because of promotions. However, I want to stress one thing. I've done it before and so I only merely remind you. If there is a time when you don't hear from me for a while it may not be because something has happened.

You wanted to know what I wore in the field while I was away. I'm sending a picture of a group of us who work together. You'll be able to see for yourself. It isn't a very stylish picture, but then you can't be very stylish on maneuvers, can you?

///////

[Charles to Billee] June 18, 1943—London

It was just a year ago that I fully realized how thoroughly and completely separated we were, and would be. Then, it had only been two months since we kissed and said "goodbye, for a little while." We knew extensive maneuvers were to prepare our 34th division for action of some sort. And, as the months passed by, and the preparations work accelerated, I became frightened. Oh, I don't think it was a fear for safety.

It was a fear that one day you would see men coming home. There would be families and girls like you there to meet them. You would be there—looking— but not for anyone in particular because you would know I wasn't coming. You would be there just because we planned it. I saw you standing there, and I was frightened.

That was last summer. In a few days another summer will be with us. I'm not as frightened as I was a year ago. And, I'm not frightened at the thought of not coming back to you because I *will* be there for you to meet. I know what you will look like, how you will feel in my arms. You are going to cry, and it is quite possible I will, too, although I can't recall when I cried last. Sometimes I wonder if I have tears.

That's what I'm thinking of tonight when the full moon, enemy bombers, sirens, guns, and noise aren't enough to take you away from me.

Now that the full moon is brightening the nights, Jerry is making stabs at London. He was over three times last week. And he's over again tonight. I say "tonight" even though it's 1:30 a.m. The alerts don't last long, only about 20 or

30 minutes. The sirens wail, 10 minutes later you hear the planes, guns bark at them, you hear a couple of explosions way off—and it's all over.

/////

[Billee to Charles] June 22 and 25, 1943—Matawan

I had a long letter from Mom [in Asheville] yesterday. She rented the apartment [in Oak Lodge] to a flight officer and his wife and daughter for quite a nice sum. She isn't giving any meals at all, for which I am more than grateful. Having to cope with the rationing, together with no means of getting the food home, changed her mind.

I'm glad you heard from the fellows in North Africa. I've been wondering and praying that they are all right—Ben and the rest.

I'd like to close my eyes right now and wake up on the terrace of the Grove Park Inn, sitting in one of those chairs with you beside me watching the moon and catching some of the mountain breezes.

Yesterday, when I went to the station there was a wedding party there seeing the bride and groom off. You should have seen all the rice. Made me a little envious.

I read where a congressman said how important the soldier vote was going to be in the next election and that the majority of them would be home to vote. I love guys who talk like that.

/////

[Charles to Billee] June 26, 1943—London

The small portable—Bing Crosby's "When Day is Done"—your letters, smoke curling up to the shade of the table lamp, my sweetheart and Ben's wife smiling from their pictures. That's what you would see if you were sitting across the room.

Your picture is one of those enlarged snapshots that came today. It will probably take me hours to write this because every minute or so I stop to look—look—at that picture.

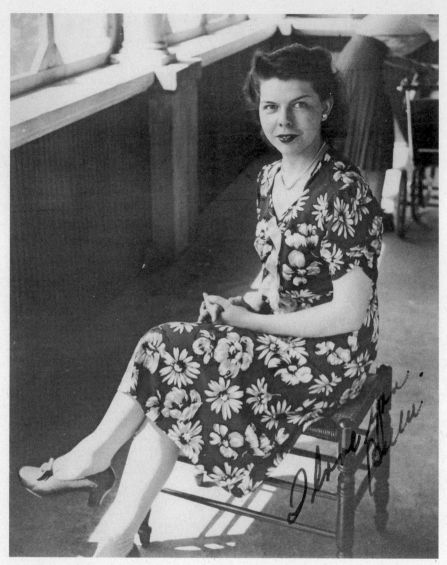

Billee—Matawan, May 1943. (Kiley Family)

Here's a new one for you, honey. One of the five WAACs I met when they arrived called me on the phone yesterday. Said she wanted to see me before she returned to her station after a 48-hour leave in London. I met her at the Washington Red Cross club and learned she wanted me to "ghost write" a story for her. One of the WAAC officers wanted the best article written by one of the five girls to put on one of the wires home; she told the girls they could get help if they wanted to. This one said I was the only newspaperman she knew and, rather embarrassed, asked me if I could help her. I asked her a flock of questions, bought her a "coke" and wrote the story in the office. It was a hurry up job, but if you see the WAAC story "written" by Joy Dunlop—that's me! That's the best yet, "ghost-writing" for a WAAC.

/////

[Billee to Charles] July 5 and 6, 1943—Matawan

The christening was Sunday at one o'clock. Annice [the baby] was very good; in fact she slept through most of it. Eddie and I went along with your Dad.

You should see Father John. He hangs over the bassinet. If she moves wrong, he picks her up. El swears she's going to brain him. He's to be home for three weeks so you can imagine how he's going to spoil her. Incidentally he calls her "Butch."

Father John is so put out, he forgot to rag Eddie about the girl in Tennessee. Your Dad and Bette asked him about it. He told Bette, "Don't be worrying. I'm not marrying her. Just writing to her." He told Pop he had one in every state. We did learn, though, that she is blonde with blue eyes.

You have probably heard that Eddie has left the division he was with. Seems he doesn't have much opportunity of being advanced to a Staff Sergeant, and since you have made the grade he isn't resting until he gets the extra bars. He looked swell, GI haircut and all. I hope you don't have one of those.

/////

[Charles to Billee] July 8, 1943—London

Just back from a four-day sortie to Air Force fighter stations and Service Command posts. Caught two good stories at a P47 (fighter) field on the second day and phoned them in.

A squadron of P47s came in from a sweep over Germany. We watched them, and saw one of the strangest sights I've ever seen. Instead of clambering out of their ships and reporting for interrogation, they immediately refueled the planes and took off again. We went to the control tower to see what it was all about and were told the boys were going back over the same ground they just covered in search of their missing 28-year-old squadron leader, Col. Arman Peterson. They didn't find him. I had a hell of a time getting the stuff cleared by censors before I phoned it in, eventually being forced to wait until the following morning when 8th Air Force HQ announced Peterson was missing.

[FROM THE *STARS AND STRIPES*, July 8, 1943]

P47S RETURN IN VAIN FOR LOST CHIEF:
THE MESS IS KEEPING VACANT PLACE FOR MISSING PILOT

[No byline]

A USAAF FIGHTER STATION, July 7—Returning from a sweep over enemy territory, pilots here immediately refueled their planes and with hardly a word spoken flew back over the ground they just covered in search of their commander, Col. Arman Peterson.

The "double sweep" in tribute to the 28-year-old squadron leader from Flagstaff, Ariz., was revealed yesterday when Eighth Air Force HQ announced that Peterson was missing in action.

Peterson was last seen after he had spotted enemy planes below and reported over the inter-com:

"There they are; here we go."

Peterson's fliers swooped in at 90 degrees and they think they saw him vanish into a cloud.

Not until they arrived back at their base did Peterson's men realize he was missing. Without orders, they refueled their planes and took off.

They returned to the area over which they had fought, looking in vain for the missing pilot until gas ran low and they headed home for the first time without Peterson's whimsical voice telling them to "scram!"

There was a vacancy at the head table for mess but they maintained there was always the chance he'd be back.

///////

So here we are after a six-hour train ride from Blackpool. The wee radio is playing "Louise" and it carries me back to June of 1930, I think, and one of our high school plays.

The mail has been good to me this week. Aside from yours, there were others from Eddie and Father John. I never fail to get a special kick from Eddie's letters. He mentions getting a cable about the baby and says innocently, "They say it's 8 lbs., 5 oz. I don't know much about those things but it sounds good."

Eddie Kiley holding El's daughter, Annice—Jersey City, June 1943. (Kiley Family)

Coming back on the train today I figured I've traveled about 15,000 miles in England, Scotland, Wales and Ireland during my eight months with the paper. This past trip, for example, covered about 700!

"Jerry" pulled a funny one tonight, just as our train got in. The ceiling was practically zero, it was raining a little but he came over, in daylight. I could hear the planes passing overhead, later heard a few blasts in the suburbs, then our fighters streaking after them. Because we are so near the Channel coast we don't get much warning. The sirens scream and half a minute later the planes are overhead.

Talk about Father John being enthusiastic about my promotions . . . He started off his letter, "Dear Lt." He doesn't know that getting a commission over here is really something. We have one OCS 90-day course, which leaves us out. We couldn't possibly go away for that long. Most OCS boys go home, which also leaves us out. If there are any commissions at all they will have to come by direct appointment. If that day comes, you'll know it was really earned. During the year and a half of publication only Bob Moora got a 2nd Lt. commission, and he really did earn it. He's the "brain" of the office on the news desk. Incidentally, Bob censors my mail by saying, "to Billee?" and signs it without reading it over.

[Billee to Charles] July 8, 1943—Matawan

I think I'll follow in your footsteps and start a column something like this:

"Advice to the Girls They Left Behind," or "How to Keep That Man Overseas . . ." send a "glamour snapshot" enclosed in your letter and see what happens.

I can see where I should have sent pictures long ago.

While we are on the subject, the proofs [of a formal portrait] came yesterday from Charles Todd [photographer] in Arlington with a nice little note asking me to please come in for a re-sitting, that something went wrong with the camera mechanically and he wasn't satisfied with the proofs. See what a girl you have. She goes around breaking cameras with that puss of hers.

[Billee to Charles] July 10, 1943—Matawan

If you could see me, all you'd be able to call me would be lazy-bones because here I am stretched out in a sun chair in my shorts and halter trying to get a little tan, battling the flies and occasionally a bee that comes my way. I still am not used to the idea of Saturdays off, but I like it very much.

I've turned around now and am cooking myself on the other side, so I'll be done to a turn by the time I go in. It's been a long time since I've spent a Saturday like this. When I was a kid and we lived in Massillon I used to spend the majority of the time swimming. By the end of the summer, I was like nothing less than an Indian.

Here comes a pair of silver wings, quite low, too. Wonder where it's going. The thought came to me that aboard one of those I could be in your arms about twelve or fifteen hours from now, not even a day.

More planes going over and all so low. We are in one of the lanes through. That's why we see so many. I'm about airplanes like some people are about fire engines.

[Billee to Charles] July 13, 1943—Matawan

Since I wrote last, Sicily has been invaded. I can imagine how excited you all must have been. We've been hanging over the radio and everywhere you see people poring over the newspaper. I'm praying that it is what Roosevelt said, "the beginning of the end." I've been reading John Steinbeck's articles in the *Herald Tribune* the last few weeks. A couple of them I clipped out. They are very good. I never liked his writing before, but these are excellent. One in particular he wrote about the boys in England and Independence Day that struck me just right. Incidentally, he is in England as a correspondent for the *Herald Tribune*.

[Charles to Billee] July 20, 1943—London

Let's you and I have a few words on the WAAC insofar as you are concerned. I won't say you should, or, you shouldn't go into the WAACs, WAVEs or any of the other services. You said [your] Mother wants you to go into the WAACs. If you want to join, go ahead, but please don't be misled by recruitment posters.

Earlier in the night I was glancing over the list of dead in the war and published in July 5 *Life*. There was a familiar name, Page Beeman from Minnesota, Co. H. bugler, killed in North Africa. His horn got me up early on many a cold morning, and how many times did we say, "Oh, how I'd love to murder the bugler." It all doesn't seem very funny now.

/////

[Billee to Charles] July 20, 1943—Matawan

Father John has been considering the army again. He really feels like a slacker when there is such an urgent need for chaplains now. I don't believe he will go, though, because as he said, if something should happen to your Dad that would leave the girls there alone. He is being practical about it, but that isn't much consolation when you feel about it the way he does.

You speak of a daylight raid as if it were a tea party. Don't you make for a shelter any more or are you afraid you'll miss something? We haven't been hearing much about London raids now. The Sicilian campaign has pushed all that kind of news to the inside pages. If only the rest of the "push" to Berlin could be as easy as this seems to be. There are so many stories in the papers, almost unbelievable, of whole companies of solders surrendering to a few of our soldiers. This morning brought the news of the bombing of Rome. Of course, Axis reports state that St. Lorenzo was seriously damaged. That seems to be the only non-military objective mentioned as being hit.

Eddie was so interested in the baby's [Annice's] christening. He wasn't going to miss that. He said to me, "You know, I've never been to one of these before."

I had a letter from my brother yesterday. He graduates this week as a radio mechanic and with a Staff Sergeant's rating. Nice going. Did I tell you Mom bought him a service watch for his birthday and graduation? He was so tickled and is so proud of it. You remember my telling you about him getting engaged? In this letter he breaks the news to me that in a letter he had just received from the girl she tells him that she's been engaged for two months to an ensign in the Navy. Poor kid, you can imagine how he feels. He says, "Shall I go on a three day binge or hang myself?" I'm anxious to see now where he will be sent.

/////

[Billee to Charles] July 21, 1943—Matawan

I had a long letter from Mom today, too, along with yours. She doesn't tell me to come home but she keeps telling me how the Postal Agency there needs girls and that they pay $1620 a year and $360 extra a year for working Saturdays.

I finished early again today and decided to take in a movie: *Bataan*, very good but anything but diverting. They had a Harry James short and guess what they played? "You Made Me Love You." I all but cried, because it was his recording we danced to.

I suppose you've seen where Knox [William Franklin "Frank" Knox (January 1, 1874—April 28, 1944) was an American newspaper editor and publisher and the Republican vice-presidential candidate in 1936, as well as Secretary of the Navy under Franklin D. Roosevelt during most of World War II] predicts the war will last until 1949. If that's the case, I might better join the WAAC or WAVE. At least I might accidentally get to see you.

/////

[Charles to Billee] July 22, 1943—London

I told you in the air mail letter that the WAACs had arrived. There were 557 of them, and the Air Force got them all. They will be attached to the 8th Air Force, working as stenographers, telephonists, plotters at operations stations, etc. Another fellow from the office and I were among several correspondents, mostly women, to make the trip to a Replacement Center where they are rested and processed after the voyage. They took part in a formal review during their first day and really looked swell. The job lasted three days, plus another spent in doing the stories.

I splurged last night after I was finished in the office and saw *The More the Merrier*, with Jean Arthur and Joel McCrea. I wondered if your "dorm" was as crowded as theirs. When I see pictures like that I get nostalgic.

/////

[FROM THE *STARS AND STRIPES*, July 20, 1943]

557 GI JANES HERE FOR DUTY WITH AIR FORCE: GIRLS WILL RELEASE SOLDIERS FROM CLERICAL JOBS FOR COMBAT DUTY

by Charles F. Kiley, *Stars and Stripes* Staff Writer

WAAC REPLACEMENT DEPOT, England, July 19—The First Separate Battalion of the Women's Auxiliary Army Corps—557 strong—is in Britain to relieve men of the Eighth Air Force for combat duty.

The girls slipped quietly into this camp without publicity or fanfare save a rousing welcome by a small group of soldiers on duty and a GI band that played, "Let Me Call You Sweetheart."

The battalion will remain here about a week, easing sea legs and being processed, before going to Air Force units as stenographers, telephonists, plotters at operational stations and in other duties for which they are, or will be, trained.

The first complete WAAC unit to reach the ETO—it is the largest of two expeditionary forces serving overseas—represents all 48 States and the District of Columbia. The girls range in ages from 21 to 45—average 27—and are blonde, brunette and redhead.

Led by its commanding officer, Capt. Mary A. Halleren, of Lowell, Mass., the battalion was welcomed at the port of debarkation by the WAAC commander in the ETO, Capt. Anna Wilson of Studio City, Cal., who with several other officers and five enrolled members preceded the battalion to Britain during the last several months.

Although the government bill, approved by Congress and the President, making the WAAC an integral part of the US Army, does not go into effect until Sept. 30, the WAACs in this theater will receive 20 per cent overseas bonus and V-mail privileges. They will not be eligible for government insurance or Class "E" allotments until Sept. 30, however. Capt. Wilson also said the WAACs here would be sworn into the Army sometime before Sept. 1.

When they arrived by train at this station the WAACs demonstrated their military training and discipline by taking 12 minutes to adjust packs, clear the platform and start marching to their barracks.

The WAAC contingent included girls who only a few months ago were students, secretaries, models, telephone operators, chorus girls and the good-looking kid who served them "off the arm" in Max's Diner on US Highway No 1.

Some have husbands, sweethearts, and brothers in service, already buried on foreign battlegrounds or who are prisoners-of-war, like blonde Margie Simpkins, of Christiansburg, Va., who is waiting for a USAAF P38 fighter pilot sweating out the war in a German prison camp.

/////

[Billee to Charles] July 24, 1943—Matawan

Missing you so. It all began with hearing "Tonight We Love" today. My knees started to shake and I had to sit down and hear it through. Is it good when music does that to you? I don't know. I always get such a choked feeling when I hear it.

The time goes quickly but still it seems like an era since I saw you last. Funny, the memories are so vivid, each moment of the time we spent together stands out alone until I know almost to a sigh what we said and did and yet it seems like such a long time ago.

I almost forgot. The quietness of the day was broken by the blaring forth of the radio telling the world of the ousting of Mussolini, which makes us all wonder, What now? Is it for the good? Is the Pope behind it? Is it a cover up for Mussolini and Hitler?

/////

Back from a four-day trip to Wales and southwestern England and a chance to spend a beautiful evening with you. My trip wasn't very productive from a news-gathering standpoint, but it did give me an opportunity to see Britain when, in my opinion, it is wearing its nicest colors.

I started out with a short plane hop to save about five hours but traveled the rest of the way by train. Wales was a bit damp. I stayed a day in Cardiff and then set out for the English coast, Penzance, Land's End, Plymouth, Torquay, Brighton and Bournemouth.

Night before last, you were never closer to me. I stood atop a cliff overlooking the Channel, in the warm, lush purple twilight. Below the water rolled over the uninhabited beach and far away a gold bar, running from north to south, stopped the sky from dropping into the water on the horizon.

And, I was lonely, very lonely.

In my train compartment today were a man and his seven-year-old daughter, as well as a woman and a two-months old baby. During the trip I confess to have taken part in holding the baby for almost a half hour while the mother went to the dining car for tea and then mixed something in a bottle with water and came up with milk, and escorting the seven-year-old junior miss (named Doris) to tea. Perhaps it was because she had a wee nose and dimples that I "fell in love" with Doris and asked her father if I might take her to tea.

Honestly, I thoroughly enjoyed both. I must have looked odd holding the baby. The man asked me if I had any of my own and although I answered in the negative, I added that I had plans to be carried out if the blasted war would hurry up.

When I got home tonight the first question I asked Benny was, "Any mail?" His answer was, "Charlie, it looks like nobody loves us anymore. I haven't heard from Jane [his wife] since a July 12 letter." So, without new "bits of heaven" to read, I went back over your old ones. Even went so far as to count them again. 145 received since April 20, 1942.

///////

[Billee to Charles] July 27, 1943—Matawan

Nothing new about Mussolini so far tonight. His whereabouts still seem to be a mystery. I wish they'd hurry and decide what they are going to do.

An amusing incident today . . . While waiting for the train, a young sailor picked up a conversation with Marge and me. Just a kid, and he had just returned from his boot training in the Great Lakes. You never saw anyone so bubbling over. He told us practically his life history. An Irishman, too, by the way. He was going to Matawan "to see his darling."

We played records tonight. I mentioned before that Agnes had so many good ones. I don't think she enjoys hearing them so much now. She and Jack bought them together and spent many happy hours together listening to them. She's had no direct word from him since a year in April.

CHAPTER 5

AUGUST–DECEMBER 1943

*Your wandering boy is back, safe and sound. It was quite an
experience. The target was Frankfurt, about 600 miles from Britain
and 100 miles inside Germany . . . . Back on the ground, we
discovered we were hit in two places but no serious damage. Other
planes weren't so lucky.*

[*Charles to Billee, October 1943.*]

/////

The War: In August 1943, General Eisenhower ordered volatile General
Patton to apologize for his physical abuse of certain soldiers in hospitals.
Later that month, as Messina fell to the Allies in Sicily, secret negotiations
began in Portugal toward an armistice with Italy, which was signed in Sep-
tember. As they left Rome, German troops looted the city's art treasures, and
Hitler ordered a captured Mussolini freed by German paratroopers.

In Norway, the Germans executed the Oslo police commissioner and
rounded up Norwegian officers in response to widespread Norwegian civilian
defiance of German occupation. The same scenario played out in Denmark.
Civilian unrest in these two countries was partially incited by Allied infiltra-
tors, forcing Germany to send troops away from battlegrounds to maintain
order: fifty thousand troops were sent to Denmark alone.

Seven thousand miners defied an order that banned labor strikes in the
United Kingdom and struck in Scotland for better pay. In August, riots broke
out in New York's Harlem neighborhood over the consistent refusal to give
black people decent defense industry jobs; the *New York Times* reported that
110,000 war prisoners held in the United States were being used to relieve manpower shortages.

Russia launched an offensive on a 1,300-mile western front as German forces retreated to Crimea, prompting the propaganda genius Goebbels to formally admit the enormous danger facing Germany.

In November, a torpedo fired in error by a US destroyer narrowly missed the *Iowa*, carrying President Roosevelt on his way to the Tehran Conference. Also that month, more than five hundred B-17 bombers devastated the German Naval base at Wilhelmshaven, and over three days 764 RAF bombers dropped several tons on Berlin, killing more than three thousand people.

In the Mediterranean, off the coast of Algiers, the German Luftwaffe attacked Convoy KMF 26, sinking the troop transfer SS *Rohna*, killing 1,100 American troops.

In late November, Roosevelt, Churchill, and Stalin met in Tehran to discuss a victory strategy, one that included establishing a second front in France.

[Billee to Charles] August 1, 1943—Jersey City and Matawan

We had a little excitement today listening to *The Stars and Stripes* [*The Stars and Stripes* in Britain, a weekly radio show hosted by Ben Lyon]. When Ben Lyon was giving the buildup for Andrew Rooney I thought it was going to be you. They switched the program from the WAAC back to London and the way he announced it, I thought sure it was going to be you or Philip Bucknell.

Expanding the paper as Andrew Rooney described will make more work for all of you. He said there would be a magazine section on Friday, with short stories, etc. Hearing him talk about the familiar names of Bob Moora and Bud Hutton made you seem so near. I wondered if you were there at the broadcast.

I'm missing you again tonight. I wish I was at the Replacement Depot, so I could call up and say, "Meet me in London at the Washington Red Cross Club."

[Charles to Billee] August 3, 1943—London

After seeing Eddie with his GI haircut you wondered if I had one and if so, to make proper adjustments. While I was in Ireland, it couldn't be helped and I had one for six months. One of the company clerks was a barber. Now, although I've had my locks shorn by barbers from London to Plymouth to Liverpool to Glasgow to Oxford to Edinburgh, it doesn't look too bad.

As far as boarding a ship and heading this way after the war, as per advice from John, you've got me in the same boat with Benny. He's trying to figure out some way to get his wife over here now, he's that bad.

[Billee to Charles] August 5, 1943—Matawan

Can you imagine Asbury Park dimmed out? It was my first visit tonight. They have a heavy canvas screen all along the boardwalk to keep in what light there is. Only in one place, away from all the lights, did we [Agnes and Billee] find a place to see the surf. We sat for a while watching it, both of us lost in our thoughts. I was seeing you atop the cliff above the channel, and sharing your loneliness, too.

Your trip sounded like a pleasant one. Mom will enjoy hearing that you were in Cardiff. Both her parents came from there as children.

How in the world are you going to get all those letters home? 145 of them . . . enough for a book almost, isn't it?

The fall of Mussolini has seemed to change the whole course of events, together with the conquering of Sicily almost complete. Catania fell today.

My brother is getting his furlough this week and going to Massillon. He expects to be sent somewhere here in the East and mentioned Mitchell Field. Mom is going to Massillon to meet him.

[Charles to Billee] August 8, 1943—London

I wish I could tell you how much your letters mean, Billee. You see, they not only tell me those things precious to us but I'm beginning to rely on you to tell me just about everything taking place at home.

You asked me if Col. Peterson, who failed to come back from a P47 sortie the day I was there, has been found. No word that I know of.

Axis reports claimed the San Lorenzo basilica was hit during the Rome raid. The reports were correct but even at that the bombardiers did a remarkable job.

The raid was rehearsed for weeks and special crews picked for the job and hitting only one non-military target is amazing. The British press scream when a church or school is hit and I'm not being at all unpatriotic in saying they're all wet. I've talked with bomber crews about it and I have never heard one, either RAF or USAAF, say they could tell a church and school from any other building at a bombing altitude, or even at low level going at high speed. The targets are designated by areas, and if a church or school happens to be in the area it's just a case of bad luck. Still, there is evidence to the contrary in London. Churches have been demolished in places where other buildings were comparatively untouched. In many cases, though, buildings have been repaired whereas churches have not and that makes them stand out so much.

[Billee to Charles] August 10, 1943—Matawan

I just finished talking to Mom. We're still awaiting word of Warren's furlough. She says I'm to come for a weekend. She gave me h— about my part-time job [Billee was working Saturdays waiting tables at the Buttonwood Manor in Matawan], I should come home, etc., but I'm not going home. I'm staying right here on the Jersey Shore 'til Hitler shows that white flag. We'll have to wait and see what Churchill and Roosevelt cook up in this "pow-wow" [the Quebec conference, August 14–24, 1943, during which FDR, Stalin and Churchill decided on the D-Day invasion strategy].

I'm an airplane spotter. Agnes and I, every other Thursday, report to our post from ten 'til two p.m. The first time will be next Thursday. Between now and then we have to learn the types of planes by sound so we can report them correctly.

/////

[Charles to Billee] August 12, 1943—London

Bombers going out over the Channel again tonight. Lots of them. Thank heavens they are ours. I happened to be "on the spot" last night when Jerry took a crack at what the papers first called "a south Anglian town."

These raids aren't like the hit and run London affairs. They mean it in Plymouth, which has more property destroyed than in use, I'm sure. I got back to town about two hours ago after a few days in "south Anglia," principally Newquay and Plymouth.

I'll have to tell Rooney you caught the broadcast. Yes, maybe one of these Sundays you will get a break and I'll be on one, but don't hold your breath. Andy's done a couple of stories for the weekly magazine supplement he mentioned. I've been too damn busy getting local stuff to turn in anything for that.

/////

[Billee to Charles] August 12, 1943—Matawan

Follow up on the *Memphis Belle* in today's paper. He is to wed a girl from Texas now. I mean that Capt. Robert Morgan. He didn't waste much time after the Memphis belle broke the engagement. [The *Memphis Belle* was one of the first B17 bombers to complete 25 missions with her crew intact. The plane and crew were sent back to tour the United States; two movies have been made about this story. The plane was named for Morgan's Tennessee fiancé, who wound up marrying someone else.]

Did I tell you about the young commando that is back? He went over about the same time you did. I think in the same convoy. He's only 21 or 22. He was in the Dieppe raid. [Even though the Dieppe raid in August of 1942 was a British and Australian effort, a handful of American Rangers also participated.] It was there that I think he was wounded. He was sent to Massachusetts for a while and then home. He has a savings account in our bank and he came in soon after he was home to draw some money. He had such a funny look about him. My heart ached for him. Since then, he has been married and is working in an air-craft factory. He came in today to change his account to a joint one and he is so changed. That look is gone and he seems more natural. The war is over for him.

Did I tell you my vacation time has been definitely settled? Two weeks beginning October fourth. I'll spend a good part of it with you, in Asheville.

PS: the papers are filled with post-war plans.

[Charles to Billee] August 16, 1943—London

I started to tell you about the raid I was caught in last week but forgot to finish it in my last letter.

The papers said it was Plymouth so I can identify the city. It's on the south coast where fighter-bombers can get in and out without much trouble. They hung around for an hour while I and a dozen others took refuge in a basement under a huge oak table.

Brig. Gen. Osborn, head of Special Services in Washington is here on tour and had an informal conference with about 20 *Stars and Stripes* men this a.m. He's our big boss and evidently a good one. Congratulated us on putting out Army publications in any theater and he didn't make it sound like soft soap.

[Billee to Charles] August 17, 1943—Matawan

I started typing a V-letter tonight but the typewriter is acting up so you'll have to put up with the next best thing. I'm wondering if one of these days I'll be getting a letter like one Warren sent me. "For heaven's sakes," he says. "Can't you write a little plainer? All the words look alike." I won a prize once when I was in the sixth grade for penmanship. Today I'd probably get the consolation prize. . . .

According to the paper, sudden activity along the southern coast of England gives the impression that we might be approaching that long-awaited eve of invasion. They are evacuating civilians from those coastal towns. Rickenbacker's [Eddie Rickenbacker, WWI American fighter ace and co-founder of Eastern Airlines, had just returned from a fact-finding mission to Russia] report in tonight's paper says that unless a miracle happens, Germany can hold out another year.

Don't look now, but I think we're going to have a blackout. Just heard a siren. . . . Guess the siren must have been a false alarm. Blackouts usually last an hour and by that time, I could have my letter written.

Tomorrow night, or rather Thursday, we go plane spotting from ten 'til two.

/////

[Charles to Billee] August 21, 1943—London

Benny and I took a stroll along the Thames embankment this afternoon on our day off. But I left him to come home and read, and write, and miss you.

You mentioned Russ Jones being on the radio. Yes, he made a recording at the same time as Andy Rooney. He went to Africa in December with Ralph Martin and the rest. He came back when trouble started between the London and Algiers editions. I never did tell you about that, did I? Briefly, a Lt. Col. who went down to take over as CO of the detachment wouldn't give the fellows a free hand in putting the paper out. Relations between the men and CO became strained and we brought back all who wanted to come. Only Ralph stayed. While the paper is doing a swell job down there it doesn't compare with ours, mainly because we have far more experienced men up here and the brass doesn't interfere.

Tying together a lot of loose ends surrounding activity by the Air Force and ground force over here. I can foresee a lot of action from here in about two months. So far, more of it has originated from N. Africa and the Middle East, but I'm sure our turn isn't far off.

I'd like to tell you more, but can't. Most of the Air Force sorties have been to enemy airfields lately, especially those in the coastal areas. That always has been part of pre-invasion plans. Furthermore, Germany is reported to have rushed 40,000 to 50,000 troops to Denmark [to put down civil unrest in that occupied country]. It might well be that a strike from the west will be coordinated with the usual Russian winter offensive in the war.

/////

[Billee to Charles] August 23, 1943—Matawan

I was reading about the illustrious Major Morgan of the *Memphis Belle* in yesterday's *Sunday News*. His name and face have been familiar to me and still, I couldn't place him in Asheville. Now I know . . . his father owns the Morgan Manufacturing Company at Black Mt. They are pretty wealthy, but they really aren't from Asheville. I'm sure the home is in Black Mt. It was a furniture factory before the war but now it's defense. He must be quite a guy . . . 24 and married and divorced three times.

We got Agnes off to Sea Island, Georgia, on Saturday. We all had a hand in packing her off. I never thought she'd make the train. She got word from the Red Cross that she could send Jack a package on the *Gripsholm* so now the sailing date has been advanced and Marge and I have to get it together for her this week . . . has to be in New York by Friday. According to the address they gave her, he is interned in the Philippines. [The *Gripsholm* was used by the US Department of State during WWII to repatriate and exchange Axis and Allied civilians, as well as to carry mail and packages to military prisoners of war.]

Had a letter from my brother Saturday. Twenty-seven days after he graduated from radio school, he's still in the same place doing fatigue duty (whatever that is) awaiting a furlough and shipping orders. Is he disgusted!

I didn't tell you about our airplane spotting . . . did I? It was exciting. An observation post out in the country with the sky for a roof. The stars were so bright and so numerous that we had a time distinguishing planes from the stars. One in particular we saw a long time before we heard it and it was so low . . . just missing the trees that I almost reported the damn thing as a glider. We didn't hear it until it was over our heads. We drank coffee … seems like gallons of it, to keep warm and ate tomato sandwiches to help pass the time away. Next Thursday I'll know better and wear my woolen slacks and a sweater besides the coat.

[Billee to Charles] August 27, 1943—Matawan

I had a note from Warren. He will be in Massillon the 30th, so I guess I will spend Labor Day weekend in Massillon. It will be swell being with them all again, if only for a few days. As a good citizen, I should stay at home but heaven only knows when I'll have another opportunity to see him.

[Charles to Billee] August 30, 1943—London

Tell me more about your plane spotting.

You said you had to learn to tell a plane by sound. Who is responsible for those instructions? I want to meet the person who can do that, even after years and years of actual work on planes. It takes tedious study to even tell one from another in pictures let alone identify them in the air, and they want it done by sound!

By tomorrow or the next day I'll know whether or not I go away for a while for an aerial gunnery course. Don't get excited. It's just that we feel there should be more than one in the office with the training. Bud Hutton plans to go and is checking to see if the Air Force will take two of our men. If so, it will be me.

[FROM THE *STARS AND STRIPES*, August 27, 1943]

ACK-ACK GUNNERS TRAINED HERE
AIR FORCE SCHOOL RUN BY MAJOR
WHO WAS "TOO OLD TO FIGHT"

by Charles F. Kiley, *Stars and Stripes* **Staff Writer**

US ANTI-AIRCRAFT SCHOOL, England, Aug. 26—A 58-year-old major who thumbed his way across the Atlantic with the Air Force, after the Field Artillery told him he was too old to fight, will probably go through the second war without firing a shot at the enemy.

But he's doing the next best thing: teaching others how to shoot, and in the last nine months has trained thousands of soldiers to defend US installations in the ETO against attacks by enemy aircraft.

The major—lean, leathery Walter S. Jones, of Milwaukee, Wis.—is boss of this anti-aircraft school, the only one of its kind operated by US forces in this theater. He gets clerks, mechanics, riflemen, engineers, and artillerymen for courses and sends them back to their units equipped to drop pencils, tools, rifles and shovels, and get behind ring-railed, water-cooled .50 caliber machine-guns—and use them.

Primarily an instruction center for Air Force personnel who have to defend their own USAAF stations, the school also trains men from every branch of service, the theory being that a bomb would just as leave come to rest in the Infantry's back yard as it would on an Air Force station.

Made up of three phases, the course includes aircraft recognition, mechanical function of a water-cooled .50 and practical range work against sleeve targets towed by RAF monoplanes. That's making a long story short because the schedule lists such detailed training as safety precautions, manipulation of gun and mount, gun pointing and tracking, individual tracer control, dispersion and hit expectancy, calculation of leads, assembly and disassembly, mounting and dismounting, stoppages and immediate repairs.

In other words, if you don't know all there is to know about a water-cooled .50 when you leave this school—you should.

Looking around for a man to do the job, officials pinned it on Maj. Jones, who had a reputation of getting things done. The reputation resulted from an incident that took place while the major commanded an Air Force unit of ground personnel. A guard, who accidentally fired a round, caused Maj. Jones to conduct a one-man investigation of his unit's weapons training. In less time than it takes for him to tell about it, he had every man in his command on a British range for long hours of rifle firing.

Head of the aircraft recognition department is a rotund sergeant whose chief interest for the last 14 years has been telling one plane from another and who has done nothing else during his 17 months in the army but teach aircraft recognition.

Jim Handy, the 35-year-old expert from Denver, Colo., was on the payroll of Lockheed Aircraft for 12 years as a camouflage instructor and for 14 years has made a hobby of aircraft recognition. If anybody can teach novices the difference between a FW190 and a P47 or a Me109E from a P51, it's Jim Handy. His identification course here covers 57 types of US, British and German aircraft—all that the Air Force permits him to cover in this theater.

No. 1 aide to artilleryman Maj. Jones at this Air Force school is an infantry officer, Capt. Leonard E. Pauley, of Lake Charles, La., which exemplifies cooperation between the branches of the service.

Capt. Pauley, who says he didn't get his second bar because he married his CO's daughter, supervises "dry run" training with a secretive device instituted by the British in their AA training, besides joining the staff for other instruction.

All the preliminary training leads up to the practical range work, covering a minimum of eight days, six hours a day.

No chair-borne commander, the major is on the firing line every day with his men, barking fire orders and frequently getting behind a gun to show them how it's done.

It isn't hard for the 58-year-old major to remember the comical look he had on his face and the feeling that somebody kicked him six inches below the belt when they passed on that "too old to fight" sentence. But he feels a little better about it now that he can tell his daughter, a captain in the WAC, and his two boys, both second looeys, he's doing a helluva sight more in this war than he did in the last one as an OCS instructor back home.

/////

[Billee to Charles] August 31, 1943—Matawan

You never mentioned the strained relations in the N. African office. That's too bad because I imagine the fellows down there really look forward to the paper. Seems a shame there couldn't be cooperation. They should have sent a new CO there to take over. I was wondering if Ralph Martin was still there.

I almost forgot to tell you I'm leaving Thursday night for Massillon. Mom left Asheville Sunday and arrived about the same time Warren did. Warren is being shipped to the West Coast so heaven only knows when we'll see him again.

/////

[Charles to Billee] Early September 1943—London
[DATE TORN OFF LETTER]

Ben's wife sent him a dozen snaps of herself in various attire, a couple of them real "cheesecake."

While I'm writing this, you are probably on your way to Massillon to visit Warren. Tomorrow is Labor Day but merely another working day in the Army.

For the first time in years and years, I hear a ukulele playing. Must be one of the Associated Press fellows in the apartment. He's playing "Sweet Sue" and I'm sure there isn't an Englishman with that much jive in him.

Remember I told you about the gunnery school? It still isn't settled but I may have final word on it tomorrow.

The RAF just went out, taking 50 minutes to fly over London. Just a constant roar overhead. Once in a while, a squadron leader flicks his signal lights on and off, but otherwise nothing can be seen. While you are plane spotting, think how long it takes for a few planes to pass overhead and you'll have an idea what this is.

[Billee to Charles] September 6, 1943—Jersey City

It was good to be with the family again. We had a regular reunion. Mom arrived last Monday and Warren came in Tuesday night. I got there Friday morning. Warren has gained weight and looks so fit, quite dashing in fact. He's a gunner and second radioman on a bomber, a B25 I think. He likes it very much and thinks he'll stay in after the war. This really wasn't a furlough, instead a delay between orders. He goes to Salt Lake City to receive his orders. He had all his equipment with him, flying suit and even his parachute.

Little Billy, the one who had infantile paralysis, is remarkably well. He doesn't walk but he crawls quite a bit. Funny, he's only three and a half and it's been nearly a year since he was stricken, but he can remember when he walked. He gets braces this week and a pair of crutches.

Warren is to take three months combat training and then he expects to be shipped out. When that time comes, I promised him I'd go home and stay with Mom.

[Billee to Charles] September 8, 1943—Matawan

The most important news today is the surrender of Italy. I heard it at twelve-thirty. Everyone was jubilant. Guess they had quite a demonstration in New York. That's one down and two to go.

We have a hint that my cousin Fred may still be alive and a Japanese prisoner. They have found a Marine that was with him after the date he was reported killed and he saw him captured by some Japs with eight others; another Marine from Fred's home, who is still in the islands, has checked and there is no grave for Fred. I have never given up hope. [The family learned later that he had been killed in 1942.]

Agnes received two cards from Jack, one Saturday and one yesterday, the first word directly from him. They are form cards but with his signature and she said that it is definitely his. She gave a talk this morning on the War Bond Drive for Public Service in Newark. Her husband had a very good job there for a number of years. One of the girls brought her radio in and we heard it this morning.

Our plane spotting was neglected last week because of my trip to Ohio. We had to get someone to take our places. About telling the type of plane, we tell from the sound if they are one, two or four-engine planes. That you can tell from the sound, especially out there because all you hear are the planes. With gas rationing and the OPA [Office of Price Administration, which managed the rationing program] you don't hear many cars.

I called El today since we are getting together on your Xmas box. She had bad news, poor kid. Tom called her Tuesday and said he was on his way out to an embarkation point. Said he had been issued clothes, etc.

/////

[Charles to Billee] September 11, 1943—London

It's too early to tell much about the Italy affair. Germany will naturally fight a delaying action and hold the country as long as possible. It is probably in control in the northern area and grasping what it can in the center. Yesterday it was rather well established that Rome was in German hands, and that means more bombing.

The tempo in the office was up 100 percent this week with the capitulation of Italy, the American landings, etc., and I worked until at least 11 o'clock and sometimes 12 every night. It was natural for me to sleep late today, take in a movie and come home to relax. Not that I ever do more on my day off.

In conjunction with the recent shakeup in the office, Hutton and Moora transferring to different posts on the staff with Benny and Len Giblin (a new name to you) taking the desk jobs as news and city editors, things have been a little confusing.

Ordinarily, I'd be in and out of town but with routine a bit disorganized for the present I stayed in all week to help take the strain off new men, and doing the lead story on Italy since the capitulation, handling Russia, the Pacific and Balkan unrest at times. And when the paper went to bed last night, I sighed with relief at the prospect of a holiday today.

That moon is going to waste, darling. Benny is homesick for Jane tonight, too, so you can easily picture what a happy household we have. All we need is a body and we'd have a funeral.

//////

[FROM THE *STARS AND STRIPES*, September 9, 1943]

ITALY SURRENDERS
EISENHOWER ANNOUNCES ALL ITALIAN ARMED FORCES GIVE UP UNCONDITIONALLY

[No byline]

At 5:30 p.m. Gen. Eisenhower announced that a military armistice had been signed "by my representative and the representative of Marshal Badoglio and it becomes effective this instant. Hostilities between the armed forces of the United Nations and those of Italy terminate at once."

Eisenhower's statement asserted the terms of the armistice he had granted as Allied commander-in-chief in the Mediterranean had been approved by the governments of Britain, Russia and the United States . . .

The Allied blitz was kept up until the very end. British troops made new landings at the Gulf of Eufemia, while other Eighth Army forces chased Nazi rearguards up the Italian "boot." And in the air Flying Fortresses blasted Foggia airdrome anew, while medium bombers hammered away at roads and bridges.

On the Calabrian peninsula British and Canadian forces were slowly advancing practically unopposed. A six-mile advance along the west coast from Palmi, and an advance 12 miles inland by another column, were reported by Algiers radio.

Contact with Axis troops was also reported by Algiers radio, which said that an enemy rearguard had been encountered by our troops advancing from Palmi, but opposition seems to have been only very slight.

The main body of the enemy was still well ahead of the last town occupied by Allied forces, and civilians reported that the Germans had moved out two or three days before the Canadians arrived.

Almost everywhere the Allied troops are treated as liberators rather than as conquerors, and the welcome the British troops are getting becomes warmer the further they advance.

Details of the terms of the armistice have not been announced but Gen. Eisenhower said in his radio announcement from Allied Force Headquarters in North Africa that "the Italian government has bound itself to abide by these terms without reservation."

The story of the negotiations leading up to the surrender was revealed by Algiers radio.

Some weeks ago the Italian government approached the British and American governments with a view to concluding an armistice. At a meeting in neutral territory the Italian representatives were told that they must surrender unconditionally and on this understanding the Allied representatives were empowered to communicate to them the military conditions they would have to fulfill.

Another meeting was arranged, this time in Sicily. Finally, on Sept. 3, the armistice agreement was signed at Allied HQ, Sicily.

In spite of the fact that the Italians had thus surrendered, the possibility of the Germans preventing the surrender from becoming known among the Italians had to be taken into consideration.

To meet this eventuality it was agreed that one of the senior Italian representatives remain in Sicily. Another precaution was to have Marshal Badoglio send a copy of the proclamation he would make to the Italian people to Sicily, in case the Germans prevented its being broadcast.

The Germans, however, did not prevent its being broadcast, for Rome radio tonight broadcast the proclamation, which Italians heard in Badoglio's own voice.

Obviously, the Germans will not leave whatever part of Italy they now virtually occupy without a fight . . .

/////

[Billee to Charles] September 13, 1943—Matawan

I called El today and Tom was home over the weekend. She's already had a card from Uncle Sam changing his address to a New York APO. Tom is in Massachusetts now but has been issued heavy clothing suitable for either Iceland or Greenland.

Do you realize that actually we weren't together but five weekends? You can't even call it ten days because we only had a part of those days together. I've often wondered, did you think after awhile I'd get tired of writing and we'd just drift apart? I imagine other people did even if you didn't.

I almost forgot to tell you about my dream. I could see a plane and knew you were in it, and they told me it exploded in the air and that all aboard were gone. I was crying and the next thing I knew you were there holding me, and that it was all a mistake. I could see you and feel your arms around me. Then, I was seeing you off at a station somewhere and the train was made up of flat cars carrying troops and the last I saw of you going down the tracks with the rest was your handkerchief waving to me.

[Charles to Billee] September 16, 1943— "Somewhere in England"

I'm writing this from an Eighth Air Force base where I've been taking the aerial gunnery course. That was the trip I mentioned in my last letter. This is my fifth day and I took the last of my exams this evening. Since Sunday, I've been going from 8 a.m. until 9 p.m. plus a couple of hours each night for study. I didn't want to say anything in my last letter until the course was over.

I received my grades an hour ago: 82 in aircraft recognition, 96 each in sighting, operation and emergency repair of the caliber .50 machine gun, 92 in first-aid. The course also included skeet shooting plus lectures on security, use of oxygen at high altitude, ditching, etc.

Don't worry. If and when I go on a mission you will know about it. As in the case of expectant fathers, the Fortresses haven't lost a correspondent yet. Sorry. They did lose one, but it was an exception.

Tomorrow we are making a proactive flight in a Fort for target practice and to get familiar with the use of oxygen at 30,000 feet. Our pilot, co-pilot and navigator are all 25-mission men. Incidentally, I've earned "wings," too. I'm entitled to wear them, but I won't. Like the rest of the correspondents, I feel only the real combat men should wear them.

So much for gunnery, and please don't worry because there isn't anything to worry about. I'm just telling you all this because we don't hide anything from each other.

Somehow, the night reminds me of the surprise I mentioned a few letters ago. I'll go a little further and tell you you'll have to wait until Christmas. It's the best Christmas present I can think of.

[Billee to Charles] September 18, 1943—Matawan

Thursday night we went airplane spotting. An awful night with ceiling zero so there wasn't much traffic. It would clear and then cloud up and rain a while. Part of the time we spent outside until we were a little on the wet side and then we went inside. I couldn't help but think of you doing guard duty in the rain that week I was in New York.

Sitting out the other night on duty, with the sky for our roof brought you so much closer. I like doing that. Gives me a lot of satisfaction. The fellow that relieved us laughed when we picked up our weapon to go home. It's a wicked-looking thing, one of Mr. Heuser's garden tools [Marguerite's father]. We've not had the occasion to use it but it's nice to have around, just in case. Heaven help whoever's on the receiving end of it!

[Billee to Charles] September 20, 1943—Matawan

Finally, word from my brother. He is still at Salt Lake City and expects to be there for another two weeks; then, he will be assigned to a bomber crew as second-radio man on a B17 or B24. He has grown up so for his nineteen years, I can hardly believe he's my kid brother.

You should see all the girls with these handbags made in Africa. They must be doing quite a business down there with our boys. Our telephone operator has had one for several months that her boyfriend sent. He's in Sicily now, I believe. The bags run around five or ten dollars, I believe all handmade and all leather inside and out.

[Billee to Charles] September 22, 1943—Matawan (V-mail)

I called El today and Tom was home again over the weekend but rather suspected it would be his last. Eddie was home, too, so it was like old home week. I'm going in next week one day. El is going to get me a ham to take home with me on my vacation [to Asheville]. You'd die if you could see what I have to take with me. Ed, Marguerite's brother, is trying to find me a pint to take home. Mom can't get it down there except from a bootlegger and she doesn't like to be without it in the house so I'm going to have to get that, and besides, I want to put some in your fruitcake. The ham is for her, too. Seems like it's hard to find ham down there, more than here for some reason or other. Can't you see me boarding the streamliner with a pint under one arm and a ham under the other? It won't be quite that bad. The ham I'm going to send ahead by fast express but the pint is going to be where I can keep an eye on it.

[Billee to Charles] September 24, 1943—Matawan (V-mail)

Speaking of Ben's wife sending shots of her in "various attire and some were cheesecake . . ." since I'm not familiar with the expression, you'll have to explain. Then I'll see whether or not I can send you any "cheesecake shots."

We go spotting again next week. It's every two weeks, but it sure rolls around quick. This month has flown by. Hope my two weeks' vacation slows it down a bit. I'm leaving next Saturday on the one-thirty train from Newark. I couldn't get reservations on the streamliner going down or coming back so I'll go "sit-up" in the coach train.

Billee—September 1943. (Kiley Family)

[Charles to Billee] September 27, 1943—London

I don't know how many of my letters, especially the recent ones, have been based on a sympathetic theme, the sympathy being rather personal. Whenever

I begin to write, the first thought in my mind borders on something akin to the whole world being against me, and us.

I suppose I should be trying to make you smile, instead of looking across the ocean at you with sad eyes. Your picture came today, and I wouldn't be at all surprised if that started me off.

There ought to be a law against pictures like that; either that, or a law against Billee Ruth Grays. You are so alive in that picture I can almost hear you talk, and that isn't good for people in my condition. I told Ben if the war isn't over pretty quick, there will be a one-man rampage around the globe.

I'm working on a story of a 25-mission man, a gunner whom I brought home with me for the weekend. Somehow, Ben wangled a chicken somewhere, and actually cooked it for us.

So, Warren flies in a B-25. That's a "Mitchell," named after the late Gen. Billy Mitchell, and the plane used for the Tokyo raid. It's a twin-engine medium bomber. They don't use them over here, or haven't so far. The B-26s, "Marauders," have done the bombing by mediums.

Jim King, a fellow I know with Associated Press here, did a piece on the *Stars and Stripes* last week and sent it back. He was in for a visit with Ben and me Saturday night. Like some of the other civilian correspondents, he either stops in the office or home to pick up leads for stories they can't get from troops the way we can, or to get soldiers' reactions to things.

[Billee to Charles] September 27, 1943—Matawan

I had a long letter from Mom today. She said the President of the Wachovia Bank contacted one of the girls I used to work with to find out where I was and if she thought I'd be interested in a job there. I'm afraid to go back for fear I'll be shanghaied. Ivey's called Mom and wanted to know if I'd come home to stay— that they certainly needed me—that they'd pay anything I asked. As I told you before, the only time I'll go back is if Warren is sent out of the country. I can't get the picture of my aunt, the one whose son was reported killed at Guadalcanal, out of my mind. The last time I saw her she hardly knew me, and my sister told me when I was home that she is worse.

We all think that it's time you had a leave—a 30-day leave. It would be awfully hard to see you go back again, but I think seeing you for five minutes would be worth it all.

/////

[Billee to Charles] September 30, 1943—Matawan

It's really a terror out. We're at the observation tower, or trailer I should say and I wouldn't be surprised to see the top go right off. If there are any planes out tonight, somebody is crazy.

We have a pot-bellied stove in here that's really throwing the heat. I'll have to shed a sweater or two. So far, we haven't had to go outside.

It has started to rain now, to make it an even more pleasant evening.

We just had a visitor, the first since we've been "spotting." We heard a knock on the screen door. I parked by the telephone with our "weapon," a really wicked-looking thing—one of the farm implements—behind my back. He just wanted to know where a certain highway was, so that's all there was to that.

Tom called El yesterday and obviously the line was open and someone was listening. All he said was that he wouldn't see her for a while.

I see we have a new censor; is he as nice as Bob Moora, or is he the nosey type?

/////

[Charles to Billee] October 3, 1943—Fortress Bomber Base, England

I've been here for a week now, with the exception of yesterday, "sweating" out my first mission.

Here's the story:

Bud Hutton, Andy Rooney and I are flying from the same field on the same mission; the first time a stunt like that has been pulled. That is, having three men cover one mission first hand. We came here a week ago, were grounded by bad weather and then ducked into London yesterday, after it appeared as though we would be inactive for another day. While we were gone, they did go out, and raided the naval base at Emden in Germany. So, we hot-footed it back again today.

The *Stars and Stripes* bomber, with the drawing on the nose by Dick Wingert—England, October 1943. (US Army/The *Stars and Stripes*)

In one letter, you said you hadn't heard from me in two weeks. By now, you know it was because I was too hasty in sending mail to Asheville. I should have waited a bit longer.

There was also the paragraph about the bad dream you had, the mistaken news that I got tangled up in a bomber accident. If this is going to affect you like that, I'm going to call the whole thing off and stay on the ground.

I was up on two practice flights last week while we were waiting for the real thing. The crew I'm with is swell. The pilot, Lt. McIlveen, is quite capable and the gunners, well, you can tell they know their stuff by just talking to them. The ship I'm flying in is called *The Stars and Stripes*, named for the paper and making its maiden flight after we christen it tomorrow. One of our artists, Dick Wingert, is here to paint the name and the characters on the nose of the ship. Bud is flying with the *Lady Susie II*, piloted by Lt. Sam Dickson, son of the ex-governor of Alabama. Andy is going with the *Mission Belle*, but if we go tomorrow, he'll go in another ship. The *Mission Belle* crew is due for a leave starting tomorrow.

I haven't done much writing in the past week or so, waiting for this trip to come off. However, I am working on a story built around a kid who has completed 25 missions. He was one of the boys who sat in on Benny's chicken dinner feast. It is to run this week and I haven't even started getting it in shape. I started to work on it tonight but I was thinking of you so much I just had to get this off.

I just looked in my pocket to make sure I had a few things with me. They include the four-leaf clover you gave me so long ago and the picture of you in the leather case. They go with me wherever we go.

/////

[FROM THE *STARS AND STRIPES*, October 2, 1943]

"25-MISSION" MAN

Twenty-five mission men are not rare in the Eighth Air Force, but without exception each one who has sweated out and completed 25 trips to and from enemy territory has a rare story. Some have been told in part. Some are more colorful than others. This is the story of Thomas Joseph McGrath, Flying Fortress waist gunner, who had more than an average share of thrills, flak and Focke-Wulfs from the morning he took off on his first mission to Romilly-sur-Seine until the afternoon eight months later when he came back from the Ruhr on his 25th. Although he has been decorated with the DSC, DFC, Purple Heart and Air Medal with three Oak Leaf Clusters, he doesn't consider himself a hero. But then, most 25-mission men don't.

by Charles F. Kiley, *Stars and Stripes* Staff Writer

If you read the newspapers you remember the "Unmentionable Ten," the Fortress that came back from Lorient on less than a wing and a prayer with two gunners severely wounded, three crewmen sharing two oxygen lines, an injured navigator on the floor charting a course home from landmarks called off by the bombardier and the ship riddled with more flak and 20mm fragments than Boeing thought a B17 could carry in her frame.

That was Tom McGrath's ship and his 23rd mission. The 23-year-old waist gunner had rough trips before—St. Nazaire's "flak city," Brest, Bremen, Wilhelmshaven—but not like that one. He was bowled over twice by cannon fire and flak, and when they carried him off the ship flight surgeons weren't certain it wasn't his last trip anywhere except to wherever dead waist gunners gather for that last briefing.

They had Mac on the operating table for three hours, picking shrapnel from two ugly wounds in his right arm and in a gaping hole in his side. Despite the almost fatal injuries, he had twice crawled back to his gun and kept firing until the last Nazi fighter was out of sight.

Mac doesn't think he did so much and the blond, curly-haired Irishman doesn't talk about it. But the Air Force said he was largely responsible for the deflection of enemy attacks and for the subsequent safe return of the aircraft and crew. He was awarded the Distinguished Service Cross, America's second highest decoration for valor.

A typical combat crewman, Mac doesn't regard his action as extraordinary because he remembers the men who lived with him in the same hut, those with whom he played cards and joked about the second thing they were going to do when they got home, the familiar faces he knew from the crowded briefing room.

He remembers the days when they didn't come back.

Like most combat crewmen, Mac was cocky on his first mission. Hell, nothing could happen to him. He had a good pilot in "Big" Adams, didn't he, and a good crew? Besides, he could take care of himself. FW190s and Me109s weren't so hot. What was all this about flak anyway?

Like most combat crewmen, Mac also learned the hard way—that German flak was all they said it was and Nazi fighters had good ships and knew how to fly them. After his first three missions to Romilly-sur-Seine, the heavily protected sub pens of Lorient and Brest and the Wilhelmshaven naval base, Thomas Joseph McGrath was a man separated from the boys.

It was on the way back from St. Nazaire that Mac first saw a Fortress queen die and to him she didn't look like she was dying proudly.

"It was one of the toughest missions we had," he says. "Over the target the sky was pocked with flak as far as I could see. Fighters were all over the clock. Shortly after we headed home, a ship from another group came down from above to fly on our right wing. Its No. 3 engine was burning and the wing wrapped in flames. It went along like that for five minutes before anybody jumped. Then one man bailed out. Two others followed him but they were too late. The wing came apart and their chutes were caught in the wreckage. They didn't have a chance. It was the first time I'd seen a ship crack up and I'll never forget it. My stomach turned over, made me sick."

Mac never paid much attention to his parachute until then. Some gunners don't bother to keep them handy. They have to see somebody lose his life before they realize what it means, he says. Mac remembers the day he saw a man bail out and drop right through his harness because a buckle wasn't hooked. It wasn't a nice sight . . . someone frantically grasping at air to pull himself up. Another telegram to be sent by the Adjutant General.

When you have done 25 missions it isn't easy to remember everything, but Mac hasn't forgotten the second time he went to Wilhelmshaven. After leaving the target a piece of flak cut the oxygen lines and electrical wires behind the pilot. The oxygen ignited and burst into flames. The navigator and bombardier bailed out, thinking the ship was doomed. Then the pilot started to pass out from lack of oxygen and the co-pilot, Lt. Henry McMurry, had to take over with the controls shot out. They used to kid McMurry about his piloting, but he brought the crippled Fort home.

Mac had another close call in a subsequent mission when somebody called fighters at 12 o'clock. He stuck his head through the waist window and a 20mm. shell exploded over his head, driving him to the opposite side of the plane. He got back to his gun just as a FW barrel-rolled through the formation and zipped past him. Another 20mm. hit his gun-mount, narrowly missing him.

The first time the Forts hit Bremen on Apr. 17 they lost 16 but brought down 62 fighters. Mac saw one B17 group below him, and to the left, disregard a wall of flak and fly right through it to make their bomb run. Says he, "It's a wonder any of them got through. I'll bet there were a lot of gunners on those ships who wished they joined the Infantry . . ."

Mac was grounded for three months after he was shot up on his 23rd mission. But he had it in him to go on two of the toughest jobs in which the Eighth Air Force took part when he was back on combat status. They were the raids on the Nazi rubber factory at Hanover and the synthetic oil plants at Gelsenkirchen, Wesseling and Bonn in the Ruhr. The black tape on the briefing board stretched long to those targets.

He's a 25-mission man and the Air Force says he's a hero.

Says Mac, "All I'm interested in is my wife and the honeymoon that's waiting, together with a chance to get a job after the war."

[Billee to Charles] October 5, 1943—Asheville

It's good to be home, to look up and see my mountains, to see Grove Park Inn and remember "our moment" there.

Mom has five permanent-party air flight boys with her, besides three nice girls in the apartment that work for the Postal Agency. She also has the cottage rented to two business girls. Thank heaven she isn't serving any meals.

One of the boys here was at New Caledonia [in Melanesia; it was the Pacific headquarters for the US Army and Navy in 1942]. He had the misfortune to contract jungle fever so he was sent home in August. From his conversation, it must have been pretty awful down there. He doesn't like to talk about it. One of the other fellows has been here several months. He's been in the service for three years with a year and some months spent in Greenland and then back here for thirty days, and then again to the arctic region in Canada. The cold finally got him down and he was transferred to the States.

The hospitals around here are filled. You see quite a few of the convalescents on the street, some with crutches. They have five hundred air flight boys that go to school in the City Hall besides all the postal employees, so that brings a lot of extra residents here.

We had a letter from Warren yesterday. He was due to be sent from Salt Lake City to his new post within the next few days.

/////

(l–r) Bud Hutton, Charles, Andy Rooney, before the bombing run to Frankfurt—England, October 1943. (US Army/The *Stars and Stripes*)

[Charles to Billee] October 5, 1943—London

Your wandering boy is back, safe and sound. I've just returned from the bomber base, and in keeping with my promise, I'm getting this off without delay.

I heard the Associated Press sent back a story on the raid, how the *Stars and Stripes* covered it, etc., so you may even know by now that everything turned out all right.

It was quite an experience. I don't believe we could have handpicked a tougher mission. The target was Frankfurt, about 600 miles from Britain and 100 miles inside Germany. It was one of the deepest penetrations made by Fortresses, roughly a 1,200 to 1,300 mile flight.

I waited a week before weather permitted a mission.

We were awakened yesterday morning at 2 a.m., had a quick breakfast and gathered with our crews to be briefed. The target was said to be a tough one. Ground defenses should be fairly strong and fighter opposition could be expected. It was to be a seven-hour flight, five of them on oxygen. You see, above 10,000 feet you have to have oxygen and we were at 25,000 most of the time.

We took off at 7:30, gradually forming with other formations until the sky seemed to be filled with Fortresses. When we crossed the Channel and went over Belgium, I had my first look at continental Europe. When we reached Germany, the ground defenses opened up on us and there were a couple of fighter attacks just before we reached the target. On the homeward flight, it was a little rougher, but not bad.

Inasmuch as our ship was in a lead element, we didn't have it so bad. The fighters concentrate on the rear groups, usually. Six Focke-Wulfs made a pass at us over Holland but a turret gunner in the ship next to us shot one down and scared the rest away.

It was pretty cold up there, 29.7 below zero, and I was glad to see the English coast again. The oxygen was starting to get me, too. I rode all the way in the nose of the ship with the navigator and bombardier and, while we had a heater up there, it was still rather chilly.

Back on the ground, we discovered we were hit in two places but no serious damage. Other planes weren't so lucky. We lost 15 Forts in all but claimed quite a few fighters and really plastered what used to be Frankfurt. The RAF went back there last night, and guided by the fires we started, finished the job.

So here I am. Nothing to worry about, see?

I was too busy to think about much besides what was going on but while we were between Frankfurt and Holland, I had the craziest idea that you would love to see the pattern of continental Europe from 25,000 feet.

Andy's ship got back without a scratch, but Bud's had to turn back shortly after we took off because of mechanical trouble. Consequently, he was a bit disappointed.

Now, I'll be able to tell our "ball club" about the day Daddy "bombed" Germany.

My story for the *Stars and Stripes* wasn't so good (I'll make excuses now) mainly because I had to dictate it over the phone. By the time the crew was interrogated and I was able to get a long distance call through to London, there were only 20 minutes until our deadline.

However, they did run a 2-column picture of Andy, Bud and I with my story. Andy didn't even have time to do one.

Our chief purpose in making the flights, though, was to get background material for future stories.

Forgive me if this is a bit shaky, but I still have a bit of a headache from using that oxygen and I am so, so tired.

///////

[FROM THE *STARS AND STRIPES*, October 5, 1943]

RAID CHRISTENS B17 "STARS AND STRIPES": STAFF WRITER ALONG FOR BAPTISMAL OF BULLETS, FLAK

by Charles F. Kiley, *Stars and Stripes* Staff Writer

A HEAVY BOMBER STATION, Oct 4—Flak burst over the nose of 1/Lt. Clarence S. McIlveen's Fortress *The Stars and Stripes* to christen the ship today as Eighth Air Force bombers struck deep inside Germany.

One of the first ships over the target, the big B17, named for the US forces' newspaper in the ETO, toted a load of high explosives—and someone to write the story.

Almost as uneventfully as delivering the soldiers' morning newspaper on time, the newly christened Fortress pegged straight to the target, dropped its bombs on a major link in the Reich's system of air defense, and then headed home through flak and fighter opposition.

Flying in the nose of the ship with 1/Lt. Bill Williams, bombardier from Barnsville, Ga., and Navigator 2/Lt. Eugene Shober, of Ottumwa, Ia., I waited for the flak with which Nazi ground defenses shake up invaders, and for the Luftwaffe fighters.

But there was no flak or fighter opposition to hinder outward flight until shortly before we reached the target. Then a few fighters made passes at the Fortress fleet. The absence of fighters and flak gave us a break over the target, but Nazi ground defenses tore at formations behind us.

We made our bomb run, and shortly after starting the homeward flight, our ship was hit in two places by flak. One fragment nicked the left wing near the nose and another fractured the oil line feeding No. 1 engine.

Then, all the way back to the coast, FW190s and Me109s hacked away at the formation in twos, threes and fours. Our gunners didn't claim any enemy fighter by way of celebrating the ship's "christening," but their fire kept the Nazis at long range.

S/Sgt. Eddie Barrett, our tail gunner from New York City, and at 28 the oldest member in the crew, had a crack at a Focke-Wulf which attempted to get through the suicide circle that is a Fortress formation, and watched a gunner from another B17 finish him off. The Nazi pilot bailed out when his plane went into a spin.

Nearing the Dutch coast, a swarm of FWs made the final attack, a formation of six coming in at 11 o'clock. Just as the others, they were driven off.

/////

[Billee to Charles] October 7, 1943—Asheville

Today I helped Mom with the work; then, I walked almost all the way to the Inn. I walked around slowly to the terrace, trying to catch your presence, and I did. I stood on the terrace and looked across the mountains, then I walked a little more, still feeling you so near. I started to go then, but decided to go to the cocktail lounge. Perhaps I'm an incurable romantic, but I sat in our same corner and ordered a champagne cocktail. I whispered a toast to you, with my love; then, I drank another one for you. I sat a little while longer, then made my way to the bus. That's the first time since you left that I've been there, and that's the first cocktail since we had ours together. While I was drinking your cocktail, the radio played "As Time Goes By." Really.

/////

[Charles to Billee] October 7, 1943— London

Isn't it strange how that number "4" came up again? The mission taking place on Oct. 4, I mean. It certainly has been significant in our lives. Do you think there is a possibility of it meaning we will only have four players on our team?

Perhaps it means we will have four boys and four girls. Or, better still, four sets of twins.

When you told me of the dream you had, in which the plane exploded, I came very close to passing the raid up. I couldn't see the justification in it if your reaction was along those lines. Then, I realized you wouldn't be very proud of me if I backed down.

I'm surprised you don't know what "cheesecake" is. You'll make a swell newspaperman's wife.

///////

[Billee to Charles] October 10, 1943—Asheville

I just got in from the canteen dance. I danced quite a bit, more than I have in a long time. My feet hurt now and they are a little bruised from being stepped on. I shagged with a sergeant, a master sergeant. He was amazed that I could, and I had to confess that I was just following him, that I'd never done it before.

Then I met a young intelligence—not officer, but a Pfc. in the Intelligence Division. A nice enough fellow, but did he think he was something. I felt like sticking a pin in him. He was just my age but had a good enough education and should have grown up a little more by now. He danced with me quite a bit, I guess because I was a good listener. I did get a word in now and then, but what an effort!

The Pfc. was just your height and I couldn't help but wish he could trade places with you, if just for one dance.

///////

[Charles to Billee] October 12, 1943—London

We had a pretty good show here the other night. A force of German bombers, said to be only 15 but I believe there were more, got through the outer defenses to London. They caught three of them in the spotlights and fired everything in the book at them. There must have been blind men on the A.A. guns because they didn't hit any of them. There weren't any bombs dropped on the city but they did drop some in the suburbs.

I had a good seat for the hour-and-a-half show on the outskirts of the city. Together with several others, I was driving back after covering the first WAC-soldier wedding over here.

Warren is flying in the heavy bombers, is he? It's a favorable break for him to be shifted from the B25s (Mitchells) to the B17s or 24s (Fortresses and Liberators) because the heavies are much safer ships to fly in, I think. Wonder if he'll come over here.

Billee, I don't have any doubt in my mind that my operational work with the Eighth Air Force is worrying you. I can tell it even before I get your reaction to the raid I went on. So, I'm going to make you a promise. Before I go on another one, I'll wait for a verdict from you. I don't have to go. It's an Air Force rule that no one can make you fly. From our standpoint, it's strictly a voluntary job. And, as Andy Rooney says while thinking of his wife, "There really isn't any justification in it."

[Billee to Charles] October 14, 1943—Asheville

You know, for some reason you're awfully popular. There are four boxes on the way to you, or at least there will be by tomorrow. In Mom's package is your fruitcake and "a Christmas tree." Mom will throw a fit when she discovers a branch from her shrubbery is gone.

I couldn't get the Xmas spirit last year when I fixed your box. They told us we couldn't wrap anything and that spoiled things. Then, I couldn't think of things to send. Now this Xmas is almost here and I was so sure you'd be home by now.

In an article today, they were saying that demobilization of troops would take from four to five years and that married men would be mustered out first.

[Billee to Charles] October 15, 1943—Asheville

My vacation is nearly over. I'll leave Friday or Saturday and spend Sunday at 195. It's been swell.

Mom went to the doctor yesterday and the report wasn't the best. She'll have to take it easy for a while so I guess as soon as I can I'll return home to stay until a certain Sgt. Kiley comes to claim me as Mrs. Charles Kiley.

She hasn't asked me to come home but it's so plain that she needs me. She is already better than when I came home last week. She has too much time alone to worry about Warren. She doesn't eat right either, just having herself to cook for. I think it's best that I come home.

/////

[Charles to Billee] October 17, 1943—London

Now that you are back from vacation, I'm anxiously waiting to hear about two things. The first is your stay with Mother and the second your reaction to my escapade in the Fortress.

While I'm on the subject of Asheville, Miss Gray, your very jealous suitor sincerely hopes his sweetheart didn't look more than once at soldiers while she was in Asheville. Mother said there were quite a few of them there, including those who stayed at "412" [Oak Lodge was located at 412 Merrimon Avenue].

Sure, I have more faith than that in you, but you can't stop me from being jealous. There isn't anyone any worse than Charles Francis when it comes to that.

Your speculation on a promotion for me as a result of the office shakeup is way off. At least, I don't know anything about one. I'm quite happy to be roaming around the country instead of working out of the office. Of course, if they want to add another stripe or ten, I'll take them. But we do have only so many ranks and must abide by them. After all, with my four stripes I'm only 11 promotions removed from a four-star general like Eisenhower.

I'm going away for a week tomorrow. There's a good story, I think, on an "assault training center" and I'm going through the training for a week in order to get material first hand. Can't ever say I don't work for my stories. Perhaps I have a little soldier in me and enjoy getting out in the field with the boys once in awhile.

///

[Billee to Charles] October 17, 1943—Matawan

I arrived in Newark at 6:30 a.m., so I freshened up and decided to go out to Blessed Sacrament. I surprised Father John. That's the first time I've seen him since July. His first words were, "What do you think of the bombing mission?" He proceeded to tell me all about it since I haven't received your letter.

I hardly know how to explain my feelings—dismay, anxiety and relief all at one time. Then I thought, how many more times will it be?

Eddie was home this weekend. He looks well. He's still in Pine Camp.

I have the clipping of your mission. You rated the front page but then, why shouldn't you?

///

[Charles to Billee] October 23, 1943—London

Back from a week with the infantry and its final amphibious assault training. I use the word "final" because I'm certain the next move will be one that counts. I don't know when that move will take place but they are putting the men through training that adds up to one thing, "rehearsal for invasion."

Yes, it's good to be back after a cold and wet week of mud, tents, rugged living, and no mail. While I was away I had an opportunity to ride in the amphibious Jeeps and larger "ducks" for the first time. It felt strange, speeding along a hard, sandy beach then plunging into the sea to continue the trip.

Later, I accompanied a detachment during a practice assault on pill boxes and became a casualty. I had a tumble, skinning the knuckles of my right hand.

Had a letter from Ralph Martin, so I'm able to give you a late report. He's well again, apparently, and anxious to go to Italy. [Martin had contracted malaria while in Africa.] He said he wrote a piece for the *N.Y. Times* Sunday magazine section and got $100 for it. It had to do with junior officers in the field.

Believe me when I say I can't do anything anymore without associating you with it. Ben is like that, too, in regards to Jane. I guess that's why we click, because we have so much in common. When some of the boys go out to let off a little steam, we just find our way home to you.

/////

[FROM THE *STARS AND STRIPES*, November 4, 1943]

OBJECTIVE: HITLER'S WESTERN WALL
YOUNG EXPERT ON GERMAN TACTICS BRIEFS US ASSAULT TROOPS FOR INVASION IN AMPHIBIOUS BATTLE EXERCISES

by Charles F. Kiley, *Stars and Stripes* Staff Writer

Along the continental European coast . . . behind what is probably the strongest and most deliberately fortified first line of defense against invasion in the world . . . the Wehrmacht is waiting.

For three years the heiling warriors of Field Marshal Gerd von Rundstedt have been digging themselves in behind walls of concrete and steel, hundreds of miles of wire, pillboxes, road blocks, mined beaches and fortification . . . ever since Hitler called them back off the docks of France muttering in his beard something equivalent to "damn Spitfires."

The Allied High Command makes no secret of the fact that it will take an "unparalleled attack" to crack that western wall of Festung Europa, and it likewise makes no effort to conceal the fact that its plans are already blueprinted.

Here along a stretch of English coast, topographically similar to many points on the German-held shores of Europe, thousands of American assault troops are preparing for their part in springing the lock on Adolf's front door.

The preparations are intense, and in most phases severe. Every type of weapon and vehicle necessary for a successful stroke is used in the most extensive amphibious exercises undertaken by US forces in Britain, at least, and in all probability anywhere else.

Hand-picked by the War Department for the job of briefing these troops—

no specialized units but ordinary infantry and armored forces designed and trained for assault purposes—is a 37-year-old Nebraskan who knows more than most military masterminds what Pvt. Joe Blow is going to find when he scrambles into the surf from his LCVP and over the beaches where the Wehrmacht is waiting.

Young, able Co. Paul W. Thompson spent several months with units of the German army, as recently as 1939, during service as an assistant military attaché in Berlin. Author of numerous articles on German tactics, chemical engineer and expert on amphibious operations, Col. Thompson carefully planned his invasion technique before adopting it for the Assault Training Center.

The West Point graduate surrounded himself with a staff of capable and experienced officers from every branch of the Army, gathered commissioned instructors skilled in their work, many of whom were battle-trained in war zones. He reproduced enemy fortifications all over this maneuver area. Then Col. Thompson went to work.

The technique employed in assault landings is not for publication. At least not that which is to be employed in the liquidation of the Western Wall when the Allied High Command sets its watch on "H" hour. But the equipment used in the operation will be the best and most improved hurled against the enemy in the war.

The fortified area under attack consists of 11 concrete pillboxes, two of which are reinforced with steel, a number of open emplacements, slit trenches, observation posts and fox holes. Surrounded by bands of tactical double apron wire, ranging from two to six bands in depth, the area is planted with anti-tank and anti-personnel mines, tank traps and other obstacles.

Launching the hedgehog attack are medium bombers of the Air Force Ground Support Command which blast "enemy" positions with HE [high-explosive] bombs. Batteries of 105mm howitzers fire over the heads of advancing troops, M4 tanks and M10 tank destroyers add their supporting fire. Mortars lay on objectives and provide smoke screens. Under cover of the screen, the assault companies, tanks, destroyers, and anti-tank units deploy for the attack.

Nothing stops the drive until it is finished. Injured are treated or removed under fire.

The reaction of the troops to this invasion rehearsal, according to Col.

Thompson, is that it is "tough and exacting," but they are enthusiastic. No chair-borne leader, he gets into fox holes with the men, prods them with questions and gets first-hand reactions.

The training of assault troops here will continue through the winter and beyond, Col. Thompson said. Billeted at present in "tent cities," troops will soon move to Nissen hut areas now under construction.

The Wehrmacht is waiting . . . how much longer it will have to wait is a question causing anxiety not only to the defenders of Festung Europa but to Pvt. Joe Blow who has to go in and dig them out.

///////

[Billee to Charles] October 26, 1943—Matawan

What an experience. No wonder Father John was so excited when he talked to me.

After lecturing you, I'm at a loss for words because I'll sound like a hypo-crite, but this is the impractical side of me revealing itself; the Billee that wanted to drag you off to a preacher that Sunday night in Penn Station. It must have been exciting and I'd give a million dollars or more to have seen it with you.

You didn't say whether or not you were scared or aren't you talking? I wouldn't like it if you weren't scared.

Now that you are back safe and sound, and I'm reassured by your letter that everything is all right, I wouldn't have had you miss the experience for anything. Please, don't rush right out and do it again, though.

I'll bet that's the reason you went on the raid, just so you could brag to our "ball club" about your bombing of Germany. Four sets of twins—now that's going some. We've really set a goal for ourselves, I can see. I can see where I should have played "hard to get." I'm not very smart, I guess. The first meeting left me in a daze. Say, do you throw all the girls you meet for such a loop? If so, the girls "over there" must be in a daze now, and really badly off.

I think you're mean not to tell me what "cheesecake" means.

[Billee to Charles] October 26, 1943—Matawan

My brother is in Ephrata, Washington. I don't know whether that's a jumping off place for the Pacific theater of war or not. I haven't had anything but a post-card. I've been elected to carry the news to Mom in the event he is shipped out.

So you're the jealous type? Heavens, you must have been green when you read about my going to the canteen dance. Maybe it's a good thing I didn't tell you I had an escort home that night. I failed to tell you, too, that the soldiers stationed in Asheville are definitely not 1A.

So you're anxious to know my reaction concerning the Fortress raid.

My sense of everything that is sane and sensible rebels at the idea of any-thing so risky, but then the other side of me is envious to say the least of you being a part of anything so exciting. Let's listen to the sane side of me. It is risky business, especially when it isn't necessary, since you say if it worries me too much, you'll give it up. Too many things can happen up there and we have so much to look forward to.

Anyone that has covered the territory you've covered, taken in the Ranger training, field maneuvers I don't know how many times, besides a gunnery course and now a new assault course (whatever that is) for the sake of gathering material for the paper shouldn't have conscience trouble. You should know as well as I do how necessary that paper is to those boys over there and certainly just not anyone could be doing your job. You and a few others happen to have that gift that is put to use in helping the war effort in that way, instead of on the battlefield. Certainly, your job is as important.

I picked up the *New York Times* magazine Sunday and a familiar byline caught my eye. Sgt. Ralph Martin, under a heading, "What the Soldier Thinks About." Very good. I'll save it for you.

/////

[Billee to Charles] October 30, 1943—Matawan

I just heard something wonderful today. Seems my dentist's niece is married to a sergeant and he has been stationed in England for many months. One evening last week he walks in the house. Just like that, with no warning. It seems he had orders to board a transport and report to a commanding officer in a camp near here. When he reported, the officer failed to have any idea why he was supposed to report and the sergeant didn't have any idea either. The outcome is that he gets a thirty-day furlough and goes back. I wish they'd make a mistake where you're concerned.

/////

[Charles to Billee] November 4, 1943—London (V-mail)

We had a big day here yesterday. Eighth Air Force sent out over 1,000 planes in daylight raids on the German naval base at Wilhelmshaven and three airfields in France. The 1,000 included the largest force of Forts and Liberators ever dispatched by the Eighth to hit Wilhelmshaven. Thunderbolt and Lightning fighter escort and Marauder medium bombers to hit the airfields. The best part of it is we lost only five heavy bombers, two fighters, and two Marauders. The RAF big boys then went out last night to pay a visit to Dusseldorf and Cologne making the total tonnage of bombs dropped by all bombers for the day—more than 4,000 tons. I don't know how much it means to you, but it's an awful lot of grief to whoever caught it.

I've been out with the infantry again. I know you approve of that more than the Air Force. I was going to send you clippings of a couple of the pieces I did but since all mail seems to be going by boat I believe you'll get the papers just as quickly. Bud did a swell piece on his trip to Bremen in yesterday's magazine section. When you see it, you can get a good description of what I was trying to tell you after my trip. The fellows he mentioned were all quartered in the same hut with [us] while we were at that bomber base. He also speaks of Lt. McIlveen, pilot of *The Stars and Stripes*, who took me over, and what is more important, back again.

/////

[FROM THE *STARS AND STRIPES*, November 4, 1943]

SWEATIN' IT OUT—THAT'S THE TOUGHEST JOB OF ALL GI TALK IN NISSEN HUTS BEFORE THE MISSION AND OVER THE INTERCOM IN THE THICK OF BATTLE TELLS A STORY THAT THE FORMAL PHRASES OF THE OFFICIAL COMMUNIQUE CANNOT CONVEY—A STORY THAT GIVES THE INSIDE DOPE.

by Bud Hutton, *Stars and Stripes* Staff Writer

The communique said that strong formations of US Eighth Air Force Flying Fortresses and Liberators attacked Bremen and Vegesack. It said that 130 enemy fighters were shot down by the Forts and Libs and another 12 by the Thunderbolts. It said, finally, that from these operations, 30 bombers and 3 fighters were missing.

But communiques are written in the stiff phrases that high commands mostly use on both sides of the Channel, and there isn't any way for them to tell about the people who went to Bremen and Vegesack and shot down 130 enemy aircraft, nor about the 30 and 3 . . . And since, in a communique, you can't talk about men in a Nissen hut, waiting to go to work, nor about men who laugh at very simple things while the 110s and 88s are pressing in, nor about "sweating" or the rest of the things that go to make up a Fortress gunner, this is the way it was.

In the evening the mist began to lift from the far ends of the runways and a sergeant from operations came into the hut and said, "Standby alert, you guys." The gunners went out to stand in the mud the three days of rain had left . . .

"It'll clear," somebody said.

They argued awhile about the clouds against the southeastern night horizon . . . Back in the hut, the blackjack game started again, and some of the gunners went to bed and a couple wrote letters. The rest of them sat around on the bottom tier of double edged bunks and made the smoke thicker in the yellow light of the one bulb.

The crew of *Lady Liz* had a new left waist gunner, so Pete Bobulsky, the right wing gunner from Cleveland, went over to the new guy's bunk and sat down for a cigarette ... He began to talk about flying helmets and the new type of microphones which fit in a flier's oxygen mask, and the new gunner never realized until the next day that all the time Bobulsky was checking over his equipment and making sure the new gunner would be all right for his first job in *Lady Liz*.

Harry Edgins, the Georgia tail gunner, threw down in disgust four cards that just totaled 22. "Sweatin's always the hardest part of it," he said.

No man had been talking about "sweating," but everyone knew what Edgins meant and they picked up the conversation there ...

The blackjack game went on.

After 11 another sergeant from operations came into the hut and this time it was, "The alert's on, you guys. Cerrone's crew and Binks' and McIlveen's in here. Chow at two ayem, briefing at 2:45."

... and the blackjack game went on.

Bill McDaniel, the top turret gunner from Atlanta, Ga., rolled over beneath a pile of gray and brown blankets and told everybody to shut up ... Everyone who wasn't playing cards went outside to look to the sky again.

Often it's pretty good—fried eggs and pancakes and the coffee is black as hell. More often it's just breakfast—scrambled dried eggs and pancakes and the same coffee.

Jim Reed, the ball turret gunner, lounges back over coffee and talks for a while with the new gunner ... no one at these breakfast tables is crabby. They don't even insult the cooks before they leave the mess hall and go to the square room with the blackboards and movie screen.

It's like the coach talking to you before you go out for the first half, except that you never think of that simile until a long time after you're home from Bremen.

On the way into the briefing room Pete Bobulsky had a look at the long stretch of tape marking the route for today.

"They must've run out of tape," he says, softly.

"Gentlemen, the target today presents possibly the most interesting task yet."

The briefing officer is a major, Mr. S-2 himself.

... he talks for five or six minutes before you hear the word Bremen. He talks about flak and fighters and what the target means in the big scheme of things in the air. He says who's going and how many. It's a lot and the gunners relax a little until the talk gets onto flak . . . they'll take fighters all day long but that flak gets them.

. . . the major finishes his briefing and you wait to hear him say, "Let's go get 'em, men" or something like that but no one does and the gunners just get up and start hauling the piles of clothing to the planes.

They leave the zippered bags full of heated suits and shoes and parapher-nalia on the circle on concrete on which *Lady Liz* stands and head for the arma-ment shop.

. . . the gunners take the caliber .50s out of their covers and break them down to clean them. The armaments men did this whole job on the same guns just a few hours before and they stand around watching the gunners trying to find clean patches or more oil.

Back at the ship they put in the guns and recheck their gear, and about that time Darren Cerrone, who is a first lieutenant and the pilot of *Lady Liz* arrives in a truck with the other three officers, 2/Lt. Dick Proctor, the Matamoras, Pa. navigator, 2/Lt. Bon Selby, the Rockford, Illinois, bombardier, and 1/Lt. Novo Maryonovich, co-pilot, from Gary, Ind.

The sun came out . . .

McDaniel lay down on the concrete and went to sleep. Maryonovich handed out the emergency kits and Bobulsky and Reed checked the new gun-ner's gear once again, just for the hell of it.

Then it was time that they got in and Cerrone and Maryonovich took *Lady Liz* down the runway and climbed up to join the rest.

"Pilot to navigator. Pilot to navigator. Go ahead."

"Go ahead, pilot."

"You all squared away?"

"Roger."

Lady Liz kept on climbing. McIlveen's guys were just below to the left in *The Stars and Stripes*. Binks' ship led, up above and in front. Strung out across the English sky the rest of four or five thousand gunners and pilots and bombar-diers and navigators were talking about the same things.

The fields down there grow small. They don't look a bit like checkerboards, though.

"Pilot to crew. We're getting up there now. Better go on oxygen. Check in, will you?"

The answers start with a Georgia drawl from the tail and move up through the ship. Up ahead, a navigator in the lead checks course and the formations go away from England.

"Co-pilot to gunners. Try 'em out now if you want to."

The inside of the B17 is filled with the comfortable sound of pounding as the top turret and the ball turret open up.

The gunners check in, and for a long time the interphone is quiet. They've all been scanning the sky . . . the talker sounds again.

"Gettin' in there now, you guys. Better be on watch."

The P47s show up, but until they formate out on the wings and overhead no one is sure they're 47s. After they've been there awhile Jerry arrives. "Fighters at 2 o'clock, high."

McDaniel's guns begin to pound and this is where the communique starts to get written.

The rest of it is hard to describe, because on paper there isn't any difference between a guy saying "Fighters at nine o'clock" and "fighters at nine o'clock," but mostly the rest of the crew can tell whether the fighter at nine o'clock is coming in or not from the way the gunner says it.

"Well, there it is ahead of us."

That's Cerrone. Everyone can't see what he's talking about, but Maryonovich clears it up.

"Let's see us on the other side."

Somebody—no one remembered who it was later—came on the talker:

"That stuff's thick enough to fly through on instruments."

Lady Liz goes into the flak, which comes up all around. The fighters go away, and some of the gunners watch the flak and some don't because this day Bremen earns the title of flak champion and it isn't easy to look at it and not want to run away.

"Anybody want to get out and walk?"

That's Cerrone, too, and this time the whole bunch laugh like hell because *Lady Liz* is right in the center and the bombs are just gone away and that's a good thing. But for some of the others it has not been that way, and back in the tail Harry Edgins is calling out in a flat tone the B17s that have been hit.

... The orange and black Ju88s come up and take a swipe, and the Me110s cut in with their twin fins high. The Me210s slash at a squadron while other 110s and 210s lay back on the edge of the sky and peg rockets in orange arcs at the Forts.

The Forts are on the way home, and once when a gunner sights down his .50 at an 88 passing under, the corner of his eye sees the pattern of the fields 'way down there. They're just like the English fields.

That bunch of fighters goes away ... Then the fighters come back and this part will be the end of the communique.

A pack of 110s gangs up on a Fort that's limping on three engines. Flame sifts out of another engine and the Fort starts to slide off to the south. Out of the ship come little black dots that are men you ate breakfast with a million years or so before. Their parachutes open and they go down ... the Fort ... lumbers along, losing a little height and still smoking, and the last you see, it is a lumbering giant shuffling down a long hill into the mist. It isn't good to watch.

They come back, all but the 30 and 3. The gunners and the bombardiers and the navigators and pilots talked to intelligence officers who put down what had happened and sent it to command. Command put down what the intelligence officers had sent and handed it over to HQ. And after that, the communique was written, in the stiff phrases that high commands use.

/////

[Billee to Charles] November 6, 1943—Matawan

You will probably know by the time this reaches you that Tom is in Greenland and not England. El had a letter from him Wednesday dated Oct. 25 and sent ordinary mail. Not bad. He has a good chance of coming home in months from there instead of years, because of the climate.

[Charles to Billee] November 7, 1943—London (V-mail)

You said Warren was moving again. I sent him a letter and a card to the Salt Lake City address. I'll wager they don't reach him.

Haven't had much of an opportunity to even think about making another flight, but I did get in two practice trips over the weekend. Both of them were in Marauders (B-26s). The two-engined planes rock and roll a good deal more than the big fellers. Personally, I like the big boys better. Feel safer in them because they are so big. I guess. Or maybe it's just that it was a first love.

[Billee to Charles] November 10, 1943—Matawan

Today brought a letter from Warren. He expects to leave around the first of the year, for the same place you are, so don't be surprised if you look up some day soon from your desk and see Sgt. Warren Gray. There is a family resemblance, they tell me, but I couldn't see it, in case you are thinking he might look like me. So, since I promised him I'd go home when that happened, you can see what is going to happen. That gypsy you picked out to be Mrs. Kiley will be on the jump again.

I made a trip to 195 yesterday. Father John got in just a few minutes before I arrived and stayed for dinner. You should see Annice stick her tongue out at him. Your dad taught her that. The best one was, though, Father John giving her a ride on his knees, singing "Pistol Packin' Mama." El looks better now that she has heard from Tom.

Eddie is mad because he hasn't been sent over. He says he's been in longer than Tom. By the way, he's expecting a 15-day furlough over Christmas.

[Billee to Charles] November 12, 1943—Matawan

Marguerite and I made the 8:30 express to New York, uptown. We went over on the Ferry from Jersey City and I loved it. Saw the Statue of Liberty on the way over.

We had dinner about 2:00 in McCreery's Big Top Restaurant and had supper in the Savarin, an oyster stew and did it hit the spot! We made Radio City by 7:15 and by 7:30 were comfortably seated watching *Claudia*. The stage show was super, the best I've ever seen.

Claudia is a simple story about a newly married couple. There was a line in the script I want to remember. In a conversation with his wife, the young husband says, "when you like the person you love, that's marriage." The whole foundation of a happy and successful marriage is in that one line.

Of course, we didn't get out in time to make a decent train home so we saw a little more of the picture over and walked from Radio City to Penn Station down Fifth Avenue. The moonlight was so bright, even the effectiveness of the "brown-out" in New York was faded.

Speaking of the new "brown-out," you can see where you are going now but I don't think they should have lifted the blackout yet. It makes people more optimistic than they should be.

I keep telling you how much I miss you. According to these articles on "How to Write to Your Serviceman," letters should be cheerful and so I shouldn't let you know how I feel.

By the way, I know what "cheesecake" means. So it's "cheesecake" snaps you want, hmmmm.

/////

[Charles to Billee] November 13, 1943—London

Two of the boys of *The Stars and Stripes* crew were in London on a pass over this weekend and stopped in to see me last night: Danny Sullivan and Charlie Rotunda. Today, Benny and I took them to see *This Is the Army,* the original stage production which Irving Berlin has on tour over here. It was a great show. During intermission, we met Eddie Barrett, *The Stars and Stripes* tail gunner. After the show we went to the L'Aperitif restaurant for dinner, and between us did away with a quart of Johnny Walker. It was a swell reunion and a grand day. The boys said they have installed a special intercom connection (inter-communication with the crew and other planes in the group) in the nose of *The Stars and Stripes* for me, when I can go out with them again.

I also heard some bad, and good, news. Lt. McIlveen's brother, who co-pilots a plane at the same field, went down last week, but he's safe. My "Mac," the boys say, is really a "hot" pilot right now. Other skippers regard him as one of the best at the base.

You thought Ephrata might be a springboard to the Pacific for Warren. Not necessarily, Billee. Most of the fellows I know here went through Salt Lake City and Ephrata. I don't mean to sound pessimistic, but you should know. From Ephrata he should go overseas although it's difficult to say when. He may even go east to Maine like some of the crews have before coming here.

Since this letter seems to be all Air Force, I may as well stick to it and answer some more of your queries.

Was I "scared" on my trip? I won't disappoint you. From the time we were "briefed" at 3:00 a.m. until we took off at 7:30, I thought of a million things, mostly about you and us. I was jumpy but once we were in the air, I was honestly too busy doing and seeing things to be concerned about safety. Once, when four Focke-Wulfs zipped down and in close, my breathing stopped for a moment, and when a formation above us and to the right dropped their bombs, I didn't know where they were coming from. They appeared to be awfully close, and I gulped. Otherwise—well, it was a "nice" ride; as nice as any bomber mission is.

Leaving the Air Force, you wanted to know if I "knock all the girls for a loop" over here. There was the WAC whom I helped do a story for her home-town paper. She said I was "sweet," and cooed like a sick calf, if calves coo. Then, there are Mrs. Taylor and Mrs. Saltmarch, the "glamour girls" who keep the apartment tidy. Every day when they come in, Mrs. Taylor says, "Charlie, m'love, you been 'upstairs' again? Blimey, I wish you'd stay on the ground so I wouldn't have to worry 'bout you."

So, there you are. If that's "knocking them for a loop," I must be slaying 'em.

And, how about you? How about the escort you had home from the canteen dance?

[Charles to Billee] November 16, 1943—London

Your Nov. 4 letter made me say, "ouch." In it you said, "I'll feel a lot better if you don't go up again." So, here I am with a tale to tell and I don't know how to tell it. However, I'll tell you everything in an airmail, when I get back in a few days from a trip to Liverpool. The story is I went out again with *The Stars and Stripes* yesterday to—of all places—Norway. The ship was doing its 13th trip and I did a piece on it. All I'll tell you now is that it was nothing but a long, frigid trip. No fighters, no flak, almost like a practice flight. But, I'm beginning to see your way and you have my promise not to go again if I "can get out of it gracefully without my conscience bothering me."

Had a long talk with a chaplain while I was at the fort base. Only a young fellow, 26, and a Protestant chaplain. The boys call him "Chaplain Jim." Last name is Kincannon, and a Kentuckian. He talked of the letters he receives from families, sweethearts and wives of boys who go out and don't get back. Even showed me some of them. I guess that was what I needed to open my eyes. One fellow whom I knew, a 1/Lt. and a pilot of a ship, was lost about two months ago. He has a three-month-old daughter he had never seen and the letter from his wife was a story in itself: calm, sensible, but still so full of anguish and sorrow.

[FROM THE *STARS AND STRIPES*, November 17, 1943]

FORT STARS AND STRIPES FINDS 12B (AWRIGHT, 13) LUCKY TRIP

by Charles F. Kiley, *Stars and Stripes* Staff Writer

AN EIGHTH BOMBER STATION, Nov. 16—*The Stars and Stripes* thumbed its plexiglass nose at superstition and winged its way over Axis territory for the 13th time today, joining in the second bombing of important military targets in Norway by Eighth Air Force heavy bombers.

If there was any hard luck riding on the Fortress it was in the form of heavy bombs which cascaded down on the unlucky objectives. Otherwise mission No. 13—or 12B, as the flying trade calls it—was just a long frigid trip for the B17 which 1/Lt. Clarence McIlveen, of Portland, Ore., and his crew named after the servicemen's newspaper in the ETO.

Aerial photos and reports from crews at this station, commanded by Lt. Col. Elliott Vandevanter, Jr., of Washington, indicated that the target bombed by this group was destroyed.

In a position to note the damage, 1/Lt. Earl Mazo, of Charlestown, S.C., who flew in the *Raunchy Wolf,* said the bomb loads from *The Stars and Stripes* and other Forts dropped straight across the target.

The group reported no flak over the target. A few enemy fighters were reported over Norway on the outward flight and over the North Sea on the way back, but none was seen.

The Stars and Stripes, which started ops in the Lorient raid Sept. 23, has never turned back from a mission because of mechanical difficulties, thanks to the ground crew.

[Billee to Charles] November 17, 1943—Matawan (V-mail)

Yesterday brought a long letter from my brother. He is definitely coming over to pay you a visit after the first of the year. Incidentally, they have changed his position in the crew and made him a tail gunner. I wanted to write last night but the letter from Warren kind of got me. He is such a kid and that is such a dangerous position. I have the task of breaking the news to Mom when he leaves and as I told you before, I promised Warren that I would go home, so my days in Jersey are numbered.

I called El this morning and she received a twenty-two-page letter from Tom written on his trip to Greenland. He gave it to a merchant marine to mail so it wasn't censored. I can imagine it is quite interesting. El said he didn't leave anything out.

[Charles to Billee] November 18, 1943—London

This is my report on "Norway."

Before going into the trip, let me say that I'm not flying for the thrill. I know that isn't your impression but some people who have written seem to think it's just a "Coney Island" roller-coaster ride.

First of all, I don't have to fly. In fact, all the generals in the Army can't make a man fly. But in my case, although Andy says, "there isn't any justification in it," it's our job to get the best stories, and get them right.

The two trips I've made were for specific purposes: not only to get stories on those particular raids but to also get background material for future use.

We never know whether it's going to be a big raid on an important target or a "milk run" as the boys call the easy ones. Fortunately or unfortunately, it's been my fate to draw big ones.

But, and you'll favor this, today Col. [E. M.] Llewellyn, our CO, told me I was to concentrate mainly on ground force material. He said it before but made it a little stronger this time. Seems as though we aren't getting all the ground force stories we should and he has put part of the problem on my shoulders. So, in a day or so, I'm going to start seeing more of the infantry, armored troops, etc.

Now, for Norway.

Lt. McIlveen and the crew were taking *The Stars and Stripes* on her 13th mission. I went up to the bomber station and made arrangements to go. It was a cold, cold morning when they awakened us for briefing. The target was a chemical plant in Rjukan, a bit west of Oslo.

It was a long ride over the icy North Sea, and while the temperatures varied between 40 and 55 below zero at high altitude, we were fairly comfortable with our heavy, heated clothes.

Yes, I was riding in the nose again with Gene Shober, the navigator, and Bill Williams, the bombardier. We didn't see a sign of enemy fighters until we crossed the Norwegian coast; then, a few of them showed up and disappeared.

The snow-covered mountains were beautiful. Here and there, we passed over wee villages with pretty little white houses.

The target looked like a new, white-bricked high school, but after we passed over there wasn't too much left of it. The part I didn't like was the destruction of some of those "doll houses" surrounding the plant. But we can't help that.

On the way back, I saw a lone house on a mountainside and had a crazy thought. It seemed a perfect spot for us!

All the way back over the North Sea we didn't see a thing but water. Eddie Barrett, the tail gunner, called "aircraft at nine o'clock" over the intercom once but they were Liberators that were out to hit an airfield in Norway that day. Back at the base we talked with one of our crews that never left England. Their ship developed engine trouble and they had to bail out only 50 miles from the base.

Lt. Earl Mazo, the public-relations officer at the field, went along on the raid with a crew that was finishing its tour of operations.

Earl is here at home with me now, writing to his wife in Charleston, S.C., asking her to forgive him for going. You see, he just likes to fly, although he doesn't have to. He's going to stay with Ben and me for a few days while he's on leave.

I had that "cold sweat" feeling again before takeoff, thinking of you.

[Billee to Charles] November 19, 1943—Matawan (V-mail)

I had another letter from Warren yesterday. He may get a five-day leave around Christmas time so he will go home. He seems quite enthused about his new position. Their colonel and the instructors have just returned from the European Theater so they are learning all the newest tactics. He says it's very near the Real McCoy; that is, their practice missions. He is still waiting for your letter and is quite anxious to meet you. To quote from his letter, he wants to make sure that I'm not just sitting around waiting for just any "GI Joe."

[Billee to Charles] November 26, 1943—Matawan

So, you like the big Fortresses better. I can imagine they would be steadier. I'm trying to remember the sensation of my first and only airplane ride. It was a Fourth of July, the one before I met you. We were at the airport, a couple of girls and me. A friend of one of the girls had part interest in a Piper Cub and he took all of us up that day. I loved it. We rode quite a ways over the mountains and back again. Then, just before we landed, he decided to do a little stunting: a barrel roll. The plane was such a little bit of a thing.

Funny thing. High buildings bother me. Remember the day we went up in the Empire State Building? I couldn't wait until we got down to street level again, and I couldn't look over that railing, but up in the airplane, it never bothered me.

Hey, did you read about the girl that stowed away on a plane from England to Canada? Canada is treating her royally, they say. Gave her a job and she has permission to stay six months. Think I'll go to La Guardia and hang around.

/////

[Charles to Billee] December 1, 1943—London (V-mail)

You wanted to know if you should write your own style or follow the method advised by "morale experts." Listen, Mrs. Kiley-to-be, if you start sending me those stereotyped letters that make everything sound rosy, I'll divorce you, so help me.

About Warren being a tail gunner, don't start worrying over little things like that. There isn't any position on the ship any more dangerous than the others. In fact, of all the tail gunners I know there isn't one who would change his job.

I suppose my Irish temper should boil over and curl my hair after hearing that Warren wants to make sure his sister isn't waiting for "just any GI Joe" but I don't blame him. Brothers have to be pretty careful these days.

I was a little disappointed about Tom's letter to El. I'd like to kick him where it would do the most good. Last week I met five gunners who had just finished their tour, have been decorated with DFCs, Air Medals with three clusters, and two of them with Purple Hearts. Ordinarily, they'd be on their way home soon. But, they are awaiting a court martial for sending home uncensored mail. The outcome will probably be reduction to privates for all and three to six months in the guardhouse.

[Billee to Charles] December 2, 1943—Matawan

Did I tell you Warren received your letter and enjoyed it very much? You'll probably have an answer by now. He wants a new uniform for Christmas. How about that? He's planning on seeing New York before he goes over.

I'm wondering how the meeting with Stalin is going to come out. I feel like I'm sitting on Mt. Vesuvius and I guess everyone else does, too. From the reports tonight, Japan is in for the next offensive. How do they feel over there about it? We've heard rumors that all the lights are going on again at Christmas time. Speaking of lights, there goes the air raid siren. Lights out! . . .

All clear after forty-five minutes. I couldn't help but think what the sirens mean to you all over there. Thank God, we don't have to hear the sound of anti-aircraft fire. Just came over the radio that Berlin was bombed again tonight. The last report [said] Berlin was already in shambles.

[Charles to Billee] December 7, 1943—London (V-mail)

I was out last week to get a story on our "flying nurses." They call them the glamour girls of the Air Force and I can understand why. They are stationed temporarily at bomber bases here waiting for the invasion from the West when they will evacuate wounded soldiers by air from the front. They have been doing great work in Africa, the Pacific and Alaska. They aren't pilots, but nurses who are charged with keeping severely wounded personnel alive until they can reach hospitals.

I have some more pictures. While I was away, I had some taken of *The Stars and Stripes* crew. The following day, Harbison, the ball turret gunner, flew with another crew on a raid and didn't get back. They think he might be safe, though, because some of the boys saw a flock of 'chutes come out of the ship. Dick Yoder, pilot of the plane on which Andy Rooney flew to Frankfurt, also was lost with his crew on the same mission, his 23rd.

I had Lt. McIlveen, my pilot, as an overnight guest last night. He came to London on pass and stayed the night with Ben and me. I told you his brother went down, didn't I? That was about two months ago and Mac has never talked about it. It's easy to see what he feels.

Perhaps I shouldn't talk about these things because you'll probably worry more about Warren.

/////

[FROM THE *STARS AND STRIPES*, December 9, 1943]

FLYING NURSES GET SET IN ETO TO CARE FOR INVASION CASUALTIES

by Charles F. Kiley, *Stars and Stripes* Staff Writer

American flight nurses, trained to evacuate wounded soldiers by air from battlefronts, are in England ready to move in with the Allied invasion of Europe from the west.

Stationed temporarily at US bomber bases, the "glamour girls" of the Air Force are getting practical experience in the care of battle casualties by attending fliers cut up on raids over enemy territory.

The flying nurses are attached to Air Evacuation Squadrons and are part of the organization which sent girls to Africa, the southwest Pacific and Alaska to nurse litter cases over thousands of miles, from front lines to hospitals in the rear.

To most of the flight nurses, air travel isn't new. Many were commercial airline hostesses.

All, however, are graduates of a rigid six-week course in air evacuation at Bowman Field, Ky., through which all flight nurses pass before receiving assignments to combat zones.

They call them "glamour girls" for obvious reasons. Those in Britain, at least, are long on looks and figures. But the girls do not consider their work very glamorous. To them it's a job necessary to save the lives of wounded men who might otherwise be lost through lack of immediate treatment.

At Bowman Field the flight nurses learned methods of Arctic, jungle and ocean survival; climates and customs prevalent in various war theaters; administration of first aid, including blood transfusions at high altitude; how to steer clear of booby traps and to use a parachute, if necessary.

In order to earn their wings—miniature flight-surgeon wings with a block N in the center—flying nurses must weigh less than 135 pounds, be over five feet tall and pass the Form 64 medical examination given all flying personnel.

The biggest job handled so far by a flight nurse in the ETO was the evacuation to America of the 12 prisoners of war who were repatriated from Germany last month.

Commanded by Maj. W. K. Jordan, flight surgeon from Macon, Ga., the Air Evacuation Squadron here is made up of six male officers, 25 flight nurses and 61 enlisted men. Twenty-four of the EMs are surgical technicians, each of whom teams up with a nurse to attend as many as 18 litter cases per plane.

For the most part the squadron uses C47s, converted into flying hospitals. The ship has no armament; the chief purpose of air evacuation is to keep men alive until they can be properly treated.

/////

[Billee to Charles] December 9, 1943—Matawan

I had two long letters from Warren. Morning after morning they drag him out at 2:30 a.m. as if they were going on a mission. It's pretty definite he's leaving. He even went so far as to name a date, so I will go home about the fifteenth of January and break the news to Mom. He was telling me about the Marauders and how he likes the Forts better. He compared being in a Marauder to riding on a whip. Too, he was telling me about the first time he was sick up there. Several of them got sick that day and he said they were all ready to transfer to the motor pool when it was over.

I couldn't help but be amused. He used to take a drink now and then like most kids these days. Now he's decided drinking and flying don't mix so he's definitely on the wagon.

[Billee to Charles] December 12, 1943—Matawan

Another raid, and the thirteenth at that. Not that I'm superstitious but I'm glad that's behind you, even though it was rather on the uneventful side. I realize only too well that it isn't just excitement or a thrill to you. In my estimation, Sherman found the right words for his definition of war. ["I am tired and sick of war. Its glory is all moonshine. It is only those who have neither fired a shot nor heard the shrieks and groans of the wounded who cry aloud for blood, for vengeance, for desolation. War is hell." William Tecumseh Sherman.]

I don't know who the people are that think you are just out for a thrill, but it seems to me they don't know you very well.

I've had us in my "dreams," in just a spot as you mentioned seeing in Norway. I've had us so many places but I like this one place. It's a cabin-like house, comfortably built with an enormous fireplace. There's no one around but us.

You probably know Eddie has been moved from Pine Camp. We are waiting a new address and rather expect an APO to be the new address, from what he says.

My letters seem to arrive at the wrong time: the one about the dream just before you went on your first raid; and again the one telling you not to go again after you'd just been.

[Charles to Billee] December 12, 1943—London (V-mail)

Received two letters yesterday, one from my favorite angel and the other from her brother. Give you two guesses who they are.

Warren repeated your news in the probability of him coming over here soon. I liked the way he boasted about his crew and his modesty in admitting, "the crew is green but we're all willing to learn." Don't worry; he'll get by. He didn't say anything about being anxious to make sure his sister isn't waiting "for any old GI," but said he was looking forward to the time when he meets yours truly. He thought you would be going back to Asheville "after the first of the year." He didn't have to tell me why. I should mention some of the flattering things he said about his "big sister" but I'm afraid you would puff up with pride and burst.

///// |

[Charles made no mention of this story in a letter to Billee; it is just one of the stories printed in the *Stars and Stripes* that shows the close and intimate relationship between American soldiers and British civilians.]

[FROM THE *STARS AND STRIPES*, December 13, 1943]

CHRISTMAS WILL FORGE NEW LINKS WITH BRITISH YANKS PLANNING PARTIES FOR KIDS ALL OVER U.K. INFANTRY TO PLAY SANTA TO 9,500; TONS OF GIFTS ON HAND FROM US

by Charles F. Kiley, *Stars and Stripes* Staff Writer

American soldiers sitting with families in chairs left empty by British sons gone to war . . .

Under-privileged English children, to whom Santa Claus and Father Christmas are almost forgotten memories, as guests of Yanks at Yuletide parties throughout the United Kingdom.

Thousands of America's fighting men grasping moments of holiday spirit during a few hours of relief from aerial combat, invasion preparations and other Army duties . . .

This is a broad picture of what Christmas 1943 will be in Britain for the second AEF 3,000 miles and more from home.

For the most part, the soldiers' Christmas spirit will be showered on kids too young to know why, but who have been orphaned and left wanting since war flooded the world more than four years ago.

In British homes, too, will be forged new links of Anglo-American friendship when average American soldiers sit down with average British people, each with something to give.

The children's parties will be conducted on a larger scale than last year, mainly because of the increase in US personnel in the British Isles.

Appeals by soldiers to families in America, some of which were turned into newspaper campaigns, have brought tons of children's gifts in packages that would otherwise contain Christmas presents for the men. These gifts, to be distributed at parties, have been supplemented by thousands of toys manufactured by soldiers themselves in their spare time.

Probably the biggest job of spreading Christmas cheer undertaken by a single unit is the series of 40 parties for more than 9,500 British, French and Belgian evacuated and refugee children.

They will be staged between Saturday and Jan. 5 by men of a US infantry division and directed by Chaplains James R. McAllister, of Boydton, Va., and H. F. Donovan, of Baltimore, Md. Women from the American Red Cross and British welfare organizations are undertaking a vast baking program, soldiers are dusting off Santa Claus outfits, and candy rations are being collected. When the material gifts run out, cash presents will be made to the children from a $2,000 fund voluntarily raised by the men.

Another of the bigger parties scheduled is one being arranged for Dec. 24 by officers and men of an Eighth Air Force Service Command station, who will entertain 1,000 evacuees and orphans at dinner and movies.

Units of ETO headquarters are starting children's parties as early as Dec. 18, when a US general depot entertains under-privileged kids from London's East End.

Four hundred children from Paddington will be guests of the Yanks Dec. 23 at Portchester Hill, London, thanks to a couple of master sergeants who conceived the idea of defraying expenses for the party by tossing pennies into a glass in pubs near Paddington. The sergeants are Clifford J. Moran, of Madison, Wis., and George A. Lawton Jr., of New York, who head an Anglo-American committee in charge of the party. They also rounded up 50 GI volunteers to wear white whiskers and red suits while distributing gifts. The Mayor of Paddington leads the civilian committee.

On the afternoon of Dec. 24 patients, officers and nurses of a station hospital are entertaining 25 orphans of British merchant seamen.

Christmas preparations and children's parties are not confined only to soldiers. The WACs at ETOUSA headquarters are entertaining 80 sons and daughters of Red Cross volunteer workers Dec. 22 at the WAC service club, 47 Charles St., London. Toys made by WACs in the Eighth Air Force will be distributed at the party.

The first war orphan sponsored by the WACs through the *Stars and Stripes* War Orphan Fund will be the guest of honor at the party. The orphan, seven-year-old Muriel, whose father was an RAF aerial gunner killed during an attack in April on Cape Bon, Africa, will be dressed in a WAC uniform made from salvaged clothing.

For their own Christmas the girls working out of ETOUSA headquarters will have "Open Night" for guests at their billets on Christmas night.

For the entertainment of soldiers, the American Red Cross is arranging elaborate holiday programs for Christmas. British families have filed more invitations with Special Service Sections than there have been applications by soldiers.

This will be Christmas. In Berlin, the people have been told they will not have Christmas trees because of a manpower shortage. In Britain, the US Quartermaster Corps will deliver a Christmas tree to every American unit by Dec. 25.

[Charles to Billee] December 18, 1943—London (V-mail)

This is another of our Saturdays but I'm afraid we won't have our customary date. You see, today is also a wedding anniversary for Ben and since he hasn't Jane to help him make whoopee, or whatever married people do on anniversaries, I'll have to fill in. It won't be a whoopee for me, unless you call dinner at an Indian restaurant and a show exciting.

A letter from the boys of Co. H in Italy carried a little bad news the other day. It included a message from five of them. The bad news told of Harold Gee, an old buddy who lives in Winston-Salem being wounded, and of Tom Scott being taken prisoner. Jack Donnell sent his best. Sounded as though they are all getting a little tired and would certainly welcome a furlough.

[Billee to Charles] December 18, 1943—Matawan

At long last, you've finally done something that I had just about given up hope for. It kept getting worse and worse until the last time it was almost impossible. I was beginning to get impatient with you but everything is all right now. I know the Army must be as happy as I am about it, especially those that had to handle [your stories]. You finally put a new ribbon in your typewriter. Thank you.

[Charles to Billee] December 22, 1943—London (V-mail)

I've been reading a book sent to me for Xmas, *God is My Co-Pilot*, written by a Col. Robert Scott about his life, including action as a fighter pilot in Burma and China. From what I gather, it's a best seller in the United States. I get a funny reaction from it. He described personal experiences that are supposed to be "breathtaking," if you get what I mean. Hell, bomber crews and fighter pilots over here go through more in one mission than he did in four months in China. I don't know why it is, but papers at home play the Pacific theater more than the European. I guess it's because most Americans feel the war against the Japs is their own and that the one over here belongs to England and Russia. Still, fliers who have been in combat in the Pacific as well as here call the European theater the "Big League." You can easily make the comparison by the losses we suffer in the air. The best feature of the losses, however, is that an average of 50 percent of our crews that go down live to tell about it. Besides, the German prisoner of war camps are 100 percent better than the Japs'.

[Billee to Charles] December 23, 1943—Matawan

The article on the flying nurses sounds interesting. They're doing a swell job and I envy them; they had the pleasure of you interviewing them.

I thought surely by now they might receive some word concerning Lt.

McIlveen [brother of *The Stars and Stripes* bomber pilot]. I imagine the prisoner of war lists are slow coming through, and then it probably would come here first. I do worry about Warren even now and he hasn't left yet, but I want to hear about everything, so keep telling me.

Only tonight and tomorrow, and then I'll know what my surprise is, I hope. The next time you start three months in advance telling me about a surprise I'm going to crown you.

One of the girls that works with me—married and quite nice—I tell her little things you write. She says we must have a good time back and forth with our letters. She just doesn't know, does she? They are much more than letters. They are our life.

[Billee to Charles] December 1943—Matawan

I'm not dating this letter because I want it to be a special letter.

I'm sending my love, all my love, on this Christmas Day with a prayer that it doesn't find you feeling too lonely. I'll be with you. I'll be taking out our memories—yes, those I so foolishly said we were reliving too much, and remembering them all. For instance: our first few minutes along in Evelyn Fragge's car that memorable January 17, the Sunday afternoon you put all the nickels in the music box and we just sat and listened and shared each other's thoughts—you held my hand, too—the moments we spent in "our corner," you kissing me good morning so nonchalantly in my own living room, having breakfast together. Then there are our memories in New York. All my dreams coming true in one Saturday night. They are like Christmas presents, each one more memorable than the last, all done up in ribbon and bright paper. I almost forgot one special memory: "our moment" on the terrace of the Inn. I could feel your rebellion that night as you held me but it only matched my "it isn't fair." I'll be thinking, too, of the new memories we'll be making together when the lights go on again.

At the Lamb and Lark: (back row, left) Charles with one of the landlord's daughters; (back row, center near post) Benny Price, with the landlord's other daughter—London, December 1943. (Kiley Family)

[Charles to Billee] December 25, Christmas Night—London

I wanted to be able to turn my head a little to one side and see you looking at me quietly without saying a word, just smiling. I wanted to be able to say, "Good morning, glory and Merry Christmas, angel." I wanted to see your nose wrinkle a little, to reach for you and hold you and kiss you, to put my head down and hear your heart beat, to stay there forever.

Yesterday I met Andy Rooney and we paid a visit to the Churchill Club, and poked through the library there for a couple of hours. After dinner at a French restaurant, L'Aperitif, we headed for the Lamb and Lark. That's the favorite pub near the office. Most of the editorial crowd were gathering there.

This morning, I took an early train to Beckenham, Kent, for my Christmas with the Frost family. Mr. Frost, his daughter Doris and son Gordon met me at the station. Before going to the house, we stopped for an hour at a country tavern for a few tankards of brown ale. It was a cozy, picturesque place and while I hoped a grizzled, round-bellied tavern keeper would be there to complete the picture, I found a couple of very modern maids behind the bar.

When we reached home, Mrs. Frost and Lorna, the thirteen-year-old baby of the family, were waiting for us. You know what a passion I have for fireplaces. Well, I had one today. We had a big turkey dinner, a bit of wine and later went for a two-hour walk. In the evening, we just talked and listened to the radio. Doris, a wireless operator in the WAAF, and a very interesting speaker, and I compared notes on the RAF and Eighth Air Force. We heard a recorded broadcast of Roosevelt's "Fireside Chat" in which he named the second front leaders, then a Christmas "Command Performance" program from Hollywood.

All in all, it was swell just being with a family. Often during the day, I stared into the fireplace and thought of other Christmas days, as well as ones to come. Once, Mrs. Frost offered the "penny for my thoughts," and I told them you were worth much more.

[Billee to Charles] December 25, 1943—Jersey City

I could say you shouldn't have done it, that the other ring, your ring, suited me fine but I'm very proud and happy that you did surprise me with my "blue-white" [a diamond ring in a platinum setting; Charles had commissioned his brother to buy Billee her engagement ring]. No one ever had a lovelier ring. Father John has excellent taste. The simplicity of the mounting sets the diamond off beautifully and the engraving makes it perfect.

When you come home, we'll pretend you've just given me my blue-white and you can put it on my finger.

[Charles to Billee] December 27, 1943—London

Besides your letters, there was other big news: the appointment of Gen. Eisenhower to command Allied invasion forces with British Air Marshal [Arthur]

Tedder as his deputy and Gen. [Bernard] Montgomery leading British Army units. It's a good team. I have heard Jimmy Doolittle will be brought up from the Mediterranean to replace Gen. [Ira] Eaker as boss of the Eighth Air Force. That will mean Warren will have a new boss.

Gen. [Carl] Spaatz, another good man, is also due in Britain from Africa to lead all US air forces here. Looks like Eisenhower is bringing his gang with him. Eaker, who has done a terrific job with the Eighth Air Force will probably take over where Spaatz left off down below.

It sounded odd to hear you talk of "air raids." I'm sure the sirens do not convey all that a raid means. I also agree with you that most people at home haven't the slightest conception of war as it really is. Even those who lost husbands, sweethearts or brothers. To them the loss is a blow, but I hardly think it tells the story of war.

I've talked to numerous men who took part in the African, Sicilian and Italian campaigns. It was pretty awful and it will be much, much worse, I think, when the real invasion gets under way.

You said Berlin "must be a shambles." It has experienced something like 85 raids, had thousands of tons of bombs dropped on it, but it is hardly a shambles. It took much more than that to reduce Hamburg, which is a much smaller city.

[Charles to Billee] December 28, 1943—London (V-mail)

Judging by your remarks, Warren is getting ready. He might as well become accustomed to getting up at 2:30 a.m. for practice missions because he'll do a lot of it over here. Only he'll be getting up before that most of the time. I know what he means by airsickness. I've never had it bad. In fact, I only had symptoms of it once while flying from here to Ireland over the Irish Sea about seven months ago. After that, I never had any trouble.

My predictions of Gens. Doolittle and Spaatz came true today. And, Gen. Eaker went south together with Gen. [Jacob] Devers, who had been ETO commander. Gen. Eisenhower, who was here prior to going to Africa, takes over again. Can't understand the Doolittle-Eaker swap because the latter has done a tremendous job here with strategic bombing, whereas Doolittle was the tactical air force man down there. Strategic bombing means precision bombing by heavies. Tactical means use of mediums and fighter bombers for support of ground forces. With the naming of Air Marshal [Trafford] Leigh-Mallory of the RAF (head of RAF Fighter Command) as chief of Allied air forces in on the invasion it looks like everything will be centered around support for the ground forces. See? I'm getting to be an armchair strategist already. Can't you picture me in my old age fighting these battles all over again with my grandchildren?

/////

[Billee to Charles] December 30, 1943—Matawan

One more day left to this year and the papers are screaming "Victory in '44". Last night I couldn't help but think of the radio reports of the preparation being made on the English coasts for invasion and I get an awful sick feeling knowing what it is going to be like. I'm wondering, too, if you will take part in it and I've been praying so hard, Charles, that maybe you wouldn't.

On the fifteenth I'll make tracks for home and that will be that until you come home for me, and please let it be soon.

CHAPTER 6

JANUARY–FEBRUARY 1944

The fellows claim I'm a jinx because every time I come up to make a trip with them, I bring bad weather with me and they stay on the ground for a week or more. The last time I was up, I waited for four days before giving up and returning to London.
                                        [Charles to Billee, February 1944.]

The War: In early January 1944, after leading Liberator bombers on a mission over Ludwigshaven, actor and USAAF pilot Major Jimmy Stewart took heroic action to give fire cover to bombers that had lost their bearings home and which he guided back on course. Also that month, the RAF staged its heaviest raid on Berlin, dropping eighty tons of bombs per minute for more than half an hour—the raids continued into February.

On the ground, General Eisenhower appointed General Omar Bradley to command the US Army, and on January 21, Eisenhower gathered his commanders in London to start a round of planning meetings for the invasion of France. Russian troop advances continued to weaken German lines, finally breaking the siege of Leningrad and encircling sixty thousand German troops south of Kiev.

In the Pacific, US forces attacked and landed on the Marshall Islands in early February, followed by US and New Zealand forces retaking the Solomon Islands.

On February 2, Frank L Kluckhohn in Australia wrote, for the *New York Times*, a story concerning the dismay of war correspondents who obey military rules to withhold certain information and then find that the information had gotten back to the states and into newspapers. Kluckhohn was concerned that leaks might lead to tighter censorship of war correspondents.

Also in February, the United States finally acknowledged the November 1943 sinking of a troop transport ship in the Mediterranean, blaming it on a submarine torpedo. The government did not identify the ship by name until June 1945—the British SS *Rohna*. It had been hit by German bombers dropping radio-guided bombs. It was the largest US troop convoy ever lost.

[Billee to Charles] January 1, 1944—Matawan

I haven't heard from my brother since before Xmas. I'm hoping it's just the mail held up and that he hasn't been moved yet. I'd love to see him before he goes.

Still more reports on the coming invasion. I think that, more than anything else, is sending me home. I have the picture of Mom by the radio listening and knowing Warren will be "over there" somewhere.

All my life, since I can remember, I've wanted to see New York on New Year's Eve. Here I am an hour away and here I sit, but it wouldn't be any fun without you.

[Charles to Billee] January 2, 1944—London

Forgive me for being a little late, but all the very best for the New Year is what I'm sending to you tonight, with hopes that we will be together this time next year—and my love.

Coming back to town today gave me an opportunity to see more Americans in London than I've ever seen before. Sunday is usually "movie day" here and to get the proper picture you'd have to see it yourself. There were literally thousands of people in lines of threes and fours waiting to get into at least 12 theaters I passed, and for seats ranging from $.80 to $2.10! There were so many Yanks it looked like New York. And naturally, for every Yank there was a girl.

Looked positively fantastic to see civilians and British soldiers walking in male pairs, trios and quartets, and then see our guys with all the women. The films which are currently attracting the crowds are *Jane Eyre*, *This Is the Army*, *The Nelson Touch*, *Sahara*, *Best Foot Forward*, *North Star*, *For Whom the Bell Tolls*, and *Cry "Havoc,"* all but *Jane Eyre* having a war angle to them.

Have you been reading of the proposed bill to give soldiers mustering out pay up to $500? I did an opinion roundup last week and found 25 soldiers spending it already.

/////

[Billee to Charles] January 3, 1944—Matawan

Had a letter from Warren today. He's still at the same place. Your letters are meaning a lot to him. The whole crew is enjoying your letters. To quote, "He writes a very intelligent letter. The boys really like them. In fact, the minute I open one they know who it was from and snatch it from my hand and read it aloud, but I don't mind."

I'm praying he'll be sent somewhere near you.

/////

[Charles to Billee] January 5, 1944—London

Here is part of my photo collection. The pictures of *The Stars and Stripes* with her crew were made just in time. Jimmy Harbison is missing now. Eddie Barret, tail gunner and Bill Williams, bombardier were in the hospital when these were taken. Incidentally, the plane is no more. Another crew took her up last week and, well, there isn't any more of *The Stars and Stripes*. However, Mac is getting another ship and he's calling it *The Stars and Stripes, Second Edition*.

Captain McIlveen (kneeling, right) and his crew, with *The Stars and Stripes, 2nd Edition*—England, January 1944. (US Army/*The Stars and Stripes*)

/////

[Charles to Billee] January 9, 1944—London

I saw you in a dream last night. Strangely enough, I was coming home in it. You were with the family at home when I arrived, wearing a black skirt and white blouse. You had your hair done in an upsweep with lots of curls. I can't remember the rest of it, but at least I remembered what you looked like.

I had a letter from Warren today. He still maintains he'll be on his way soon. He'll have a new boss when he gets here. You probably have read that Gen. [Carl] Spaatz will be US Air Force chief here with Gen. Jimmy Doolittle as head of the Eighth Air Force.

/////

[Billee to Charles] January 10, 1944—Matawan

I had a letter from Warren and they are to leave there the sixteenth or seventeenth and proceed to a staging area and then, about the first of February commence the hop across. He sent me his will. I get the chills. I know it's only a matter of form but still I don't like it.

We think Eddie has left. We haven't heard a word since Christmas week, after he left on the 26th and he said he'd be in over New Year's if he were still there.

/////

[Charles to Billee] January 12, 1944—London

Are your mountains as beautiful now, in January, as they were two years ago? I wonder if they have snow-capped peaks like they did when we last saw them together. Strange as it sounds, that was the last snow I saw. That is, aside from about six seconds of snowfall here a month ago.

Remember how you pictured London in winter? To me, snow and London went together. I guess we'll have to blame Dickens, Shakespeare, Charlotte Bronte and other writers of old England for the illusion. On the other hand, snow wouldn't be so good now. Too many men in the field would have an additional hardship. In their last letter from Italy, the old gang said they had seen enough snow for a lifetime. What started me on this subject, anyway? Nevertheless, I'll bet those mountains look good, snow or not.

///////

[Billee to Charles] January 13, 1944—Matawan

Not such good news today. A letter from Warren tells me that he is being moved to a staging area somewhere in Nebraska and that the prospects of seeing you are slim, since now he's afraid he will be sent in the opposite direction.

That's going to make it doubly hard to tell Mom. She has said before she could take his going to Europe all right but the Pacific Theater of War . . . never.

///////

[Charles to Billee] January 17, 1944—London

I got back from my most recent trip today.

My return coincided with the first appearance of Gen. Eisenhower in London since his appointment as Allied Chief of Invasion Forces. During a press conference, he named Lt. Gen. Omar Bradley, veteran of the Tunisian and Sicilian campaigns, as the American ground invasion forces leader. Gen. Montgomery, as previously announced, will command British ground forces.

With these rather important news breaks, I had to forsake the rest of the day off and do a background story on Gen. Bradley. With that to start me off, I pitched in and did a 2,000-word piece on a story I uncovered on my trip. Between you and I, I believe it was one of the best I've ever turned in. It was the story of a fantastic personality, a soldier called "Molotoff" who performed incredible feats during the African campaign. He was killed but his story will live long with the men who knew him. I'll send it to you when we use it.

/////

[FROM THE *STARS AND STRIPES*, January 18, 1944]

GEN. BRADLEY IS CHOSEN TO LEAD U.S. GROUND TROOPS IN INVASION; PRELIMINARIES OVER

[No byline]

Lt. Gen. Omar N. Bradley, who commanded the American Second Corps in the campaigns in Tunisia and Sicily and was one of Gen. Eisenhower's chief assistants in the Mediterranean theater, has been named commander of American ground forces in the European theater preparing for the coming invasion of Europe, it was announced yesterday.

Gen. Bradley, who is recognized as one of the foremost infantry experts in the US Army, was given a large share of the credit for the American successes in the African fighting and was credited with holding casualties in the final battle for Tunisia to a minimum.

Gen. Bradley has been an infantry officer so long that he is known today as "the doughboy's general." Fifty years old, with graying hair and a square-hewed chin, he was graduated from West Point as an infantry lieutenant in 1915, served through the last war as a foot soldier and was in command of Fort Benning when the United States entered this war.

Meanwhile, the picture of Allied might menacing Hitler from the west and south, as well as the east, grew clearer as Gen. Eisenhower disclosed that the pre-invasion task already was far advanced in Britain and Gen. Sir Henry Maitland Wilson, Allied commander in the Mediterranean, hinted of blows in fresh quarters in that theater, possibly in southern France.

Gen. Eisenhower, in his first press conference as commander-in-chief in the west, gave warm praise to the air forces for the blows they were inflicting now on the enemy, and paid particular tribute to the infantrymen in the United Kingdom who, he said, "are getting themselves ready and toughened for any job that lies ahead."

Gen. Maitland Wilson said that southern France, like any other along the Mediterranean front, might be turned into a battlefield if the opportunity for successful operations there developed. He disclosed that he was to confer with Gen. Charles de Gaulle tomorrow.

Gen. Eisenhower, whose arrival in England after conferences with Prime Minister Churchill and President Roosevelt was announced only 24 hours earlier, made it clear to the press at his first conference that things were not just starting with his arrival.

The new Allied supreme commander told correspondents that "fundamentally, public opinion wins wars," and asked the fullest and frankest possible reporting of operations in this theater.

Striking strongly at any idea that an apology is needed in connection with Allied progress in the Mediterranean theater, Gen. Eisenhower said the troops there "have become extraordinary fighting men—navy, air and ground."

/////

[Billee to Charles] January 17, 1944—Asheville

I found Mom better than I hoped. [Billee had fulfilled her promise to Warren and moved back to Asheville to be with her mother.] Warren is expected home tomorrow for a leave, so I guess everything is set. I haven't told her yet [that Warren was being deployed]. I thought I'd wait until he came.

Home is just the same, [only] a bit brighter on the outside with some new paint. Incidentally, nothing but a Marine and his wife here in the way of soldiers. Relieved?

/////

[Billee to Charles] January 18, 1944—Asheville

Warren came home this morning. How happy Mom was to see him. He has a date with an old girlfriend tonight. He hasn't been in Asheville in several years now. We had a chicken dinner for him, and one of the fellows that stayed with Mom came in and had dinner with us.

He seems so terribly young to me and old at the same time. He looks swell and how he loves his work. Now, besides being tail gunner, engineer and second radio man, he's doing some flying.

We've been discussing the war and the termination today. They aren't as optimistic as I am.

Billee, Warren, and Elizabeth Gray—Asheville, January 1944. (Kiley Family)

[Billee to Charles] January 19, 1944—Asheville

I have a job already. A letter from the bank wondering if I'd be interested in an opening. The guy almost passed out from shock when I called him because he thought I was in Jersey.

I can start Monday at $125 a month, more than Perth Amboy, so maybe I can save a little money for that four-star wedding that's on my calendar for 1944.

My heart jumped to my throat when I read about your *Stars and Stripes* [bomber]. What a tragedy. You didn't mention how many survived. I know how you must have felt. I'm relieved to hear about Lt. McIlveen [*Stars and Stripes* bomber captain's brother, who had been shot down over Germany in 1943]. It's wonderful that he's been reported a prisoner. At least it's better than just "missing."

Looks as if the stage were set for the big day. Just any time now. You still haven't said what your role will be.

The big puzzle is this rumor of a German-British separate peace. What's the answer to that? Propaganda? [The Russian news agency Pravda published rumors of separate peace talks between Britain and Nazi Foreign Minister Joachim von Ribbentrop, which were denied by British officials.]

[Charles to Billee] January 25, 1944—London (V-mail)

Not much excitement around the office these days. One of the best stories of the war broke yesterday, though. Lowell Burnett, 24-year-old INS correspondent who first was listed as missing from the Dec. 2 RAF raid on Berlin, then later was changed to prisoner of war, not only escaped but sent a story out called "Inside Nazi Europe." It told of the raid, his experience in parachuting from a Lancaster, his capture and escape. Also that he was in hiding and will soon do a piece on the aerial destruction in Germany. He's got a million $ waiting for him when he starts telling about his experiences.

[Charles to Billee] January 25, 1943—London

I hate to say this but I'm listening to Berlin Radio and enjoying it. It has been playing some of the best recordings I've heard since I left home. It plays about 10 minutes of recordings, then gives about five minutes of news. Now and then, I hear words like "London," "Italy," "Americans."

Just now, a swell band with a hot clarinet sounds good but the British are trying to "jam" the program. I'm waiting for the news in English to find out what we didn't do today.

The announcer just said something about Hamburg. I didn't think there was anything left there to talk about.

I should bring you up to date on my work, Mrs. K. I picked up half a dozen stories in the infantry last week, one a magazine feature, and did a bit of Air Force re-write in the office, a bit more on the soldier vote bill, a story on the Lowell Bennett piece from "Inside Nazi Europe" that you must have read about, and today, a feature on some WACs who came to the ETO with Gen. Eisenhower from Africa.

Last night I sat down with nine WACs to get the material. I enjoyed it insofar as comparing their lives in Britain and in Africa.

/////

[FROM THE *STARS AND STRIPES*, January 26, 1944]

BENNETT ESCAPES, GETS THE STORY OUT

[No byline]

One of the most graphic stories of the war, written "inside Nazi Europe," was published in newspapers of America and in London's *Daily Express* yesterday when INS Correspondent Lowell Bennett recounted his experiences of parachuting from a stricken Lancaster bomber over Berlin and his ultimate capture and escape from a prisoner-of-war camp in Germany.

Bennett, 24 years old, was reported missing following the Dec. 2 RAF raid on Berlin, but last Saturday the International News Service bureau in London received from him a letter written apparently from a German P/W camp before his escape.

The arrival of his spectacular story was the first indication that Bennett had escaped. His present whereabouts are unknown, and the channel through which his dispatch was sent was not revealed.

Using the dateline, "Inside Nazi Europe," Bennett told of his take-off from a Lancaster base in Britain, of encountering flak from Nazi defenses off the Dutch coast and of "searchlights by the hundreds" near Hanover.

Going into the bomb run over Berlin "right through the center of a shield of a hundred shell and rocket explosions, scores of weaving, fingering searchlights and dozens of fighter flares," Bennett told how one of the bomber's gunners called of an enemy fighter "climbing toward us from starboard."

Despite violent evasive action by the pilot, the night fighter pressed home his attack, Bennett related.

Bennett wrote, "The world seemed to burst into an inferno of flame. Our plane shuddered and rocked violently. Cannon shells had ripped into the starboard wing, and both engines exploded into furious fire."

The pilot said: "OK boys—bail out—sorry." Then later, after the crew buckled their parachutes: "Hurry up, boys, can't hold it much longer." The crew followed each other into the bombardier's compartment, tore away their oxygen masks and spilled out into the cold air."

Bennett said. "Flak spangled the darkness around me. My ears rang with concussion and explosions; my head whirred with the wildness of mad nightmares. Beneath me the fires spread larger and clearer.

I was certain I was going to drop into one of them. A nearby shell-burst rocked the parachute and for a moment I thought it had been pierced.

"A wild panorama of the Battle of Death—crazed symphony of bombs, planes, guns. A tumultuous jig-saw of color, sound, consuming fear, bewilderment, wonder.

"The bag strapped to me was twisted around my throat, and with frozen fingers I could not move it, so I could not look downwards easily.

"Then suddenly I hit, smashing through thick reeds, and sinking waist-deep into the mud, chest deep in water."

Bennett was picked up by two men in a rowboat and taken to a cottage in a German village where two sergeants from a nearby searchlight battery came for him. That afternoon, he wrote, he was taken by truck to a camp near Berlin with two other members of his crew who had been picked up.

"Sometime later, during another transfer, I escaped," Bennett said. "The details of that and my subsequent travels and my present location must remain secret until I have reached a safer point for dispatch."

Bennett, a resident of South Orange, N.J., once before was imprisoned by Germany after the occupation of Paris. He saw action in the Finnish-Russo war and with the French and British armies in France. He accompanied invading US forces to North Africa in 1942 before being assigned to the INS bureau in London.

[FROM THE *STARS AND STRIPES*, January 27, 1944]

SOLDIER VOTE BILL "FRAUD"—FDR

[No byline]

WASHINGTON, Jan. 26—President Roosevelt again stepped into the Congressional wrangle over votes for soldiers today with a sharp criticism of the measure passed by the Senate last month and a demand for "adequate legislation." In a message to Congress, the President described the bill, approved Dec. 3 by the Senate and now pending before the House, as "meaningless."

The bill to which the President referred and which passed the Senate 42–37, limits Federal action to the distribution and collection of ballots printed by the states. The bill also provides for the use of state absentee voting processes, which, according to an Associated Press story, are of "questionable" value in 18 states.

"I consider such proposed legislation a fraud on soldiers, sailors and

Marines now in training and fighting for us and for our sacred rights," the President declared.

The President's blunt demand brought Republican guffaws in the House and a cry in the Senate that he had delivered "a direct insult" to the lawmakers.

The President endorsed substitute measures proposed by the Democratic Senators Theodore Green (R.I.) and Scott Lucas (Ill.) and by Rep. Eugene Worley (D. Tex.), which would provide simplified Federal ballots on which soldiers could write the name of their choice for President, Vice-President, Senator and Representative. This idea was rejected by the Senate as "unconstitutional and a violation of states' rights."

There is nothing in this bill violating the rights of the states," the President declared. "I am sure I express their (the troops) wishes in this matter and their resentment against the discrimination being practiced against them."

[FROM THE *STARS AND STRIPES*, January 27, 1944]

INTRODUCING THE CHIEF'S LADY AIDES
14 WOMEN, 9 OF THEM EMS, HERE AFTER SERVING IN
NORTH AFRICA WITH GEN. EISENHOWER

by Charles F. Kiley, *Stars and Stripes* Staff Writer

WACs were not available in France in 1917 so it is not on the record what "Black Jack" Pershing thought of having female personnel working for him at AEF headquarters.

But 26 years and another war later, Gen. Dwight D. Eisenhower has found women to be invaluable at his Supreme Allied Command HQ in Algiers and London.

When America's No. 1 soldier in this part of the world was appointed Allied chief of invasion forces and brought his varsity team back to Britain from the Mediterranean—Montgomery, Spaatz, Bradley, Tedder, et al—he also brought 14 women who occupy positions on his winning combination.

The distaff side of Gen. Eisenhower's office, who recently arrived in London to take up their duties where they left off in Africa, include nine enlisted and three commissioned WACs working as secretaries and stenographers for members of his staff, a WAC captain who is secretary to the general and a British girl who has been the chief's personal secretary and chauffeuse since he first came overseas in May 1942.

The lone non-military member of the general's feminine force is Kay Summersby, an Irish-born Londoner, who has held the joint position of personal secretary-chauffeuse for Gen. Eisenhower for almost two years.

With S/Sgt. James (Mickey) McKeough, ex-New York bellhop and orderly-chauffeur for the general since the latter was a colonel in Texas, Kay Summersby has driven "the boss" in Britain, Africa, Sicily and Italy.

How do the WACs compare service in North Africa with that in Britain?

In Africa, they maintain, there were sunshine, summer-long swimming in the Mediterranean, no KP, sanctioned dates with officers, informal dress in hot weather, admiration and respect from all and a lot of work done willingly by the Corps.

In Britain, the food is better, dress regulations are more strict, there is no sunshine, soldiers whistle and ask "Does your mother know you're out?" and a lot of work is still done willingly without martyr-to-the-cause attitude.

The enlisted WACs in Africa were permitted to date officers, the girls said, since August. They welcomed the official OK not to date officers exclusively but as a privilege to choose their own company whether it be a general or buck private, they claim. (In Britain, WACs must receive special permission from the COs to date officers, i.e., friends from home, relatives, fiancés, etc.)

The one soldier-WAC romance that began in Africa and is being continued in London is that between Mickey McKeough, the general's GI "aide-de-camp," and Cpl. Pearlie Hargrave. They were engaged Dec. 17 in Algiers and were able to remain together with the transfer of Gen. Eisenhower's HQ. Cpl. Hargrave has driven for Gen. George C. Marshall and Lt. Gen. Omar N. Bradley, chatted with Winston Churchill, and was one of the first women in Bizerte after the city fell to the Allies. She also drove in the Tunis "Victory Day" parade.

In the short time the girls have been in Britain one of them has had a family reunion. Sgt. Rhona Laired, a secretary, met her brother a few days ago after a three-year separation.

For Sgt. Nana Rae, her transfer presents an opportunity to visit Dumfrieshire, Scotland, which she left 12 years ago to go to America.

Women supposedly are fain to talk but those at SAC have military secrets to keep and nobody has ever said they don't know how.

[Billee to Charles] January 24, 1944—Asheville

Warren left last night. My two sisters were to meet him in Cincinnati and stay during his wait for the train. Mom insisted on going to the train here. She did pretty well; better than I thought. One of her "boys" went with us so he helped. He has been swell to Mom. He always comes, since he's been at the camp, on his day off to see her.

I went to see *Guadalcanal Diary* to see if I could see Fred, my cousin. A lot of the scenes and background were actual photographs. I saw him . . . not actually but all the way through the picture, the hell he must have gone through until the end. I left the theater with a bitter, dry taste in my mouth. The two hours made me feel helpless.

[Billee to Charles] January 28, 1944—Asheville

The revealing of the Japanese atrocities to our prisoners over there is really a blow. Now what will be in store for those remaining? It would have been better to have fought to the last man than to have surrendered to a fate such as theirs. Doesn't seem possible living in a civilized world that such primeval methods of torture could exist. Agnes won't enjoy hearing or reading this latest report. She's held such faith and hope for her Jack, but with this you can't believe the cards she's received.

[Billee to Charles] February 1, 1944—Asheville

Have I mentioned a Freddie [Daddasio] in any of my letters? Don't get excited now. I'm being a good fiancé. He's one of Mom's "boys" who have been so nice to her while I was away. He lives at the camp now but spends weekends here. He's from New York and does photostatic work for the intelligence department of the Air Corps. [He was] formerly with the New York Library doing the same kind of work. His ambition is to be a member of the *Yank* [the US Army weekly magazine] staff. He's about 32. He got an awful dirty deal from one of the girls in Mom's apartment. He really fell hard and she led him to believe she did, too, until another soldier came to live here and she dropped Freddie like a hot potato. I'd like to kick her or give her a good shaking because he's a swell fellow and deserves better treatment, so Mom and I have been nice to him. Sunday we took a walk to the Inn and back in the afternoon. I didn't want to go because it's one of our special places but he was interested in taking some good camera shots of it. You can imagine what good company I was, especially talking about you as much as I do. "Charles says," creeps into all my conversation before long.

[Charles to Billee] February 1, 1944—London

I met a lieutenant who has been in the ETO for about a year. Last week he received a letter from his eight-year-old son, written (or shall I say, scrawled) in a kid's handwriting. This was the letter:

"Dear Pa, I want a baby brother. Mum says I can have one if you say I can. I sure would like you to tell her to get it while you are away. I sure wish I had been with you when you went shooting. Write soon and tell me about the baby. Your son, Buzzie."

The moral of the story: don't get any funny ideas. And since there is a lot of space between us, I can risk a playful slap in the face. Seriously, though, it's one way to keep the boys over here laughing. That kind of a letter, I mean.

[Charles to Billee] February 1, 1944—London

You wanted to know if I was doing any rewriting. Yes, quite a bit recently. I did most of the soldier-vote stuff from special cables out of Washington. That is a big issue with the men.

Big news in the Pacific today—the landings on the Marshall Islands. I think it's the biggest undertaking yet out that way. Occupation of the Marshall's will mean the Japs may have to evacuate their greatest naval base at Truk, since it will be flanked and open to air attack from the Marshalls, Gilberts and Solomons. First reports were that the landings were successful without too many casualties.

Over this way, Berlin is practically on her knees after the latest RAF raids. Our heavies have been over four days in a row.

/////

[Charles to Billee] February 5, 1944—London

Ben and I were up at 9:30, lazily enjoyed breakfast on our day off, and set out for a walk that took us along the Thames embankment from Blackfriars Bridge to Parliament and the Abbey, along Whitehall to Trafalgar Square, then along Pall Mall to Buckingham Palace and Hyde Park.

We just about ran out of gas at that point and took a cab to the Churchill Club for lunch. We spent the entire afternoon in the Club's library, after which we met Andy Rooney and Joe Fleming [another *Stars and Stripes* staff writer] and saw *Panama Hattie* at the Piccadilly Theater. Andy was given four tickets to a box by Ben Lyon (Major) before the latter left for service under Gen. [Ira] Eaker in the Mediterranean. Bebe Daniels (Mrs. Ben Lyon) stars in the show. With the tickets was an invitation to drop back stage for a "hello" and a drink with Bebe.

She was very gracious, informal, talked with us for about an hour. Before we left, she asked us to have dinner with her next Saturday night at her home. Said nights were going to be lonely with Ben away. So, we are dining with her after the show next week.

Bebe must be in her 40s but she is still vivacious. She and Ben probably have entertained more servicemen over here than any 50 people. Since our men first came over in Jan. 1942, they have been constantly having men to their home for tea and all that goes with a visit with "old friends." They could easily have gone back to America when the blitz started but stayed on to continue their radio program, one of the most popular in Britain. Ben came into service with the Air Force as head of the radio end of public relations with a major's commission. He held a commission in the service during peace. In fact, I believe he was promoted to Lt. Col. a short while ago, although I'm not sure.

[Charles made no mention in any letter to Billee of this remarkable story.]

[FROM THE *STARS AND STRIPES*, February 5, 1944]

JUST BEFORE THE BATTLE, BROTHER: DON'T BE SCARED OF BEING SCARED, VETERAN ADVISES

by Charles F. Kiley, *Stars and Stripes* Staff Writer

Sgt. Sammie Slusher has something to say to American soldiers. His message is aimed chiefly at men as yet untried in combat; men who are asking themselves the same questions he asked before he first saw action.

What is it going to be like? Will I be frightened? How will I react to killing people? Is the Nazi as cunning, as fanatical, as ruthless as they say he is? Are his weapons as good as mine?

Slusher, who went into the North African landings a wide-eyed private and came out of Sicily months later a battle-wise, hard-bitten veteran decorated with the Silver Star and Purple Heart, frankly says you will be scared stiff.

Your frame will tremble and your knees will knock. The sweat on your hands will be cold and clammy. Your lips and throat will be dry, your stomach upset and you'll wish you were a couple of thousand miles away somewhere in America.

Chances are you'll be surprised how cool you are once you get "in there." You will find you have a lot more know-how than you thought you did.

You also may not have the desire to shoot and kill, but when you see your buddies—like the fellow sitting next to you now—bathed in blood and grotesquely sprawled in death, you are likely to feel differently than you did when you started.

The Nazis' most effective weapons that Slusher encountered, and the kind you like to have on your side, are his 88 mm. gun and his automatic machine pistol. The first time you hear four 88s sound off you will think they number 500, but you will get used to them—like a number of other things. If you get your hands on a machine pistol you will want to know how it operates so you can use it yourself.

Slusher warns: (1) Don't ever turn your back on a German soldier; (2) don't pick up anything unless you are absolutely sure it isn't wired for "boom."

The Nazis, according to Slusher's calculations, probably are the most ingenious in laying booby traps. He can substantiate the reports that booby traps were placed on American dead in Africa. They were found also on fountain pens, cigarettes, toilet seats, water canteens, weapons, German cap badges likely to be picked up for souvenirs and a hundred and one other things.

Here are a few tips Slusher thinks soldiers going into action for the first time should paste in their helmets.

Take all the cigarettes, matches and lighters you can carry. You aren't likely to find a PX in a foxhole. You have heard this before and Slusher says it again—socks, foot powder, cleaning patches and entrenching tools are "musts." If you can tote more than one entrenching tool, do so.

Slit trenches offer more protection and are more comfortable, if properly dug, than foxholes. Dig one whenever you stop for more than an hour.

Never get up where an enemy can see you. An artillery or mortar barrage inevitably follows. Keep the chin strap on your helmet open as often as possible to prevent concussion in a barrage. Stay away from trees during enemy mortar fire. They are used frequently as aiming points.

Always keep your canteen filled with water and don't use it to wash wounds. Sulfa powder and gauze bandage will safely take care of a wound for as long as two days. In treating wounds of another man, use his aid packet. You might have to use your own sooner than you expect.

A 22-year-old ex-mechanic from Willard, Ohio, Sammie isn't a professional soldier. Well-built, blond and soft spoken, he is as homespun as anybody could be who came from a Midwestern town of 2,500. He wants to get home like everybody else, to the wife he married eight months before he came overseas.

He knows there are men who will feel as he did before combat. He is certain they will know what to do when they have to do it.

Like the day at Djebel Marata, in Sedjenane Valley, when the main body of which Slusher was a part was held up by a German machine-gun nest. Then a Pfc., Slusher volunteered to take five men and endeavor to knock it out. One of his men was wounded in the attack. About 25 yards from the next Slusher saw a head coming up from the emplacement. He ordered a volley, followed by a charge with fixed bayonets.

When they reached the position, eight men, including a lieutenant, came out of the emplacement hands raised in surrender. The German whose curiosity moved him to show himself was found with his head almost blown off.

That's Slusher's message and story. If absorbed in the spirit with which it was given, it may save the adjutant a little work in sending cables to next of kin come Invasion Day.

/////

[Charles to Billee] February 9, 1944—London

Let's talk about Warren. I'm glad he had a chance to get home. You have probably written another letter between the 19th and the 24th, which tells more of his visit. In any case, I know he was home.

As for his possibilities of going to the Pacific are concerned, it really doesn't make much difference. Service overseas is as good, or bad, in any theater. In fact, as flying goes, the Pacific is actually about 30 to 40 percent less dangerous than it is over here. If he does go to the Pacific, I have a lot of figures that may change Mom's opinion. I know they won't console her entirely but they may help.

[Billee to Charles] February 10, 1944—Asheville

A lone V-letter so far this week. I've been wanting a letter so very much, just a page with your writing and it hasn't come. I still don't like these V-letters. They are about as personal as Grand Central Station.

Warren's instructor was a flight officer who was shot down over Germany, interred and then escaped. Speaking of Warren, we received a letter at the bank from him, from an undisclosed place 48 hours away from Nebraska and colder than an icebox was all he could say. The letter itself wasn't even postmarked in any way. He must be at an embarkation point.

One of Mom's old guests came in last night. He served overseas eleven months during the last war. I was reading the *Stars and Stripes* when he came in. He said they used to stand in long lines to get that paper and nine times out of ten there wouldn't be half enough copies and by the time you finally got hold of one it was practically confetti.

[Billee to Charles] February 18, 1944—Asheville

Today brought two letters from Warren, "somewhere in Newfoundland," he said. "I'll be giving your message to Charles," so you know what that means.

After Mom getting the news about the tragic happening to the convoy in the ETO, she went to pieces last night but she's better today since she got the mail from Warren [the sinking of the *Rohna* in the Mediterranean]. Poor kid hasn't had any mail since he left home and you could tell he'd give his right arm for a letter from somewhere.

This latest news about the convoy is heartbreaking. A thousand boys! The news of the bombing of Japan's "Pearl Harbor" doesn't make up for that, even though it is good news [the bombing of the Japanese Naval Base at Truk Lagoon, Micronesia].

[Charles to Billee] February 19, 1944—A Fortress Base

The fellows claim I'm a jinx because every time I come up to make a trip with them, I bring bad weather with me and they stay on the ground for a week or more. The last time I was up (one which I failed to tell you about inasmuch as I didn't fly) I waited for four days before giving up and returning to London.

But this time . . . well, I'm going to stay here until we do one. We have been alerted for one tomorrow but may not go. You see, this will be the last mission for Mac (Capt. McIlveen) and I'm doing it with him. The angle? Well, as pilot of *The Stars and Stripes, Second Edition*, he rates a final story. Two of the crew, Lt. Shober the navigator and Danny Sullivan, one of the gunners, finished up last week. John Scarborough, the engineer, and Lt. Williams the bombardier, finish up with Mac. Charlie Rotunda, radio operator, will have one more. Ray Malmfelt, another gunner, will have two and Eddie Barrett, tail gunner who was in the hospital for five weeks, will have nine to go. Lt. Cygan, the co-pilot, transferred to another crew a couple of months ago and Mac has been taking different co-pilots on each trip.

I don't believe I ever told you what the "night before a mission" was like, did I?

Picture the brick hut where I am as one room, lined on both sides with double-decked beds. Between each bed is a rack where the uniforms and flying equipment for each man hangs. Ingenious as they are, the fellows have rigged up light extensions so that most bunks have "bed lamps." The lamp cover is a painted tin can. Everything is neat. Men are sprawled on their bunks, fully clothed or in pajamas. Some are shining shoes for the want of something else to do. A couple are sitting around the two stoves at opposite ends of the hut reading. Three men are sitting at the table in the center of the hut writing letters. Two are off in a corner making models of planes from the kind of a kit you'd buy a 10-year-old at Christmas. Others are talking shop. The new men listen to the "veterans" and say little, all anxious to learn what they can and hear about "that tough trip to Brunswick" or Kiel or Leipsig or Schweinfurt or Frankfurt or the "milk run" to Pas de Calais or Bordeaux or Tours.

Somebody steps outside the door to look at the sky. "Looks bad, guys. Damn snow has started again." Eddie Barrett calls across the room, "Charlie, if we don't go tomorrow so help me I'm going to ask the Colonel to ground you." He puts on his heavy jacket and wants to know if I'll stroll over to the Aero Club (Red Cross) and have coffee with him. I tell him I've got a date but if he waits I'll walk over with him.

Outside, it's dark. Real, coal-black dark. When your eyes get accustomed to the darkness you can make out the outline of the hut-tops on the skyline. A few small lights creep along the roads—GIs on bicycles. You hear the engines of a Fortress start up, coughing a little at first then falling into a smooth whirr. The sound of the engines rises and falls as the crew chief pre-flights the engines. It's a little early for pre-flighting. That doesn't start, usually, until four hours before takeoff. But in this case, a ground crew probably has been feverishly working all day and night to get a bomber in shape for the next mission. The unsung ground crews who work in all kinds of weather, faces stained with oil and dyed reddish-purple by the cold, fingers numbed, conscientious at their work. Only they know how much depends on the work done by the mechanics. The slightest bit of carelessness can cost the lives of 10 men and send a quarter of a million dollar plane to its doom.

Inside the Aero Club men in flight jackets, coveralls, and uniforms sit in pairs, trios and quartets drinking coke or coffee, munching on snacks. Somebody in the corner pecks away on the piano . . . "Melancholy Baby." Two guys lean over the counter talking to a British volunteer worker of about 20 who titters when one of the boys, obviously from Brooklyn, tells her that "these English goils can't stack up to our goils back home nohow, 'cept once in a while when you meet a nice one."

Back in the hut, Harry Edgins (tail gunner on the *Lady Liz* with 21 missions) berates his pilot in a Georgian drawl for going off on pass without telling him. "Hell, man," Harry says. "Here I am with a chance to fly tomorrow and he blows out on a pass, leavin' me high and dry. Looks like I'll have to bum a ride with another crew. Hey, John. Think Mac will take me? I'll fly the waist." John thinks Mac will take him so Harry makes a mental note to look up Mac in the briefing room in the morning.

One by one, the boys begin to "hit the sack." After a while there are only five or six still up, sitting in a wide circle around one of the stoves. Joe Carbonetti, pint-sized smoothest Latin Lover you ever did see, with a thick mustache and jet-black curly hair, and Eddie Barrett talk about the "good old days" in Salt

Lake City, Seattle, Spokane, Myers Field, etc. Harry wonders what his wife and three kids are doing. Another guy wonders what his precious bit of femininity is doing, too. Wonders what she could be doing at six o'clock in Asheville. Figures it's a darn sight warmer than it is here, too.

Everybody will be in bed soon. The lights will be out and although it will appear as if everybody is sleeping peacefully, you will only hear a few snoring in complete relaxation. For, even though tomorrow's mission may be a "milk run" they know anything can happen. Maybe it's a long haul. They won't know until briefing at about 4 a.m. If the mission isn't "scrubbed" somebody will stick his neck in the door at about three and say "Everybody listed for today's mission, hit the deck. Breakfast at 3:30, briefing at 4:15."

Nobody will say much on the way to breakfast or briefing. Can't waste time. Besides, everybody is still half asleep. It will be a good breakfast. Most everybody will be tense at briefing, veterans as well as rookies, until they hear the target. If it's a tough one, there will be a spontaneous whistle. If it's an easy one, comparatively speaking, there will be hundreds of broad smiles.

After briefing, the gunners get their 50s, climb on trucks and ride out to the perimeter where the bombers rest in the dispersal areas. There will be faint, flickering lights around the ships where ground crews are making last-minute checks, pre-flighting engines. The guns are put in, Mac will have a look, Bill Williams will check his bomb bays. Everything will be set. We'll hang around the edge of the plane, smoking cigarettes. We'll ask Mac if he'd like to be starting all over again and Mac will say, "Are you kidding?"

Pretty soon, the big boys will taxi from the dispersal areas, line up one behind the other until the fleet is assembled. We'll rumble down the runway, gathering speed until we reach the maximum, lift into the air . . . and from then on, we'll be in the hands of God.

///////

[Billee to Charles] February 21, 1944—Asheville

I just heard today that a kid I used to go to high school with—he ran around in our gang—is a bombardier, a Capt. Edgar Dickinson. Have you ever run across him? Everyone I used to know is scattered far and wide and a few won't be among those to return. They were such kids.

[Charles to Billee] February 24, 1944—London

This isn't going to be a very pleasant letter. In fact, I was going to break one of our promises and not write it at all.

If you have received the letter I sent from the Fortress base, you will be able to make better sense of this, because this is the first I've written since.

I went out to do the 25th and last mission with Captain Mac and the boys last week. Bad weather kept us on the ground for five days. Then, last Tuesday, we were "alerted" and that's when I wrote to you, giving you a picture of "the night before a mission."

The following morning we were "briefed" to raid Schweinfurt and took off. After being in the air for 3 1/2 hours, the mission was called off and we came back. The next day we started out again and once more, it was called off because of bad weather. It looked as if the bombers would be idle for a few days so I came back to London.

Yesterday, however, for the third day in succession they went out. This time they kept going and when I heard about it, I was more than a little disappointed. In the office I had already written a story on the boys' last trip, how they all would be home in a few weeks.

Last night I called the base and was told Capt. Mac and the boys didn't get back. They were hit by enemy fighters over Germany. Crews in other planes in the formation saw five to seven men bail out and saw Mac going down under control which means, I hope, that everybody got out safely. Before he went, Mac told other planes over the radio, "I won't be going back with you today, boys."

So there it is. It all made me fully realize one thing. I've made my last mission! From this day on, I'm looking out for us, and us alone.

[Billee to Charles] February 25, 1944—Asheville

Maybe, like me Charles, you get a lost feeling sometimes. It has been so long. I don't know how to say it but it kind of makes you bitter inside when you see other young couples together, living a reasonably normal life. At least they are together. So many are stationed here. They go to work at eight and finish at five. They have apartments and except for the khaki, live like civilians. One girl in the bank has been here with her husband for eighteen months.

We received a cable from Warren that he arrived safely overseas, so perhaps you'll be seeing him soon.

[Charles to Billee] February 26, 1944—London

You did give me a start when you said, "Have I mentioned Freddie in my letters?" But after hurriedly reading on, my mind was put at ease. I'm terribly jealous. You will find that out as time goes on.

Another question you asked, about my part in the invasion. I have purposely held it back until I could be more definite. As it is now, three or four men on the staff may go with the troops. Naturally, I want to be one of them and have been promised a place. But, things change quickly.

They wanted me to take a desk job, for the third time, a couple of weeks ago but I turned it down. It would be ideal if I was cut out to stay inside and wait for everything to happen but I guess I'm not built that way. It would mean editing other men's stories, but I'd rather get out and do them myself. It's bad enough when I have to put in a week or so of rewrite when an emergency arises.

Besides, I have too many good contacts in the Air Force and infantry to throw them away. No, I believe I could do a better job the way I am, and I'd be happier.

/////

[Charles to Billee] February 27, 1944—London

At about five o'clock this evening, I received a phone call at the office. The voice on the other end said, "Is this Staff Sergeant Kiley?" After I had answered in the affirmative, the voice went on . . . "This is Sergeant Gray."

You could have bowled me over with something lighter than a feather. I had to laugh over the formalities, what with ranks and all.

At any rate, Warren has just arrived at a Combat Crews Reception Center, about 30 miles from here, and I'm planning to get out and see him Tuesday.

He will be there for three days before going to a gunnery range for a "refresher" course. Then he will be assigned to an operational group. All this is a follow-up to the cable I'm sending after I meet your brother. I'll have a lot to say after I give him a chance to size up his future brother-in-law.

/////

[Charles to Billee] February 29, 1944—London

Warren and I are going to make a pair of pretty good brothers-in-law. I decided that during the first minute of our meeting today.

He doesn't look at all like you, does he?

I took an early train out of London this morning and met him at 10:30 in the gunnery office of the post where he is staying until the end of this week. After another week at an advanced gunnery range, he will move on, together with his crew, to an operational station.

I won't see him until after he is settled at his permanent base but he is sending me his address as soon as he reaches it and I'll keep in touch with him. He probably will not get a pass that would enable him to come to London for a while yet. In the meantime, however, I'm sure I'll get an opportunity to visit him. Naturally, I expect he will be spending most of his free time with the boys in his crew.

Incidentally, Warren is stationed at the same gunnery school at which I earned my "wings." I knew most of the boys who are permanently stationed there as instructors so the visit gave me a chance to renew old acquaintances. When I introduced one of the instructors to Warren and mentioned him as the brother of my sweetheart, the instructor wise cracked, "So, you came over to check up on him?" I had to smile when Warren flushed and stammered, "Not me."

Charles with Warren Gray—England, March 1944. (Kiley Family)

I'm going to say goodnight now, while looking at you smile from your picture only a foot away. May I tell you again how beautiful you are? There is a French quotation that speaks for my thoughts . . . *"J'amour plus que hier et nous que demain."* (I love you more than yesterday and less than tomorrow.)

CHAPTER 7

MARCH–MAY 1944

For the first time today, I realized fully how much of an obsession you have become with me. It has been so for a long time now, I guess, but I laid it at the doorstep of endless devotion, a deep love and a painful separation.

[*Charles to Billee, May 1944.*]

///////

The War: Field Marshal Rommel determined that the Atlantic Wall was a disaster. He tried to persuade Field Marshal von Rundstedt that the invasion would be at Normandy, but von Rundstedt believed it would be at Pas-de-Calais, and denied Rommel an armored reserve. Rommel had troops install stakes, mazes, and mines on the beaches of Normandy.

In early March, the US Eighth Air Force suffered more than three hundred bomber losses, yet intense bombing of Berlin and Nuremberg continued. On March 15, nearly eight hundred Allied bombers all but flattened Monte Cassino about eighty miles south of Rome. At the same time, travel to and from Ireland was sealed off in preparation for the Allied invasion; following that, diplomatic privileges were restricted and all embassies were under surveillance.

In late March, seventy-six POWs escaped through tunnels they had dug underneath a German prison camp at Sagan, some eighty miles southeast of Berlin. In May, fifty of the POWs were recaptured and shot by the Gestapo. This action was famously recreated in the 1963 movie *The Great Escape*.

An Allied invasion exercise, Operation Beaver, ended in utter confusion; the following month 638 American troops died in another practice, Operation Tiger. The final practice, Operation Fabius, along the southern British coast, was deemed satisfactory.

In April, while US aircraft bombed the Volkswagen plant near Hanover, US bombers mistakenly killed civilians in Schaffhausen, Switzerland. At around the same time, German soldiers began to evacuate Crimea on the Russian front.

On May 8, General Eisenhower set D-Day for June 5. On May 9, German Admiral Dönitz said that he did not expect an Allied invasion in the near future.

/////

[Billee to Charles] March 2, 1944—Asheville

Did I tell you I spoke to a lieutenant on Sunday that I used to go to school with? He's in the 12th Armored Division. I said I knew someone in the Fifth, meaning Eddie of course. He said, "Oh yes, they are due for some excitement very soon."

I went to the movies tonight with Freddie and we decided to walk home. I don't know why he hangs around. I'm not such good company but I guess it is someplace to come to that's like home. We saw *Gung Ho*, the story of Carlson's raid on Makin. Very exciting, of course. The husband of one of the girls in the bank made quite a name for himself over in France the other day. He's a Capt. Benzing, a bombardier I think, shot down three German planes.

Lately, I've felt the need of you so much. Do you get like that? Just one big ache, then you start slinging insults under your breath at everyone who's keeping us apart.

/////

[Billee to Charles] March 6, 1944—Asheville

What can I say or do? I'm so very grateful. It is the answer to my prayers that you are being kept safe. The next thing . . . what of the boys that went down? I hope you hear word very soon that they are safe as prisoners or perhaps in friendly hands, and that Mac bailed out in time. I get frightened just writing about it, Charles. I hardly know what to say. It's too big, but I'm so glad that it was your last mission.

I'm thinking too, how you must feel after knowing those men and being with them just a few nights before. I'm remembering your letter written the night before you were to go up.

We received a V-letter from Warren today written the 22nd of Feb. Mom was more than glad to hear from him. He said he was at a reception center. Didn't say much more. Poor guy hasn't received any mail yet.

These new raids are frightening Mom. It's in her face ... wondering is Warren taking part? I've told her it will probably be several months before he goes into action.

/////

[Charles to Billee] March 9, 1944—London

I love you because when my eyes first found you I tingled all over; because you are soft, tender and sincere; because you are intelligent with just enough devilry; because your eyes are sleepy and because I haven't lost the taste of your first kiss; because you like to dream the way I do and are sensitive the way I am; because you love children and because you are beautiful, even in the kitchen wearing an apron and an unruly curl on your forehead; because you are independent and could tell me to go to _____ and (maybe) get away with it; because you know a first baseman from a fullback, are romantic and enjoy good music, good books and good scotch; because you are all I ever wanted to come live with me; because you give me confidence and ambition; because you taught me faith; because you remember the little things that mean so much; because I have missed you so much the ache misted my eyes; because I wouldn't or couldn't go on from here without you; because you are all that matters to me; because your nose is tilted; because you love me! and, even if you didn't, I would still love you!

You must have heard the news of the daylight raids on Berlin. Probably played up sensationally in the American press. The receding losses on the three large-scale attacks are significant of waning enemy fighter strength, I think. We lost 68 heavy bombers in the first raid, 36 in the second and only seven in the third.

Of course, the birth of the quadruplets almost pushed the war off page one last week. It could only happen to an American soldier! We weren't allowed to print a line about it (ruling handed down from HQ) although the British papers and American correspondents went all out. I sat in on a press conference at which the fellow, a sergeant in the Engineers, issued a prepared statement saying he was going to do right by the girl, that he loved her and has asked his wife in Pennsylvania for a divorce. The girl, incidentally, was in the ATS, the British equivalent of our WAC.

Just had a funny thought: you haven't had quadruplets in your family, have you?

[Billee to Charles] March 10, 1944—Asheville

I've been awfully busy yesterday and today. The teller next to the head teller has been out sick. I don't know what he has wrong with him. Of all things, they gave me his window [with] all big commercial deposits. They really broke me in but I fooled them. Balanced twenty thousand dollars to a penny. You have to keep your wits about you, playing with that much money from nine to one. Working with money has spoiled me. Money seems to have lost its value. The only time it has value is when you come up over or short at the end of the day, especially short.

[Charles to Billee] March 12, 1944—London

Your brother just called me long distance. I couldn't imagine who it was at first because I'm not one to get calls at 11 p.m. very often.

He has been assigned to an operational group and called to let me know which one so I can track it down. We can't identify unit locations over the phone but in this case, he didn't have to. I knew where he was from the number of his group. And here is some good news: the bombardment group to which he has been assigned has the record for the entire Eighth Air Force of losing the fewest planes. Of the 112 bombers lost on the three big Berlin raids, his group didn't lose a single one. I believe it was the only group to escape completely. I'm planning a trip to his base about the middle of next week.

I suppose I should have preceded my story of today's activities with a report on yesterday, because it was one of the most interesting and enjoyable afternoons I've had over here. It was a working day but Andy and I managed to combine business with pleasure by having lunch with Lady [Nancy] Astor, Virginia-born "stormy petrel" of the House of Commons, and later sitting in on a Commons' legislation session. I'd better start from the beginning so you will understand how we got there in the first place.

Andy plans to do a story on Lady Astor, the angle being she was American-born. Years ago she married one of the Lord Astors and for a long time now, she has been a Member of Parliament from Plymouth. That is equivalent to our congressional representative. I don't know who I compare her with in our House but it is a matter of record that she has been lauded and criticized more than any other five MPs put together.

Andy made an appointment with her through her secretary and asked me to accompany him to Parliament yesterday. We met Lady Astor, had lunch with her and another female MP, talked for over an hour of a million things and then sat in the visitors' gallery of the House for a couple of hours listening to a debate on an education bill.

I came away with the impression that Lady Astor is one of the most out-spoken, sincere and lively personalities I have ever met. She is in her early 50s or late 40s, I would judge, but is as active as a girl of 20. [Nancy Astor was 65 in 1944.] If I dared write some of the statements she made I could get a tidy sum for the story.

But of course, a lot of what she said was off the record. Still, a lot of journalists have taken her at her word in the past, which gave her some anxious moments. She openly admits not being the least bit afraid of saying what is on her mind. She is sharp-witted and sharp-tongued as more than a few of her colleagues have found out. Although Churchill is a close friend and both belong to the Conservative Party (counterpart to our Republican Party) she attacked him, or I should say "opposed" him, on many issues. She smiles when she recalls the day she objected to a point on Anglo-Russian collaboration, and objected so vehemently that the prime minister called her a fascist.

"I'm nothing of the sort," she says. "And Winston knows it. As long as I am able to fight for what I think is right and have a voice in the House, they can call me anything they want to. I've called people worse than that so I guess I can take it when I have to."

[Nancy Langhorne Astor (1879–1964) was the first woman to sit as a Member of Parliament in England; she served from 1919 until 1945.]

/////

[Charles to Billee] March 15, 1944—London

Warren called again today, just by way of keeping you informed about him. You see, today was the day I was to visit him but I had to postpone it until later in the week. I figured he would realize I would be up in a few days but when I didn't turn up, he thought something happened to me and called the office long distance. Looks like he is worrying about me when it should be vice versa. He isn't on "ops" yet but will be in about a week. They keep new crews on the ground for a few weeks before putting them on operational status. He said he hadn't received any mail yet, which isn't at all surprising. Takes time to be forwarded to a new APO.

You are taking perilous chances with reports of Freddie turning up on Valentine's Day armed with a box of candy plus the acknowledgment that his presence gives you more of a "miss you" feeling than usual. Sight unseen, I'll agree with you, that this young man is all you say he is. But the mere thought of him, or anyone else, reaching the "candy and movie" stage makes me want to go over the hill and take the next bomber to Canada. Moreover, when I picture you in somebody else's arms at the camp and canteen dances, I tremble with jealous rage.

Seriously, perhaps I shouldn't want to see you getting opportunities for a little enjoyment. I do, honestly. But I love you enough to make me intensely jealous, which isn't so good from this distance, is it?

/////

[Billee to Charles] March 15, 1944—Asheville

We've had three V-letters from Warren but not anything this week. Poor kid is probably still waiting to hear from us and doesn't feel like writing.

A letter from Bette today tells me they received a V-letter from Eddie but nothing that tells them where he is. She said her Eddie [Bette's boyfriend] is somewhere in the South Pacific. I'm still very grateful you weren't sent there. It seems like such a long, long way from here.

[Charles to Billee] March 16, 1944—London

Remember me mentioning Sally Reston of the *N.Y. Times*? She called me today to say the *Times* wanted one of my stories. Fact is, she asked for it a few weeks ago and said she was sending it to New York for an ok. The N.Y. office said it would like to use it in its Sunday magazine. She confirmed the cable today and said she would let me know when it was used. She also said a check was forthcoming.

[Charles to Billee] March 17, 1944—London

Remember reading about the Fortress crew that flew a donkey with them from Africa to England last August? Her name is Lady Moe and she is the mascot for Warren's group. Bud Hutton did a story on her.

Incidentally, Bud and Andy finished their book, *Air Gunner*, and mailed it today to the New York publishers, Houghton and Mifflin.

I'm going away for two weeks on March 27. I'll write while I'm away this time, though. It's for a special course for correspondents and is being arranged to indoctrinate them with invasion tactics.

About the Capt. Benzing you said shot down three planes recently. I doubt if he was a bombardier. Sure he wasn't a fighter pilot? In these days, fellows in bombers seldom get a chance to even fire their guns with all the fighter escorts around. And it would be very unusual for a bombardier to get one, let alone three.

[FROM THE *STARS AND STRIPES*, March 16, 1944]

THE LADY MOE STILL ALIVE, KICKING

DONKEY FROM ARABIA LEADING THE LIFE OF A CHOW HOUND; NO GRASS FOR THIS ASS IS HER MOTTO; SHE WANTS FOOD!

by Bud Hutton, *Stars and Stripes* Staff Writer

A FORTRESS BASE, Mar. 15—Lady Moe, a tub-gutted Arabian donkey who mingles with mess sergeants, Grosvenor House society and other exalted people, is becoming a legend and she'll chew (literally) the tail out of anyone who doesn't like it.

The gravel-voiced mascot of this base flew to England in a B17 returning from the shuttle raid to Regensburg and North Africa last August. She weighed 50 pounds, was soft-coated, nuzzling-nosed, gentle and thin. The airmen took her to heart, bathed her, petted her, let her sleep in their huts and fed her.

Today Lady Moe is 150 pounds or more, shaggy-haired and redolent with B.O., sharp of tooth, ornery and fat-bellied enough for these Fortress men to compare her with a Liberator. She is still in the men's hearts, but they no longer bathe her, nor do they let her sleep in the huts, and she has been stigmatized with the epithet of "chow hound."

The boys still love Lady Moe. They will swear fiercely that she is the best air base mascot in the ETO, which, of course, means all the world. They will feed her (even as she bites off their hands up to the wrist because she is tired of Spam). They will pet her (even as she whirls on her forefeet and belts their shins with a pair of lashing hooves.) They will lie in their sacks and recount her exploits (even as she brays her long-eared head off at the moon to keep them awake.)

Since the day Capt. Andrew Miracle, Loyall, Ky., pilot and his crew of *The Miracle Tribe* bought Lady Moe for 400 francs from a beat-up old Arab donkeyman, made her an oxygen mask and brought her back here by way of the raid on Bordeaux, she has grown in legend in exact proportion to the now alarming extent of her cast-iron gut.

These days a gunner or maybe a line chief will be walking down the dark perimeter track after a midnight job of work on a B17. He will be maybe thinking of payday, or home-made fudge or his gal when something will jab him from behind and a hideous noise will rend the night. Lady Moe—and they still love her.

Lady Moe was shown where the mess hall was—the combat mess. She was shown once. After that belly-inflating experience, Lady Moe knew. She would be standing in green grass a mile away and when it was exactly 11:30 o'clock she would whirl, head for the mess hall past idling engines and busy mechanics, in front of visiting colonels to the chow lines.

It was all very cute, the gunners said, and they would feed her and scratch her ears. They would feed her and scratch her ears from 11:30 to 1 o'clock when the mess hall closed and then the cooks would feed her a little more. After a while, though, some of the boys found they weren't getting much time to eat themselves and they told Lady Moe to go away after the first tid-bit. That was the beginning of the legend.

Lady Moe began to nudge gunners on the part of them that stuck over the edges of the chairs. She would nudge them twice and if she still got no response, she would sink her broad donkey's teeth into that same portion that stuck over the edges of the chairs. If they had a *Stars and Stripes* stuck in their back pockets at noon chow, maybe she'd first pull that out and chew it up.

As she grew in size, Lady Moe found food harder and harder to get, even at the threat of the bared front teeth. So she began to lurk quietly in the back of the mess until some unlucky gunner put his food down at a table and went off to get coffee, or maybe jam for his bread. As soon as he had left the table, Moe would sprint to his place, lick the plate clean (spitting out any knives or forks she'd gulped) and retire. Every now and then a gunner would belt his innocent neighbor when he returned and found an empty plate.

Then there was the affair at London's swank Grosvenor House.

The Society for the Protection of Animals in North Africa president, Her Grace the Duchess of Portland, was giving a ball at Grosvenor House. They invited Lady Moe. The boys in base PTO went out to get the crate they'd shipped her in the last time and someone had busted it up for firewood, so they made another and sent her to London, resplendent in a new orange blanket.

Lady Moe was a great success at the ball. She chewed off the orange blanket, spat the pieces on the floor, repeatedly fell off the platform when benevolent-minded dowagers tried to pet her, mussed up the place in general and took a bite at the breeches of a naive individual who chewed gum in front of her. She was a very great success.

Moe rode back on a night train. There was a party at base when she arrived at the railroad station. The baggage master had dealt with Lady Moe before, so he called the base immediately, and when he couldn't find the PRO he called the MPs. About 3 o'clock in the morning the PRO staff had to get Lady Moe out of the guardhouse.

About this time there came to the relationship between Lady Moe and M/Sgt. Jasper Baker, of Jacksonville, Fla., a new deal. Group headquarters issued an order barring Lady Moe from the mess hall, and Baker heaved a reluctant (he still loved her) but relieved sigh. Moe, who had found there were three other messes besides the combat mess, tried them all. No soap.

Each day, then, Lady Moe stood wistfully at the combat mess entrance. She would sigh as the gunners went in to chow and she was waiting there as they came out. She would nuzzle them gently, stirring their memories. It was very touching. Of course, if their memories had happened to forget to being her a little sugar or maybe a piece of chicken, Moe would whirl around and kick the khaki off any stragglers. All very touching.

Moe took to playing with a pack of dogs about this time, and with Smokey, a Dalmatian owned by Col. James Travis of Portland, Ore., the group commander, would delight in racing through mud puddles as soldiers were passing.

The boys put up a tent in a hollow, bought a batch of the market's best hay. Not for Moe. She'd been sleeping in Nissen huts and she intended to continue. By this time she'd grown big as a small horse, fat, shaggy and was somewhat fragrant, and she couldn't understand why the boys resented it when she kicked in the outside doors after they'd turned her out of the hut.

She took to roaming the perimeter track late at night, and as some late-working mechanic would start for his hut in the darkness, thinking maybe of homemade fudge or a spam-less world, an ungentle nose would give him a shove, a dark shape would race away in the dark and through the still night air would go a brassy braying.

These days, Moe is out on what T/Sgt. Everett Lee, of Wenatchee, Wash., describes as "DS to the hospital because the grass is greener." She still gets to chow on time and she knows what time the PX is open. As a matter of fact, the PX is one of her favorite spots, because new gunners on the base usually can be cajoled into giving her a package of American cigarettes to chew. She's a little brassed off at the old gunners who got tired of giving her part of their cigarette ration and started to buy her English cigarettes for chewing tobacco. She doesn't like English cigarettes.

The other day a London newspaper carried a story that "Lady Moe, the famous donkey brought back from Africa by American airmen, is dead." The boys were a little alarmed, but it was all right.

It seemed there was another donkey named Lady Moe at another group. She had died. THE Lady Moe was still alive. The boys found her the very first place they looked—just outside the kitchen door at the combat mess.

Charles and Eddie Kiley—Fort Dix, 1942. (Kiley Family)

[Billee to Charles] *March 20, 1944—Asheville*

I had a long letter from El today. Eddie is in England, too. What a reunion that will be! I know how happy you'll be to see him. You'll have so much to talk over.

I didn't expect such a . . . how shall I say it? Can't find the words to express myself the way you do. I always manage to bring on things like this but in this instance, I'm glad I questioned your reason for loving me. You make me laugh and cry all with one page. You make the ache nearer and dearer for you. When you write like this, all my fears vanish.

From the reports on the radio, invasion will soon be a reality. I want to see it come because I know the sooner it happens the climax of this will come, but I'm dreading it. My imagination is such that I know what it will be like, but most of all those people that mean my whole life will be taking part—you and Warren. I feel so helpless. I'm wishing you hadn't been so dead set against the WAC and the WAVE, it would have satisfied the restlessness in me [and] the need to do something materially that would be of some help to you indirectly.

The American soldier-superman got quite a lot of copy here. What a mess to get into. I feel sorry for the guy and the girl. I hope the girl in Pennsylvania comes through and gives them a break. Not even twins in my family, so you haven't a chance to gather that kind of fame.

/////

[Charles to Billee] *March 24, 1944—London*

We have company tonight, you and I, but I don't think you will mind.

Our company is Warren. He came to London on his first 48-hour pass about an hour ago. Furthermore, he called me from the station and came straight to the apartment. He will be with me until he goes back. Just now, he is talking "Air Force" with Ben. Warren won't be able to tell you much of his work because of Air Force censorship. I'll be his spokesperson.

He has come a long way in a week. During the last six days, he has been on four missions. One more and he gets the Air Medal. He went on "ops" last Saturday, Mar. 18. The target was Augsberg. On Monday he went to Frankfurt and yesterday to Big B ... Berlin. Today he went to Brunswick. Those names may not mean much, but they are four of the toughest places he could have gone to. Everything from now on should be easy. He came through all four in grand fashion and looks swell.

I went up to his base yesterday to see him, just in time to "sweat" him out on the Berlin raid. I was there when he came in, had our picture taken together by the plane, talked through the night with him and the other fellows of his crew and stayed overnight in his hut. I came back this morning and was frankly surprised to see him tonight. He said they got the pass when they landed this afternoon and he hot-footed straightaway to Clifford's Inn. Warren's only complaint is that he hasn't received any mail yet. But he is waiting for the truckload when it comes.

/////

[Billee to Charles] March 25, 1944—Asheville

We heard from Warren yesterday. He has a permanent APO now so perhaps he will be getting mail from us. He probably told you about the fellows he is with. He says the only news he's had of us is through you.

Wonder what Churchill is going to have to say tomorrow. Cassino isn't going so good. Hitler must have his best there.

/////

[Charles to Billee] March 25, 1944—London

I was going to write last night while Warren was spending his second night with me. But two things forced me to put it off until tonight. One reason was the late hour when we broke up a talkfest between Warren, Earl Mazo, Pete Paris and I. The other reason surrounded a little overhead activity by Jerry. Nothing serious but it kept us up.

I should introduce Earl and Pete. The former, if I haven't already spoken of him is a lieutenant who recently transferred from the Air Force, where he was a public relations officer, to the *Stars and Stripes*. He has an apartment, which he insists I share with him but which I use only when occasions like Warren's visit occur.

He has a bigger place than ours so after Warren spent one night with Ben and me, he stayed with Earl last night. I thought Earl and Warren would have a lot in common to talk of, and they did.

Pete Paris, a correspondent-photographer for *Yank* magazine, is one of the most widely traveled Army correspondents. He was in Africa, Sicily and Italy before he came here.

Getting back to your kid brother. After sleeping for 12 hours Thursday, he got up at noon yesterday, did a little shopping and took in a show while I was working. Later we met for dinner and went to Air Force headquarters where I had to finish up by writing one "raid" story. The bombers (ours) were out for the 19th day this month—a record.

Before going on to Earl's place, we stopped at the Stork Club (yep, we have one over here, too) for a drink. We were at Earl's only a short time when Jerry came. It was Warren's first experience and he thought he would rather drop them than catch them.

He went back to the base this morning to leave me with the unenviable job of packing enough stuff for two weeks in the country. The trip involves some sort of maneuvers and field indoctrination for correspondents. It won't be new for me, but Bob Moora thought I should go. There will be a flock of civilian correspondents there, I'm sure. There won't be much, if any, material for stories and that is mainly why I'm not as keen about the trip as I should be. However, it will keep me out in fresh air for a while and make my cheeks rosy.

[Billee to Charles] March 28, 1944—Asheville

We're all on edge now, expecting any minute that the invasion will be announced. Mom gets more upset every day. Looking at her, I'm thinking of all the other mothers with boys over there.

I'm just hearing Doolittle's report on Nazi planes destroyed by the Eighth and Ninth Air Forces. Not bad but our losses are heavy, too.

We had some excitement. Mom and Freddie were finishing burning off the back yard, preparing for the planting. The wind came up a bit high and we very nearly had the cottage catch on fire. The fire department came and we had a merry time.

I know what's wrong. I have spring fever. That's why I'm missing you so much. This is the second one without you. Seems like we said—or maybe it was just me—that we'd be together this Easter and here we are with still so many miles between us.

I'm not listening to any more predictions. There ought to be a law or something.

/////

[Charles to Billee] March 30, 1944—"Somewhere in England"

Charles (right) during pre-invasion training course, with other correspondents—England, March 1944. (Kiley Family)

This probably will be the shortest "date" we've had, mainly because there isn't much I can tell you about this sojourn into the country. This is our fourth day out of the city and the first I have had a chance to call on you. The schedule (and I can't tell you what it is for) has not been nearly as strenuous as the Ranger or assault training courses, but it has left me with stiff muscles here and there.

This is the first time I've been to this particular spot in England and it is one of the most picturesque I have seen. We have been favored by excellent weather, making it that much more enjoyable.

[Billee to Charles] March 31, 1944—Asheville

I loved your advice. If I thought something like Freddie getting to the movie and candy stage might bring you home, I'd . . . but then, I guess I wouldn't. Mom is looking after me, though. She says, "I don't think Charles would like you going out with Freddie."

Don't be jealous. Nothing to be jealous about. I get a little twinge now and then, like at the mention of the WACs and Mr. Frost's daughter—even Bebe Daniels—but, like you, I can't see you shutting yourself off in a corner.

Poor Warren. These more recent raids worry me a bit. I've told Mom it will still be some time before he goes out on the raids. I think it's better that way.

Last night after all the moving around I was too tired to make up my bed so I fell into yours—the one in the room with the private bath—and fell asleep almost immediately. I dreamed about you, too. I don't know where we were. Seemed a foreign place, but we were together and Warren was there. The hardest part was that I knew you were only there for the one night. I'll have to try sleeping in your bed again.

[Charles to Billee] April 2, 1944—"Somewhere in England"

There is a great deal of optimism over here about a possible quick success once the second front offensive is launched. I like to hear stuff like that, because it gives me something to cling to.

You ask, "Can you be jealous so many miles away?" Billee, I wouldn't dare admit how jealous I can be, and have been, "so many miles away." When I first met Warren, I wanted to ask him who this Freddie was.

When Warren was in London we were talking of you and Ben teasingly said, "I'll bet Billee is having the time of her life with all those guys in Asheville." Warren leaped to my defense so quickly I must have blushed. He said, "No, I don't think Charlie has to worry about Billee."

[Billee to Charles] April 3, 1944—Asheville

Mom was delighted today with your letter and her first airmail from Warren. She loved reading about her pride and joy. I told her of the missions, Charles. She has to know sooner or later. She has such a fierce pride in him, though, in everything he does, even this. She can't quite grasp the idea of Warren actually taking part in the "action," but she took it very well.

One thing you didn't tell me about Warren. How did it affect him inside? Could you tell? Warren is very impressionable. I've been more worried about that aspect of it, just as I was worried about you and how being in the "action" would affect you. He still seems so young to me.

You should have heard him rave about the Kiley hospitality in London and he admitted that he could see where I could see something in you.

[Charles to Billee] April 8, 1944—London

Home again! I arrived back in London about two hours ago and with dinner and a bath behind me I want to tell you all about the past two weeks.

The purpose of the school and two-week course was to indoctrinate correspondents who may cover the second front. Ours was the first class of 16. There is another class going through now and there will probably be a third. Most of the course was devoted to stuff I knew from my Army training (I sound like a civilian). But I did get acquainted with many officers who will work with us.

GREETINGS

To whom it may concern, and others.

Know all men by these presents that *Charles F. Kiley* War Correspondent representing *Star and Stripes* has this day satisfactorily completed the prescribed course of indoctrination in Foxhole Facility.

Said Scribe has demonstrated himself to be an admirable character and a gentleman, schooled in Chow Line Etiquette and graciously mannered during Convoy Breaks. He has further demonstrated his ability to nurse Shin Splints; to Swear by the Numbers; to bear the Burdens of a Soldier, cum Entrenching Tool; to remain prone without Sleeping; and to fit his Activities into a Prescribed Time.

These abilities having been noted and approbated, said Scribe is herewith awarded this Testament of Commendation. From this day henceforward he shall be a By-Line Officer of the United States Army, and will ~~simulate~~ the rank of Captain. His arm of Service will be the Corps of Cablese; his Serial Number is Chapter *XVI*.

He will Rank from his Last Appearance at a Bar and he is herein ordered for Permanent Duty to the Deadline Battalion.

Given under my hand in London, England, this *Seventh* day of *April* 1944

P. D. Widmer.
P. D. WIDMER.
Commanding, Widmer's Weary Wainjers.

[Handwritten signatures of attending correspondents, including:]
Pierre Granovat — French Independent News Agency — 8 April 1944
Wright Bryan — 8 April 1944 — "Atlanta Journal-WSB"
Capt. Watson "Australia Truth"
Arlie Randall "Evening Standard"
George Hicks — "Blue Network"
"Free McAteer, the racketeer!" Walter Peters YANK
Bill Davidson — "Yank"
Marsh Yarrow — "Reuters"
Philip Sturm — "Evening Standard"
Jack Coggins "Yank"
Ray Kenny "Yank"
William Stringer — "Reuters"
E. R. Noderer — "Chicago Tribune"
Roy Wells, P.R.O.
G. K. Hodenfield — "Stars and Stripes"

Spoof certificate from the training course, with signatures of other attending correspondents—England, April 1944. (Kiley Family)

During most of my free time, of which there wasn't much, I spent with George Hicks, Blue Network radio correspondent who recently came here from Italy, and with Wright Bryan of the *Atlanta Journal*, a 6 foot, 6 inch "suthin' gentleman." The names of those in our class are listed on the "diploma" we received and which I am enclosing. The name on top is that of Pierre Jannarat, an English-educated Frenchman who wore his monocle even when he played ball with us.

It is a beautiful Easter eve. Now, at 10 o'clock, a golden sunset is covering everything with a lush blue-red hue. It won't be dark for another 30 or 40 minutes because of the double-summer-time [during the war, Britain shifted daylight savings, or "summer" time by two hours].

/////

[Charles to Billee] April 9, 1944—London

Your sympathies seem to lie with the father and mother of the quadruplets born over here. You say you hope the sergeant's wife makes it possible for them to be married. From what I hear, that is the popular feeling at home. But, hell: I sympathize with the guy's wife who didn't have anything to do with it and is the innocent bystander. After all, the stork didn't bring the children. Why, sweetheart . . . you're blushing!

/////

[Billee to Charles] April 10, 1944—Asheville

There's no reason to worry about Freddie. I think he likes to talk to me because I've lived near New York and he is homesick, as homesick a guy as I ever saw. Ask Warren, he'll tell you Freddie is all right. We talk about you and he takes pictures of me, and says these will be for Charles.

Truly, he only makes me miss you that much more, makes the ache a bit worse is all, so don't be jealous, please.

We have a sergeant and his wife and four-month-old baby boy in the house.

He's so cute—the baby, not the sergeant. I took him to the store in the carriage today. I felt almost like Mrs. K., buying my groceries and putting them in the carriage. One of the clerks made such a fuss over him, saying he looks just like me.

Billee on the front lawn at Oak Lodge, with the Grove Park Inn in the background (upper right)—Asheville, April 1944. (Kiley Family)

/////

[Charles to Billee] April 11, 1944—London

You asked me about Warren's reaction to the missions. They are about the same as the average gunner's. They don't regard them as thrilling or adventurous after the first two, especially if they see a lot of unpleasant sights. It gets to be pretty important business with them. And Warren is just about like that. He talks a lot about them. That is, he did about the first four, which is a healthy sign. I don't believe he will talk about them much when I see him next. You will have to be prepared to meet a more mature kid brother when next you see him. True, he's young, but as I've said before, kids grow up awfully fast in the Air Force.

Now, about the story I sold to the *Times*. I wasn't going to tell you because I wanted to have you read it without knowing what it was about. Since you are inquisitive, however, I'll give you a brief outline.

It is a story about a soldier named Karl Warner. I never met him but got the story from men of his outfit who were in Africa. Warner was referred to only by the name of "Molotoff." He was tagged with the nickname while he was at Fort Bragg. His civilian background is rather mysterious. A boastful wise guy who never obeyed orders and wore outlandish uniforms, he was generally disliked by all until he went into combat. He turned out to be quite a hero before he was killed.

/////

[Note: The *New York Times* finally published a different version of the story; following is the version published in the Army newspaper.]

[FROM THE *STARS AND STRIPES*, May 26, 1944]

MOLOTOFF FROM BROADWAY

by S/Sgt. Charles F. Kiley, *Stars and Stripes* Staff Writer

They found him face down on the side of a hill in the Sedjenane Valley. Nearby were the lifeless bodies of French Commando scouts who fell with him in a suicidal attempt to storm a German machine-gun nest. This was the end of "Molotoff," the United States Ninth Infantry Division's one-man army and one of the most fantastic personalities of the war.

His name was really Karl Warner, but on the corner of Broadway and

Forty-sixth Street, his New York hangout, he was known as "Curly." He was a private, hated and loved by officers and fellow soldiers alike, who for a long time regarded him as the poorest example of a man in uniform. But before he fell dead on that Tunisian hill, Molotoff proved himself one of the most efficient, courageous and fearless soldiers in this or any other army.

A boastful, loud-mouthed "wise guy," Molotoff was allergic to discipline. He always wore outlandish uniforms and never completed a route march. He fell asleep on guard, deserted his post and talked his way free of two courts-martial. He won fabulous sums in crap games, squawked loudly about Army life from reveille to dawn, was insubordinate to all ranks and went AWOL.

But in combat, Molotoff performed incredible feats, albeit by his own peculiar methods. He never was known to get out of hand under fire and he subjected himself willingly to combat orders, but he raised hell when a colonel told him to get a haircut. He bluffed an entire Italian company into surrender with the same persuasiveness that saved him from courts-martial. He exposed himself to enemy fire on numerous occasions to direct artillery, and once saved his company from being trapped by a superior enemy force.

Frequently disappearing on solo expeditions for days, Molotoff located enemy positions that regular observers had failed to find. He captured an Arab spy and was the first of his outfit to scale the wall of a besieged fort, where he found more than 40,000 francs, which he distributed among his buddies. He killed more than a score of enemy officers and men in hand-to-hand combat on scouting trips.

No one knew him by his real name. It was always Molotoff at roll call. It was Molotoff from the moment another soldier pinned the tag on him at Fort Bragg after deciding Warner was "a radical." About his civilian life little is known except that he lived alone in a boarding house on Forty-fourth Street in Manhattan, that he hung out at his own special corner of Times Square, seemed to have been all over the United States, claimed to have been on familiar terms with radio and screen stars, did business for and with racketeers, and once said he was "part Russian and part Jewish."

Through the French Moroccan, Maknassy and Sedjenane battles he appeared at various times in French scarlet and blue capes, in an armored sol-dier's "zoot suit," in an Italian beret with a huge, black plume, and with an Italian officer's belt.

In Port Lyautey he quickly made friends with the Arabs when others failed to make any headway. His new followers built him a tent, furnished it with rugs, tapestries, lamps, pictures, a cot and mattress, table and chairs. They dug his foxholes and brought him fruit, wine and eggs.

The outstanding feat of this "poorest example of a soldier" occurred at Station de Sened, where Molotoff's platoon was covered by a company of Italian infantry dug in on higher ground. Molotoff brazenly walked up the hill toward the Italian position. The enemy thought it was a surrender and withheld fire.

With his gift of gab, Molotoff made them believe they were surrounded by a superior American force. The Italians said they could not surrender until ordered to do so by a colonel who was then in the rear. Molotoff went back up the hill a second time and when the Italians stood fast, he was first to charge and disarm 140 men without firing a shot.

The following day Molotoff told his platoon sergeant he was going up ahead "to see what the score is." Standing atop a hill 800 yards from his company and waving his automatic above his head, he shouted "Finish la guerre, finish la guerre." The sound echoed over the hills while enemy machine guns sprayed the area with searching fire. Crouched between two boulders, Molotoff made note of the gun positions, relayed the information to the artillery and soon the enemy emplacements were wiped out.

On his final exploit, he was part of a file assigned to maintain contact between his unit and a French force on the left flank. He sent back word that he was going up with the French Ghoums to see "what the score was." His final report was of a German machine-gun nest and he was last seen on his way to wipe it out with a patrol of the French Commandos. His body was discovered by the French, who found a Nazi flag—the American's last trophy—in Molotoff's hip pocket.

When he died a hero, there were two charges pending against this "poorest example of a man in uniform." They were dropped from the record in accordance with Army policy. Even in death, he beat the rap.

[*Billee to Charles*] *April 18, 1944—Asheville*

We had letters from Warren yesterday and today. He was to get a twelve-hour pass over Easter. I'm wondering if it was granted. We heard over the air that so many of the passes were canceled. He definitely doesn't care too much for it over there.

I wanted to tell you about Sunday—my ten-mile jaunt to a place I've wanted to see ever since I've been here in Asheville. It was so much more beautiful than I imagined that I wish now I had waited to see it with you. The place I'm speaking of is called the Biltmore Estate, the home of George Vanderbilt. He has some 12,000 acres here in the mountains. Before the war there was a charge of $2.00 per person but that was just to keep riffraff out. I thought it rather stiff but I can see it was well worth it. The house itself is closed to the public, but servicemen and whoever are with them are permitted in the grounds so I was "whoever" happened to be with Freddie. It was a beautiful day and the wild flowers and the trees are all in bloom. Everything is well-taken care of but still it has an untouched look. It's a three-mile jaunt to the house. Suddenly you come upon it, like something out of a book. It's fashioned after a French chateau—only has 385 rooms. Freddie, being a camera bug, was in his glory. He was oblivious to everyone except what he saw in the camera. We even forgot to eat.

I had lunch with my girlfriend, Elise, today and I was showing her the picture of you and Warren. Know what she said? "You must have done something awfully nice in your time, Billee, to rate a guy like him."

/////

[*Billee to Charles*] *April 20, 1944—Asheville*

Guess where I went last evening? To a boxing tournament, and enjoyed it. Moore General Hospital put it on for the benefit of the recreation funds. It was held at the auditorium and quite a nice crowd turned out. Nearly all the soldiers were there but the civilians supported it quite well. I was glad to see it. They had nine three-round bouts. One was an exhibition match, both boxers being professional before turning GI.

I couldn't help but think of you when I looked down near the judges' seats and saw two fellows busy scribbling away between rounds.

Yesterday's mail brought a long letter from Warren. Seems the girlfriend here isn't writing to him so we're getting the mail. I don't mean that the way it might sound, but when Warren's life doesn't go right, I always get showered with letters.

He tells me he was awarded the Air Medal plus an oak leaf cluster, which means ten missions, doesn't it? At the rate he's going, he'll have those 25 in nothing flat. He said he was going to bed when he finished the letter and it was only 7:00 p.m. He sounded just a bit homesick in this letter. I'm glad you aren't too far away.

///////

[Charles to Billee] April 23, 1944—London

We are going to move and a lot of things have to be straightened out. Ben left yesterday for a week's stay in our Northern Ireland office, which put the domestic load on me. We aren't moving far—just from the fourth floor to the third. It is a nicer apartment, better furnished and for the same rent. While Ben is away, Andy is staying here. He lent a hand with the packing, discarding of junk acquired, etc.

Today I was up bright and early to the office for a solid day of reading, chewing, swallowing and digesting material on "how a soldier can vote." It is in preparation for a series we are running this week. Last week it was "what a soldier can and cannot write on political issues at home." Do you wonder why I like the wide, open spaces?

Warren called again today. He has fifteen behind him now. Fifteen! Because of recent restrictions on leaves, he didn't know when he would be in. He has come a long way.

I received a letter from Mac's mother the other day. She hasn't heard anything since the news-breaking cable. She asked me what happened to his personal things. I had to tell her they will be sent to her after three months. Judging by her intimations, she hasn't received the personal effects of Mac's brother yet either, and he went down last October. She has recently received a card and letter from Mac's brother, both written in November from his POW camp.

///////

[FROM THE *STARS AND STRIPES*, May 1, 1944]

THE SOLDIER'S VOTE: WHAT YOU CAN AND CAN'T WRITE

[No byline]

The soldier's vote is important. So is his opinion, not only on political issues but any other controversial subject. The new Federal Voting Law safeguards that opinion from being misused.

Under this law, effective Apr. 1, persons in and out of the US armed forces are prohibited from conducting polls of soldier opinion with reference to the choice of candidate for election. The law also prohibits any other poll of soldier opinion, unless specifically authorized by the War Department.

This restriction is aimed chiefly at civilian agencies, such as newspapers, but is also directed at servicemen for their guidance. One of the main reasons for the restriction is military security. Enemy agents are not particularly interested in an individual soldier's opinion but they are anxious to know how a group, or the Army as a whole, feels.

There is no restriction on your private opinion and you can write about it, shout it and do anything you want with it. You may not, however, say your opinion is shared by anyone else.

The new voting law further restricts the dissemination to members of the armed forces of political argument or propaganda sponsored by the Government and which may be designed to affect the result of an election for President, Vice-President, Presidential elector, member of the Senate and House of Representatives, unless it conforms to the following:

1—Newspapers and magazines of general circulation in the United States, for which the preference by soldiers has been established through a method determined by the Secretary of war, may be distributed to soldiers.

2—Books of general circulation in the United States also may be distributed. Any books purchased by the Army after Apr. 1 for distribution among soldiers, however, must be free of any or all political argument or propaganda which may affect elections for Federal offices mentioned above.

3—A political address may be re-broadcast over Government-controlled radio stations provided that equal time, if requested, is given to other political parties having candidates for President in at least six states.

4—Movies, radio broadcasts and servicemen's newspapers and magazines—sponsored or paid for by the Government may be distributed to the armed forces if they are NON-PARTISAN and NON-POLITICAL. The impartial coverage as news or information of public events and persons in public life is not curtailed or prohibited. (The *Stars and Stripes* has followed that policy ever since it commenced publication Apr. 17, 1942.)

If any such presentation allots space or time to editorial comment or other argumentative matter supporting a political party which has a candidate for President in at least six states, an equal amount of time or space must be allotted in the same issue to similar matter concerning each other political party.

5—Any individual or corporation, other than a Government-owned or Government-controlled corporation or political committee, may send to any member of the armed forces letters, magazines, newspapers or other literature addressed personally to the soldier and paid for him by the individual or group sending it. Unless such material contains information which may be of value to the enemy, it will not be removed from mail by Army censors or any other Army employees.

These restrictions have little to do with the physical execution of a vote by a soldier but are published for his general information concerning the vote.

/////

[Billee to Charles] April 23, 1944—Asheville

One of the [radio] announcers, Upton Close to be exact [a reporter out of San Francisco], said last night that whatever happens in the European theater must happen within the next sixty days. The papers are full of "jitters."

One of the girls who lives here couldn't believe that I hadn't seen you in two years. Her lieutenant is awaiting overseas shipment at Fort Dix. He's called her every day for the past week. She spent last weekend with him in Richmond. She said she didn't know how she was going to stand it. I practically laughed in her face; then, I said I'd been standing it for two years. She said the way I talked of you it was as if we'd seen each other yesterday.

///////

[Charles to Billee] April 27, 1944—London

I have long since covered all the "big" things we did together. In fact, I have relived our biggest moments so often I can go through them all, step by step, without missing a single detail.

It is true I see you more clearly, sitting at the table in the "Y" where I first saw you; in my arms that first night; dancing at Lucille's; across the table at the Inn . . . Your uplifted face in the moonlight on the terrace; in our corner. At Penn Station for our "hello" and "goodbye."

I should have told you this before but hoped it would come gradually. You mentioned Warren finishing his 25 "in no time." Well, within the last few months the number of missions making up a tour of operations has been raised. It went into effect shortly before Warren started. It was brought up at a recent conference with Gen. Spaatz and his answer was that "it was now up to the commanding officer and flight surgeon to determine when a man is through."

However, the figure has been set at 30 for heavy bombers and 50 for mediums. So, with 15 behind him, Warren is half-way through. Let's hope the second half will be as easy as the first.

///////

[Billee to Charles] April 28, 1944—Asheville

I got too restless tonight, so after the dishes were finished I donned hat and coat and took myself off to a movie all by myself. I thoroughly enjoyed *The Hour Before the Dawn* with Veronica Lake and Franchot Tone. The setting is

England. On the same bill was a short subject called "This is America" depicting the life of a war correspondent. They picked one at random: Kenneth Burns of the Associated Press. Of course, I thought of you. It showed scenes of him gathering material at the invasion of Africa.

We had three letters from Warren this week. According to yesterday's letter, he just returned from his thirteenth mission. He's homesick.

/////

[Charles to Billee] May 1, 1944—London

It started out all right—a beautiful, sunny day. But after I was in the office for a while, I had the news broken, gently but from what I can see, firmly.

Comes the "big show," the office wants me to be chair-borne, doing deskwork, instead of going in with the invaders. They explain it won't be permanent; just until they get things organized after the first busy rush. If they told me I was going to be shot at dawn I wouldn't have been more surprised.

Seems the colonel mentioned it to Bob Moora a few weeks ago but Bob hesitated to tell me, knowing how much I had my heart set on going. Too, he hoped he would be able to persuade the old buzzard to change his mind. Bob knows who can and who cannot handle the job.

But the colonel, with the shortsightedness I should have expected, figures I'll be more of an asset on the desk. I don't know why I didn't suspect it because just before and after I went to the correspondents' school, I was put on the desk more and more.

Before the fireworks subsided in the conference between the colonel, Bob and me, I was able to exact a promise to get away from the desk as soon as possible. Desk! Hell, that's for Bob, Benny and the rest, but not for me.

Speaking of Ben, he's still in Ireland and screaming his head off to get back. Meanwhile, I'm maintaining bachelor quarters. Andy took off this morning for a week with the Air Force. He made another flight last week and Earl figures to make a couple this week. And here I am chained to a desk.

Ranger training, assault training, infantry training—all for what? What an Army!

/////

[Billee to Charles] May 2, 1944—Asheville

Did you ever feel as though you were sitting on a keg of dynamite? That's me for the past week. Must be "invasion jitters." I'm afraid to turn the radio on and afraid not to for fear I'll miss something. By the time this reaches you, it may have begun already.

I hope they give Warren a rest for a few days in some different surroundings. He sounded a bit tired in his last letter. He's really had a workout. It sounds like more than his limit. He doesn't say much of his work but then perhaps it isn't permitted. His missions read like a train schedule.

This weekend we've had a captain from New York in the medical corps. He did a lot of work at Seton Hall on Staten Island. He's a surgeon and very brilliant but still very young to have come so far. He's 34. He served in the African campaign.

I must tell you we had an inquiry from a midshipman at Annapolis for a room for he and his bride. It's priceless. "Would you please send me a list of your accommodations and prices? I should also like to know what facilities are available near your establishment for athletics and other entertainment. My bride and I are not looking for a stereotype honeymoon. Leisure and comfort are our first aims. We want to live, not squander the few weeks we have together before I put to sea."

Short and to the point, and my sentiments exactly. I'm going to love answering that inquiry.

/////

[Charles to Billee] May 4, 1944—London

I got out of the office yesterday long enough to have a two-hour chat with Ernie Pyle, Scripps-Howard columnist up from Italy, who yesterday was announced as a Pulitzer Prize-winner for "distinguished war correspondence."

Pyle is a swell fellow. Probably made himself more famous than any other newsman because of his stories of real life in the Army. He knows Ralph Martin well, and worked with him in Africa and Italy. I did a piece on Pyle, which ran on page one today.

///////

[FROM THE *STARS AND STRIPES*, May 3, 1944]

PYLE, GI JOE OF CORRESPONDENTS, HONORED FOR HIS SOLDIER STORIES: GETS PULITZER PRIZE, BUT REGARDS INFANTRYMAN'S PRAISE EQUAL TRIBUTE

by Charles F. Kiley, *Stars and Stripes* Staff Writer

Ernie Pyle, Scripps-Howard columnist for more than 300 newspapers, who recently arrived in London from Italy, yesterday received two messages.

One told the diminutive gray-haired newsman he had been awarded a Pulitzer Prize for "distinguished correspondence during the war." The other, contained in a letter written by an American infantryman at Anzio to a friend in the United States and forwarded to Pyle, described the GI Joe of war correspondents as "the best reporter in the whole damn world" and wondered "how a dried-up little guy like that gets around so much."

Pyle wasn't sure which of the tributes he appreciated most.

The 43-year-old newsman, who probably has filed more copy on the American soldier at the front than any four others, was one of five named for the Pulitzer Prize awards.

Ernie Pyle has been closer to the soldier than any other writer. He started to report the war to America during the Battle of Britain in the winter of 1940–41. With the exception of two brief visits to the United States, he has been at it ever since, covering the AEF in Northern Ireland early in 1942 and later the troops in Africa, Sicily and Italy.

Pyle's reports of a soldier's life, written while living, marching and eating with troops in combat zones, earned for him the title of "the GI's own reporter." His book, *Here Is Your War*, edited from columns written overseas, has sold more than a half-million copies. The book also is being used as a basis for a motion picture portraying the life of an infantryman.

Asked to play a leading role in the film, Pyle refused on the grounds that he preferred to stick to the Scripps-Howard job he has held for 21 years.

A reporter with honest and outspoken opinions, Pyle warned America two months after the African invasion not to expect "a walkaway" with small losses. He echoed the soldiers' own belief that it would take months of fighting for US forces to gain the experience the enemy started with.

Pyle came to Britain several weeks ago from the Italian front in order to be on hand for the next show. His bed-roll is packed.

/////

[Billee to Charles] May 5, 1944—Asheville

[Billee's Asheville friend] Evelyn Fragge's sister's husband is in the Pacific—New Caledonia. He wrote and told her to buy two Civic Music Club tickets for the new season. You buy them now for the season that starts in October or November and goes through April—concerts, symphonies, ballets, operettas—whatever they can bring. He told her he wouldn't be there for the first ones but he'd see the others with her.

I had the most interesting conversation with one of my customers yesterday, an Australian who is a refugee from France. He and his wife are writers and they lived in France for years. They got over the Spanish border just 24 hours before the German tanks got there. They really saw the fall of France. Very nonchalantly he says, "Of course, my wife and I would have been shot had we been caught since we've been writing against them for years."

/////

[Charles to Billee] May 6, 1944—London

This afternoon was chiefly devoted to getting caught up on mail and one of the letters was to [your] mother. In it I gave her the latest report on Warren.

A few hours after I mailed the letter, who should pop up again in London but your kid brother. He is on his way to the Air Force Rest Home at Southport for a week. Armed with a special pass giving him a couple of days in London, he is parking his bag with me until Monday or Tuesday.

As of today, he has 18 missions behind him. Only 12 to go now! If you haven't heard about the rest home before, it is a place where combat crews, officers and EMs go to take it easy and do whatever their hearts desire for a week. Fliers go there at various times. If nothing extraordinary occurs, a crew is sent there about halfway through its tour. They also are usually sent after a ditching experience in the sea, a crash-landing, or something which may shake them up a bit. The accommodations are ideal, food of the best and entertainment galore. Fliers refer to the place as the "Flak Home" since those suffering from jitters as the result of too much nervous strain rest up at Southport. Andy spent a few days there last week, not because he needed the rest but because he was lazy and wanted a few days off.

/////

[Billee to Charles] May 6, 1944—Asheville

I think I remember seeing something about increasing the number of missions to 30. I had a long letter from Warren last Friday, written the day he got back, telling me how much he enjoyed the time with you. His friend George said it was like being home, being in your apartment. I breathe a sigh of relief when I see his letters or hear of him through you.

You know the little things I remember. You shining your shoes in the kitchen at 195. Calling to your mom and asking for a needle and thread. Us poring over the map trying to find your brother's camp in California and the kiss you sneaked. The way you looked at me standing in the bus going to Journal Square when you left your hat in the luggage rack. The way you liked chocolate ice cream. The evening you kissed me goodbye on the corner where Ivey's is. You didn't want me to go to the bus station . . .

I haven't forgotten anything.

/////

[Charles to Billee] May 8, 1944—London

Warren has gone again. He left by train this afternoon for the rest home. I promised to try to get two days off later in the week and spend them with him there but I'm not very optimistic about my chances.

We had a couple of enjoyable days together, despite the fact that I worked during the day and was able to be with him only in the evening. It's odd that I have been with Warren almost as much as I've been with you.

Ben returned from Ireland last night and Andy moved to a hotel so the old homestead is back to normal. When Andy left, he put his wife's picture with those of Jane and you, so she will have company. Her name is Margaret.

Charles with Billee's picture—London, 1944. (Kiley Family)

Charles and Andy Rooney at the Cliffords Inn apartment—London, May 1944. (Kiley Family)

/////

[Charles to Billee] May 9, 1944—London

So, you folks at home have the invasion jitters like the rest of us. I suppose it is natural. That is, for families with men in England. It will happen just as suddenly for us as it will for you; in your case, it will be that little man in Radio City who sits beside a button for 24 hours a day. One day, or night, he will push that button. Bob Hope will be cut off in the middle of a gag. An orchestra will stop playing. A politician's speech will be interrupted and the little man will try to calmly say something like: "It has just been announced that British and American troops have landed on Fortress Europe." Those few words will cause

America to stop whatever it is doing. That will be the beginning of the greatest military operation in history.

The mystery surrounding my role in future operations continues. Today I was quietly told to report to a certain office. When I got there, I discovered my correspondent's credentials had to be checked so I could be accredited to Gen. Eisenhower's headquarters. I don't get it. Too deep and too much intrigue for me.

I also was presented with a list of instructions. One of them said, "Correspondents will not arm themselves with weapons." It also said that in the event of capture by the enemy, correspondents would receive "treatment accorded to an officer with the rank of captain." Well, that's one way to get a commission.

Getting away from painful subjects, you know I appreciate how you and Mom feel. But I want to caution you on one thing. Don't ever think I, or Warren, or anyone else is doing even as much as many others. The worst thing you can do to a flier especially is to make him feel he's a martyr. It is and will be natural for you to give them ideas they may not have. It happens to most fliers, especially those who finish. I've seen so many of them practically convince themselves they won 50 percent of the war alone.

Warren has been exceptionally sensible in that respect, and you should be proud of him. He has done a lot. But in the time he has done 18 missions, others have done 30. Some go out twice a day. Warren has been fortunate in that he has had only about a half-dozen rough trips. Let's hope it continues that way.

I still haven't heard anything of Mac and the rest. I'm just beginning to worry a bit, too. Before, I was confident but it's almost three months now and the usual time to report P/Ws is almost up.

/////

[Charles to Billee] May 14, 1944—London

Yesterday put me back in the Women's Page department, with a story written as a first annual report on the WAC over here. The Corps, incidentally, celebrates its second anniversary tomorrow and I've been assigned to attend a review and dinner at Supreme Allied Headquarters. There will be more brass there than there is in a barroom rail.

[FROM THE *STARS AND STRIPES*, May 13, 1944]

THE ARMY'S BETTER HALF CELEBRATES

by Charles F. Kiley, *Stars and Stripes* Staff Writer

Starting a gala weekend of festivity, pomp and parades, upward of 4,000 WACs in England lifted canteen cups yesterday to toast the first anniversary of the Corps' arrival in the ETO, and together with 65,000 other GI Janes in America, Italy, Egypt, North Africa, Hawaii, New Caledonia, India and Australia, those in this theater tomorrow will make it a double celebration by observing the second birthday of the women's half of the Army.

It was on May 12, 1943, that five Janes and six officers disembarked from a transport in the U.K. to pave the way for the arrival two months later of the first full-strength WAC contingent in Britain.

With dignity and firm morale, the Corps grew in numbers and reputation in the ensuing year to become as much a part of operations in the European theater as any GI outfit in the Army. Moreover, as the WAC grew, the ranks of resentful dogfaces diminished until today there are few still reluctant to admit that Jane has given a tremendous lift to the AEF in Britain.

On performance, the WACs have proved themselves. The evidence lies in the frank admission by Army commanders and soldiers alike that there are not nearly enough of them over here.

Like the rest of the Army in general, that portion of it in Britain a year ago was openly apprehensive over the arrival of traditionally emotional and unpredictable females, supposedly geared to fit into a war machine girding for the biggest military operation in history.

Jane came in luxury liners and cargo boats, seasick but upright, to ETOUSA headquarters, to all branches of the Air Forces, to services mushrooming from SOS such as Ordnance, QM, Transportation, Chemical Warfare, Engineers. She plotted, teleprinted, operated switchboards, typed, filed, made maps, assessed combat films, cooked, nursed and gave "shots" to jittery Joes, drove jeeps and trucks, handled intelligence records, sweated out missions from control towers and handled many more of the 239 types of jobs for which WACs train.

On parade, the smartness and precision of the Janes caused the eyes of hardened line troops to go up and down like elevators. For many soldiers, first glimpses of US women in uniform came in England; they had to admit the gals looked good. British and Canadian officers, long proud of their own girls in service, agreed that the WACs in review were hard to beat.

Whatever they were told or dreamed about life in the ETO, Col. Wilson's Army quickly discovered there wasn't much glamor in it.

The clammy English dawn made them shiver in heatless Nissen huts and concrete barracks as much as any Joe. Only the few hundred working in London and one or two other sections were billeted in more comfortable quarters. Discipline was strict, more so than in the soldier's Army. Passes weren't too plentiful. And there was mud.

On or off duty, there weren't many essential differences between Joes and Janes. The WACs short-sheeted bunks in their huts, wore boyfriends' insignia on their fatigues and maroon robes, fastened uniform buttons on the inside with captains' bars, or pilot and gunner wings for bracelets.

They also referred to an unpopular officer in much the same manner as a soldier.

The WACs also had a Liberator, the *Pallas Athene—The GI Jane*, named after them; they sponsored war orphans, often spoke before Anglo-American groups, organized choirs and Bible classes. The Joes were glad, too, that Jane was around to brighten up Aero clubs and canteens, and satisfy their craving for jitterbugging.

Proudest of all WAC boasts in their first year in the ETO has been their good conduct. Closely observed by ever-anxious gossipers, nearby and 3,000-odd miles away, Col. Wilson's Janes set a laudable standard for staying out of trouble, one that probably is not equaled by a unit of 4,000 in any branch of service at home or abroad.

Informed of a recent press report that only three AWOLs were on the books in three battalions, Col. Wilson last week spoke up and said there "never has been a single case" where a girl has been "absent" from her unit from more than three or four hours, and the latter usually because a train was missed.

Col. Oveta Culp Hobby, chief of all WACs, once said, "I predict that all America will be proud of them."

The ETO is ready to cast an affirmative vote after the first year.

/////

[Charles to Billee] May 15, 1944—London

I've been surrounded by women all afternoon but I wouldn't trade a squeeze of your hand for all of them. I went with a press party, most of which were women, to Supreme Allied Headquarters where a couple of generals reviewed some WACs on parade. The review was part of ceremonies marking the second anniversary of the WAC. The girls looked good. You have to give them credit for being hard to beat on parade.

My companions during most of the day were Dixie Tighe of International New Service, Ruth Cowan of AP and [a] WAC public relations officer. Dixie is always good company. She must be in her late 40s but manages to look and act like a prematurely gray-haired woman of 30. She was with me when I covered my first Air Force story in January of last year. Her husband, incidentally, is the London *Daily Express* correspondent in New York. There is an unusual paradox: he's a Briton in America and she is an American in England.

I heard yesterday that Ralph Martin was in New York with several of the men from Algiers. That may mean they are getting ready to fold up the paper down there.

/////

[Charles to Billee] May 17, 1944—London

The sun, moon and stars fell on Ben today. He is virtually assured of being in New York within a couple of weeks to open a bureau for us there. Unless something goes wrong with the simple routine of having his orders go through channels, he will be on his way. Yes, naturally, I'm envious but I would rather see him get it than anyone else.

His orders will put him on detached service for an indefinite period. Following a talk with the colonel, Ben said it was intimated that the job would be worked on a rotation basis but there isn't anything definite on it.

I don't have to describe Ben's feelings after being here for 28 months and away from his wife. It is even hard for him to talk coherently.

/////

[Billee to Charles] May 19, 1944—Asheville

With the new offensive under way in Italy, I keep saying "any day now." I've just been listening to a round table report from NBC announcers in London, those that are to go in with the troops.

I wondered about the prospect of your being armed so that question is answered. I don't want you to have a commission if it has to be from eating sauerkraut. I'd much rather have my staff sergeant. I can't help but get frightened inside at what the future holds as far as the invasion is concerned, but I know you'd be terribly disappointed not to be a part of all that.

I suppose Mom and I are a bit prejudiced where Warren is concerned and what he is doing, but I can see where you are right. I haven't commented on how much he's doing. I don't know about Mom since I don't know what kind of letters she writes him. It's a little bit hard for us to understand, Charles. I don't know how to explain exactly but you're over there near the enemy and you come in such direct contact with those who are doing the fighting. All we have is what is portrayed through Hollywood and what writers like you tell us.

/////

[Charles to Billee] May 19, 1944—London

I have all the information it will be possible to get on our N.Y. bureau.

The plans, as they are now and which are always subject to change, are for Ben to leave within a week or two to establish the office in New York. He is likely to stay there. After about two months, another man will join Ben to form a two-man office. This second man will be the first of the "rotators." He will stay about two months and return to London, being replaced in N.Y. by another man.

The colonel came back this afternoon and when I tackled him on the subject, he said he could not say whether or not the plan is definite. He said it was hard enough to get one man to N.Y. and we'll have to wait to see how higher-ups feel about the rotation. He couldn't say who would be included in the rotation and in what order, either.

There isn't much point speculating on these things in the Army. I can say this: if the rotation system goes into effect I won't be any farther down the list than No. 5.

[Charles to Billee] May 20, 1944—London

Billee, I can understand the times when you thought you had lost me and couldn't seem to find me anywhere. It is the "coming back," or the finding of one again that burns love in our hearts.

I haven't ever lost you, Billee. Of that I am certain because I can feel the warmth and security of your love by just pausing to think of you. It has been like that the whole time we've been away from each other. It is what causes loneliness, aches of remorse. And you can no more change that than you can hold back a tide or stop time.

There is an "off the record" with Gen. Eisenhower coming up Monday. Do you think I should ask him to take the wraps off the invasion and get it started?

Big raid on Berlin yesterday. Wonder if Warren was in it? I imagine he was since a strong force was involved. The new attack in Italy goes well. In fact, yesterday's news was the fall of Cassino after how many months of siege? Good news in the Pacific. All good news. Never seems to be any bad, but where are we?

[Billee to Charles] May 22, 1944—Asheville

The WACs are really on a recruiting drive around here. They'll be snatching us off the streets first thing I know. I hope you had a good dinner. I guess there are quite a few of them over there now.

Yesterday was a busy day. We had twelve for dinner so you can imagine. I had to stay up until two a.m. to put five soldiers to bed. Now don't get excited. One of the USO centers in town reserved rooms for five from Camp Croft and they didn't show up until that time.

We had a private from Moore General. He served in Africa for eight months until he was wounded. He'll be discharged very shortly. He told us quite a bit yesterday, a lot about the French Moroccans and how they saved the day at Oran. He told us how they cut the Germans' ears off and put them in baskets they carried on their shoulders. He refuses to salute officers. He said he didn't care what they did to him, but he hadn't seen one yet worthwhile saluting. He told, too, how much the *Stars and Stripes* meant to them on the front lines, as much as mail from home. They practically stampeded the distributor. He was in a hospital in England some time before being brought to the states.

/////

[Charles to Billee] May 22, 1944—London

My role in forthcoming operations has changed considerably. In fact, it has changed for a lot of us. We had a conference this afternoon: the colonel, Bob and five others including myself.

About 30 men from editorial, circulation and business offices will move with our invasion forces and set up a headquarters in the field as quickly as possible. Capt. McNamara, the *Stars and Stripes* adjutant in the business office will head the first detachment of eight men. I'll go with him to get the editorial side of the plan organized. The circulation manager will also be with us to start papers rolling on delivery.

A second detachment of eight, including Earl [Mazo] and Andy [Rooney], will follow us after a few days. The rest will come later, a week apart. Bob

[Moora] will stay where he is to head the home office. Bud [Hutton] goes with the Air Force, and Phil [Bucknell] with the airborne troops.

In short, it will be my job to investigate newspapers or publishing houses wherever we go and determine how quickly we can move a full force from London to "wherever" we go and launch a continental edition. Capt. McNamara will furnish the necessary "brass" to expedite business transactions. Meanwhile, I'll be filing stories whenever I can.

We will move shortly, I imagine, to a staging area and wait.

The new arrangements will not affect my status where the New York bureau is concerned. I willingly took the job as the editorial "executive" only after a promise to pull me back when my turn on the rotation comes along. That is, if the rotation is eventually approved.

Stars and Stripes D-Day team (back row, second from left) Bob McNamara; (front row, left) Charles; (front row, right) Bud Hutton—England, May 1944. (Kiley Family)

Andy is as eager as I am. He says, if his wife only knew he was going "to war" she would have all faith in Allied power. I began getting things in shape this afternoon and will finish tomorrow. Since the rent for our apartment comes due this week, in advance, I'm moving to a hotel with Andy.

I wanted to check on Warren today but didn't get a chance. They went to Berlin over the weekend and I'm anxious to know if he went.

/////

[Charles to Billee] May 24, 1944—London

So much has taken place during the last few days that I've been confused. I couldn't make a decision whether or not I was going to be satisfied. Some aspects of the job make it look bad. Too many parts of it have to be taken care of as we go along. No definite plans in advance. Then, on the other hand, it looks good in some respects. The news of the New York office naturally makes me think of that.

Ben leaves Sunday, four days hence. I was told our detachment leaves here on the same day for a post where we will wait and wait and wait. I spent the afternoon and evening just walking and sitting and thinking—trying to take each phase and settle it in my mind. All the time, I wanted you to talk with. You aren't supposed to know the answers, but I needed you. That's when I realized you were an obsession.

Andy says our future job will work out all right. I'm not certain because of the many holes in the plans. I've questioned them in talking with the officers but they claim they are in the dark as much as I am and will be until security regulations enable them to be revealed. I want things planned and insured to be foolproof ahead of time, which may explain why I can't put all of my faith in them.

After long hours of solitude today I met Andy at about eight and went to the Eagle Club for coffee. I was in a perfect mood for reveries, and I played "I'll Get By" on the jukebox three times in succession. I've admired Andy for his outlook on "the job." He was set to cover air forces just as he always has until this week, when he learned differently. Andy is all set, and while he, too, doesn't care for uncertainties, he says, "I know all the alleys and shortcuts in the Army now. I don't think I can get trapped. If things don't work out the colonel's way, we'll make them to suit ourselves."

///////

[Billee to Charles] May 26 1944—Asheville

I had two callers last evening, a WAC lieutenant and a male private. Seems they are following up the literature they sent and I threw in the wastebasket. She came right out and called me a slacker. I told her I figured your peace of mind and Warren's meant more to the war effort than my joining the WAC. I told her I had too many home responsibilities, too. That's no lie, either. She mentioned how lovely our home was. Says I, that's one of the reasons why I'm not a WAC. I told her joining the WAC would be a vacation. The soldier with her burst out laughing. She kind of gave me a dirty look. So that's that. Guess they are getting desperate and in spite of all my reasons, I do feel like a slacker.

///////

[Billee to Charles] May 29, 1944—Asheville

I had a letter from my older sister. Young Bill took four steps in his braces alone. She said he was so proud and of course, they were more than delighted.

Things are progressing well in Italy tonight. We are still going through invasion jitters. They must be cutting down on the mail, so many that I know who have brothers, sweethearts and husbands stationed in England haven't had mail in several weeks. I still get that sick feeling in my stomach when I think what it's going to be like.

CHAPTER 8
JUNE–JULY 1944

Mom awakened me this morning at seven with the news, "It's the invasion."... I'm sitting here quietly trying to find you in all the confusion and panorama of guns, men, planes ... trying to guess where among all those beachheads established you might be.

[Billee to Charles, June 1944.]

//////

The War: On June 1, the BBC transmitted a coded message in poetry to let the French Resistance know of the coming invasion. On the same day, the Allies ended Operations Fortitude North and Fortitude South aimed at convincing the Germans that an invasion was to take place at Norway and at Pas-de-Calais.

On June 2, Operation Cover began, sending planes to Pas-de-Calais.

On June 3, a wave of RAF round-the-clock bombings hit Pas-de-Calais and Normandy.

On June 4, US troops of the Fifth Army took Rome.

On June 5, 1,136 RAF bombers hit ten coastal batteries at Normandy, and gave cover to the first invasion troops, the British 6th Airborne Division, who landed in gliders.

On June 6 at 2:40 am, British paratroopers landed. Still believing Calais was the target, von Rundstedt took their arrival as a feint. The British Naval bombardment began at 5:30 am, followed by US troop landings at Utah and Omaha Beaches. All through the morning British, US, and Canadian troops landed ashore; with them went nearly six hundred journalists from Allied countries, all of whose stories had to pass through censors.

On June 8, after capturing a set of Allied plans, the Germans finally realized that the invasion of Normandy was not a diversion.

On June 13, the first ten German V-1 rockets hit Britain, killing six in London and setting off a string of V-1 attacks that by month's end had killed nearly two thousand civilians.

By late June, more than 5,200 Allied soldiers had been counted as casualties of the Normandy invasion. On June 27, US forces took Cherbourg at a cost of nearly two thousand troops killed and fifteen thousand wounded. Discipline broke down when troops in the US VII Corps discovered a cache of Champagne and brandy and got drunk.

After Rommel and von Rundstedt tried to persuade Hitler that the German military situation was dire, von Rundstedt was replaced. In early July, a planned assassination of Hitler and his top generals, Himmler and Goering, was called off when the generals did not show up at a planned meeting. A second attempt on July 15 was foiled when Hitler left a conference earlier than expected. A third attempt on July 20 also failed. When it was learned that Rommel was in on the plot, Hitler forced him to take poison.

[Billee to Charles] June 1, 1944—Asheville

I'm anxious about you, Charles. No mail all week. I've gone longer before, but I guess it's because of the coming invasion and all, keeping us on pins and needles, and missing you so much.

[Charles to Billee] June 2, 1944—"Somewhere"

I know when this reaches you there will have been another week, at least, between my letters. It has been quite a week—working 15 hours a day mostly—up at 6:00 and to bed at 11:00, just like the old days with Company H.

You will be able to tell how little I can say to you. This is a place that is more security-minded than almost any I have ever encountered, and for a good reason.

Since we arrived there has been much more preparation and work to be done than I had imagined. But it is being done and now, after a week, we just about have our feet on the ground.

Andy and I are living together, far short of the comfort and freedom we enjoyed in London, but not too bad. If we only had beds, it would be positively swell. I'm not certain I can tell you how we are living, so until I find out you will have to simply picture me living in a house but without a bed, rising at six and dressing in leggings, field jacket and steel helmet, eating in Army mess and coming home late looking like a real soldier. [Charles and Andy Rooney had been quartered with a very unwilling family in Bristol, England, while they waited for their invasion orders; the two were provided with a piece of floor to sleep on and a roof over their heads, and that's it.]

/////

[Billee to Charles] June 3, 1944—Asheville

Saturday night—the Hit Parade is playing. Sinatra crooning . . .

Still no mail. There was a piece in the paper this morning about the restriction of mail from England. My last letter was dated May 17 and Warren's was about the same date.

We had a little excitement when the report, in error, came over the radio today that the troops had landed in France.

I think the rain has stopped now. We could go out if you wanted to but I am comfortable snuggled on your shoulder. Let's stay in. I'll make coffee and sandwiches later. Tell me all the things you wanted to tell me when I wasn't around. Those nights you stared at the ceiling making up imaginary conversations. Have you done that? Yes, so have I, by the hour.

/////

[Charles to Billee] June 6, 1944—"Somewhere"

This may be my last letter for a while.

It is after midnight now and we have been busy since eight this morning.

Today has been one we have been waiting for, for a long, long time.

The aerial bombardment and naval support preceding the landing of airborne and ground forces must have been terrific. I'm sure Warren was in on it since the announcement said bombers in "very great strength" were employed.

The amazing, but wholly satisfactory item was the statement that Allied losses in the landings were extremely light. The latest news said our forces have pushed inland seven miles.

With the fall of Rome earlier in the week, today's success makes things look good all around. I'm not optimistic enough to feel it is the beginning of a quick ending but it is a good start in the proper direction.

Your letters mean more to me than ever now. And, if I couldn't rely on anything else to give me peace of mind, you will.

Wherever I go and wherever I am, you will be by my side and closer to my heart than ever. I'll think of you more often and yearn more for the beginning of our own "D-Day." Smile, angel, and kiss me goodnight.

[Billee to Charles] June 6, 1944—Asheville

Mom awakened me this morning at seven with the news, "It's the invasion." She had a strange look on her face—confusion, relief, anxiety. I didn't know whether to laugh or cry. I did more of the latter, I guess.

Everyone is calm outwardly—all of us a little cautious. Trying not to be too optimistic. I'm afraid my mind wasn't on my work. I kept thinking of you wherever you might be, and Warren, and wondered where Eddie might be.

Words somehow seem futile. Each news bulletin comes fast and furious. The direct reports haven't been too clear because of atmospheric difficulties. We were to hear an eyewitness account just now but they couldn't get through . . .

They got through, and George Hicks is giving a blow-by-blow description and we can hear the guns.

So far, things are going too well. Doesn't seem possible that there could be so little opposition. The lack of air defense is what puzzles me. We've all felt that they were conserving the Luftwaffe for just this time.

Still no word from you.

/////

[Billee to Charles] June 7, 1944—Asheville

I turned the radio off for a little while because I wanted to be with you. Everyone is in bed or out and I'm sitting here quietly trying to find you in all the confusion and panorama of guns, men, planes—trying to guess where among all those beachheads established you might be and wondering how long it will be before I hear from you.

It's difficult to write, it should be something gay and carefree, but I feel very grave and cautious.

According to reports here, things are still quiet. No counter-offensive has begun yet today, and they are, *and* we are, wondering why.

Already you hear predictions. One of my customers today, said 60 days. The writer I mentioned in a previous letter, the one that lived in France, came in and asked me if I thought you were there. He wished you well and proceeded to tell me a little of Normandy. He lived there for some time. He said we had a tough fight ahead.

Mom is holding up. Of course, we expect Warren is in there pitching too. I'm proud of her because she is doing so well. She stays pretty close to the radio. We have one upstairs and one down.

I'll say good night, wherever you are.

/////

[Charles to Billee] June [9 or 10], 1944—"At sea"

We have been together in some strange places before, but I'm certain this one gets first prize.

I didn't intend to write until I had a better opportunity. However, as I lean against the side of the ship tonight, looking out into the gray-black night to where you are, I want to be with you in this way at least.

I am on a Liberty ship, bound for what the radio says is "our beachhead in Normandy." Looking at the map makes it appear to be a simple process of getting from England to France. But it takes longer than you may imagine. We have been aboard for 3 days now and we are just about there. The travel experience has been reminiscent of our trip from America. That is, everyone sleeps with clothes on in the hold of the ship, wears lifebelt, etc. Our meals come right out of the can, prepared ourselves. We wash out of the tin helmets, sneak in a shower in the crew's quarters, and—wait.

This morning brought one of the most impressive sights I have ever seen, as far as strength in merchant shipping and warships is concerned. Passing a US battleship and two cruisers at a 200-yard distance, we watched them fire salvo after salvo at targets miles out of sight on land.

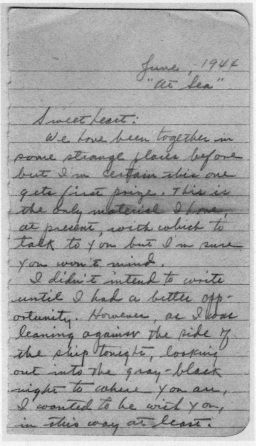

First page of the letter Charles wrote on his way to Normandy—June 1944. (Kiley Family)

Planes of every description have been soaring overhead in pairs, quartets, and large formations. In the distance, we heard shellfire on land. And in the midst of it all a chaplain spread his white alter linen over an oil-stained canvas on top of a hatch and celebrated Mass.

I'll have to apologize for not being dressed for a date tonight. My "ensemble," from shoes to helmet, are pretty grimy.

The news over the ship's radio says the beachhead has been extended along 50 miles of the Normandy coast and some 15 miles inland. Intense fighting in Caen however is still going on. When we sailed, I noticed part of Eddie's division on the way over so it looks like I might meet him again.

Thinking of you tonight, Billee, made me realize, or rather appreciate more than ever, how much it means to know someone is waiting. The mere thought of our life tomorrow brings the same feeling you get when you are wet and cold, and know that you will soon be before a warm fire.

[Billee to Charles] June 10, 1944—Asheville

I'm wondering where you are and what you are finding. I hope at this time maybe you are getting a little rest. This week must have seemed like a century.

So much excitement this week. First the news of D-Day itself, then Thursday night the dramatization of your story [the "Molotoff" story] on *The March of Time*. Did you know? I missed it. I'm so mad I could chew nails. I went to a movie and came in just as it was going off. Mom heard it all. I wrote and asked for a copy of the broadcast.

The news is good tonight. The Russian offensive has begun.

Mom is a little worried about Warren. We've heard nothing. She has his birthday cake all baked and ready to send. We're sending red, white, and blue candles for it. He'll be 20 years old, you know. Seems like yesterday he was such a kid and Mom had a big chocolate cake for him and ice cream.

I'm missing you and trying to find you in all the confusion.

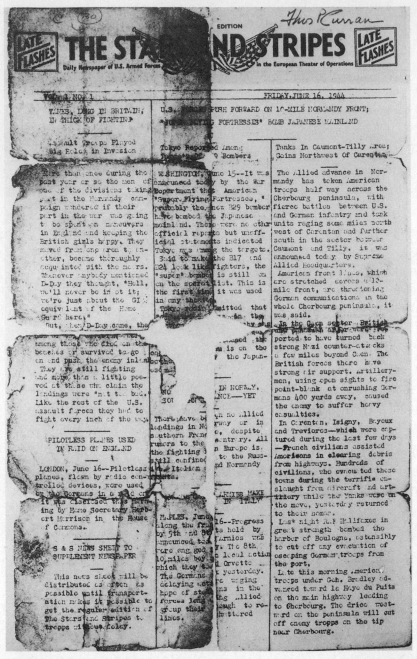

The first *Stars and Stripes* Beachhead Edition—July 1944. (US Army/The *Stars and Stripes*/New York Public Library Collection)

[Charles to Billee] June 14, 1944—Normandy

I have been here for three days now and this is my first letter from France. We just got out our first "beachhead" edition of the paper, a single page mimeograph sheet with the *Stars and Stripes* masthead, and have been working like hell to distribute it.

The first load of papers from London arrived yesterday, only two days late. We needed seven hours to deliver them but we made it. When some of the other fellows get over here, I'll have more of an opportunity to get around to some writing.

We aren't too far from the front, and are exercising muscles digging foxholes, etc. I have been from one end of the beachhead area to the other as well as getting inland as far as possible. I've been able to see quite a bit, short of the actual fighting. The French people, I'd say, belong in two classes. Those living in towns not shattered by the terrific air and ground attacks during the drive are openly welcoming the Yanks. Those in the bomb-battered towns like Carentan, Isigny and Treviers are apathetic. They are dazed by what has happened and I honestly don't know if they are certain of what's going on. The people here remind me of those I saw in Northern Ireland. They are definitely country folk, are in the poor class and desperately in need of rehabilitation. It is apparent they weren't too well off even before we came.

I learned yesterday when the colonel arrived that Phil Bucknell, one of our boys who went in with the airborne troops on D-Day suffered fractures of both legs. [In fact, it was only one leg: Bucknell had broken it just months before on a training jump, and had doctor's orders not to jump again, but he jumped with the paratroopers on D-Day anyway and rebroke the leg when he landed.] Pete Paris, whom I knew very well as a writer-photographer with *Yank*, was killed going in with the 1st Division.

You had better be in rare cooking form when I get back because I'm going to eat and eat and eat some more. I've been eating K rations, C rations and every other kind of ration; they all look and taste alike. Furthermore, the ground and floors over here are pretty hard. I know I can rely on you to know a soft mattress when you see one, come our shopping days.

/////

[FROM THE *STARS AND STRIPES*, June 13, 1944]

HOW OUTMANNED YANKS HELD NAZIS NO RATIONS, AMMUNITION RAN LOW, BUT THEY FOUGHT ON; US FORCE BATTLED 22 HOURS PAST SCHEDULE UNTIL LINKUP

by Philip H. Bucknell, *Stars and Stripes* Staff Writer

WITH AMERICAN AIRBORNE TROOPS, Ste. Mere Eglise, France, June 8 (delayed)—One-and-a-half hours after American paratroopers hit the Drop Zone (DZ) the American flag flew over the vital communications key-point of Ste. Mere Eglise.

The Americans swept into the town, winkling out the enemy from their strong points. They were reinforced by glider-borne troops. Simultaneously other units landed at other DZs in the vicinity and bottled up the road networks, holding down the line of attack for the troops, which came in by sea.

Those amphibious forces were scheduled to reach us by noon D-Day—they came in some hours later. In the meantime, the airborne troops held their positions against ever-increasing enemy counter-attacks, against artillery zeroed in on their positions and in the face of diminishing ammunition and non-existent rations. They held, and when at 10:30 a.m. on Wednesday the tanks came up, the two bridgeheads were waiting for their crossing.

Now the land forces have moved on and beyond this town, and so have the airborne troops who survived the 32 hours of incessant and savage battle.

The trip across was easy and the paratroopers took it easy. Most of the men in my plane slept until we hit the French coast. Then—"Stand up; hook up" called the battalion commander, a lieutenant-colonel whose third combat jump this was. Flak started coming up at us as we crossed the coast, and by peering over his shoulder I could see yellow and green tracers reaching up at us. On the ground, apparently, was more opposition than we had expected.

The ground began to take the shape of the sand tables we had studied back in England. "This is it, fellers. Let's go," said the battalion commander quietly.

We went.

They were shooting at us as we came down and we had to slip our chutes violently to escape the fire. That accelerates the speed of drop, and the impact of landing was too much for this reporter, who received a broken leg.

For the next seven and a half hours, I watched the campaign from the position in which I landed. I could hear combat teams forming, moving stealthily to rendezvous points. There were angry bursts of machine-gun fire and the explosions of grenades. In the distance was the sound of mortar firing and way out towards the sea was the sound of our naval fire.

Throughout the night came other paratroops, and gliders towed by the Ninth Troop Carrier Command swooped down searching for landing places.

I was not exactly lonely in my field, but I was mighty isolated.

In the morning, I was found by the medical aide men and they carried me in to a post near the chief CP, where I was able to keep up with the progress of the fighting.

The reports were good. The battalion commander, with whom I jumped, had collected a force of men and made a two-way penetration into Ste. Mere Eglise. Other forces were out on the flanks protecting communications and establishing roadblocks.

Prisoners began to come in. Some were pathetic, obviously inferior coastal defense troops, either too young or too old. Then there were some impressed troops—non-Germans. Some of them fought well and furiously—they had been told we would slit their throats if we captured them.

Soon after dawn, Ninth Troop Carrier Command C47s swooped down daringly over our positions in the face of continual fire and dropped us equipment bundles. Unfortunately, a lot of them dropped within sight of the enemy, who trained machine-gun fire on troops trying to reach them.

At 10:30 a.m. the first of the seaborne troops came through, and Sherman tanks began to arrive. And now, we advance.

This is not the complete picture.

This is just the story of how an out-numbered, outgunned force of American paratroops and glider riders accomplished the mission they have trained so long to do, and then held their positions for 22 hours longer than the plan called for.

///////

[Billee to Charles] June 16, 1944—Asheville

No more mail this week, but a letter from Warren today telling us he received our packages. He's rationing the fudge to the boys. Everything seems to go all right with him but like everyone else, we're waiting for mail written since the invasion.

The news is good on both sides this week. News of the bombing of Japan again and new landings close to Japan. The news in Normandy is good, too, except for the rift with the French.

I forgot. In Warren's letter day before yesterday he had completed twenty missions. He told us the name of his ship: *Rhapsody in Flack*, and he's with the same crew that was with him at Ardmore.

You should see our victory garden. It's beautiful. The corn is getting so high and we'll have fresh beans this week. We've already been getting lettuce, radishes and greens for the past week. It gets a good wetting once a week now that we have it started good, so there isn't so much work.

I went to a ball game at the camp out here between the Army and Navy hospitals. The camp invited a hundred sailors and marines from the hospital; most of them convalescing from wounds. The game was good. Army won 6–4.

///////

[Charles to Billee] June 18, 1944—Normandy

We have about an hour to spend together tonight before the sun goes down.

We have been having ideal weather during the last few days, which has been a boon to our operations. Today's reports were that the 9th Division, the boys I knew in England and whom I did several pieces on, swept across the Cherbourg peninsula to cut off the enemy north of their positions.

We haven't been too far from the front at any time. But there isn't what you would call immediate danger. All that befalls the boys at the front. Some of our gang went through Carentan, which was taken four days ago, and the 88s were still dropping an odd shell or two near the town. [The *Stars and Stripes* personnel in Normandy had made the first moves to establish an edition in Carentan, and Colonel Llewellyn had gone so far as to have a sign hung outside their proposed office to that effect. Just hours after the sign was hung, the building was demolished by a German shell.]

I got my first good laugh in a long time earlier this evening, listening to Jack Benny's show over the Allied Forces network. Charlie McCarthy is on now. This is a helluva war, isn't it? Only a comparatively few miles from here men are dying and we can sit here listening to radio programs and laugh.

[Billee to Charles] June 21, 1944—Asheville

Your D-Day letter arrived and what a welcome letter! By now you know I had you pictured among the first on the Normandy beaches. This eases my mind considerably, to know that there was a day or so passed before you left England.

We had a letter yesterday from Warren, written D-Day also but no mention of the invasion. The boys sent Mom a thank you note for the candy.

I went to a dance at Moore General Hospital for the patients. What an enormous place that is. Two boys I played rummy with had been in the African and Italian campaigns. One had been a German prisoner for two months. It left me a bit depressed seeing all those men crippled.

I've been following Ernie Pyle's column from France. He's so human, isn't he?

You know I was thinking the other day there are so many things we haven't done together. I've never taken your picture, we've never shared a steak dinner. I've only been to two shows with you. We have to go on a picnic together, swimming. So many things to do.

[This was the only byline story by Charles in June and July, since most of his time was spent in locating a printing plant and enough hard-to-find paper to print an edition in France.]

[FROM THE *STARS AND STRIPES*, June 23, 1944]

MOVIES COME TO YANKS IN FRANCE: PVT. ROONEY CAVORTS—BY COURTESY OF THE *S&S*

by Charles F. Kiley, *Stars and Stripes* Staff Writer

CARENTAN, France, June 20 (delayed)—This town's only movie house, Le Jeanne d'Arc, which for the last four years provided entertainment for German soldiers and their girlfriends, last night housed more than 1,000 paratroopers for the first film show staged in a theater for Americans in France.

Where a couple of weeks ago the Jerries were seeing Magda Schneider and Heinz Englemann in the Nazi-produced *Jeunes Filles*, the Yanks, according to the owner of the theater, enjoyed themselves a helluva lot more looking and laughing at Mickey Rooney (now Pvt. Rooney) in *Andy Hardy's Blonde Trouble*.

The show was staged by the *Stars and Stripes*, which besides gathering, publishing and circulating news in Normandy, also finds time to show a picture now and again with equipment ... it managed to lug across the Channel and operate until additional Special Service units get here. Shows were staged in the last week in tents and barracks, but last night marked the first time comfortable seats and a legitimate theater were available.

The movie house is owned by Marc Mouchel-Cafosse, 30-year-old English-speaking Frenchman, who enthusiastically declared it was "a pleasure, monsieurs," to open the theater for the "parachutes." The theater is equipped with American-made machinery for 35mm film, and when the *Stars and Stripes* turned up with 16mm. stuff M. Mouchel-Cafosse assigned three of his engineers to run the projector. A second lieutenant, on his way to the front, stopped off for a couple of hours to lend a hand.

The theater equipment, stocked in Paris before the war, was brought to Carentan about a year ago and used mainly to entertain the German garrisons in this vicinity. Civilians, with the exception of the soldiers' girlfriends, were barred, and all the pictures furnished by the Wehrmacht were loaded with Nazi propaganda, according to M. Mouchel-Cafosse.

There was one German-produced film in the theater when the town fell last week. It was turned over to US authorities.

Last night's show was split into two performances and the only complaint from the paratroopers was that those blonde twins Pvt. (just inducted) Rooney couldn't handle were on the screen and not in the audience.

/////

[Charles to Billee] June 28, 1944—France

Glory, glory! An armful of mail today when I returned from Cherbourg shortly after it fell! Earl [Mazo] and several of the other fellows arrived and brought it with them.

The picture in Cherbourg wasn't so nice. It was the second time in as many days that I had been up to that front and most of what I saw will not be passed on to you. Not that you can't take it, but I'd rather not talk about dead, dying, shelling, snipers, wounded, chaos, etc.

Since I wrote last, we moved for the second time. The first was to establish better headquarters. The second was because Boche shells were getting too close for comfort—next door, in fact. Now we occupy a house, which formerly housed a German HQ. The place was partly shelled and the roof leaks but it will suffice. We have engaged two French women to cook and housekeep for us and they are worth their weight in gold. The husband of one has been a prisoner for four years. One of her two sons, a six-year-old boy called Guy (pronounced "Gee with a hard "G") is the cutest kid you ever saw. The fellows have taken to him quite a bit and are spoiling him, I'm sure. He greets me with "Bonjour, Monsieur Charles," and holds out his hand. His twelve-year-old brother's name is Michel.

Writing to you like this almost makes me feel the war isn't too close but the spirit is interrupted too often by the Thunderbolts and Lightnings sweeping low overhead on their way out, and the roar of traffic from tanks, big guns and trucks is constant. In the midst of it all I can look at your picture and still say, "Hello, sweetheart. You look damned pretty today, as usual."

/////

[Billee to Charles] June 29, 1944—Asheville

To be able to hear from you at last from all that confusion and turmoil. From the pictures we've seen I have a good picture, together with your letter, of what goes on.

I've read and reread your scribbles on the notepaper and the typewritten letter. I could tell immediately how busy you are, the way your sentences were short and to the point, but I don't mind. We'll have time to settle down at a near-future date and you can take time to tell me. If you'd rather not remember, that's all right, too.

What a tough break for Phil Bucknell. The photographer from *Yank* [Pete Paris] was with you at the apartment when Warren was there. I'll tell Warren when I write. I wondered about Eddie, but presumed he was taking part, too.

Cherbourg has fallen since I last wrote. The news is encouraging on all the fronts except China.

Our papers keep telling us of all the steaks and good food and wines found in Bayeaux. They call it "Furloughville" in *Newsweek*.

Warren has his third oak leaf cluster. That must be about 25.

/////

[Billee to Charles] July 1, 1944—Asheville

Warren has been away on detached service, according to his letter of June 29 and wasn't able to write. We've been wondering if it was this recent three-way bombing run that took several days, or else perhaps they are using them to evacuate wounded from the beachhead.

You sound as if you are a bit shorthanded. I hope by this time the situation is changed. You sound tired and grim.

Some interesting news over the air tonight. Col. White, I believe his name is, who has charge of the African publication of the *Stars and Stripes* was recalled because of suppressing political news from the boys there. Isn't he the one you mentioned in a letter some months back, that the boys on the staff had so much trouble with?

According to reports tonight, the boys are holding their own in France. Ernie Pyle's column has carried a lot concerning the activities of the boys. The latest week of the *Stars and Stripes*, June 12, covered it more thoroughly than anything yet and covered it more exactly, I'd say.

I still can't understand why they try to soften the news to us. They make much ado out of the first news of any big battle and then when the reports on the wounded and killed comes through they stick it on an inside page in an obscure place, as if to tell us we can't take it.

[Charles to Billee] July 1, 1944—France (V-mail)

I have been traveling today and stopped off here for a bite to eat before heading back to headquarters. I have these few minutes on my hands and decided to have a little chat with you.

Our hopes to start publishing on the continent went up a few points during the past week but we are still circulating the paper turned out in London. I never imagined there would be so much attached to getting a paper under way and it has been more difficult here because of war damage to plants, trying to "parlay" with French labor at a time when the people are only beginning to recover from German occupation. Still, we're plugging away and if the first few editions aren't all we hope for, we'll try to work out the difficulties as we go along.

Operations for our guys—that is, the Americans at the front—have quieted down since the capture of Cherbourg. The British are taking over for the time being in their sector. The whole picture still looks like a lot of hard fighting. That is apparent by the time it took to sweep such a small part of France like the Cherbourg peninsula.

Andy got over yesterday, and with Earl here, it's like old times. Andy brought with him a postcard from Benny, sent from a lake in Wisconsin where he and Jane were enjoying his furlough. That's the way it is. Everybody else runs for a foxhole and Benny basks in the sun at a Wisconsin lake.

/////

[Billee to Charles] July 2, 1944—Asheville

We had a houseful last night, mostly soldiers. One came in from the hospital and had his wife with him. It's the first time in 14 months they have been together. He just got back from overseas. They were oblivious to everything but each other.

It's like you to reassure me that your position is not in the danger zone. In the newsreel today we saw them landing supplies at Cherbourg. We saw the king, General "Monty" and Eisenhower as they visited the beachhead, and also De Gaulle. I looked for you but didn't see you.

I had to stop again and billet—is that the term they use?—two lieutenants and wives for the night. [They are] field artillery observer pilots. What a title that is! We get all kinds from colonels down to privates.

/////

[Billee to Charles] July 5, 1944—Asheville

I went to Red Cross tonight. Someone misinformed me when I came home in January. They told me they no longer had night sessions. After D-Day, they had a notice in the paper that they had one night a week, so I presumed they started the night sessions again because of that. Now I learn that they've always had them. Think of all the bandages I could have made.

We have reports tonight that bombers have returned to England that have been gone since June 22nd on a 3-way bombing mission. They landed in Russia and Italy. I'm wondering if Warren was among them. We haven't been hearing as regularly. They mentioned no losses.

They announced last night on the late news that the first continental edition has been distributed to the boys and how you fellows had to figure out the French presses. You're making the news again.

[FROM THE *STARS AND STRIPES*, July 5, 1944]

STARS AND STRIPES GOES TO PRESS AGAIN IN FRANCE AFTER 25 YEARS

CHERBOURG, July 4—The *Stars and Stripes* resumed publication in France this Independence Day, a quarter of a century after the final edition of its illustrious weekly predecessor went to press in Paris after the last war.

The French edition of the *Stars and Stripes* for the AEF of this war is a two page tabloid daily—for a starter—published in Cherbourg by a staff headed by Lt. Col. E. M. Llewellyn, of Tacoma, Wash., under the Army Special Service Division.

The start of operations in Cherbourg brings to three the number of editions currently published by the *Stars and Stripes* in this theater—others are in London and Belfast.

Since D-Day-plus-Six, the London edition has been shipped daily to France and distributed to men all the way up to the front lines. Distribution of the London edition in France was suspended with the start of the Cherbourg edition.

The London edition of the *Stars and Stripes* was started as an eight-page weekly Apr. 18, 1942, with a staff of only seven officers and men. It became a daily paper Nov. 2, 1942, and now operates on a scale comparable to a metropolitan US daily, receiving news from its own correspondents on the battlefronts and at home, and from the major wire services. The Belfast edition was started last December.

Other service papers under the name of the *Stars and Stripes* are published in Italy and North Africa.

/////

[Charles to Billee] July 6, 1944—Cherbourg

The day after Cherbourg fell, our somewhat small editorial staff moved in. There is, or was, a small newspaper plant here and after negotiations with the owner, we decided to try and turn out our first paper in France. The mechanical facilities and incoming communications system only allowed for a two-page paper. We got the first one out on July 4 and we will publish every day until the paper stock runs out or we move to another spot. Morrow Davis, ex-*N.Y. Herald Tribune,* and I are handling the desk with Earl, Andy, and three others on the staff. Our cable news is coming direct from Benny in New York.

Until someone gets here to relieve me so I can devote my time to writing, I'll be on the desk from 7 p.m. until 8 a.m. Of course, the job is more than that. We only have one Frenchman working with us, and our work includes just about everything there is to publishing a newspaper. There isn't any engraving plant here so we can't use pictures.

We have moved into a three-story house and have two Frenchwomen and a man cooking and keeping house.

Bob Moora is supposed to be coming over soon, but not soon enough to suit me. Yet, despite all the trials and hard work, it certainly has been a lot of fun.

Getting back to our "home." It was formerly occupied by a German labor headquarters. Before that, it was possibly the home of a fairly wealthy Frenchman. There are three floors, eight bedrooms, three baths, and five large rooms for office and dining space.

There was a huge safe in one of the rooms, locked and looking a bit suspicious. Today, the Intelligence people came and calmly burned the door off. The fact that it could have contained a booby trap and blown me to kingdom come in my sleep didn't seem to bother them. The joke of it was that the safe was empty.

Andy, Morrow Davis and I occupy a room on the top floor and, under the circumstances, we are quite comfortable. The schedule operates with Andy, Earl and the other reporters covering the field and front, with Morrow and I on the desk. Hutton is stationed in another sector, writing solely for London.

One of the women in the house is a 20-year-old named Paulette. The fellows have a great time trying to make her understand English. She grasps the general idea of what we say and serves as a medium through which we talk to others.

We've also hired a young Hollander who speaks broken English and good French, and we use him as an interpreter at the plant. He was conscripted for work by the Germans and sent to Cherbourg to work for them. We are still on canned rations, but with a little ingenuity have done pretty well.

After the first week, when death was all around and everywhere I went, this has been something of a pleasant change.

Charles and Earl Mazo in Normandy—July 1944. (Kiley Family)

/////

[Charles to Billee] July 8, 1944—Cherbourg

It's a lovely night and the war isn't very far away but everything is quiet. It is just sunset time, 10:30. We are alone in the room I share with Andy and Morrow Davis, Andy having gone off to the front for a couple of days and Morrow downstairs talking baseball with Earl and a few of the others.

Our house is getting to be quite popular. The word has spread like wildfire that we have a good "mess" and invariably there are four to eight guests for meals. Yesterday we had our first female guests, two Red Cross girls and a nurse. They said they were just "passing by." And last night, three correspondents stayed all night.

After working all night on the paper I went up near the front for a while this morning, but came back early for a cold shower and some sleep. I wanted to see some of our artillery in action.

Billee, I haven't seen much on what they are saying at home but for the life of me I can't understand this "60-day surrender" business. I don't think I'm pessimistic when I say the Jerries are pretty well set here, and it is taking a helluva lot of hard work to push them back. We have been here for more than a month and we aren't even clear of the Cherbourg peninsula.

/////

[Billee to Charles] July 10, 1944—Asheville

I've seen quite a bit in the newsreel and the commentators give us a pretty vivid picture of the area so I have a fairly clear picture of your surroundings, enough that I don't like it.

At least La Boche, as you call them since being in France, keeps things from getting dull and in a rut, dropping shells on your next door neighbor, necessitating a move. Having the roof leak in your new domain isn't too good either, since the weather hasn't been on your side of late, so we hear.

You sound all settled and comfy. Two Frenchwomen to cook and clean for you. Are you getting better food? I hope so. I'm sending two packages this week. I was sure one would be mailed today but I finished too late to have them boxed. Since the boxes and the weight have to be exact, I take whatever I'm going to mail to a friend of mine in the mailing department at Ivey's and she boxes them for me. I'll send along some candy for the two little French boys, just in case you are in the same place when they reach you. I'm also sending you some very precious film.

I heard a broadcast tonight, transcribed, entitled "Dateline, Normandy," with Larry LeSeur, George Hicks and [Charles] Collingwood. Good, intimate incidents that happened among the boys taking Cherbourg.

You made me almost hear the interruptions interfering with our date . . . the tanks and the rumbling of the guns. Since hearing the transcription of George Hicks entering Normandy, it isn't hard for me to imagine what you are hearing. That was so vivid. All I had to do was close my eyes and I was at his elbow, seeing the Luftwaffe being shot down and hear the ack-ack of the anti-aircraft.

/////

[Billee to Charles] July 12, 1944—Asheville

I went to Red Cross and rolled bandages until nine, and took in all the latest methods of raising infants. I was the lone single woman among a half-dozen or more young mothers. I filed it all away for future reference. There were a lot of memories gone over tonight. I just listened to what Bill and Jim and Gene did, the little things they did around the house. So you see, you aren't forgotten, any of you. You're talked about in all the Red Cross rooms or wherever women— waiting women—gather. I thought, too, how very much alike we all are in that respect, over there or from what I've heard when you gather together, talk always goes back home and what they used to do, and about Mary, Betty, Sally . . .

I had a long letter from El. She tells me Eddie is still in England. I'll bet he doesn't like that. Tom is out on the water somewhere. He must be on patrol duty.

I saw more pictures of Cherbourg tonight and the rubble, ruin, prisoners and dead. I know why you didn't want to write about it.

A letter from Warren yesterday says he had completed 27 missions as of July 4 and that they had jumped it to 35. He had a pass and went to Southport. He said he spent it going from one bar to the next.

/////

[Charles to Billee] July 15, 1944—Cherbourg

Cherbourg isn't the romantic spot we knew in other places. Being an old city, with only 30,000 population and a port, makes it ugly in places. That's a brief picture of our "lover's lane" in France. Nevertheless, we are still very close together, always.

In one of your letters, you asked me what I had done with "you," when I scrambled up the beaches of Normandy. I had to leave most of "you" in Clifford's Inn but you know I wouldn't go more than two blocks without you in my pocket. Your big pictures were too valuable to risk damage so I brought the picture case with you and I together. That's the one I took to Frankfurt and Norway as well as on most of my trips.

Bob Moora and three more fellows arrived from London during the past week, which makes the job more than a little easier. Bob will take over the No. 1 spot on the desk, with me as No. 2. I thought I would get a chance to get out and write but the colonel says no. However, Bob and I are going up to visit the press camp at 1st Army this afternoon and will return tomorrow. Ralph Martin, in a letter from New York, gave me a message to pass on to Ernie Pyle and there are a few others I want to see. Meanwhile, Andy says he'll write to you while I'm gone. I'll bet he does, too.

/////

[Charles to Billee] July 17, 1944—Cherbourg

It's 3:30 a.m. here at the office and there's a lull in the work so it might be a good idea for you to drop in, sit on the edge of my desk, and let me have a look at you.

I had two letters from you today, by way of marking our anniversary, but they are back in our "chateau." I meant to bring them down with me but not only forgot them but my pen and ink as well. I'm afraid this nightlife isn't agreeing with me. I never was able to sleep much during the day and I've been trying to do it for the last two weeks.

I had the plaster removed from my chest and back yesterday afternoon and let me give you some advice. Don't ever have your chest shaved. Come to think of it, I don't believe I told you about that. Nothing serious, but a couple of weeks ago I had to make a dive to safety and in the process of doing so strained my back and chest. Adhesive tape was all that was needed to fix me up. But that gets us around to the chest-shaving department. The doctor shaved my chest (all five strands of hair) before taping it and now I have to scratch my chest so often it looks as if I have something.

We have a radio here in the office, which gives us music all night. We get New York on short wave occasionally but mostly it's German stations. Berlin Betty is on now. And I could almost love her for playing "Ain't Misbehavin.'" She sounds like an American and besides playing records, also sends messages to the American people from GI prisoners of war.

/////

[Charles to Billee] July 23, 1944—Cherbourg

I believe I told you we have a teletype here that runs direct to the *Times* in London. Well, this afternoon while I was in communication with London, one of the boys broke in on the transmission to say he had an important message for me. I assumed it was a routine answer to some of the things I have been asking London to send here. But, this is what came over: "URGENT TO KILEY: Warren Gray has finished up and is going home."

[Note: Warren "finished up" because he had a public breakdown right before his ship and crew were about to take off on another mission, and he was shipped home. He completed around thirty bombing runs in just over three months, most before he was twenty years old—his crew called him "The Kid." His breakdown was never discussed in the letters and never referred to in conversation even after his family learned the facts; his mother never understood how it could have happened, and she never forgave him.]

During the past week, I started to worry again. I hadn't heard from Warren for a spell and almost every night the wires told of "more than 1,000 American heavy bombers today attacked targets in Munich, Leipsig, Sweinfurt, Regensburg . . ." They are all pretty tough runs, and we have been losing a few, although not so many in view of the large force we sent. Last night when we lost 36 on a run to Schwienfurt and Regensburg, I got to thinking again. He should be finished by now. Maybe he finished up last week. Why don't I get some word about him?

Now we just have a couple more to "sweat out." I heard part of Eddie's outfit got in today but haven't been able to check where they are.

Got a letter from you today, too, which made it a good one all around. And, with the sudden reports of revolt in Germany, Hitler almost knocked off, the Russians rolling along like a steamroller, our guys invading Guam. Wow!

///////

[Billee to Charles] August 7, 1944—Asheville

Lloyds of London give 8 to 5 that victory in Europe will be by October 31, 1944. Tonight's news says we're 110 miles from Paris. The news in the Pacific is good, too. The campaign for the Philippines is starting now. What are the odds on our being together for Xmas? What a Christmas present that would be.

We're worried about Warren. Not a word since a week on Friday when he called. I can't understand what goes on. He said he'd be there for a week or maybe two, but he'd let us know. I'm afraid he might be sick or something.

INTERVAL

AUGUST–NOVEMBER 1944

The War: The tide of war had turned decidedly in the Allies' favor. The Allied efforts in France led to the liberation of Paris on August 25. The *Stars and Stripes* Cherbourg edition was moved to Paris. By September, General Eisenhower had taken direct command of Allied forces in Europe and set up the Supreme Headquarters Allied Expeditionary Force command at Granville. Elsewhere, Brussels had been liberated, and US forces had captured Liege; Denmark was on strike; the Allies marched into the Netherlands; and US Army units brought the fight onto German soil.

As Russian troops swept through the Balkans, the Allies liberated much of Greece.

Confident the war in Europe was near its end, Roosevelt and Churchill met in Quebec in September to discuss what to do about Japan.

Hopes for an imminent end to the war were dashed when British and Polish forces surrendered to the German Panzer division at Arnhem in the Netherlands, followed by strong continuing German resistance in Italy as well as rounds of V-2 rockets over Britain.

At home, Roosevelt won his fourth presidential term, with Harry S. Truman as vice president.

Around August 10, Charles unexpectedly arrived in New York, with a thirty-day furlough and a two-month assignment to work in the newly established *Stars and Stripes* New York City bureau. Billee arrived by train from Asheville a few days later and Charles met her at Penn Station, after a separation of twenty-eight months.

Charles and Billee on their wedding day—Jersey City, August 1944. (Kiley Family)

Billee and Charles were married in Jersey City on Thursday morning, August 17, exactly thirty-one months after they first met. Billee wore a wedding dress borrowed from Charles's sister, Eleanor, because there was no time to shop for a new one. Charles's brother, Father John, performed the ceremony and then ran outside to shoot 8mm color film footage of the wedding guests and newlyweds in front of the church. In the film, Billee and Charles are incandescent. They entertained fifty of their guests with a wedding breakfast and champagne at a nearby hotel; the total bill for this reception was $43.

They traveled to Ohio and to North Carolina to visit Billee's family; then they spent nearly three months together living in a sublet studio apartment on 14th Street, near Union Square in Manhattan. Charles worked in the *Stars and Stripes*'s New York bureau and Billee found a job at *Time* magazine. Charles briefly traveled to St. Louis to cover the Browns/Cardinals World Series. He also started a US sports roundup column for the paper called "Once Over

Lightly." (After Charles was sent back to Europe, the column was taken over by the next staff writer rotated to the New York Office—Andy Rooney.)

The *Stars and Stripes* New York bureau—New York City, October 1944. (Kiley Family)

In September 1944, Charles once again interviewed Ernie Pyle, back in the United States for a break before traveling to the Pacific to cover the war there.

[FROM THE *STARS AND STRIPES*, September 21, 1944]

A TIRED MAN IS HOME: PYLE CAN'T EXPLAIN, WOUNDED KNOW

by Charles F. Kiley, *Stars and Stripes* Staff Writer

NEW YORK, Sept. 20—Like any man in uniform who has been in the war business for two and a half years, Ernie Pyle came home very tired. And typical of the "GIs' war correspondent" he passed up a speedier, more comfortable Atlantic crossing by plane to make the trip with a boatload of wounded soldiers half his age.

The "skinny, dried-up little guy," as one soldier reader characterized him in a letter, decided in Paris a few weeks ago he couldn't go any longer without a rest. So after a few days here Ernie is going to Washington for a week, thence home to New Mexico, stopping in Indiana for a brief visit with his father.

Pyle isn't finished with the war, though. He figures a couple of months of sunshine and home cooking will fix him up for the Pacific.

At his hotel today, Pyle didn't look any different outwardly than he did in London last spring when he came up from Italy to get in on the landings in France or when he was working out of the First Army press camp in Normandy.

"It's a hard thing to explain to anyone here who hasn't been through it," Pyle said. "After the breakthrough at St. Lo in July I think I knew it was coming. Except for a slight cold I think I was all right physically. But inside I felt awful. In Paris it really got me. The Germans came over one day and pasted hell out of us. I'd been through thousands of bombings but that one did it. I knew then I'd have to get some rest."

But Ernie wasn't through yet. On the boat coming back the wounded who could get around asked him to go below and talk to the bedridden. Typically, Pyle went and talked with hundreds of them. They had read his farewell column in the *Stars and Stripes*, he said, and wanted to tell him they understood.

"There I was standing over those kids with arms, legs and eyes gone, all battered to hell and they told me they understood," he said. "But they knew what the score was and that helped. They were amazing, always cheerful and kidding. One kid with his eyes gone would push a boy without legs in a wheelchair, the legless one guiding him. They were all together and they were going home. But a year from now they'll be separated and a lot of them will be forgotten. There's the great tragedy. You live with those kids for awhile and you know what the war's about."

Soldiers often talk about the first thing they're going to do when they get home. Well, here's the first thing Pyle did. There was a kid from Nebraska aboard who had lost his leg. His folks only had the notification that he was "slightly wounded," following the War Department's classification of wounded as "slightly" and "seriously." He didn't know how to tell them and thought Ernie could do it for him.

When the boat docked, that was the first thing Pyle did. "Your son is healthy, happy . . . don't feel too badly about him." Simple—gentle—typical of Pyle.

Ernie didn't bring much back with him except his sidekick, Clark Lee, of INS, who was stricken with illness aboard, and his familiar little wool cap—which he's discarded for the time being for a beret a la Paree—and a beat-up shovel which has been with him since Africa. He intends to take the shovel to the Pacific with him because "there'll be some holes to dig out there, too."

At the end of November, Charles was reassigned to the *Stars and Stripes* Paris office; on November 24, he had to leave Billee behind in New York and go back to the war.

CHAPTER 9

NOVEMBER 1944–APRIL 1945

I've carried your grief in my heart. I have only my love to comfort you
... at this great distance. I've thought of you so since the news... tried
to find my way to you to ease any bitterness you might hold ...
[Billee to Charles, January 1945.]

/////

The War: In December 1944, General Patton took the Third Army across the Saar River; a few days after that, a German line around Metz surrendered, and another fell a few days after that.

East of the Belgium/German border, a battle that began in September still raged in the Hurtgen Forest and became the longest battle of the war on German territory as well as the longest battle ever for the US Army. It had begun as a diversionary offensive to prevent the German Army from reinforcing the battle at Aachen.

On December 11, raging, trembling, and pale, Hitler ordered a major Belgium offensive in the Ardennes, in what came to be known as the Battle of the Bulge. On December 24, Liege was the target when the Germans unleashed the world's first jet bombing raid. On December 31, Eisenhower ordered General Montgomery to mount an offensive attack in the north of the Ardennes. The Battle of the Bulge had pushed the fierce Hurtgen Forest battle into the background.

By mid-January 1945, Hitler was forced to concede the Ardennes offensive. Later that month, the Russians were just one hundred miles from Berlin. German civilians in Berlin were put to work digging trenches around the city. By February, Allied bombing raids over Germany and Austria faced little resistance—in a controversial raid, the RAF destroyed the city of Dresden.

In the Pacific, US forces invaded Iwo Jima on February 19 with thirty thousand troops, raising the US flag on February 23. On March 3, the Allies cleared the final resistance at Manila. In Japan, US B-29 raids killed more than eighty thousand people in Tokyo and then bombed Nagoya, Osaka, and Kobe.

By mid-March, the big three Allied forces were nearly ready to meet in German and East European locations, but Eisenhower ordered the Allies not to advance beyond the Elbe River, giving Russian forces first crack at Berlin.

On April 12, Franklin D. Roosevelt died at Warm Springs, Georgia.

///////

[Charles in New York: farewell message before returning ETO]
November 1944

I know I wasn't able to say all that I wanted to say when we made our "bye-for-a-whiles" but I knew you felt what I had in my heart. Because of your unfailing love, it was easier to go this time. At the same time, I know it was harder for you.

///////

[Billee to Charles] November 24, 1944—New York City

Tonight you're soaring somewhere close to the stars. So far and so near. I know that I'm going to be all right. It's good Jane and I are together. [Ben Price's wife, Jane, and Billee were sharing an apartment in Manhattan.] We're keeping each other's chin up.

I thought maybe I might feel like "Billee Gray" again, not having you here, but I'm Mrs. Kiley whose husband is away.

We're reading the Sunday papers and the *Tribune* Book Review has a half page ad devoted to *Air Gunner* [by Andy Rooney and Bud Hutton].

[Charles to Billee] November 24, 1944—En Route to ETO

My letters to you have been written in and from more than a few strange places. So this, written in a C54 at 8,000 feet or so shouldn't be too unusual. We took off exactly four hours and 31 minutes after I had spoken to you. Fortunately, we are making the 16-hour trip in a "plush job." That is to say, we are in a "luxury" air liner complete with super-comfortable seats, etc. There are only 12 passengers, which makes the ship practically a private compartment.

Sitting across the aisle from me, and munching a sandwich, is Col. Phil [Flip] Cochran. You are more familiar with him as "Flip" Corkin in *Terry and the Pirates* [popular comic strip by cartoonist Milton Caniff, which he drew from 1934–1946]. He can't be much older than I, perhaps a few years, but he has more silver in his hair than I'll have at 50. Want to bet?

When I left two and half years ago in the bottom of a transport, my spirit meter registered minus. Today, knowing you are mine and that we'll always be one has made a world of difference . . .

Sunset again. First time I've been able to see the sun go down and the moon come up at the same time. Pretty soon we'll be back in the ETO . . .

London once more, and it hasn't changed a bit. There are a few new faces in the office but still some of the old ones. And, of course, Gertie and Alf are still going strong [landlord of The Lamb and Lark pub and his wife]. We spent about five hours in the Lamb and Lark today passing out the gifts we brought and having a "few" for "auld lang syne."

[Billee to Charles] November 26, 1944—New York City

We received the welcome message of your safe arrival in London. Now I'm concerned about getting you to Paris. The sooner the better, what with those buzz bombs. The first time I've been in the [New York *Stars and Stripes*] office without you was today. I took your glasses up so Carl [Larsen, a *Stars and Stripes* staffer managing the New York bureau] could stick them in the envelope going over. I wrote a little note and stuck it in the bottom of the glasses case. I also invited Carl for spaghetti Thursday night. He has been hesitant about coming up; said he didn't like the idea of eating up our groceries, and wanted to know if he could bring something.

We're checking on the French lessons. I think it will be the Berlitz School. [Both Billee and Jane wanted to get jobs that would take them to Paris.]

I think the best thing to do is try and get into one of the government agencies.

/////

[Billee to Charles] November 29, 1944—New York City

Your Dad finished *Air Gunner* and enjoyed it. Didn't care too much for the coarse language but said that must be the way they are. Eddie's Purple Heart arrived, though the poor guy still hasn't received any mail. [Eddie had been wounded during the first days of the Hurtgen Forest battle.]

Received a long letter from Warren, but no mention of being grounded. He just finished reading *Air Gunner* and it made him homesick, says he, but he still doesn't want any part of it.

/////

[FROM THE *STARS AND STRIPES*, November 29, 1944]

A PEEK AT THE USA OF TODAY

By Charles F. Kiley, *Stars and Stripes* Staff Writer

You have your own idea of the America you want to find when you go home. It may be different than the one we hoped would be there after 2 ½ years. But if it is the same, your USA will be your hometown, your family, your friends, the house with the white flagpole in the front garden and the girl who promised to wait—and did.

Your America will be the one place in the world you will be glad hasn't changed much and the one place you will want to go back to.

There will be some changes of course. Your father will look a little older. Mother has passed away. Your sister will be married, and the mother of the healthiest kid you ever saw. Your kid brother, who was a civilian when you last saw him, will be in a field hospital in France. A lot of your friends will now be married with children. Some will have as many overseas stripes as you have. People you know will be making good money—$75–$100 a week, but they will not be making much headway, what with taxes and the war-time cost of living.

If you live in the city you will spend hours just looking at the restaurants and the bars, because you had almost forgotten there was food and drink aplenty, even in America. And you will add about 20 pounds to your frame on the home cooking by the family who will shovel it into you knowing you have had your fill of spam, potatoes, Brussels sprouts and powdered eggs.

There will be several things to make you uneasy. Like Bud Hutton said a few months ago, people will proudly boast of the War Bonds they bought while you were away, of the donations they made to the Red Cross and the time they put in at the local USO. They will tell you how much overtime they put in at the war production plant, all the while trying to make you feel like America at home did its part. It will all seem like a pretty small contribution by comparison. But if you look at America as this reporter did you will bear with them, because in a couple of years it will all straighten out.

You will discover that your family, in particular, will want to make a big fuss over you when you get home. It will be embarrassing, but you will be able to stand it.

You may go home with the idea that there are still a lot of guys, healthy and young, who are still wearing civvies. You won't, however, find too many of them. When you see service flags in four of five windows on your street, you will realize that Uncle Sam is getting just about everybody in sight.

There will be football games, baseball, basketball, hockey, good shows, beautiful women, steaks, ice cream, bourbon, rye, green mountains, fishing, clear lakes. Why go on—you know it all.

[Charles to Billee] November 29, 1944—London

This will be my last night in London if the flying weather remains clear. I booked passage to Paris this morning and am due to leave tomorrow afternoon.

I did a story on my reactions to the "home front" yesterday, then went to Beckenham to spend the rest of the day with the Frosts. Mr. Frost showed me around to see the awful destruction caused by the V-1 bombs. It was terrible. They haven't had any V-2s fall there yet and it's a good thing. Mrs. Frost worked at an emergency rest center for bombed-out families during the five months of the bombings and for a period of ten weeks didn't see Mr. Frost at all. She was working all night while he worked all day. They were fortunate in only having the ceilings in two rooms fall, a few holes in the roof and windows smashed by blast. They sleep in a shelter during the night.

/////

[Charles to Billee] December 2, 1944—Paris

While Benny is dipping cheese tidbits into a jar of his peanut butter and passing them along to me I'll try to give you a picture of the setup here.

The office occupies four floors of the Paris *Herald* building. The editorial room is on the second floor. Col. Llewellyn is back in the states and a Maj. Goodfriend with whom I was friendly is the big boss. Bud [Hutton] is running the Paris desk at present.

We are billeted in a fourth-rate hotel, two men to a room with hot water about three days a week. Still, it's better than most others have here and nobody is kicking.

I'll be in Paris for about two weeks as things look now. Then, a team of about 12 will go to either Liege (Belgium) or Luxembourg to open another edition. Eventually, this edition will be the one servicing frontline troops while Paris will service troops in and around Paris. Bob [Moora] and Benny will remain in Paris and work on the desk here.

Earl [Mazo] and I had quite a long talk last night. He was just back from the front and anxious to get news of home. Joe Fleming was with us; he'll be in the next group to go home.

Charles and Earl Mazo—Paris, December 1944. (Kiley Family)

Incidentally, we have our meals in a restaurant near the office. It is staffed by French help supervised by an Army mess sergeant with GI food served. For entertainment, there are two GI movies, a couple of good French shows like the Folies Bergere, which I'll probably never see. There are plenty of spots for a beer or two now and then. Beer is about 25 cents a glass, cognac is 80 cents and champagne is 12 dollars a bottle.

/////

[Billee to Charles] December 3, 1944—New York City

This was quite a Sunday. Lunching with a Lt. Colonel, and what an old goat. [Colonel Llewellyn took some *Stars and Stripes* wives out to lunch.] He tried to be at his best, what with four women in tow. He played the part of "one of the boys" and "slap you on the back" attitude. A lot of big talk that we simply let go in one ear and out the other. He rattled on about getting promotions for you all and how the office is going to be enlarged; even proposed that one of us take over the secretarial position open but we returned the idea as not practical. I can't think of anything worse than working for him. What a tactless so and so he is.

One thing he said about you—you were the only guy he knew that could sleep in a foxhole all night and get up in the morning with your pants pressed.

/////

[Charles to Billee] December 4, 1944—Paris

I had my first experience with the French language this morning when I set out for church. The manageress of the hotel gave me directions to "l'eglise" first. After walking about half a mile I asked a man to direct me to "la Catholique eglise." On I went for a mile and after one more query found myself in St. Augustin Cathedral, about two and half miles from the hotel. I found my way back all right after Mass and learned the church I should have gone to was only two blocks away.

/////

[Billee to Charles] December 4, 1944—New York City

I went to the Red Cross today and had an interview. I didn't give her any information and only asked if you could select the theatre to be sent to, and the answer was no. Tomorrow I'm going to check on the International Business Machine Co.; they have an office in Paris. Jane is so positive there will be a way.

/////

[Charles to Billee] December 5, 1944—Paris

Orders are being made now for the return of Joe [Fleming], and one of the sports writers named Gene Graff. They expect to be home before Christmas.

The boys are still calling me "Butterball" because I look so much heavier now than I did four months ago. I met one of the captains coming into the office this afternoon and he remarked, "Charlie, you are the healthiest-looking thing I've seen in the ETO." I didn't know whether it was a compliment or a dig at my double chin.

/////

[Billee to Charles] December 5, 1944—New York

Carl and the Colonel have pestered the daylights out of me about taking the job in the office. I wish I could talk to you for five minutes to get your reaction. There are so many pros and cons. I still come back with the same thought, that you wouldn't appreciate my being there. The job itself I know I would love and I know I could handle it all right, but . . . Oh well, I'll just say no again and tell them that's final. The money is good, too, but I have a feeling the hours will be long. I wouldn't mind that though . . . Again, it's no.

We tried a couple more leads today. You know, you shouldn't be surprised if I turn up at the office one day, maybe for lunch.

/////

[Billee to Charles] December 7, 1944—New York City

When I hear about things like the V1 bombing and the results I get sick inside because I've done so little: rolled a few bandages, [donated] a few pints of plasma and a little money. Waiting for you is the extent of the effect of the war on me. Warren, of course, too. I've done nothing of any real benefit. That leaves an unsatisfied feeling.

/////

[Billee to Charles] December 9, 1944—New York City

Tonight walking down 14th from the subway I wanted so to continue down to 309 [14th St., where Charles and Billee lived while Charles was working out of the *Stars and Stripes* New York Office in October and November] and find you waiting for me.

We registered at Berlitz today and we start Monday with a 2 1/2 hour lesson then go on Wednesday and Friday. I'm anxious to hear about Liege. Carl and Andy seemed surprised that you were leaving Paris. [Andy Rooney was on leave and working out of the paper's New York office.]

/////

[Charles to Billee] December 10, 1944—Paris

By now, you must know Joe is home. He should have reached New York early today. If he has delivered the package to you, it is evident that you aren't to open it until Dec. 26 [Billee's birthday], and I do mean Dec. 26!

I had a day off yesterday. I started the day by visiting the Louvre. The world-renowned art treasures haven't been restored yet but there is still much to be seen, especially in the way of sculpture and centuries-old stone from Egypt, Rome, Athens, Persia, etc. It would take a week to cover the whole of the Louvre so you can imagine what I saw in two hours. [The most well-known items in the Louvre collection, including the Mona Lisa, had been quietly removed from the museum in 1939 and remained hidden in various locations throughout France and out of the hands of the German occupiers until the end of the war.]

From there I went to Notre Dame and was a little disappointed, not at the cathedral because its age makes it magnificent. But, it was the commercial stain that sort of deflated me. As soon as you enter the door, someone eases up and asks if you want a guide—to walk through a church, mind you. Further on is an enclosed alcove with a relic of the true cross, sundry chalices donated by kings and emperors down through the years; a beautiful collection of all the popes in cameos in there; relics of several French saints. Frankly, I was a little awed. But I had to pay some man five francs to see these things. Of course, they do the same thing in the Westminster Abbey in London, but that still doesn't make it right.

In the afternoon, I slummed around Montmartre. It all looked pretty dirty to me. Ah, then the "piece de resistance." Last night, I went to the famous Folies Bergere—and enjoyed it a lot. Perhaps I should say there were too many women appearing and disappearing throughout the show with nothing but complete nakedness from the waist up—but that's part of the Folies Bergere, they say. The chorus was pretty, lively and talented, the scenes were beautiful, the leading comedian excellent and the comedienne exceptional. The music also was very entertaining. It was the scenery and tableaus, I guess, that lifted it from the burlesque level. I was lucky to get a box seat (I would, wouldn't I?) for 130 francs ($2.60) since the theatre always is sold out for at least five days in advance. My good fortune came from someone who cancelled a reservation.

I'm working on the sports page and makeup until I move on to Liege. Incidentally, Bud and I together with Bill Spear, a desk man, are making a four-day trip to Liege, starting tomorrow. It's an eight-hour trip by jeep so we're getting an early start. It's been rainy and cold but I'll be well-protected on the trip. Long johns, wool pants and shirt, sweater, leather jacket, lined all-purpose coat, boots, gloves, wool cap, and a couple of blankets. I'll try to write while I'm up there but we have a helluva lot of work to do in the short space of time and I don't know when I'll have 15 minutes to write.

[Billee to Charles] December 12, 1944—New York City

Funny, starting the French lessons gave me a strange but good feeling that I had taken a step closer to that day.

It's only a little over two weeks since the 24th and it seems like that many years since I saw you. The "miss you" seems to get worse instead of better.

They received your letter at 195. Pop is still anxious about Eddie. That was the first thing he asked.

/////

[Billee to Charles] December 13, 1944—New York City

Tonight added another of the members of the *Stars and Stripes* to our little circle in the person of Joe Fleming and he is just as I imagined.

First off, he handed me your letter that I was so happy to see, since there wasn't one in our box this evening.

We learned a little more in our French today. Our vocabulary now consists of about twenty nouns and about a half-dozen adjectives that we can shift back and forth in sentences. The instructor keeps saying "tres bien" so I guess we're doing all right.

For the first time since that last afternoon in your arms I broke down tonight when I read your letter. I made a beeline for the bathroom and locked myself in.

/////

[Charles to Billee] December 14, 1944—Paris

I got back from Liege tonight after an eight-hour jeep ride in freezing weather. I've been thawing out for a couple of hours.

The trip to Liege had a lot to do with the sting of disgust that has come over me in the last week. I started to feel it after being here only a couple of days. Paris, and all of France, for that matter, may have been nice places before the war. I hope so, because if there is anything cheaper, dirtier or low it is Paris right now. I don't mean to say all of it is like that. But I haven't seen a square inch of the continent I liked yet. It is mainly a struggle for existence with everybody. I wouldn't trust a soul in all of France, or Belgium for that matter, as far as I could place-kick him. The worst of many stories I have heard concerns about 250 officers and men in the Army, attached to a railway unit, who have been nailed after carrying out one of the biggest black market rackets in history. Men are losing the most priceless thing they have—life—while this handful of skunks sell their food, cigarettes, gasoline, medical supplies and God only knows what else to our "liberated Allies." In Liege, where signs are being hung all over the city hailing the "liberators," it isn't safe to leave a monkey wrench down in fear of it being stolen.

People say it's all part of war but I never expected to see humanity degraded as it is here. I have all this in mind when I think of you wanting to come over. I want you as near as possible and as quickly as possible, but if you were to ask me tonight what I thought of you coming tomorrow, I believe I'd say, "no."

//////

[Charles to Billee] December 16, 1944—Paris

Will you forgive me for being in such a nasty mood last night when I wrote the "book" on "les miserables" of France? I'm not completely over the mood. Don't expect to be on that subject, but I feel better about everything in general today. Maybe it's because it's raining *again*.

I'm off to Liege for good in three days. We hope to turn out the first edition there on Dec. 26. Benny, as I said before, is staying in Paris with Bob. Hutton and I, together with eight or nine others will go to Liege. Bud is going to stay there only two weeks, he says, and go back to covering the war from the field. He misses his byline in the paper.

By handling the sports desk and makeup, I won't have to answer to anyone and I won't be over-burdened with responsibility. In this business, I find it's much nicer to stand on the outside and watch everybody else wrangling. I don't think it would be the *Stars and Stripes* if complete peace reigned in the family. And, as such, I don't think it would be as much fun as it is.

Two good features about Liege are coal and ice cream. It may sound like a strange paradox but since Liege is a coal-mining district, we can get more there than here and consequently be much warmer. The ice cream hasn't much of a flavor to it but it isn't bad.

/////

[Billee to Charles] December 20, 1944—New York City

Carl told me yesterday that you had left for Liege and casually added that he hoped you arrived before the Germans did. The news last night was that all travel to the front had been canceled. That included travel to Belgium. Since they received no word today concerning you, I don't know where you are and I don't like the feeling.

/////

[Billee to Charles] December 21, 1944—New York City

Still no word and no mail, so you can guess the rest. I know service is bad during the holidays and I should expect it but still I look. I would like to know where you are.

/////

[Billee to Charles] December 23, 1944—New York City

195 has received one letter so far from Eddie written November 21. There's no way of knowing where he is, I suppose.

Tom [O'Connor] is still in Maine. After two weeks of silence, he called El the other night. They are waiting for a plane. He had to take a guard to the phone with him and they wouldn't even pay the fellows for fear they'd take a powder. If there is a way possible and he's still there, he'll be home for Xmas. The plan is now that he will go to Greenland for 14 months! [Tom was being punished for having gone AWOL to see his daughter.]

Joe Fleming left an enormous box yesterday while I was at 195, with "Do Not Open 'til Dec. 26."

/////

[Charles to Billee] December 23, 1944—Paris

Back again from Liege! This time I'll be here in Paris for an indefinite period. It all depends on the German counter-offensive. We reached Liege, all 10 of us, last Tuesday night only to discover that the tactical situation there wasn't very healthy. Nevertheless, we pitched in and got everything in the office squared around and ready to publish. All that was missing was a Paris-to-Liege cable circuit for our teletype. Without a teletype it is impossible to operate, since we must depend on Paris to relay all news, about 20,000 words daily, from New York. The cable circuit was taken by First Army, which naturally has top priority and isn't likely to turn it over to us until the present situation at the front changes for the better.

While in Liege we also had to put up with those things we were ducking in London [V-1 rockets]. So, since we couldn't work, it was decided that our gang would return to Paris and continue to help out there until we can open in Liege.

You probably are wondering how serious the counter-offensive is. From what I could see, it wasn't serious in that the First Army was in a chaotic state. They bent before the rush of German armor in several sections but they were holding together while giving ground. Unfortunately, I suppose a lot of our guys were overrun and taken but I seriously doubt if the push will lose more than another week. Patton already has jumped in to help Hodges by attacking from the right flank.

Earl came back from Third Army yesterday and said Patton was exploding with, "Hell, why didn't those _____ come at me? If they want to pick on somebody, I'll take care of those _____!!" Sure enough, the Germans are using the same tactics that Patton used to run through France and old "Blood and Guts" says "they must have some smart men running this show." Earl doesn't like him but gives him a lot of credit for getting things done.

While in Liege, I had hoped to track down Eddie but honestly didn't have time with the work we had to do. However, I had one of our fellows at First

Army checking for me and he reported Eddie's outfit as not being involved in the counter-offensive.

/////

[Charles to Billee] December 25, 1944—Paris

Last year in London, I remember I awoke and wanted to stretch my arm and feel you close to me, to turn my head and know you were there. Today . . .

You may have heard from Carl that a paper comes out seven days a week now. Everybody is working seven days, until the situation at the front changes for the better. Then, we will probably work out a schedule whereby we will get a day off now and then.

So, now, it's just another "goodnight, sweetheart," the way it has been for almost three years and will be until the end of our lives.

/////

[Birthday note from Charles enclosed with his gifts; December 26, 1944]

I hope these few things will help bring me a little closer on another of your birthdays we will be apart. The vase, Lalique glass, or some such word as that, is said here to be the most exquisite in the world. I wouldn't know but it was priced high enough to be exquisite. The scarf, a little gaudy, perhaps, but it is Schiaparelli. The hankies, compact, powder and doll to remind us I was once in gay Paree.

Happy birthday, sweetheart.

/////

[Billee to Charles] December 26, 1944—New York City

I guess I'm the luckiest girl in the world including the ETO. I'm practically wordless. Why didn't you just wrap up the department store in pink ribbons?

You've made it a beautiful birthday; my first as Mrs. K.

/////

[Charles to Billee] December 26, 1944—Paris

I could make this an awful letter buy going into detail on a "snafu" which has wrapped itself around the *Stars and Stripes*. But, none of it is worth getting all hot and bothered about. Let me just say that my interest and enthusiasm for the paper is at a new low. Every time I turn around some piece of brass, from a brigadier general to a lowly captain, is trying to play little games with the paper. My attitude may change when and if we get to Liege and away from all this brass.

Morrow [Davis] and Earl went back to the front today. Almost wished I was going with them.

Benny received a letter from Joe today. He told of having a spaghetti dinner with you and how very nice both of you are. He advised us to throw away the pictures we have of you because they don't do you justice. Joe also said you'd be "perfect" if *you could only cook*!

/////

[Cable from the Stars and Stripes *to Charles] December 26, 1944—*
New York

PRESS WIRELESS

PRO KILEY EXLARSEN SORRIEST RELAY MESSAGE EXSPOUSE YOUR FAMILY NOTIFIED TUESDAY BROTHER ED KILLED DANSGERMANY DECEMBER ELEVENTH STOP BILLEE VISITED FAMILY DANSJERSEY LAST NIGHT POSTRECEIVING NEWS END = LARSEN STARSSTRIPES

[Cable from Billee to Charles] December 26, 1944—New York

LC CHARLES KILEY STARS AND STRIPES CARE PARIS HERALD PARIS

EDDIE KILLED DECEMBER 11 IN GERMANY ALL MY LOVE

AND PRAYERS ARE WITH YOU MY DARLING AGAIN I CANT BE
WITH YOU
   BILLEE KILEY

Eddie Kiley—England, 1944. (Kiley Family)

/////

[Billee to Charles] December 26, 1944—New York City

I wish I could write as if we didn't know any of the heart-breaking news. By the time this reaches you, you will have received the two cables. Darling, darling . . . if only for five minutes I could be with you tonight.

/////

[Charles to Billee] December 27, 1944—Paris

I have been a little lost I must admit. After I received the cable, I tried to keep working. But it was no use. The other fellows all knew. Benny did his best for me, but he didn't have words either. Earl was here too. I got out of the newsroom and went for a long walk. I didn't get very far, though and went into the church near the office.

If I said I never expected it, I would be a liar. John and I talked about it before I left, and we knew he was going to be in the thick of the fighting. I immediately thought of Pop. I know he isn't the same since Mom passed.

It just drives it home more for me how much I have to come home in one piece. I'm not taking any chances I don't have to. I will do my job. But no glory seeking. The only thing that matters to me at this point is coming home to you. I'm going to try and find out the details. I'll relay them to you and John as soon as I have them.

/////

[Charles to Billee] December 28, 1944—Paris

I'm much better today. I've been keeping busy trying not to think too much.

I went out to do a story on two fellows who just came out of the line after being caught in the counter-offensive for nine days. It made me feel lots better. I'll say this. No matter what I do or where I go, there won't be the slightest possibility of me getting "hit on the head." If I have to sacrifice anything and everything, that comes first.

/////

[Excerpt from a letter from Charles to his brother John, sent December 29, 1944]

I can go back to June when I received a letter from Eddie saying he thought he was on his way to France pretty quick. I remember, before I finished the letter, something came over me to make me feel he was never going to get through. I can't say why I put the finger on him, more than any of the other thousands. But I did. It may have been that I had seen fellows dead and dying in Normandy before I got that letter from Ed. But there it was.

Yesterday, it all started to sink in and I couldn't keep my mind on anything. Always it was some thought in connection with him. Today it isn't so bad. All I know is that I'm so fed up, sick, sore and disgusted with anything with a war angle to it I can hardly sit still.

I try to think of the couple of hundred thousand other kids who went the same way all over the world. It doesn't do much good.

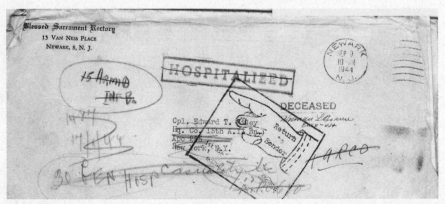

Letter returned unopened to Charles's brother, John, showing the course of Eddie's final months. (Kiley Family)

/////

[Charles to Billee] January 2, 1945—Paris

The war has swung again in our favor, even though it isn't much to brag about. Patton has counter-attacked in two places and has won back one-third of the Bulge lost to the German counter-offensive. At least, the war is pushing forward again instead of coming back at us.

One day a week, I cover the war and write the lead story. Another day I do the "outside war" pieces on Pacific, Russia, Italy, etc. Then I work on sports and make up a couple of pages on the other days. By "make up" I don't mean I daub powder and lipstick on the pages.

During the last week, our end of *Stars and Stripes* has taken over three editions in Marseilles, Dijon and Strasbourg, which were operated by men who came up from Italy with the 7th Army on the invasion of southern France. Too, we're still planning to open the new one in Liege. I seriously doubt if I'll leave Paris for a while and IF I do it will be to Liege, the best deal of all.

/////

[Billee to Charles] January 3, 1945—New York City

I'm sorry Joe didn't like my cooking. It was spaghetti, just as I made for the four of us. Andy ate all his. Mrs. Rooney picked, as usual. After hearing about Joe's appetite, I didn't expect to satisfy him. I told him the other night to come back after his trip to see Margaret and I'd have a baked potato for him.

Please, don't let the *Stars and Stripes* get you down. You know I've never had any letters like these from you before, but I know you are sharing the good and the not so good with me and that makes me very happy inside because I want to be a part of everything.

/////

[Charles to Billee] January 7, 1945—Paris

I may go to Liege for a few days, return to Paris, and then maybe go up there to work on the desk. Liege is out of danger now so don't worry. You sounded awfully concerned in one of your letters, after Larsen told you I'd gone up there. And, I can imagine your anxiety but it wasn't nearly as bad as the picture that was painted. In fact, there never was any real threat to Liege at all, except a few buzz bombs flying over. Just remember, I know where it's safe and where it isn't and even if you hear "accurate" reports, believe me I'll be anywhere but in danger if something happens.

[Billee to Charles] January 9, 1945—New York City

We received the *Stars and Stripes* edition with your home front story. It was wonderful—so simple. I'm speaking of your writing. So simple yet you get everything down and it's all so easy to understand.

We're to be hounded by the V-2s sometime this month or next. It's very possible darling but I'm not too concerned. Might be good for a few of these people around here. I'm sorry, I shouldn't say things like that.

[Billee to Charles] January 11, 1945—New York City

Rita [Mazo, Earl's wife] is quite upset about Earl now, afraid he got tired of waiting for his orders and decided to go on one last mission or something while waiting. She hasn't heard anything else since his message for her to be in New York on the ninth. In the meantime, she's resting comfortably on our sofa. It's nice she's so tiny.

[Charles to Billee] January 13, 1945—Paris

I arrived back from Liege this morning at 2:00 after a frigid trip. In a way it was a beautiful trip—snow all the way through France and into Belgium. The Ardennes Mountains were like winter portraits. The bad feature, of course, was the condition of the roads.

I came back to take care of a few more details—communications, supplies, personnel, etc.—and figure to go back up there within a few days to get the paper out at long last. The weather here in Paris and in Liege has been really cold these last few days but I'm well protected and have been inside with the exception of the round trip. I bought an officer's combination field coat, lined and all, for $30 dollars, which leaves me a little off balance for the month but it was worth it. I won't need the money, though.

/////

[Charles to Billee] January 14, 1945—Paris

You asked if the Congressional investigation will have any effect on me. No, it won't. In fact, the powers that be here welcome the investigation because it is felt we would be able to clear the picture once and for all. However, the feeling is that the investigation will never come off. I think we can forget about it. The chief squawk, made by visiting Congressmen, was that the Paris edition didn't publish enough unbiased news from home. When they were here, the paper was a four-pager due to the shortage of newsprint but for the last month it has been an eight-pager seven days a week. And, there has been plenty of news from home.

I'm moving up to Liege on Tuesday. We'll have a limited but capable staff to begin with and I know we'll do a good job. Our paper will service the First and Ninth Armies plus troops in Holland, Belgium and part of France. By "troops" I mean rear echelon, medical, signal and other units not part of armies.

[Charles to Billee] January 14, 1945—Paris

These are simply a few lines to accompany the small gifts Earl will give you. They aren't much, angel, but just about the best you can do in Paris these days. The Schiaparelli, I have been assured, is tops. The Chanel is questionable. You'll have to judge for yourself. I'm just hoping it doesn't evaporate during the air trip.

I'm awfully envious of Earl and Morrow. I'd give anything to be going back with them. And, that's the way they felt when I went home.

In a few days it appears as if I'll be in Liege for good. That is, I'll work out of there mostly. Now and again I'll come to Paris and get together with Benny but Liege will be my job. It's okay up there now except that it's cold with lots of snow.

/////

[Billee to Charles] January 15, 1945—New York City

Saw an ad yesterday. They would like airplane mechanic trainees at La Guardia field. Starting salary while training is $158.00 a month. If I can't get a job paying a decent salary, don't be surprised if I do something like that. I think it would be kind of fun. Something new and I'd be around airplanes.

That wonderful meat market on 8th Ave., where you used to go, must like Jane and I because today he sold me lamb chops and ham, and there isn't any meat at all in so many places. I'll never get over Jane coming home Saturday with a whole pound of butter and a pound of bacon.

Rita is amazed at the long letters we write every night. She's afraid she's been neglecting Earl with her short ones.

/////

[Charles to Billee] January 18, 1945—Liege

I received a report on Eddie's death today. I contacted the public relations officer of the 5th Armored and asked him to find out what he could. He couldn't find out where Ed is buried, which is what I wanted to know most of all. But here is the report he got for me.

"Cpl. Kiley was a member of a mortar platoon until he was evacuated during the fighting near Wallendorf in September. He was wounded at the time by a bullet, which struck the mount of a machine gun near his head. According to one of the men in Kiley's platoon, he returned to the outfit about a week before the battalion was committed to action on the Roer front. He was killed during that engagement on Dec. 11, the morning of the first attack. He was standing in back of his halftrack near the line of departure east of Klenhau when a barrage of mortar shells was thrown in on them by the enemy. One of these shells landed only a few yards from Kiley and he was killed instantly. According to an eye-witness, shrapnel from the shells also killed five other men but did not touch Kiley. He died from the concussion."

They say it was pretty tough up there.

/////

[Billee to Charles] January 20, 1945—New York City

We were gad-abouts tonight. Andy was simply wonderful. [He] took Jane, Rita and me to dinner with he and Marg [Rooney, Andy's wife] at Toots Shor's and then to a newsreel. We all wanted to pay our own checks. After a bit of fussing he settled it with, "You all don't mean a damn to me but your husbands are my best friends." Also he added that maybe he could like us eventually.

We walked down Broadway after we left Andy and Marg and were pushed around quite a bit. We stopped in the Brass Rail and had a drink and watched the crowds come in and out. That's really a place.

/////

[Charles to Billee] January 21, 1945—Liege

Gen. [Oscar] Solbert showed up yesterday and said we were doing "a great job," which doesn't mean a damn thing, coming from somebody who doesn't know a newspaper from a three-base hit. Still, it was nice having company.

The *Stars and Stripes* office; Charles is seated, second from left—Liege, January 1945. (US Army/The *Stars and Stripes*)

/////

[Billee to Charles] January 22, 1945—New York City

Earl arrived this a.m. but I didn't see him, about 6:30 I guess. Jane heard the doorbell first. Since I had washed my hair last night and was all pinned up (only you have the privilege of seeing Mrs. K. in that getup) I stayed out of sight while he called Rita at the hotel. I'm so grateful she wasn't here. I don't think I could have taken a meeting like that.

Earl told Jane, too, that he was so anxious to meet me, that according to you I must be perfect.

I went to the blood bank this a.m. Feel fine and had a long talk with one of the women there. She said they need hospital staff assistants in the New York vicinity. I think it pays about $150 a month. I called Jane and she called the employment officer.

I had a letter from Warren today, finally. He gets a 15-day furlough beginning Feb. 1st and asked if I would be here so perhaps he plans on spending part of it here. He has been assigned to radio maintenance—emergency work. Seems to like it, too. His letter is a lot more cheerful than I hoped to get.

/////

[Billee to Charles] January 23, 1945—New York City

I talked to Earl on the phone tonight and he delivered your love. That's a heck of a way to get it. We are all meeting at the English Grill, the Rooneys and Mazos, Mrs. Price and Mrs. Kiley. I might even take more than an hour of *Times'* time. [Billee was still working at *Time* magazine.]

Sometimes "over there" doesn't seem very far away but tonight it seems as if it were the end of the world.

/////

[Billee to Charles] January 24, 1945—New York City

Today was the luncheon with the Mazos and the Rooneys. It was the next best thing to seeing you. Earl saw you on Saturday and this is Thursday. I asked him a million questions and he obliged me with all the answers. Kept calling me "child." He's a regular guy and I like him. When he comes back from Charleston [where Mazo's family lived], he wants to go over to 195 and spend the day, he says. He brought back the *Stars and Stripes* camera and film and he plans on taking pictures.

Also I delivered the details about Eddie [to Earl].

Pop is well, darling, but he has a little older look about him since the news.

/////

[Charles to Billee] January 25, 1945—Liege

I used to think I got tired at night back in New York. But it was nothing compared to these nights. Right now, I'm a weary old man. I try to think what it was I wanted to say to you, and I can't think. I try to keep at a letter and I start thinking what I should get up tonight for tomorrow's paper.

/////

[Charles to Billee] January 30, 1945—Liege

I would have loved to have been with Earl when he got home. He said he was just going to take his little gal and hide her for three days; not let anyone even see her. I'll bet he did, too.

(You'll have to excuse me for a bit, hon. Paris just called with a late report from a German source that the Russians are only 40 miles from Berlin. They are checking the story for some kind of confirmation and if it's worth anything we are going to make over our Page One. Incidentally, it's 12:45 am now. See you in a bit.)

I have a little more time. One of the boys hopped in a jeep to go after one of the Belgian linotype operators and bring him back to set the new stuff. While we're waiting for him and the confirmation call from Paris, I'll stay with you. Can I persuade you to make me a cup of coffee, in the meantime? Getting sleepy now and a hot cup would fix me fine. Might as well warm a roll or two.

One of these days, or nights, I'm going to get off a real, honest-to-goodness love letter and I'll surprise myself. You are always very much in my heart, dearest. There goes the phone.

/////

[Billee to Charles] January 30, 1945—New York City

I'm glad to hear about your living quarters and the Turkish bath. A nice substitute for no hot water. But tell me, (your curious wife), what did you mean when you said you could "bathe, etc." in the Turkish bath. What else do they do in a Turkish bath? [Charles's first letter about his accommodations in Liege has not been found.]

/////

[Charles to Billee] February 8, 1945—Liege

"What do they do in Turkish baths?" I guess I tried to cover a lot of territory with the "etc."

The "etc." in this case meant being able to shave with hot water. But, for a week now there hasn't been any bath or shower facilities in the Turkish bath because it can't get any coal to heat the water. To meet the emergency, Bill Spear and I bought an electric coil gadget, about the size of a saucer, so we can have hot water for washing and shaving. I have tried taking a bath in absolutely cold water (a performance I will never repeat, believe me) and sponging myself down with a cold towel since the baths have been closed. However, today I found a solution. I know the [Allied Military Government for Occupied Territories, or AMGOT] Town Major, who incidentally is not a major but a lieutenant, and he gave me the key to his hotel room, which has a tub and plenty of hot water. There must be a GI shower place around town someplace but I haven't been able to find it. American installations are the only ones with coal, and therefore hot water. I suppose the civilians get a little coal, but it's not very much, despite the fact that this is a coal-mining sector.

Now, about the Paris blowoff.

Major Goodfriend, who just became a Lt. Colonel, and the man who succeeded Llewellyn, has been writing the editorials. He wrote one supporting the National Service Act. [President Roosevelt had called for the compulsory military training of youth after the war.] The boys in Paris (apparently led by Bob, Bud and Benny) revolted and said no one man should speak for the four million soldiers in the ETO, and that the *Stars and Stripes* policy always has been "hands off" on controversial matters. By supporting the Bill, the *Stars and Stripes* would be, unofficially, stating the viewpoint of every solder over here. And, who are we to be able to say what they think?

The editorial was held out, temporarily. A conference of the Paris staff and Goodfriend was called. The news leaked out to the civilian correspondents and they filed stories of an "uprising." At least, that's the second-hand information I got over the phone.

Goodfriend then called a press conference of the civilian writers, the outcome of which I don't know. Bob said he couldn't say much on the phone but intimated that Goodfriend successfully explained his position to the writers. Bud got on the phone and said he was sending me a detailed report on the "blowoff" as he put it. I'll get it tomorrow, and when he writes like that I can only think that possibly a lot of the fellows are ready to quit.

[Billee to Charles] February 8, 1945—New York City

The Parisian bickering between the brass and staff has come to the front in the paper this time. I'm wondering what will happen. Don Hallenback of NBC was talking to Jane about it. He says it's obvious that the staff is right, that Goodfriend has no right to impose his editorials on the GIs. The item in the *Sun* went on to say that a meeting of the staff members had been called. I'm glad you're out of that deal at least for the time being.

[Billee to Charles] February 13, 1945—New York City

5L [the number of Billee and Jane's apartment] must look like Clifford's Inn tonight since we are going to put up both Warren and Joe. I haven't exactly figured out how but I can assure you that we aren't going to flip a coin.

Warren arrived this a.m. and since he was only going to be here today, I took off. We sat in the Little Campus this afternoon with Joe and Warren, practically all afternoon, the fellows drinking scotch and soda and me, rye. I skipped a couple. I cooked dinner for all of us and I'm so pleased Joe cleaned his plate nearly so that sort of redeems my failure before.

I think Joe and Warren enjoyed the afternoon talking over the London days. Joe is a little lonesome, I'm sure.

Warren and I talked to Mom just a bit ago and she is fine [and] looking forward to Warren's arrival to finish out his furlough. Fifty days this makes since his return. Also I talked to Pop tonight. He received another Purple Heart medal for Eddie. I don't know, but I don't think they should send those things after it's all over. Only opens up the hurt again.

Jane just made coffee and we're making preparations to rig up some kind of bed for the fellows. It will seem strange to have men around here.

I hadn't realized I was homesick for someone that belonged to me 'til I saw Warren getting off the bus. He looks wonderful and I think he likes what he's doing.

/////

[Billee to Charles] February 14, 1945—New York City

You're liable to get a report from the apartment that we're shacking up. I never thought a thing about it 'til Joe and I got in the elevator this morning to go downstairs. The elevator operator raised his eyebrows. Jane thought of it, too, going down with Warren a half-hour later. As Jane said, it was like a boarding house slumber party except we had an ex-tail gunner and the New York chief of the *Stars and Stripes*.

/////

[Charles to Billee] February 14, 1945—Liege

I talked with Andy on the phone yesterday. [Andy had returned from his leave.] He said he and Bud were coming up this way tomorrow or the next day. Andy will work in the field out of First Army (which is in our sector) and Bud will just roam around. Carl is staying in Paris doing a little bit of everything, I guess. And, incidentally (between us) Bob and Benny were chastised for their part in the revolt last week. Bob was removed (again) as head of the news bureau and put in charge of America copy only. Benny was put back as picture editor for Paris only. He's way down in the dumps.

[Charles to Billee] February 24, 1945—Liege

A fellow I knew in J[ersey] C[ity] (Ed McGovern) stopped in to see me the other day. He told me he thought he could find out where Ed was buried from First Army Graves and Registration. He called three hours later and gave me the information. So, the following day (Thursday) I went out to the First Army Press camp at Spa, met Andy and we drove to Henri Chapelle, in Belgium on the road to Aachen. It's practically on the Belgian-German frontier. There is a huge American cemetery there, about 15,000 graves, and Eddie's was Grave 138, Row 7, Plot LL. It wasn't fixed as well as it will be in a month or so. But there it was with one of his dog tags on the white cross. The officer at the cemetery said the thaw had caused a lot of the graves to sink a little and they aren't going to plant grass or fix any of them until the ground is thoroughly thawed out.

Later we drove through Aachen (my first trip inside Germany). It was the worst blitz I've ever seen and that covers a lot of territory. Aachen was a fairly large city, but I doubt if there was a building or house with a roof or inside left to it. Picture, if you can, a city about the size of half of Cleveland just laid to ruins.

I stayed overnight at the Press camp, met George Hicks (just back from the States) and others I hadn't seen in a long time. I had an opportunity to sit in on the briefing for the big offensive, then went to bed while Andy took off for the front at 11 p.m.

We were jammed trying to get all the coverage on the offensive but we did a good job. Ralph Martin (now up in our territory with the 9th Army) came in with a good piece, Andy did a good one from First, fellows named Leiser and Lee came through with good yarns and Larry Riordan, our photographer, enabled us to turn out a full page of pictures on it.

We have a "farewell" here tonight. Bill Spear is leaving for Paris, from where he'll take off by boat for the New York office. It was good working with him. Look him up when he gets settled in NY, sweetheart. You'll like him. I turned down the top desk job in Bill's place. Maybe I'm selfish, but there aren't enough good copyreaders and headline writers here to turn out the kind of paper I'd want to have and rather than be the top man on it I said I'd rather continue to do what I am doing.

//////

[Billee to Charles] March 2, 1945—New York City

I've gotten so I don't wait around in meat markets anymore but with Earl, Rita and Joe coming for dinner Sunday, something had to be done. You'd die if you could see the price of meat. I had something like chicken in mind but no go so I ended up with a pot roast. I only asked for four pounds, darling, but it looks just enormous.

I'm greatly enlightened on Turkish baths. How I hope the situation is relieved and you don't have to go around borrowing bathrooms and no more cold, cold showers.

//////

[Charles to Billee] March 3, 1945—Liege

Andy came in tonight. We talked a while and he went back to the press camp in order to get an early start up front tomorrow. He intends to get into Cologne with the advance troops. Bud has been around here a bit, but mostly up front.

When Benny called me, he devoted about 15 minutes to explanation of a potential new setup in Paris with a Lt. Col. just over from Washington, taking over Goodfriend's job and shaking up the organization. He wanted to know if I would consider coming to Paris as "war editor" for all editions.

I know how Benny jumps at conclusions. I'm sure he's wrong, so I'm continuing being happy here and working hard. Carl is on the desk, knows little or nothing about making up pages, so I'm now making up six instead of four as I did when Bill Spear was here. As soon as I can get someone here to handle sports, I'll work in with Larsen and run the "war" end of the paper.

We were here until 4:30 yesterday morning conferring with Elmer Roessner, the civilian consultant to *Stars and Stripes*, on our problems. There aren't many problems but we need two more men, better ink for the presses, etc.

Benny just this minute called from Paris to tell me he's writing Jane. Somehow it reminded me there was a bottle of champagne under my desk. One of the boys brought it from the front. So I opened it and poured two glasses. Just by way of having one for you.

/////

[Billee to Charles] March 5, 1945—New York City

Jane and I were up fairly early yesterday [and] gave the apartment a good cleaning. Joe arrived just in time not to help us. Rita and Earl came about an hour later. It was a good day. Things went along pretty smoothly. The pot roast was a success, my very first. I had to use lemon pie mix because we didn't have sugar enough and the pie didn't turn out very good, but everyone ate it.

We left about five-thirty to go to 195. Earl decided he wanted to take the ferry over so we did. It took us an hour and a half to get there. Pop laughed when we told him how we came. Funny . . . we asked a cop at Liberty Street about the ferry. I wasn't sure and he tried to persuade us not to go to Jersey City.

Earl as well as some of the others all asked the same question, if I find you hard to live with. Seems you led them a hard life with your neatness and cleanliness. They told about having to isolate Andy, he was so much to the other extreme.

I have a new job. I answered an ad today at Hattie Carnegie, Inc. I had one of the most sensible interviews for a position I ever had. He asked me what I could do and how much I wanted. He told me the nature of the work and weighed my qualifications against the requirements, decided I'd do and I start Friday at $35.00 a week, 5 days a week, with Saturday mornings twice a month.

Billee with Jane Price on the Jersey City ferry—New York, March 1945. (Kiley Family)

[Charles to Billee] March 7, 1945—Liege

Everything happening at once.

The First Army took Cologne yesterday, the Third Army rushed 60 miles to the Rhine today and the Russians started a new drive to Berlin.

Days like this mean a lot of work, late hours, etc. But I'm not minding it. I thrive on work, as you must know by now.

///////

[Charles to Billee] March 10, 1945—Liege

Andy blew in from the front earlier in the night and is talking with Marg on the typewriter across the room. He turned in a couple of good pieces on the Rhine crossing. Stuck his neck way out to get them, too. He'll be going back up on Monday.

I've been as busy as the devil all week again, mainly with the Rhine crossing and getting a four-page VE supplement ready. Consequently, my correspondence with everybody is suffering badly.

///////

[Billee to Charles] March 11, 1945—New York City

Called *Time, Inc.* and told them I wouldn't be back. Friday I started my new job. Let's see . . . Thursday night I met Jane and Joe at NBC and we went to Louis' [restaurant] for dinner. We met Marg later and tried to see Lena Horne at the Capitol but there were too many with the same idea, so we saw a newsreel instead. Very good, too—the pictures of Iwo Jima. We came home and talked for hours. It's really funny the way Joe always ends up in our company, but kind of nice. At least we know he approves of us.

Did I tell you Joe decided you should have been the priest instead of Father John? I'm awfully glad, of course, that you aren't.

///////

[Charles to Billee] March 13, 1945—Liege

I heard from Paris that Joe had his time extended until Bill Spear was ready to take over the bureau.

We were given a rough idea on postwar plans for *Stars and Stripes* here, and it seemed to include only one 16-page paper, but published in the section of Germany occupied by American troops. It also included a very large staff working in New York.

I'll have to confess that I didn't tell all about the Turkish bath. In Belgium, or Liege, at least, it seems to be quite natural to have woman attendants in the baths. They direct you to a private locker, then turn the key on it when you head for the shower. In the shower room you find another woman regulating the hot and cold water, frequently reaching into the shower to turn them on and off, while the shower is occupied.

What's more, they move from shower to shower *washing the backs* of those inside. Naturally, with a lot of soldiers in there every day, a state of confusion existed for awhile. Most of the GI customers follow through with the custom and have their backs washed. Not me, however. I still have a certain amount of modesty. The entrance to the pool is off the shower room, so I wear a pair of trunks to the shower, then into the pool. Andy and I had a swim the other day before he went back to the front. I did something I wouldn't do ordinarily, and that was to let him use the gloves you sent to me, the Abercrombie & Fitch mittens. He said he was using an old beat-up pair of GI wool gloves, so I offered him mine, since I won't be using them now.

Earl's last letter mentioned the dinner you had for them, and the subsequent visit to 195. He said I should have been the priest and John the *Stars & Stripes* man.

///////

[Billee to Charles] March 15, 1945—New York City

Benny finally broke the silence from Paris after six days of no messages. We were all beginning to wonder. Seems the new Colonel is trying to cut down on expenses.

Marg is still waiting to hear from Andy. When you mention Andy or talk about him, I always tell her but that's a poor substitute. She doesn't know where he is at all now.

I know how lonely you are, darling, when you pour out two glasses of champagne. Remember, it tickles my nose.

/////

[Charles to Billee] March 17, 1945—Liege

'Tis embarrassed I am, when the likes of Swedes like Larsen, Hungarians like Zumwalt [a *Stars and Stripes* staffer], Dutchmen like Moora can point a veritable finger of scorn at the homeland of Eire, which has maintained its peace of mind through the war. And my cheeks blush as red as a rose of Kilarney when I hear of an Eisenhower and a Scotch-Englishman like Patton making the news of a day. Worst of all—and my heroic ancestors who sacrificed themselves during the "trouble" with the bloody traitors of England are spinning in their graves—a North of Irelander like Montgomery is in the thick of the fight.

Where, oh where, are the fighting men of the old country on this St. Patrick's Day?

/////

[Billee to Charles] March 17, 1945—New York City

Happy St. Patrick's Day.

Joe, Jane and I went to the Commodore and had a scotch and soda by way of celebrating our seventh [month] anniversary, then came home. I baked a cake to take over to 195.

Joe will go back a week from Monday. Bill Spear finally arrived at Ft. Hamilton today after spending fifteen days on the water. He must have been paddling a canoe. He's getting a two-day pass and will report to work right away so there'll be no need for Joe to stick around. We're going to miss him. He's spent an awful lot of time with us especially since Carl went back.

Mrs. K. is among the ranks of the unemployed. The job at Hattie Carnegie's didn't work out. I'll tell you about it sometime. [Billee quit because she got a good look at the working conditions for the people making the clothes and hats, which were deplorable.] I'm liable to end up on an assembly line.

[Billee to Charles] March 19, 1945—New York City

Marg, Joe and Bill Spear are due to arrive and they can put this in tomorrow's mail.

I think I have a job. At least I start Wednesday morning, right around the corner between 7th and 8th Avenues in a branch office of Standard Oil. Goes under the name of Stanco Distributors. It entails working with the company auditors. The salary isn't as much as I wanted but being able to eat here at the apartment will make up for a lot.

The girl I talked with today at the employment service says she has several overseas jobs but the one drawback is that your husband must not be serving in the same field. She offered me a job in the Far East.

[Billee to Charles] March 23, 1945—New York City

Let me tell you about my job. So far so good. As I told you, it's being a clerk and typist to the auditors who are doing the books of four companies all owned by Standard Oil. They are in an eight-story building around the corner. I have a desk in an office with the two head auditors, both very nice: a Mr. Walton, the head who was in the AEF World War I and part of the Army of Occupation for a year.

I think he's about 54 or 55. The other auditor in the office is quite a character. His name is Mr. Tweddle, no kidding, and veddy, veddy English. He was the foreign representative in Europe for many years for Standard Oil before the war. His humor is very dry of course. He never misses an opportunity to rub it in about my name being Irish. He hasn't much use for women in business; thinks they should be at home where they belong. He's nice underneath it all. We've had some very interesting conversations. Mr. Tweddle, by the way, is sixtyish.

We're due to go to a party tomorrow night to wish Joe a bon voyage. Bill Spear and his wife are borrowing the Mazos' apartment while they are in Washington and we're to go there. I hate going out like that without you.

/////

[Charles to Billee] March 24, 1945—Liege

As of today, I'm finished with sports here. Paul Horowitz came up from Paris to take that worry away from me. Now, I move into the "slot." Between the two of us, when and if Larsen steps down I think I'll take over the paper. I hesitated to take it twice before, but the staff has shaped up 100 percent better in the last couple of weeks and now I believe I'll be able to do something with it. Meanwhile, I'll be chief of the copy desk, handle four correspondents in the field and continue to do the organizing.

/////

[Billee to Charles] March 26, 1945—New York City

I had Saturday off. Jane came in about three and Joe wandered in about four. We were all to go to Bill Spears' for the sendoff party for Joe. Marg came in about six and we all went out to dinner to a new place, Armenian on East 27th St. We had something called Shish Kebob that was very good. Even Joe liked it.

We were the first to arrive at Bill's. Soon after [*Stars and Stripes* staffers] Bob Wood and wife, Herbie Schneider and [Phil] Bucknell made their entrance in a body, all with a nice glow on. Bob Wood and Herbie Schneider I met for the first time. This is supposed to amuse you. Never having met Bob before I couldn't really appreciate his actions. He jitterbugged, did a striptease for us, after a fashion, which amounted to unbuttoning his shirt and was the life of the party. I thought Joe would die from hysteria he laughed so much. Everyone was feeling very good before the evening was over. Marg danced with Bob. Neither of them knew how to jitterbug but the attempt was a riot. We all had fun. Mrs. K. behaved herself like a lady. I had three rye and sodas very early in the evening and no more. We left around three o'clock, I guess. Bucknell was quite stiff, more than I've ever seen him. We all piled into a cab and went downtown, stopping at the respective stops. We left Buck in the cab at 5L and he made his way from there.

Marg stayed with us. We sat around 'til nearly five drinking coffee and discussing the party. Marg still hasn't received any mail from Andy. She told Joe she guessed she'd write to him instead of Andy.

//////

[Billee to Charles] March 28, 1945—New York City

Word came this morning that Benny and Moora have gone to Frankfurt to start an edition there or look the situation over. They are still fighting in Frankfurt as of tonight. Joe also arrived in Paris this morning.

Marg still has received no mail from Andy. She's afraid now that it's being tampered with. A reassuring message from Andy has stopped her from being angry with him. She's only worried now.

The Turkish bath is right out of this world. I can just see you flitting around modestly in the trunks. I'm glad, though, that you are washing your own back.

//////

[Billee to Charles] April 3, 1945—New York City

Marg came over last night and brought the letter you wrote her. A good letter, too—so informative. At long last she received a letter from Andy today.

Today is Marg's birthday. I have a cake all baked for her and as soon as Jane comes we'll have cake and ice cream. Marg is staying with us tonight. While we were in the vicinity of her hotel, we picked up some of her laundry to do. The hotel is nice where she is. A large part of it is taken over by the Navy [and] fairly bristles with officers, Marine and Navy. Nice looking, too, not that I'd be interested. It's nice she has attractive atmosphere around. Suppose we could make Andy jealous so he'd write to Marg more often.

[*Charles to Billee*] *April 7, 1945—Liege*

The Frankfurt paper (actually published in Pfungstadt, about 15 miles from Frankfurt) came out day before yesterday. Benny, Bob, and about four others are up there. There are a lot of things to straighten out before they will be operating full-scale. Communications will take another week or so, and that's the big headache.

The plan now is for all editions to continue until Frankfurt is on its feet. Then, Liege and Nancy papers will fold with Frankfurt servicing all four armies: First, Third, Seventh and Ninth. The Frankfurt staff will have to be strengthened and about a dozen more men will go there. Larsen, Dick Jones, Art Force and myself have been tentatively scheduled to go. Perhaps more from here. The rest will come from the Nancy and Paris editions. That may be in 10 days or weeks, depending on how long it takes to get Frankfurt in 100 percent operation.

The front is now more than 300 miles from here and Nancy. Frankfurt will be closer and more centrally located, and it sounds like the best idea from the standpoint of getting papers to the front quickly.

Now, there were some post VE-day plans also discussed while Goodfriend was here. And here they are:

He said MacArthur already is on record as not wanting anyone from the ETO like the *Stars and Stripes* coming to the Pacific. Apparently, if he wants a paper there he will organize it himself. Meanwhile, for all intents and purposes, *Stars and Stripes* will remain at ETO publication without any plans for the Pacific.

When the European war is over the *Stars and Stripes* will continue to function for "maximum of a year and a minimum of eight months," according to Goodfriend, as a result of his conversation with Gen. [Frederick] Osborn [head of Special Services]. London edition will probably fold about three months after VE day since the Air Forces are expected to leave quickly. Nice will continue because troops will pass through there en route to the United States and the Pacific. Paris will continue to service troops who will be given additional training for the Pacific. The German edition, wherever located, will continue for the occupational troops as well as some of those who will remain for additional training.

I haven't any idea where I fit in after VE-day, except that I'll try to get New York-wards. If not, then I believe I can have my choice of the others and it really wouldn't matter where it was.

As much as I hate to say it, let's just figure your old man is going to be here for about eight or ten months after VE day.

A soldier in the 1st Infantry Division, who had been overseas and in combat almost continuously since the invasion of Africa—Sicily, Italy, Normandy, France, the Bulge, Germany—was due to go home on a 30-day furlough. A patrol was scheduled and he was part of it. He had his choice to stay back. It wouldn't have meant much, but he went out that night. He was wounded once, could have come back, but stayed with the patrol after giving his bad arm first aid. He was wounded again, slightly in the leg, but stayed with the patrol. One of his men was wounded and in trying to help him, the soldier who was going home . . . was killed.

Perhaps, I should think I've been in this long enough. Let someone else do it. But even though I can't do anything but stay until I'm told I'm through, I don't feel too badly about it.

///////

[Charles to Billee] April 13, 1945—Liege

You are going to be awfully sorry you married a newspaperman before another week or so passes. In fact, you are going to regret having a managing editor in the family. I've been starting to tell you for five days now without getting beyond the first sentence. It's that much of a scramble around here.

To begin with, I am managing editor of Liege. I know now why I didn't want the job before. It's a swift but short life.

Yesterday morning I took over, and after putting out a decent eight-pager was sitting at my desk at about midnight sorting through papers, etc., and getting ready to write the letter I had been trying to get at for days.

The teletype machine was "out," as it had been for two days and the telephone buzzed. It was the Paris communications office hysterically relaying the "President Dead" flash.

It took me a minute to gather my wits, let the shock sink in, then start the machine working here. I had the presses stop (just like they do in the movies), had them "kill" 60,000 papers that had already been printed, then proceeded to make over pages 1 and 8. By the time we got the presses going again at 1:30, it was necessary for us to kill off pages in order for the presses to finish the run at 10 a.m. I got out of here at 6:15, was up again at 10:30 and in the office again.

I got out a darn good paper tonight, if I may pat myself on the back, with all the follow-up details on the president, past and present, solid page of obituary, page of pictures, etc.

That wasn't bad enough but at 11:00, when I was getting normal again, one of my underground agents tipped me off that Von Papen, Ribbentrop and von Rundstedt are now "guests" of Eisenhower. At the same time, [Henry] Stimson [Secretary of War] came through with an announcement that war may be over soon, and nobody knows where Ike is.

All of which means I dare not leave here until about 4:00 when it becomes almost impossible for us to make any changes.

That's not all. Another flash from Leiser at the front says the Ninth Army may be in Berlin or on the outskirts by tomorrow.

I'm just having the time of my life.

[Billee to Charles] April 14, 1945—New York City

It was after I finished my letter to you that we heard the startling news that Roosevelt was dead. Even now it seems unbelievable. Everything has seemed at a standstill since the news came over the air about six. The radio has carried nothing but news and funeral music since then.

We'll have to get along as best we can without his leadership. I have all the faith in the world that we will. There's a long road ahead and sometimes I wonder if we're going to see what we're fighting for.

We've been hearing rumors the Liege edition is being abandoned. Certainly, you can't be supplying the 1st and 9th now. They are miles beyond you now. I'm assuming that very likely some change is being made since there's been no mail in some time. The last I had was written over two weeks ago. It doesn't sound like long ago but seems an age to me.

/////

[Billee to Charles] April 17, 1945—New York City

Earl called me a few minutes ago at the office and said he'd wait while I brought the things you asked for to him this evening. Seems he's taking off in the morning.

Thought it would be nice if he could take a letter back to you. Make the distance a wee bit shorter when we can do things like this.

I'm remembering too that according to your promise, you should be home four months from today. Don't you think you and "Ike" could get together and fold this thing up? Maybe we could all mutiny as Joe suggests. Anyway, four months from today makes nice dreaming material.

CHAPTER 10

APRIL–JUNE 1945

This is so strange. I think sometimes it is all a wild dream. This morning I was driving and walking through what is left of a completely destroyed Berlin. This afternoon I sat at a table outside a sidewalk cafe on the Champs Elysees, watching one of the most unbelievable and colorful sights I'll ever see . . .

[*Charles to Billee, May 1945.*]

/////

The War: By mid-April Allied forces had all but encircled Berlin, sending Hitler to his bunker; he ordered all military and industrial installations destroyed to deny the Allies possession. His armament minister, Albert Speer, and army officers blocked the directive.

On April 18, Ernie Pyle was killed by a Japanese sniper just west of Okinawa.

S.S. leader Heinrich Himmler offered a German surrender to the British and United States, excluding the Russians, on April 22. Seeking unconditional surrender, the Allies refused the offer. Desperate and nearly incomprehensible, Hitler ordered Himmler's arrest. He had Goering arrested too.

Mussolini was arrested in Italy and on April 28, his mutilated body hung upside down in Milan. Two days later, Hitler and Goebbels committed suicide. Admiral Dönitz, the man who did not believe the Allied invasion was imminent in 1944, took control of the Third Reich.

At the end of April, US and Russian forces met by the Elbe River.

At the Dachau death camp, US troops, angered by what they witnessed and before an officer could stop them, executed more than one hundred S.S. troops.

After nine days of battle in Berlin, Russian troops took the city on April 30.

Mastermind of the death camps, Heinrich Himmler, soon went on the run, but was captured outside Hamburg by a British patrol, after which he swallowed cyanide.

On May 1, it was reported that von Rundstedt had been captured; the following day, Germans surrendered to the Russians in Berlin; German troops surrendered in Italy; and the Baltics were in Allied control. On May 4, the Germans surrendered in northwest Germany, the Netherlands, and Denmark, but the war continued.

On May 7, 1945, German officers signed a formal unconditional surrender to the Allies at Eisenhower's headquarters in Reims, France. The following day, a second signing took place in Berlin between the Germans and the Russians, officially ending the war in Europe.

Celebrations broke out in major cities of Allied countries on May 8. That same day, President Truman reminded the world that the German surrender ended only half the war. Not ready to celebrate, Truman turned his focus to Japan and the Pacific, where war continued for four more months.

[Charles to Billee] April 18, 1945—Paris

This is like old times. Benny is sitting across the desk from me writing to Jane.

I got in from Liege about an hour ago, after a seven-hour drive in an open jeep with a hot sun.

After a couple of days in Paris, I'll be going to Pfungstadt. Three others from Liege are going with me. Benny was to go to Nice but today he was informed the deal was changed and he'll possibly remain in Paris. Meanwhile, Bud is going to Nice with most of the fellows I had in Liege. I don't even know what kind of a job I'm supposed to do in Pfungstadt.

Getting back to Liege. I was managing editor for the last five editions. Did pretty good, too. I wrote to you after the Roosevelt news, expecting other big stories to break. Sure enough, the Von Papen thing came off as expected although Rundstedt and Ribbentrop remain mysteries.

/////

[Billee to Charles] April 19, 1945—New York City

We're stopped right now with the darn State Department ruling but we're hoping that they may lift it after VE Day. The ruling, as you no doubt know, is that you can't be sent to the same country or same theatre of war that your husband is in. The reason: because it isn't fair to the other wives of GIs.

I full well know how the telephone call giving you the news of the president's death must have affected you. You were right on the beam, getting everything out. We are expecting the VE day news any hour of the day or night. NBC says it won't be until June. They've been paying for a direct wire for weeks to the Astor roof overlooking Times Square to get the reaction of the crowds.

/////

[Charles to Billee] April 19, 1945—Paris

Today I changed my opinion of Paris to a more favorable one than I had a few months ago. But, the opinion only concerns the appearance of Paris. It's beautiful. Of course, the people look much better in the spring than they do in the winter and there is a lot of color to the passing parade along the Champs Elysees.

I stopped in the office long enough to talk with Col. Goodfriend about what I am supposed to do in Germany and the word is that I was asked for especially by Capt. Schouman, who will be editor (brass) and a guy named Rogosta, who will be managing editor. They want me to be the No. 2 man, whatever that is.

After talking with Goodfriend I walked along the Champs, admiring the women (but not too much) because you can't help it. There are 50 women to one man, it seems, and women naturally dominate the parade. I sat in the park, soaking up sunshine and reading some *New Yorkers*. I stopped in two sidewalk cafes for some vin blanc, and in general felt thoroughly relaxed for the first time in ages. I'll be in bed early tonight, perhaps after I see a show. Last night I stayed up until 2:00 with Benny, Joe and a couple of the boys. We were in an "American bar" having a few drinks—not many. It was good to talk, lean back and listen, have a drink to play with. Now I know, for the first time I think, what relaxation can do for you. I feel now that I worked harder in Liege than in anywhere or at anything before, because I never felt so completely tired as I did when we finished up there.

/////

[Charles to Billee] April 21, 1945—Paris

In my letter to you yesterday I told of getting ready to go to Germany. Well, the whole picture changed in less time than I can take to talk about it.

Jim Grad, to begin with, has been with Gen. Eisenhower for quite a few months. He is going home now. Yesterday, the Col. called me into his office and asked me if I would like the job. It sounded good, inasmuch as I wasn't too keen about going to Germany and working with fellows I don't know. So, I'm off to cover the ***** General. I'll meet Grad this afternoon at the General's forward headquarters. This morning I saw the general's naval aide, Capt. Butcher, here in Paris. Also a couple of colonels connected with public relations. I believe I'll meet the boss himself before I'm at his headquarters very long. The job boils down to this:

Rather than have an entourage of newsmen following the general around, one man is selected to represent the world press and radio in reporting the general's activities. Gen. Ike insisted that one man be from *Stars and Stripes* . . . that was Grad and now me.

/////

[Billee to Charles] April 22, 1945—New York City

The [*Stars and Stripes* New York] bureau is such a wonderful deal, else I'd wait for days 'til I knew this but as it is, almost as soon as you know, I know. What I'm driving at is the news that you are going to take over Jim Grad's job at Eisenhower's headquarters. I think it's wonderful. I couldn't help but be awfully excited when Jane called this evening before she came home and told me. Marg had called her a bit earlier. [Marg Rooney had taken the secretarial position at the bureau.]

I'm glad that the Russians are taking Berlin. Perhaps that will be a few less of our guys who will be slaughtered. I know it's for another reason but nevertheless, I imagine it will save a few lives. More and more of the atrocity stories are being published. They're hair-raising.

Would you like me to tell Gen'l Ike what a nice guy you are?

[Charles to Billee] April 23, 1945—"France"

I am certain you will be terribly confused by events of the past week: First, the closing in Liege; second, the trip to Paris; third, preparations for Germany; fourth, sudden change to Gen. Eisenhower. And now, on the job. All in five days!

Jules Grad left for Paris this afternoon, leaving me on my own to take over.

I met Gen. Eisenhower this morning, by way of introducing me and saying goodbye to Jules.

Col. Gault ushered us into the General's office and left us there. We saluted, he shook hands, told us to sit down, then talked for five minutes or so. He said he was sorry but it looked as if he might be "stuck" here for a few days and would not make any "news."

The General told Jules he was glad to have had him with him, wished him luck and told me he'd be "seein'" me.

He was waiting for a call from Churchill, he said, so we shook hands again and made our exit.

The General looked tired around the eyes.

The beauty of this job is, when I check in with Col. Gault at 9:30 or 10:00 a.m. and he says "nothing doing," the rest of the day is mine. If something suddenly comes up, I can always be reached at one of three places: the office, hotel or the apartment of the General's air crew.

Expenses here are very reasonable. Breakfast at the officers' mess costs only 20 cents, lunch and dinner, 40 cents. I'll get $1.50 a day for meals.

Charles (left) with General Eisenhower, meeting repatriated Allied POWs—
France, April 1945. (US Army)

/////

[Charles to Billee] April 24, 1945—"France"

It is my fourth day here, but actually my first "on the job" as it is the first day
Jules is not here.

So far, it has been a holiday as far as work goes. I checked with Col. Gault
at 9:30 this morning but he said there wouldn't be anything doing.

This afternoon I thought we would be in for a "quickie" when the air crew,
got a rush call to get to the airfield in 20 minutes. Leo and I were with them at
the time. Leo called Col. Gault but the word was that it wasn't anything for us.

I hope you get the list of names I'm sending so you'll know these people
when I talk of them.

The Family

The Boss: D.D.E. [Dwight David Eisenhower]

Chief of Staff: Lt. Gen. Walter B. Smith

Kay: Lt. Kay Summersby, WAC secretary to the boss

Nana: Nana Rae, chief clerk and Scottish-born WAC in the office

Leo: Lt. Leo Moore, the boss's photographer with whom I live and work

Col. [James] Gault: military assistant to the general; British and with the general since North Africa

Capt. [Harry] Butcher: Naval aide and right-hand man to the boss

Mickey: Mickey McKeough, driver and orderly to the general

Larry: Maj. Larry Hansen, 27-year old pilot of the general's plane

Dick: Capt. Dick Underwood, co-pilot

Charles (in background, second from left), with members of the US congressional group investigating Nazi atrocities, who had arrived at Reims airport just in time to see twenty German generals captured at Ruhr being loaded into a C-47—Reims, April 1945. (US Army)

[Charles to Billee] April 26, 1945—"France"

You are probably wondering about the "France" dateline. It is because this place, Gen. Eisenhower's forward headquarters, is strictly on the "stop" list as far as location is concerned.

I missed last night's date, I guess, because I worked for a change. Maybe it was the shock of writing a story. I could scarcely remember when I wrote the last one.

The group of senators and members of the House of Representatives who are over here to see evidence of German atrocities reported to the General yesterday and I sat in on the hour-long conference. Today, 18 newspaper publishers and editors, here for the same purpose, came in and it was another conference. Tomorrow the International War Crimes Commission will be here.

My routine is to call in the story to the office, then put it on the HQ teletype here, which gets it to HQ in Paris for distribution all over the world.

You are likely to see my stories in the New York papers from time to time, some perhaps with a byline. If they don't have a byline, you will be able to recognize them with a dateline of "Supreme Headquarters Forward CP" or "With Gen. Eisenhower's Forward CP." The "CP" part of it is "Command Post."

There were more stars around here today, than there are in the sky. It's commonplace to rub elbows, practically any day, with Gen. [James] Doolittle, Gen. [Carl] Spaatz, Gen. [Walter Bedell] Smith, Gen. [Lucius] Clay, Gen. [Benjamin] Lear—who may not sound like much but they're top men in the war.

It's funny. Tonight I went over to the officers' club and sat at a table with three majors, two captains and three first lieutenants. One of the majors was Larry Hansen and the other Gen. Smith's pilot.

Everybody calls everybody else by first names. Hansen calls me, "Chuck." Can you imagine?

/////

[Charles to Billee] April 28, 1945—"France"

There has been more than a little excitement around here for the last few hours and I don't feel ready to go to sleep yet. I am afraid I have been the cause of the excitement, too. Not the direct cause, but I had something to do with it.

We were at the air crew's apartment last night (Saturday) playing cards and talking. At 10 o'clock, I was getting ready to leave and "see" you before I retired. At that moment, Paris called to give me word that they had an idea something big might break soon and to "stand by." I waited until 2:30 a.m. and decided it was too late for anything to happen tonight. As soon as I got home, Dick Underwood came rushing over in a Jeep to get me and Leo. He said Paris called and wanted me to call back immediately. We came back to the apartment, I called Paris and Bob gave me the report that the Associated Press had quoted a "high official" at the San Francisco Conference as saying Germany had capitulated to the United States, Britain and Russia.

My job, of course, was to see what the general knew about it. It was going to be a delicate job, I knew, at 3:00 a.m.

Dick drove me first to HQ and nobody was around. Then we went to the general's house. After convincing a couple of guards we were ok, we got Col. Gault. He brought us to the general who was just getting ready to retire. Generals, it seems, keep late hours.

The General had not heard of this latest report, although he had heard an earlier one that Himmler had "reportedly" offered to surrender to the United States and Britain. Frankly, he was a little perplexed. I can see how he wouldn't have had word so quickly since the report originated in San Francisco and not here. Thinking over the situation, he said he didn't believe it, although it "would be an ironic climax to this war if it was over and I didn't know about it."

His aide put through a call to 10 Downing St. in London and received the reply that it had heard of the report but did not know of the surrender. The general thanked me for bringing the news to him and said I could quote him as saying he had received no report of any surrender.

When I called Bob back, he said they had been talking to New York by phone and learned that Pres. Truman also had denied the report of surrender.

Personally, I can't figure it out. Associated Press would not start a wild rumor, I'm sure. It quoted the "high official" in San Francisco as saying Sec. [of State] Stettinius had received word from Washington about it. There also were reports that newspapers in the United States had used the story of "Nazis Quit." In Paris, the word got around and everybody was celebrating peace.

I do know this, however, that at 3:00 o'clock this morning, the man who should know, Gen. Eisenhower, did not know anything about it. And, I also feel that the "big people" who circulate these stories without them being official ought to be hung. We were ready to start a wild celebration of our own until it all turned out to be nothing more than a rumor.

///////

[*Billee to Charles*] *April 28, 1945—New York City*

On Saturday Jane and I went shopping for the week over to the A&P. Bought out the place, but we decided it would be a good idea so we wouldn't have to make so many trips downstairs to the deli and we really save a little buying there. Didn't have supper 'til after eight or so—waffles. In the middle of supper we heard the surrender communique. We couldn't believe it, and it's a good thing, though we all did get excited in spite of ourselves. We waited and waited for some confirmation, then a lieutenant from ANS called and said he had just talked to Benny. It seems everyone in Paris thought it was over but they couldn't get any confirmation so Benny called New York to see if they knew any more here.

///////

[FROM THE *STARS AND STRIPES*, April 29, 1945]

TRUMAN AND IKE DENY IT'S OVER

by Charles Kiley, *Stars and Stripes* Staff Writer

Reports that Germany had surrendered unconditionally to the Allies were denied flatly early this morning by President Truman and General Eisenhower.

The reports, some emanating from the San Francisco Conference, said that Heinrich Himmler had offered complete surrender to the United States and Great Britain, that the offer had been rejected unless Russia was also included, and that Himmler thereupon agreed to complete capitulation to the three major powers. . . .

. . . General Eisenhower told the *Stars and Stripes* about 3 o'clock this morning that he knew nothing about any surrender offer. He said he had heard the press reports of the Himmler offer yesterday afternoon, but knew nothing of such negotiations. Word that President Truman had called the rumors absolutely unfounded was relayed to the *Stars and Stripes* by telephone from its New York bureau at 3:30 am today.

The President's announcement came even as thousands of persons jammed the streets outside the White House and crowds milled in joyous demonstrations in Times Square, Chicago's Loop, and in cities all over America. . . .

. . . The news spread everywhere, and in Paris clubs and on the boulevard civilians and soldiers danced, kissed, shouted in a joy that was to last only until morning brought the denial by press and radio. . . .

/////

[Billee to Charles] April 30, 1945—New York

I do believe you have the luck of the Irish. Where does this "Chuck" business come in?

No more exciting news tonight but I feel sure it will happen very soon. The message from Benny said the phone call saved their neck. They were all ready to make a spread of it, that it was over, when Benny decided to call and make certain.

The news came of Mussolini's execution along with the others. That's one down. The pictures are horrible.

Tonight's latest said the news would be flashed from the White House as soon as it arrives. You can imagine how excited we all are, and yet still a bit wary to get too excited.

/////

[Charles to Billee] May 2, 1945—"France"

Earl arrived in Paris the other day. I spoke with him on the phone and after the usual greetings, he remarked, "You sure have one of the sweetest girls in the world." That description came after I asked him, rather breathlessly, how you were and if he had any message for me.

He said he was going up to the Ninth Army and will stop here and stay overnight with me on the way up. I am expecting him this evening, together with mail for two weeks and the things he brought over for me.

There hasn't been much for me to do since my "middle of the night" interview with the General. Last night we heard by radio of Hitler's reported death and this morning the report is that von Rundstedt has been captured.

The events of the last week or so have been amazing.

1. The Russians in Berlin
2. The Russo-American linkup
3. Himmler's surrender offer
4. The reported end of the war
5. Mussolini's death
6. Hitler's reported death and succession by Adm. Dönitz.
7. Capture of von Rundstedt.

What next?

All I can do is stay close to HQ, in case something involving the General happens. In that event all I can do is hope it won't be so "top secret" that I'll be left behind. Because I'm almost constantly in the company of the air crew, or at the office, I'm sure I'll be aware of anything upcoming but I can only hope I'll go along, whatever it is.

[Billee to Charles] May 6, 1945—New York City

The *Stars and Stripes* keeps us up all hours. Honest, we don't know how to get out of it. Seems these guys who are back now haven't had furloughs. They are at loose ends not knowing anyone at all around here so of course, they always feel as if they can come here and sit around and chat, and you know how long they chat.

No matter who comes back and regardless of who they are they never have anything but nice things to say about you, even those you probably disapprove of, and they know it. They seem to say them in all sincerity. Art White said something last night, though, that I hadn't heard from anyone. Perhaps this isn't very nice, but it makes me believe the nice things he says about you. He said you were the only guy he ever knew that could loaf and still look as if he were working.

/////

[Charles to Billee] May 7, 1945—Reims, France

So sorry I had to kiss you awake again so early. It's five o'clock.

But, I'm sure you wanted to be awakened because the war against Germany ended two hours and 15 minutes ago. Yes, it's really over this time.

I know. I was there when the unconditional surrender terms were signed in the war room of Gen. Eisenhower's headquarters at 2:45 a.m.

I had been on top of the surrender since it first developed Saturday.

Adm. Friedeburg, the German Commander in Chief of Naval Forces, arrived here then.

I was the only correspondent here all Saturday and yesterday until 18 correspondents and radio men came up from Paris at 7 o'clock last night. As representative of the combined press and radio I had to cover for everybody until they got here.

All during the preliminary negotiations between the Germans and Gen. Smith, Chief of Staff to Gen. Ike, I was in a room adjacent to Gen. Smith's office. The only part of the surrender which any of the rest covered was the ceremony of signing in the war room.

I'm so tired, sweetheart. Been up at 6:00 the last couple of days and on the go. I have some of my stuff written but I want a little sleep before I continue. I'll do about 2,000 words for the combined press and radio for those who weren't here and want to use it. Then there will be another 1,500 or so for *Stars and*

Stripes. I've tried to cover everything down to a rustle of paper during the last couple of days. Hope I haven't missed anything.

The story is not to be released until tomorrow afternoon although I'm certain it's going to leak out before then.

Admiral Friedeburg arriving at SCHAEF headquarters in Reims for the German surrender negotiations—Reims, May 1945. (US Army)

/////

[Charles to Billee] May 7, 1945—Reims

Well, you know all about it now. That is, you have read the report of the surrender. When I spoke with you early this morning I felt the unconditional surrender would leak out ahead of time. And it has.

The Associated Press is reported to have told of the surrender here early this morning. The news was not to be released until tomorrow (Tuesday) afternoon. But apparently Ed Kennedy of the AP, one of the 18 correspondents and radio men who came up here last night from Paris for the ceremonies, managed to get word back through some devious method, avoiding censorship. Probably got through a phone call to London, which wasn't monitored. London AP called Stockholm AP and cabled New York. That's how I see it and I'm wondering if Kennedy will be punished in any way. It was a direct breach of security. Had it been me, I would have been court-martialed. But that's the penalty of being a soldier.

As I said, everybody knows about it now. Reports say New York is celebrating; London and Paris likewise. Even the French paper in Reims has a big headline. But the *Stars and Stripes*, for example, can use the AP report but nothing else.

All the background and color of the surrender will probably have to wait until after Washington, London and Moscow make formal announcements tomorrow.

In my letter this morning I said I had been on top of the whole surrender story since it developed, beginning Saturday when Adm. Friedeburg arrived here. Then, Gen. Jodl arrived yesterday and in no time at all the surrender terms were laid out and signed.

It all happened so suddenly it seemed like a long day's work. No dramatics, except Jodl's last address to the Allied signers in which he asked that generosity be shown to the German people.

I had a call from the Press Room HQ in Paris this afternoon complimenting me on the job I did for the combined press. I'll have to wait until *Stars and Stripes* is able to use the stuff before I see how it got over down there.

Incidentally, I may be going on quite a trip by air tomorrow. If so, I'll tell you about it when I get back.

/////

[Billee to Charles] May 7, 1945—New York City

It still isn't official, but there was enough excitement today to make it official.

A great many places closed, but I worked and I was very glad I had something to do to hold me together. Oh, darling, it's actually over.

Not too long from now we'll be together. I think I'm still dazed from the last few weeks' activities in the news. Naturally, it didn't come as a surprise since we've been expecting it hourly. There wasn't as much hysteria and wild excitement as there would have been if we hadn't been prepared.

Jane called me at noon and said we were supposed to meet at the *Stars and Stripes* [office] this evening, but I couldn't face any celebration without you and somehow it didn't seem right. I couldn't help but think of Eddie and the report that Gen. Patton's army was still fighting, and the Pacific still looms in the background, so before anyone could call me I took off for 195 right after work. I wanted to be there.

Edward Kennedy has been suspended.

At least I know where you are now, at or near Reims. My heart is so full tonight. So many things I want to share with you. I've been numb practically all day.

[FROM THE *STARS AND STRIPES*, May 8, 1945]

DETAILS OF THE SURRENDER NEGOTIATIONS: THIS IS HOW GERMANY GAVE UP

by Charles Kiley, *Stars and Stripes* Staff Writer

REIMS, May 8—The Third Reich surrendered unconditionally to the Allies at Gen. Eisenhower's Forward HQ here at 02:45 hours on Monday.

The terms of surrender, calling for the cessation of hostilities on all fronts at one minute past midnight (Double British Summer Time) Wednesday, May 9, were signed on behalf of the German Government by Gen. Gustav Jodl, Chief of the Wehrmacht and Chief of Staff to Fuehrer Karl Dönitz.

Under Jodl's signature were those of Lt. Gen. Walter Bedell Smith, chief of staff to the Supreme Allied Commander; General Ivan Suslaparov, head of the Russian mission to France who was authorized by Moscow to sign on behalf of Soviet forces, and General Francois Sevez of France.

The surrender was signed in five minutes in the war room at Supreme Headquarters here, 55 miles east of Compiegne Forest where Germany surrendered to the Allies in the last war, November 11, 1918, and the scene of the capitulation of France to the Third Reich in this war June 21, 1940.

The terms of surrender were signed less than ten hours after the arrival of Jodl by plane from Germany, and 34 hours after final negotiations had first begun with the arrival Saturday of Gen. Adm. Hans-George Friedeburg, Commander-in-Chief of the German Navy, who on Thursday had headed the Nazi delegation which surrendered to the 21st Army Group all German armed forces in Denmark, Holland and northwestern Germany.

Eisenhower did not take part in the actual surrender. He remained in his office with his Deputy Supreme Commander, Air Chief Marshal Sir Arthur Tedder, during the ceremonies.

Flanking Jodl at the surrender table were Friedeburg and Major Gen. G. S. Wilhelm Oxenius, Jodl's aide.

There were no dramatics during the surrender. It was conducted on a business-like basis. Correspondents, cameramen and photographers already were in the war room when the first group of high ranking Allied officers entered at 02:29 hours. In that group were three Russian officers, General Carl A. Spaatz and Lt. Gen. F. E. Morgan, Adm. Sir Harold Burrough and Air Marshal Sir J. M. Robb. One minute later Maj. Gen. H. R. Bull, Assistant Chief of Staff, entered the room.

At 02:34 Smith entered, walked to his chair and talked with Morgan and Burrough. Sevez and Col. Pedron arrived at 02:35 and went to their seats. Two minutes later [British] Major General Kenneth Strong, who had taken part in all preliminary discussions with the Germans as interpreter for Smith as well as in his official capacity as G2, SHAEF, arrived and informed Smith the German delegation was ready.

Smith answered curtly: "Bring them in."

The Germans were escorted by Brig. E. J. Foord, SHAEF chief of operational intelligence. Friedeburg came first, followed by Jodl, erect and expressionless, his uniform neat, his boots highly polished; he walked straight to the center of the huge wooden table, and faced Smith. Friedeburg and Oxenius fell in on both sides of Jodl. The Germans and Allied officers took their seats, Strong standing behind Jodl to interpret.

The formality of the surrender got under way as a copy of the surrender terms was handed by Smith to Suslaparov, who listened while his interpreter read it to him in Russian.

At 02:40 hours Suslaparov handed the copy back to Smith, nodding his head in agreement with the terms.

Smith then handed Jodl four copies and told him to sign all four. The copies went from Jodl to Smith to Suslaparov to Sevez for signatures.

Cameramen darted all over the room, climbed ladders and stood on chairs. Flashbulbs went off every second. Motion pictures hummed to record the historic event.

Jodl's face was impassive as he affixed his signatures. Only Friedeburg appeared disturbed by the commotion caused by the photographers.

At 02:46, Smith stood and spoke a few words to Jodl, which could not be heard.

Jodl stood, faced Smith.

"General," Jodl began.

"With this signature the German people and the German armed forces are for better or worse delivered into the victors' hands.

"In this war, which has lasted more than five years, both have achieved and suffered more than perhaps any other people in the world.

"In this hour I can only express the hope that the victor will treat them with generosity."

Jodl broke halfway through his address, and appeared on the verge of tears. He regained his composure, however, and finished with a strong voice. His hands were trembling when he finished.

Smith simply nodded his head and the three German delegates left the room to be taken to Eisenhower in the Supreme Commander's office.

Eisenhower and his Deputy Supreme Commander, Air Chief Marshal Sir Arthur Tedder, were waiting for the Germans.

There was no exchange of salutes. Jodl, Friedeburg and Oxenius stood at attention before Eisenhower as he sternly asked them:

"Do you understand the terms of this unconditional surrender and are you ready to comply with them?"

Jodl, in the center of the German trio, clicked his heels and bowed his head in the affirmative after Strong interpreted the Supreme Commander's question.

The Germans left the General at 02:57, after a two-minute audience.

Suslaparov led the Russian officers into the Supreme Commander's office and firmly grasped Eisenhower's hand. The Supreme Commander beamed and said, "This is a great moment for all of us."

Suslaparov spoke and when his words were interpreted, Eisenhower replied: "You said it."

Congratulations were exchanged among all the officers present. Eisenhower putting his arm around Tedder's shoulder, grasping his hand and saying, "Thank you very much, Arthur."

The Supreme Commander, enjoying his greatest moments since he was given command of Allied Forces, refused to pose for pictures until his "gang," including the officers present at the surrender, his naval aide and close friend, Capt. Harry C. Butcher, and his personal secretary, 2/Lt. Kathleen Summersby, were gathered around him.

Later, Eisenhower went to his war room for the first time during the night, where the Germans had been able to see the huge battle maps and air operation maps on the walls while they were surrendering, to have his "Victory Address" recorded.

In his address, the Supreme Commander said, "Just a few minutes ago Germany surrendered all of its land, sea and air forces. It has been thoroughly whipped!"

Eisenhower then told how the event completes the mission and plans laid by President Roosevelt and Prime Minister Churchill at Casablanca in January 1943. He said the defeat was accomplished "with the aid of our Russian allies," and that it was fitting that the surrender should take place in the heart of France, where resistance movements and valor had been inspirational. Eisenhower also said that the victory was achieved by the help of "every oppressed nation in Europe."

To the soldiers, sailors and airmen of all services of all Allied nations, Eisenhower said he owed a "debt of gratitude that can never be repaid."

Negotiations for the unconditional surrender began Saturday evening when Friedeburg, a short swarthy man of about 60 with deep-set eyes and bushy eyebrows, arrived. He was accompanied by tall, nervous Col. Fritz Poleck, a member of the Ober Kommando Wehrmacht (OKW), the Nazi equivalent of the War Department or the British War Office. Poleck, who played no actual role in the surrender, was also present when Friedeburg on Thursday surrendered more than 1,000,000 German forces in Denmark, Holland and northwestern Germany to the 21st Army Group at Luneberg, south of Hamburg.

Friedeburg conferred with Smith and Strong for 22 minutes but it was clear from the outset that he was not empowered to sign an unconditional surrender of what was left of the Third Reich.

Friedeburg finally dispatched a message in SHAEF code to Fuehrer Dönitz. The message was transmitted to British 2nd Army HQ and taken by courier to German HQ.

The message said that Eisenhower's chief of staff had put forward two proposals:

1—That Friedeburg receive full authority to make complete and unconditional surrender in all theaters.

2—That Dönitz send his chief of staff and commanders in chief of the Army, Navy and Air Force with the necessary authority to make the complete surrender.

Friedeburg, in the message, also outlined the conditions restricting the movement of surrendering troops, aircraft and ships and the demand that OK W guarantee the forwarding and execution of the Allied Command orders. He also pointed out that he was informed that the new German government would be charged with the guilt of continuance of hostilities unless they agreed promptly to surrender terms.

The second stage of the surrender was set Sunday, May 6, 11 months to the day after the Allies invaded the West Wall at Normandy. Eisenhower received word that Jodl requested a visit to Supreme HQ and he was promptly flown from 21st Army Group to Reims.

Jodl arrived at the airfield at 17:08 hours accompanied by Oxenius. They were allowed to confer with Friedeburg and Poleck for 30 minutes before Jodl and Friedeburg were summoned for discussions with Smith and Strong.

The conference between Smith and Strong, Jodl and Friedeburg lasted 65 minutes. At 19:20 hours, Smith left his office and went straight to Eisenhower. Strong, meanwhile, sent for Suslaparov.

Jodl and Friedeburg returned to the office assigned to them and joined Poleck and Oxenius.

At 19:39 hours, Smith returned to his office, where he conferred with Jodl and Friedeburg briefly for six minutes. At 19:45, the German representatives retired to their office.

One minute later Suslaparov and Colonel Zenkovitch entered Smith's office and were advised of the situation. Seven minutes later, Smith came out of his office to order coffee.

The German delegation left Supreme HQ at 21:12 hours and were taken to a house reserved for them and remained there until they were called to headquarters for the actual signing of the surrender terms.

Friedeburg suddenly came into the picture last Wednesday. It was then that the 21st Army Group established contact with a German delegation, which on the following day surrendered Denmark, Holland and northwestern Germany. Friedeburg headed the German group. The surrender was purely a tactical, battlefield surrender, authorized by Eisenhower and carried out by Field Marshall Sir. Bernard L. Montgomery.

After this surrender had been completed, it was made known by the Germans that they wished to discuss the surrender of the whole of the German armed forces.

Accordingly, Eisenhower instructed that the German representatives be brought to his headquarters at Reims on Saturday.

Friedeburg and Poleck left Luneberg at 08:00 hours by plane on Saturday. They were accompanied by Lt. Col., the Viscount Bury and Maj. F. J. Lawrence, both British officers with the 21st Army Group.

The party changed planes at Vorst, Germany, and headed for Reims, but rain and strong winds forced the plane down at Brussels. After a lunch of Spam sandwiches and Scotch ale at a RAF snack bar the party drove to Reims in an automobile driven by Pvt. Bobbie Alexander, an ATS girl from Inverness, Scotland.

Friedeburg fell asleep in the car almost immediately, having had little sleep for the past ten days. He had also slept on the plane, while Poleck remained awake throughout.

Friedeburg, Poleck and their escorts arrived at Supreme HQ, formerly an industrial college, at 17:04 hours. Their arrival coincided with the announcement of the surrender of three German armies to General Jacob L. Devers's 6th Army Group.

The Germans were met at the entrance of the headquarters by British Brig. E. J. Foord, chief of operational intelligence at Supreme HQ. The visitors and Foord exchanged military salutes.

Friedeburg and Poleck were taken to the first floor of the building and granted requests to wash before meeting the Chief of Staff. Friedeburg hummed softly to himself while washing. Poleck appeared slightly dazed.

At 12:00 hours, Strong escorted Friedeburg to Smith's office. The German naval chief did not salute, but came to attention as he passed a group of high-ranking Allied officers outside Smith's office.

At the beginning of his discussions with Smith, Friedeburg was required to show his credentials and authority to represent Dönitz.

Although it was clear that Friedeburg was not authorized to negotiate an unconditional surrender, he was allowed to study the Allied terms of surrender prior to communicating to Dönitz.

Dönitz's answer was Jodl, his chief of staff, who brought to Supreme HQ the proper credentials and authority to act on behalf of Dönitz.

After Jodl had conferred with Smith, communications were dispatched once more to Dönitz, informing him that Jodl had studied the surrender terms and was ready to sign.

Not until some time after midnight was Dönitz's answer received. When it arrived no time was lost in bringing the unconditional surrender to climax.

[Billee to Charles] May 8, 1945—New York City

VE-day is nearly over and it's been a quiet day, at least for me, and I think for a great many other people. I didn't go uptown and get in the mob. Jane says there were lots of people but they were not hysterically happy, especially not today. Edward Kennedy provided them with the excuse for a celebration yesterday with his unofficial dispatch.

I took our radio over to the office so we could hear the overseas broadcasts. I especially wanted to hear Eisenhower because I knew somewhere in the background you were there and I could be a little closer to you that way.

We received word tonight that Stalin had declared VE-day after midnight. It was after six o'clock our time. They are still fighting in some sections, however.

I liked the way the General spoke. He has such a confident voice. There's something very good about it.

Jane and I heard the president make his official proclamation. I've wanted you so many times today to share all this with.

/////

[Charles to Billee] May 9, 1945—Paris

This is so strange. I think sometimes it is all a wild dream.

This morning I was driving and walking through what is left of a completely destroyed Berlin.

This afternoon I sat at a table outside a sidewalk cafe on the Champs Elysees, watching one of the most unbelievable and colorful sights I'll ever see. Thousands and thousands of Parisians, and solders of all nations just walking in a solid mass along the wide boulevard. Traffic is closed to the Champs today, the second holiday of the VE Day celebrations. Off to my right the Arc de Triomphe is a picture to behold. It stands almost alone, towering and somehow symbolic of this victory. Flags that must be the largest ever flown anywhere hang from the top of the Arc down almost to the Tomb of the Unknown Soldier below.

It is a warm spring day. The glass of wine I have in front of me tastes like something I have never tasted before, like the best of all vintages. It is a happy day. [But] there is something missing. Yes . . . you. I want you so to be with me. Wanted you to be with me when I came back from Berlin.

I'm awfully tired but I'll try to give you the complete picture from the beginning:

Last Saturday I was told by phone that I was to work on what may be the unconditional surrender. The message came from SHAEF headquarters in Paris and from Col. [R. Ernest] Dupuy, public relations head. As the combined press and radio man, that would be my job. For the present, no correspondents would be notified of impending developments. The message came over what is called a "garbled" phone. The person on the other end talks in the clear, the words are scrambled over the wires but I hear the man perfectly on this end.

Saturday evening, Adm. von Friedeburg was flown from Germany to Reims to start negotiations. I was kept informed of everything. The following day Gen. Jodl, German Chief of Staff, arrived and thereby set the stage for the surrender. I had written about 3,000 words on the background, which was distributed to 16 correspondents who were flown at the last minute from Paris to Reims. From that point we were on our own.

The surrender ceremony started at about 2:15 a.m. Monday morning and was over shortly afterward. There were scenes in Gen. Eisenhower's office and other offices at HQ, so that it wasn't all over until about five.

I slept for three hours, got up and started on my stories. I filed them from here shortly after noon, then heard about the AP's violation of the release. It was a terrible breach of ethics, with the man, Ed Kennedy, deliberately filing the flash after being informed nothing was to be released until after 3 p.m. on Tuesday.

I thought the job was finished until I was notified at 8 p.m. Monday night that I was going to Berlin next morning. The Berlin job was to be a ratification of the first surrender and a show for the Russians.

Eight correspondents, none of whom had been at the Reims surrender, flew in one plane, Leo Moore and I flying with Air Marshall Tedder and the official Allied party in another.

We made a rendezvous with the three German chiefs of the Army, Navy and Air Force at a former German airfield in Stendal, 50 miles from Berlin, then continued on to Templehof airfield in Berlin.

The sight of the city was appalling. I can just ask you to picture a huge city completely destroyed. That's the simple picture.

The negotiations went on all afternoon and night before the ceremony started after midnight, Berlin time. After the ceremony came the official victory banquet with Marshal Zhukov as the host. I'll never forget that one, angel.

After 24 toasts, no sleep for gosh knows how long, vodka, champagne, cognac, wine, caviar, squab, Russian cigarettes, the picture of hopeless people, weary refugees streaming through Berlin, smoldering fires still in evidence, I was pretty well done in.

Air Marshall Tedder (Deputy Supreme Commander of Allied Forces) with British naval and Russian military guests inspecting bomb damage—Berlin, May 1945. (US Army)

We drove through the center of Berlin—Unter den Linden, the Chancellery, Kaiser's Palace, Tiergarten—so many more places just skeletons of buildings, rubble, brick, dust, twisted girders, charred wood.

Without sleep we flew down to Paris in three and a half hours. I started my stories on the plane, finished them in Paris and then proceeded to stay up until now: 2:35 a.m., Thursday morning.

My surrender stories got page one, in all *Stars and Stripes* editions, and were played very well. Today's paper had a page one note that I was the only correspondent at both surrenders.

I can hear the crowds still parading and yelling, planes overhead all day and night shooting flares, buzzing the Champs at 200 feet (French planes), red flood lights beautifying the Opera, water fountains spraying 50 feet high around the fountains at Place de la Concorde.

This is the Paris I wanted to see and I'm satisfied there isn't another place like it.

Charles (right), Eisenhower's co-pilot Dick Underwood, and Signal Corps photographer Leo Moore (center), with Russian photographers at second German surrender—Berlin, May 1945. (Kiley family)

/////

[Billee to Charles] May 9, 1945—New York City

I was right and you were present at the surrender. You're in the papers, hon.

El called me today and said the *Jersey Journal* carried the AP release, but of course, added a little color to it.

At supper time the little Italian girl I worked with at *Time* called me and told me that it was in this a.m.'s *Tribune*. Luckily Jane had brought hers home and I found it. I'm saving the different coverage of the "incident" because I thought you'd be interested.

I must tell you how wonderful Broadway looked all lighted and the Times Building's new headlines.

Soon we'll be together and the waiting will fade into a shadow.

/////

[Charles to Billee] May 15, 1945—Paris

If you have been following the redeployment stuff in the paper you know about the point system.

The way it stands now the only people who will be considered for discharges are those with 85 points and over. And, even they will not be able to make any plans for discharge until the latter part of June, at the earliest and probably not for four to eight or ten months. The entire picture is very hazy. In any case, I have at least 88 points and may possibly wind up with 98. That puts me under the wire with plenty to spare.

You would get a kick out of the way people are scrambling for points. Larsen, for example, needed two or three and the brass is putting him in for a Bronze Star medal, which would give him five more.

They tell me I'm in for one but it hasn't gotten me the least bit excited. Aside from the point value, they are as worthless as a Good Conduct ribbon.

Bob, I think, needs ten points so they are putting him in for a Bronze Star and, get this, a Croix de Guerre.

Seems you also get five points for each foreign decoration approved by the War Department and the Croix de Guerre is one of them. The medal should be for a "feat of arms" and the brass, notably Col. Eldridge, today was trying to dream up an excuse to get the medal for Bob.

It's enough to make you ill.

/////

[Charles to Billee] June 12, 1945—Frankfurt

It seems ages and ages since my last letters to you. That's because so much has happened in the last few days and I've been kept terribly busy.

On Sunday, Marshal Zhukov and a Russian party visited the general here and it kept me busy all day. There was a presentation of the Soviet Order of Victory (platinum, diamonds and rubies said to be worth anywhere from

$15,000 to $100,000) by Zhukov to Ike and Montgomery.

Then there was an air show of 1,700 planes, a luncheon banquet and entertainment. Yesterday we flew to London where the general today received the city's highest honor, the Freedom of the City of London, in a most impressive and colorful ceremony.

It was all Britain paying tribute to the general and he was driven in an open, black, horse-drawn carriage through the streets. There were tens of thousands packed along the route.

He was only the fifth American ever to receive the "Freedom." The others were U. S. Grant, Teddy Roosevelt, Gen. Pershing and a philanthropist named [George] Peabody.

All of the officials were in their fur-trimmed scarlet and blue robes; some wore the old-style wigs that befitted their position.

I thought the general would break down when he started to speak during the ceremony, he was that much overcome.

London looked good after the mess of what used to be cities in Germany. I stopped in the office. Moreover, I slept in my old bed in Clifford's Inn, too.

And one of the strangest of all incidents happened this afternoon after the ceremony, while I was writing my story. In London for only a day and for the first time since when, and there was a telephone call for me. It was Cliff McIlveen, brother of the Mac I flew with. He has been a P[O]W since about November 1943 and [was] on his way home. He said while he was in London he thought he'd call me. Didn't know I haven't worked out of London since June 1944.

Cliff hadn't had a letter from home in nine months, didn't know any of the details about Mac going down—just that he went. I wanted to see him, if only for a minute he sounded so lonely, but I had to rush to the airfield to be on time for my plane back here.

Day after day after day, I miss you more. This morning, walking down Fleet Street toward the Thames I thought back to the days I used to take that walk and dream across the ocean to wonder where you were and what you were doing and wishing you were with me.

It won't be long, now.

[Just a few days after this letter was written, Charles flew to Washington with Eisenhower to cover the general's welcome home ceremonies; then, back home for good, he took the first train he could to New York, where Billee met him once again at Penn Station.]

Billee and Charles—New York, Summer 1945. (Kiley Family)

EPILOGUE

AFTER THE WAR

STARS AND STRIPES STAFF WRITERS

After the war, Ben Price worked in public relations in the airline industry, but, when he died in 1994, on his death certificate his occupation was listed as "newspaper editor." Jane Price died in 2003.

Bob Moora went back to the *New York Herald Tribune*, working in various editorial capacities, including Sunday editor and news editor of the paper's Washington bureau. In 1957, he joined the press relations staff of RCA. He died in 1971, an apparent suicide.

Joe Fleming married a German woman and stayed in Germany after the war. He was a fixture in journalism in that country for decades and was named bureau chief for UPI in both Berlin and Bonn before his retirement. Fleming was renowned for such idiosyncrasies as knocking the ashes off his cigarette into his pants cuffs. He died around 2005.

Ralph Martin became a bestselling author of political and celebrity biographies, and was the author or co-author of thirty books. His most well-known work was *Jennie: The Life of Lady Randolph Churchill*, a two-volume biography of Winston Churchill's American-born mother, later made into a television mini-series. He also wrote *The Woman He Loved*, about King Edward VIII and Wallis Warfield Simpson, and *Seeds of Destruction: Joe Kennedy and His Sons*. Martin was a member of Adlai E. Stevenson's presidential campaign staff in 1952 and 1956. He died in 2013.

Earl Mazo served for a year as deputy assistant Secretary of Defense during the Truman administration and later worked for the *New York Herald Tribune* as chief political correspondent, when he got to know Richard Nixon. In 1959, Mazo wrote

Richard Nixon: A Political and Personal Portrait. In 1960, Mazo investigated cases of voter fraud in Chicago and Texas during the presidential election that he felt had fraudulently given the election to Kennedy. He planned a twelve-part series on this story; four parts had been published in newspapers across the country when Nixon himself asked Mazo to stop because, in Nixon's words, the country could not stand a constitutional crisis at the height of the Cold War. Mazo later became a fellow at the Woodrow Wilson International Center for Scholars and worked for the congressional Joint Committee on Printing in the 1970s. He died in 2007.

Charles Kiley's closest *Stars and Stripes* friend remained Andy Rooney. During the war, Rooney wrote two books with Bud Hutton, *Air Gunner* (1943) and *The Story of The Stars and Stripes* (1946), about the unlikely group of citizen-soldiers who produced the Army newspaper. Shortly after the war ended, he started working in television, writing for Arthur Godfrey, Victor Borge, and Gary Moore. He wrote scripts for *The Twentieth Century*, a series of documentaries narrated by Walter Cronkite.

Rooney's long association with CBS started in 1962, at first writing for Harry Reasoner and afterward writing and appearing in a series of special programs; one of these, *Mr. Rooney Goes to Washington*, won a Peabody Award. He appeared in the first episode of *60 Minutes* in 1968, and later joined the program as a commentator from 1978 to 2011. His appearances on *60 Minutes*, called the most successful program in television history, as well as his syndicated columns which ran in newspapers for thirty years, and his bestselling books, made Andy Rooney a household name. Rooney mentioned Charles a number of times in his WWII memoir, *My War*. In Tom Brokaw's book, *The Greatest Generation*, the section on Andy Rooney is illustrated with the same photograph of Rooney with Charles and Bud Hutton that appears in this book.

Charles and "Andrew," as Charles called him, shared a love of football and were both ardent Giants' fans; they watched many games together in all weathers at Giants' Stadium. Charles's son, David, accompanied Rooney to the 1991 Super Bowl between the Giants and the Buffalo Bills in Tampa. Ten years later, David and Rooney were again in Tampa for another Giants Super Bowl when David got the news that Charles had died. In 2011, just a few months before his own death, Rooney told David that Charles had been the finest man he had ever known.

BILLEE'S FAMILY

Billee's mother, Elizabeth Gray, continued to operate Oak Lodge until 1963. After she sold the property, the house was demolished. Elizabeth died in 1982. Warren Gray was haunted by his war experiences for the rest of his life. He died in 1996. William "Billy" Strohaker, her nephew, has continued to suffer from the after-effects of polio. His grandson, Pfc. Teddy Rushing, died in Iraq at the age of 25, on November 11, 2011—Veteran's Day.

CHARLES'S FAMILY

Charles's father, Pop, continued to live at 195, sharing the house with Eleanor, Tom, and their children until he died in 1963. Charles's brother John worked and studied in Rome for two years in the early 1950s, and later founded the *Advocate*, the newspaper of the Newark, New Jersey, archdiocese, as well as a support organization for homeless men in Newark. He died in 1985.

CHARLES AND BILLEE

Charles and Billee Kiley were married for fifty-seven years and raised six children.

After the war, Charles had a twenty-year career at a job he loved nearly as much as he loved Billee, at the *New York Herald Tribune*. He started as a reporter, then worked in rewrite and as night city editor. He was made assistant managing editor in the early 1960s and held this position until "The Paper," as it was affectionately referred to by all its employees, folded in May 1966. Charles then worked as managing editor-in-chief of the *New York Law Journal* until his retirement at the age of seventy-five. In 1974, Charles was ordained a deacon in the Catholic Church, assigned to his home parish in Westfield, New Jersey, part of the Newark archdiocese. For the next twenty-five years, he married and baptized a generation of church members, ministered to the sick, and served as instructor and board member of the diaconate program in the archdiocese. Inevitably, he also wrote and published the program's newsletter. In his last years, he volunteered as a driver for a local group of Missionaries of Charity, the order of nuns founded by Mother Theresa. Charles died in January 2001, fifty-nine years almost to the day after he and Billee met at the Asheville YMCA.

Like many World War II veterans, Charles did not talk very much about his war experiences. His bound copies of the *Stars and Stripes* newspapers, that he had helped to produce at such great personal cost, were stored away and only occasionally dragged out by his children. He also had an album of photographs taken by Signal Corps Lt. Leo Moore during the time Charles was assigned to cover General Eisenhower, which included photographs taken at newly liberated concentration camps. These photographs were more interesting to his children, but when they had nightmares about the images, the album was also put away with little explanation.

The letters that Charles and Billee had exchanged for so many months during the war were only rarely discussed. The Kiley children all knew the story of how their parents met and that they had written the letters through their long separation, but the contents were never shared with them until after Charles's death.

After the war, Billee became a strong and enduring force in her church and community; she and Charles lived in the same house in Westfield for fifty years. She loved to travel; after Charles retired they toured the country and, to her delight, went to Wales to see the place her mother's family came from, and to England to revisit the places Charles had known during the war. She was the centerpiece of a large extended family who had to share her with an ever-increasing circle of friends, with all of whom she kept in close touch . . . by writing them letters.

Billee died on August 17, 2007— her sixty-third wedding anniversary.

Billee and Charles—1996. (Kiley Family)

BIBLIOGRAPHY

Ardman, Harvey. *Normandie, Her Life and Times*. New York: Franklin Watts, 1985.

Beekman, Scott. *William Dudley Pelley: A Life in Right-Wing Extremism and the Occult*. New York: Syracuse University Press, 2005.

Connaughton, Richard. *MacArthur and Defeat in the Philippines*. New York: Overlook Press, 2001.

Copp, DeWitt S. *Forged In Fire: Strategy and Decisions in the Airwar over Europe, 1940–1945*. New York: Doubleday & Company, 1982.

Forde, Frank. *The Long Watch: History of the Irish Mercantile Marine in WWII*. Rev. Ed. Dublin: New Island Books, 2001.

Goldstein, Richard. *Helluva Town: The Story of New York City During World War II*. New York: Free Press, 2010.

Green, William. *War Planes of the Second World War: Fighters, Volume Four*. New York: Doubleday, 1964.

Hutton, Bud, and Andy Rooney. *The Story of the Stars and Stripes*. New York: Farrar and Rinehart, 1946.

Lucas, Sharon. *World War II: Day by Day*. Rev. ed. London: DK Adult, 2004.

Overy, Richard, ed. *The New York Times Complete World War II: 1939–1945*. New York: Black Dog & Leventhal, 2013.

Pfau, Ann. *Miss Yourlovin: GIs, Gender, and Domesticity during World War II*. New York: Columbia University Press, 2008.

Simon, Jean-Yves. *The Stars and Stripes in Normandy*. France: self published, 1980; New York: New Roads Media ebook, 2013.

The Stars and Stripes. US Army: European Editions, 1942–1945.

INDEX